Cursor-Movement Keystrokes

Cursor Movement	Keystroke
Left one character	←
Right one character	→
Down one line	↓
Up one line	↑
Right one word	Ctrl →
Left one word	Ctrl ←
Beginning of current line	Home
End of current line	End
Right to next tab setting	Tab
Left to previous tab setting	Shift-Tab
Top of current document screen	Home, Home
Bottom of current document screen	End, End
Down one screen	PgDn
Up one screen	PgUp
Beginning of current document	Home, Home, Home
End of current document	End, End, End
Beginning of current document, spreadsheet, etc.	Ctrl-Home
End of current document, spreadsheet, etc.	Ctrl-End
Right one cell or field	Tab
Left one cell or field	Ctrl-Tab
Down one row	↵ or ↓
Up one row	Ctrl ↵ or ↑
Right one screen	Ctrl →
Left one screen	Ctrl ←
Top of current column	Ctrl-PgUp
Bottom of current column	Ctrl-PgDn

Understanding
PFS:
First
Choice

Understanding
PFS:®
First
Choice

Gerry Litton

SAN FRANCISCO • PARIS • DÜSSELDORF • SOEST

Cover design by Thomas Ingalls + Associates
Cover Photography by Michael Lamotte
Series design by Julie Bilski
Chapter art and layout by Ingrid Owen
Screen reproductions produced by XenoFont

To Carol, whose constant patience and encouragement led me down the road to write this book.

Acknowledgments

Many thanks to all of the SYBEX people who helped put together the various parts of this book, making a coherent whole out of the bits and pieces with which I started.

Very special appreciation is due Cheryl Holzaepfel, who miraculously managed to keep track of the myriad loose ends that kept cropping up, and whose great sense of humor made this project a constant joy.

And to the rest of the staff who helped keep the wheels oiled and moving: Dianne King, for getting the project off the ground; Elizabeth Kim, copy editing; Ami Knox, proofreading; Jeff Green, technical editing; Winnie Kelly, typesetting; Anne Leach, indexing; Sonja Schenk, screen reproductions; and Robert Scott-Reynolds, word processing.

I am also very grateful to the staff at Software Publishing Corporation for their help with this project. In particular, Beti Turner was very generous with her time and assistance on numerous occasions.

Contents
at a
Glance

Introduction		**xxix**
Chapter 1	Word Processing Basics	**3**
Chapter 2	Advanced Editing and Formatting	**37**
Chapter 3	Managing Your Database Files	**77**
Chapter 4	Advanced Database Features	**127**
Chapter 5	Creating Reports	**153**
Chapter 6	Getting Started with Spreadsheets	**191**
Chapter 7	Using Formulas	**233**
Chapter 8	Creating Graphs	**285**
Chapter 9	Communicating with Other Computers	**339**
Chapter 10	Transferring Data between First Choice Modules	**367**
Chapter 11	Using the Calculator, Bookmark, Macros, and Disk Utilities Features	**391**
Appendix A	Installing PFS: First Choice	**415**
Appendix B	Printers Supported by PFS: First Choice	**437**
Appendix C	Using Forms Programs	**445**
Appendix D	Creating Presentation Graphics	**465**
Index		**473**

Table
of
Contents

Introduction   xxix

Chapter 1   Word   *3*
                Processing
                Basics

        Working with Menus   **4**
            Useful Keys   **4**
            Selecting a Menu Item   **5**
        Exploring the First Choice Word Processing Screen   **6**
            The Text Cursor   **6**
            The Ruler Line   **7**
            The Information Line   **7**
            The Menu Bar   **8**
        Getting Help   **9**
        Word Processing Basics   **10**
            The Keyboard   **10**
                Insert and Overwrite Modes   **12**
        Creating a Document   **12**
        Entering Text   **13**
        Making Text Corrections   **14**

Moving the Cursor   **14**

Changing Text   **15**

Creating Blank Lines and New Paragraphs   **17**

Combining Paragraphs   **18**

Adding Text   **18**

Deleting Text   **19**

Working with Blocks of Text   **21**

How to Define a Block   **22**

Moving a Text Block   **23**

Using Speed Keys with Text Blocks   **25**

Copying a Text Block   **25**

Deleting a Text Block   **26**

Saving a Copy of Your Document   **26**

The Directory Assistant   **27**

Creating a File for a New Document   **29**

Printing Your Document   **30**

How to End a Word Processing Session   **32**

Summary   *33*

Chapter 2   Advanced   **37**
Editing and
Formatting

Retrieving an Existing Document   **38**

Replacing an Existing Document   **39**

Keeping Several Versions   **40**

Enhancing Your Document with Special Effects   **40**

Boldfacing Existing Text   **41**

Boldfacing Text as You Type   **42**

Selecting Other Styles   **42**

Changing Page Appearance   **45**

   Working with Rulers   **45**

   Changing Left and Right Margins   **46**

   Changing Tab Settings   **47**

   Creating an Indent   **48**

   Setting Top and Bottom Margins and Page Length   **49**

   Headers and Footers   **51**

   Line Spacing   **53**

   Centering Text   **53**

   Starting a New Page   **54**

Keeping Your Place with Bookmarks   **54**

Checking Your Document for Spelling Errors   **55**

   What the Spell Checker Checks   **56**

   Starting the Spell Checker   **57**

   Creating a Personal Dictionary   **58**

   Spell Checking a Block   **59**

Using the Thesaurus   **59**

Searching and Replacing Words   **60**

   Replacing Words   **61**

   Finding without Replacement   **62**

Setting New Defaults   **63**

Making a Backup Copy of Your Document   **64**

Deleting a Document   **65**

Working with Other Types of Files   **65**

Saving Documents in Other Formats   **66**

Retrieving Files in Other Formats   **67**

Combining Several Documents   **67**

Working with Long Documents   **69**

Printing Long Documents   **69**

Advanced Printing Features   **70**

The Print Options Menu   **71**

Printing Part of Your Document   **72**

Printer Capabilities   **73**

Summary   **74**

Chapter 3   Managing   **77**
Your
Database
Files

First Choice's Computerized Filing System   **78**

Advantages of Computerized Data   **79**

How to Create a Database File   **80**

Selecting the Information to Store   **80**

Designing a Database Form   **83**

Creating the Database Form   **86**

Selecting Field Types   **90**

Adding Records to a Database   **92**

Effective Data Entry   **93**

Repositioning Field Names in a Record   **93**

Adding Space for Long Data   **95**

Entering Data in a Record with Style   **95**

The Ditto Feature: a Data-entry Shortcut   **95**

Erasing a Record in Progress   **96**

Saving a Record   **96**

Retrieving an Existing Database from a Disk   **97**

Changing the Design of a Database   **98**

Making a Backup of a Database   **98**

Working with the Information in a Database   **103**

Browsing through Records   **104**

Editing a Record   **105**

Deleting a Record   **105**

Printing a Record   **106**

Printing Part of a Record   **106**

Converting a Record to a Document   **106**

Generating Tables   **107**

Displaying a Table   **108**

Customizing Your Tables   **110**

Printing a Table   **111**

Copying a Table to a Spreadsheet   **111**

Copying a Table to a Document   **111**

Finding Selected Records in a Database   **112**

How to Use Search Instructions   **112**

Types of Search Instructions   **114**

Printing Selected Records   **121**

Previewing the Printout   **122**

Saving Paper   **122**

Summary   **123**

Chapter 4   Advanced   **127**
Database
Features

Making Copies of Records   **128**

Making a Copy of a Database Form   **128**

Copying Groups of Records   **129**

Removing Selected Records   130

    Deleting a Database   132

Sorting Records   133

    Specifying Sort Instructions   134

    Sorting with Search Instructions   136

Printing Sorted Records   138

Copying Sorted Records   139

Using Bookmarks   139

    Placing a Bookmark   139

    Jumping to a Bookmark   140

Using the Calculator   140

Text-Editing Aids   140

    Using the Spell Checker and Thesaurus   140

    Using the Search-and-Replace Feature   141

Communicating with Other Systems: ASCII Files   141

    Creating a Delimited ASCII File   142

    Reading a Delimited ASCII File   145

    Creating a Fixed-length ASCII File   146

    Reading a Fixed-length ASCII File   147

Dialing a Telephone Number in a Database   148

Summary   149

Chapter 5   Creating   153
                     Reports

An Overview of Report Generation   154

    Main Features of a Report   154

    The Elements of Report Generation   157

Creating a Set of Report Instructions   158

Getting Started   **159**

Selecting Print Options   **159**

Using Fields in Your Report   **162**

Choosing Headings and Specifying Calculations   **166**

Entering Search and Sort Instructions   **171**

Saving the Report Instructions   **172**

Generating the Report   **172**

Sending the Report to a Disk File   **173**

Viewing the Report on a Disk File   **173**

Creating a Report with Derived Columns   **174**

Specifying Derived Columns   **174**

Derived Column Formulas   **175**

Working with Derived Columns   **177**

Using an Existing Set of Report Instructions   **177**

Using Instructions with Different Databases   **179**

Generating a Summary Report   **180**

Improving the Appearance of a Report   **180**

Editing the Report   **182**

Printer Enhancements   **182**

Printing the Enhanced Report   **182**

Changing the Database Form   **183**

Sample Applications   **183**

Summary   **186**

Chapter 6   Getting   **191**
Started with
Spreadsheets

Spreadsheet Fundamentals   **192**

The Basic Spreadsheet Display   **192**

How to Move around the Spreadsheet   194

Creating a Spreadsheet   196

Entering Column and Row Headings   196

Entering Data   198

The Quick Entry Feature   199

Entering Row and Column Headings   199

Copying a Single Value to a Range of Cells   201

Using Formulas   201

Examples of Formulas   202

How to Enter a Formula into a Cell   203

Changing a Cell Formula   206

Assigning Names to Cells   206

Storing Your Spreadsheet in a File   207

Saving the Spreadsheet   207

Retrieving the Spreadsheet   208

Manipulating Spreadsheet Data   208

Selecting a Range of Cells   209

Erasing Cells   210

Moving a Group of Cells   213

Copying a Group of Cells   214

Copying One Cell to a Range   214

Inserting Rows and Columns   215

Changing Cell Styles   216

Changing the Global Style   217

Setting Individual Cell Styles   221

Setting the Style of Groups of Cells   221

Outputting a Spreadsheet   222

Printing Your Spreadsheet   222

Improving the Spreadsheet's Appearance   **224**

Printing a Wide Spreadsheet   **225**

Printing Part of a Spreadsheet   **225**

Outputting a Spreadsheet in 1-2-3 Format   **226**

Inputting a Spreadsheet in 1-2-3 Format   **227**

Merging an ASCII File into a Spreadsheet   **228**

Summary   **228**

Chapter 7   Using   *233*
Formulas

Performing Arithmetic within Formulas   **234**

How First Choice Evaluates a Formula   **235**

Copying and Moving Formulas   **236**

How Formulas Change When Copied   **238**

Maintaining a Constant Cell   **238**

Copying Formulas with Quick Entry   **240**

Automatic and Manual Recalculation   **241**

Automatic Formula Adjustment   **241**

Working with Functions   **243**

Arithmetic Functions   **244**

Financial Functions   **253**

Date Functions   **257**

Time Functions   **262**

Table Functions   **265**

String Functions   **269**

Logical Functions   **277**

Summary   **282**

Chapter 8   Creating   285
            Graphs

            Introducing the Graph Types   286
                Bar Graphs   286
                Line Graphs   288
                Point Plots   289
                Area Graphs   290
                Pie Graphs   291
                High/Low/Close Graphs   292
            How to Build a New Graph   293
                Using the Graph Module   293
                An Overview of the Graphing Process   293
                Entering and Editing Data   294
                Creating Bar Graphs   298
                Creating Line Graphs   307
                Creating Pie Graphs   308
                Creating Area Graphs   313
                Creating High/Low/Close Graphs   314
                Changing Graph Types   315
            Storing and Retrieving Graph Data on Disk Files   316
                Creating New Defaults   317
                The *Graph Format   318
                Retrieving Existing Graph Data from Disk   319
            Displaying a Graph On-Screen   319
            How to Print Graphs   320
                Printer Checklist   322
            How to Plot Graphs   323
                Using the Plot Graph Options   323

Graphing Spreadsheet Data   *325*

    Transferring Data to the Graph Module   *325*

    Graphing Data Directly from a Spreadsheet   *327*

Outputting Raw Graph Data   *332*

    Printing Graph Data   *332*

    Using the Data as a Document   *333*

    Moving Data to a Spreadsheet   *333*

Using Special First Choice Features with Graphs   *334*

    Bookmarks   *334*

    The Calculator   *335*

    Quick Entry   *335*

Summary   *335*

Chapter 9   Communicating   *339*
with
Other
Computers

Getting Started   *340*

    Using a Modem with First Choice   *340*

    Accessing Information and Bulletin Board Services   *341*

Setting up Communications Options with the Service
    Menu   *342*

    Using an Existing Entry   *343*

    Entering the Telephone Number   *343*

    Selecting the Communication Speed   *344*

    Selecting the Terminal Type   *345*

    Adding a New Entry   *345*

Connecting to a Remote Computer   *346*

Automatic Dialing   *346*

Manual Dialing   *347*

Failing to Connect   *348*

Signing On to a Remote Computer   *349*

Communication Services   *349*

Electronic Bulletin Boards   *349*

Personal Computers   *349*

Using First Choice during Two-way Communication   *350*

The Working Copy   *351*

The Transmission Line   *351*

Communicating by Special Keys   *351*

Monitoring Your Online Session   *352*

Interrupting Data Transmission   *352*

Saving a Copy of the Session   *353*

Watching for Memory Overflow   *353*

Printing the Contents of a Session   *354*

Transmitting and Receiving Files   *354*

Preparing the Remote Computer   *354*

Preparing First Choice   *355*

Ending a Communications Session   *355*

PC-to-PC Communication   *356*

Exchanging Messages   *357*

Transferring Files between PCs   *358*

Making Your Computer the Host   *360*

Automating the Sign-on Procedure   *360*

Summary   *362*

Chapter 10   Transferring   *367*
Data between
First Choice
Modules

Creating Personalized Form Letters   *368*
   Building the Form Letter   *368*
   Choosing the Database and Specifying Print Options   *370*
   Selecting Records and Printing the Letters   *371*
   Merging Long Fields into the Text   *372*
   Outputting to Screen or Disk   *372*
   Adding Style to the Form Letters   *372*
Producing Mailing Labels   *373*
   Setting Page Length and Margins   *373*
   Selecting the Database and Choosing Printer Settings   *374*
   Selecting Records and Printing the Labels   *375*
   Adjusting Printer Settings   *375*
Combining Data from Different Files   *375*
   Transferring Data with the Clipboard   *376*
   Merging Documents   *377*
   Merging Database Information into a Document   *378*
   Merging a Spreadsheet into a Document   *380*
   Combining a Graph with a Document   *382*
   Transferring Data to a Spreadsheet   *383*
Summary   *387*

xxiv

Chapter 11 Using the Calculator, Bookmark, Macros, and Disk Utilities Features   **391**

Using the Built-in Calculator   **392**

What the Calculator Can Do   **393**

How Results Are Formatted   **393**

Using Bookmarks   **394**

How to Set a Bookmark   **394**

Jumping to a Bookmark   **395**

Deleting Bookmarks   **396**

Using the Disk Utilities Module   **396**

Displaying Lists of Files   **397**

Copying Files   **399**

Renaming Files   **399**

Erasing Files   **400**

Creating Directories   **400**

Removing Directories   **401**

Formatting Disks   **402**

Copying Disks   **403**

Using Macros   **404**

Creating a Macro   **405**

Rules for Macro Creation   **407**

Playing Back a Macro   **407**

Changing or Deleting a Macro   **408**

Creating a Macro with a Pause   **408**

Running a Macro from the Main Menu   **410**

Setting Up Macro Files   **411**

Summary   **412**

Appendix A   Installing   **415**
PFS: First Choice

Hardware Requirements   **416**

Making Backups   **417**

Making Backups on a Hard-Disk Computer   **418**

Making Backups on a Floppy-Disk Computer   **419**

Installing PFS: First Choice   **420**

Starting PFS: First Choice   **421**

Starting First Choice on a Hard-Disk Computer   **421**

Starting First Choice on a Floppy-Disk Computer   **422**

Customizing PFS: First Choice for Your Computer   **423**

Making Selections from the Setup Menu   **423**

Exiting the Setup Menu   **432**

Using Multiple Devices with COM Ports   **432**

Installing a Mouse   **432**

Choosing a Port for the Mouse   **433**

Starting the Mouse   **433**

Using the Mouse with First Choice   **433**

Appendix B   Printers   **437**
Supported
by First
Choice

Appendix C Using Forms Programs   **445**

  An Introduction to the Forms Programming Language   **446**

  The Language Elements   **448**

    Variables   **448**

    Program Statements   **450**

    Functions   **455**

  Writing and Editing a Forms Program   **455**

    Creating a New Program   **456**

    Editing an Existing Program   **457**

  Storing and Retrieving Existing Programs   **457**

  Using a Program to Make Global Changes   **458**

  Using a Program to Recalculate Selected Records   **458**

  Looking at a Sample Program   **459**

    Using the Sample Program to Check Existing Records   **461**

    Using the Sample Program to Change New Records   **461**

Appendix D Creating Presentation Graphics   **465**

  Creating the Slide   **466**

    Entering Text for the Slide   **466**

    Displaying the Slide   **467**

    Saving the Slide Text   **468**

    Printing and Plotting the Slide   **468**

    Editing Slide Text   **469**

    Creating Font Commands   **469**

Including Graphs in a Slide   **470**

Producing a Slide Show   **470**

Viewing Slides Manually   **470**

Automating a Slide Show   **471**

Controlling Slide Orientation   **472**

Index   473

Introduction

If you've just purchased PFS: First Choice (or if you're considering purchasing it), you probably know that this set of programs offers an integrated approach to computerized processes. With First Choice, you can do word processing, build databases and spreadsheets, write reports, make graphs, and communicate with other computers. But now you're faced with the challenge of learning how to do all of this quickly and painlessly. That's the purpose of this book—to help you learn about all of First Choice's features.

So why do you need a book to learn to use the program when you have the manual that comes with the software? The manual is excellent, and this book isn't intended to replace it, but *Understanding PFS: First Choice* does have several features that the manual doesn't offer. To begin with, the book is designed to be used in two ways. You can use it as an on-line tutorial and create the many useful examples as you learn about each feature. For example, as you learn about the word processing module, you'll create a document, enhancing it bit by bit as you practice using each new word processing feature.

You can also use this book as a reference guide. You'll find descriptions of just about all of First Choice's features, and the table of contents and index will help you find the section you need. After you've read the general description, you can follow the exercises to learn more about the topic. And, as an additional reference aid, tables and summaries that serve as quick guides to frequently used keystrokes and commands can be found inside the front and back covers.

But, unlike most software manuals, this book is more than just a description of features. Particular attention was given to the order in which the topics are introduced. With each major subject (word processing, database management, and so on), the simpler aspects are discussed first, followed by more complex items. Furthermore, the word processing features are discussed before any others, because word processing forms the foundation for using other First Choice modules.

This book also alerts you to some pitfalls that you might encounter when using First Choice. I can't guarantee to keep you completely out of trouble, but through notes in the margin, I draw your attention to particularly important or confusing items to help you avoid problems whenever possible.

HOW TO USE THIS BOOK

This book addresses the latest release of First Choice—version 3.0. Earlier versions don't have many of the features described here, but you can still use this book as a reference.

If you haven't yet installed First Choice, you should turn to Appendix A first. It gives you step-by-step instructions for installing the software and customizing it for your system.

After you've installed First Choice, read Chapter 1, because it describes the basic features of the word processor, which underlies operations in all of First Choice's modules. Some of the topics covered include basic text entry and editing, cut-and-paste operations, and document storage, retrieval, and printing.

Chapter 2 describes the advanced word processing features, including spell checking, using the built-in thesaurus, automatic search-and-replace, and advanced printing techniques. These operations can also be used in most of the other modules.

Chapter 3 introduces the database module. This chapter covers the basic operations of creating a database, entering records and modifying existing data, and searching for specific groups of records. Also discussed are database storage and retrieval, as well as printing the contents of selected records.

Chapter 4 covers more advanced topics related to the database manager. These include moving records between databases, deleting selected records, sorting records, and transferring data between First Choice and other software packages.

Chapter 5 explains how to generate reports based on information in a database. It also tells you how to use the word processor to enhance a report.

Chapter 6 introduces the spreadsheet software and basic spreadsheet concepts. It describes how to create a spreadsheet, how to store and retrieve spreadsheet data, how to manipulate data, and how to output spreadsheet data as a report.

Chapter 7 explains how to use formulas within spreadsheets. Included in this chapter are detailed descriptions of all of the built-in functions (predefined series of complex operations) available with the software.

Chapter 8 shows you how to use the graph software. The chapter begins with a survey of the basic graph types, then shows you how to generate each of these. Included are details on printing and plotting graphs, as well as on outputting graphs to disk for use with different software packages. Finally, you'll see how to generate graphs directly from data within a spreadsheet.

Chapter 9 explains the use of the communication software. The topics include how to connect to various types of remote computers, how to use the word processor as a background tool, and how to send and receive files.

Chapter 10 is devoted to the subject of sharing data between different types of First Choice files. You'll learn how to generate form letters and mailing labels, how to combine two or more documents, and how to incorporate various types of data—such as spreadsheet information or graphs—into a document.

Chapter 11 explains four special First Choice features: the bookmark, the calculator, disk utilities, and macros. All these features are designed to provide you with quick and convenient methods for using First Choice to its fullest advantage.

Appendix A covers the nuts and bolts of setting up First Choice for use with your computer, and Appendix B lists the printers compatible with First Choice and their features. Appendix C describes one of First Choice's most advanced features—how to write programs to enhance database information—and Appendix D shows you how to use First Choice to create graphics for presentations.

ABOUT PFS: FIRST CHOICE

First Choice is an extremely well-integrated package: you give instructions to the program by selecting items from various menus (a system referred to as *menu driven*), and the same set of menus is used throughout all of the modules. Each menu is always used in the same sense, so that you soon develop a feel for which menu to use in any given situation. As much as possible, the menu items have been made identical—or at least as similar as possible—for all of the modules. For example, the steps for saving a file are always the same, regardless of whether the file is a word processed document, a spreadsheet, or a graph.

As a result of this integration, you'll find that after you have become familiar with one part of First Choice, you'll be on comfortable ground as you begin to learn about the others.

Because First Choice is completely menu driven, hardly any memorization of commands or keystrokes is required. The menus are layered, and all selections are clearly labelled, so that you can easily find the correct choices for any operation. With a little practice, you'll be performing the more common procedures automatically. And, for many tasks, you can bypass the menus entirely with a couple of keystrokes by using First Choice's special *speed keys*.

One of First Choice's strongest integration features is that the word processor underlies all of the modules: exactly the same steps are used for entering and editing data, whether you're writing a letter to your stockbroker, adding records to a database, entering data on a spreadsheet, or communicating with a remote computer in Oshkosh.

Another outstanding feature of the software is the ease with which information can be transferred from one type of file to another. For instance, spreadsheet or database information can quickly be transferred into an existing document. This feature is implemented in several ways, including the use of a clipboard for temporarily holding any type of data.

A QUICK SURVEY OF PFS: FIRST CHOICE MODULES

The word processor is used for generating and editing documents. All word processing operations are done very quickly—even on a "slow" computer. Though the size of individual documents is limited to approximately 20 pages, documents can easily be linked to form an opus of any length. As with the other modules, the word processor achieves a happy compromise between ease of use and flexibility.

The database manager works with files, each of which contains groups of similar records. Defining a new database structure to First Choice is quite intuitive, and addition and modification of data is also straightforward.

The report writer is used for producing summaries from information in a database. Standard reports are in columnar format, and they can contain totals, subtotals, averages, and subaverages. As with most report writers, the user has very limited control over the output format. Because of this, First Choice includes a clever feature that allows you to output a report to a disk file. It can then be retrieved into the word processor and edited in any desired way. This same feature can be used to enhance the output from any of First Choice's modules.

First Choice's spreadsheet software is sophisticated, but quite easy to use. Even if you're unfamiliar with features such as formulas, global and individual cell formatting, automatic and manual recalculation, and automatic column-width adjustment, you'll find First Choice's approach easy to learn.

A variety of different graph types can be generated using the graph software. You can input raw data directly to this part of First Choice, or you can transfer it from a spreadsheet. Graphs can even be tied directly to a spreadsheet, so that when the data for a graph changes, the graph is automatically updated.

First Choice's communications software is in a class by itself. The ease with which its many features can be used is really outstanding. With this software, you can establish a direct connection between your computer and another in a remote location. This gives you access to many public computerized information services, and to hundreds of independently operated bulletin boards available throughout the country. The communications module can also be used for making a direct connection with another microcomputer to exchange messages and files.

First Choice offers the unique combination of the convenience of well-integrated programs coupled with ease of use; this book will guide you through the learning process so you can quickly enjoy the benefits of this excellent package.

Chapter

1

Word Processing Basics

One of First Choice's main tools is its built-in word processor, whose primary function is to create, store, modify, and print documents. A *document* can be anything from a one-line message to a 20-page manuscript.

The word processor also has another important function: when you use First Choice's other modules, such as the file manager or report writer, you'll often be entering and updating various types of information with the word processor. Consequently, a great deal of what you learn in this and the following chapter will have direct relevance throughout the remainder of the book.

In this chapter you'll be introduced to the basics of word processing and to the various types of menus that are an integral part of First Choice. First, you'll begin by learning how to use the Main menu. You'll then learn how to create a new document, enter text in it, and make corrections. You'll also do some electronic cutting and pasting. Finally, you'll save a copy of your document and print it.

If you plan to read the first two chapters as a tutorial, I suggest that you do all of the exercises. Or, you may prefer to begin working with the word processor on your own, referring to Chapters 1 and 2 as needed. In this case, the table of contents and index will help you quickly locate any topic.

Let's get First Choice running. If you need to refresh your memory about how to do this, refer to "Starting PFS: First Choice" in Appendix A.

WORKING WITH MENUS

After First Choice is running, the Main menu (Figure 1.1) will appear.

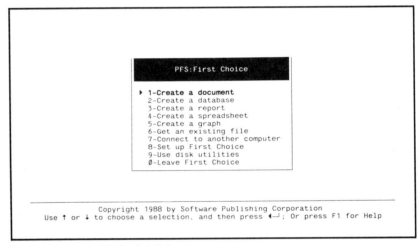

```
                        PFS:First Choice

                   ▸ 1-Create a document
                     2-Create a database
                     3-Create a report
                     4-Create a spreadsheet
                     5-Create a graph
                     6-Get an existing file
                     7-Connect to another computer
                     8-Set up First Choice
                     9-Use disk utilities
                     0-Leave First Choice


            Copyright 1988 by Software Publishing Corporation
     Use ↑ or ↓ to choose a selection, and then press ◀─┘; Or press F1 for Help
```

Figure 1.1: First Choice's Main menu

The Main menu is typical of many menus that you'll see as you work with First Choice: a series of items presented on the screen. When a menu appears, the cursor is set at the first item. In the Main menu, the cursor is positioned at *Create a document*.

USEFUL KEYS

When working with menus, you'll find a few keys especially useful. At the bottom of the Main menu, you'll see a reference to most of these keys.

■ In this book, the ◀─┘ symbol is used to indicate the Enter key.

Enter   This key is usually labeled either Enter, ◀─┘, or both. On some keyboards the key is labeled Return. This key has a variety of uses within First Choice. In menus, it's often used to select the item at which the cursor has been positioned (see below).

These keys are also used for moving other kinds of cursors used by First Choice.

Cursor keys	Four keys are used to move the cursor up, down, left, and right within a menu. These keys are usually labeled ↑, ↓, ←, and →. On some keyboards, the same keys may also have numerical labels (1, 2, 3...).
Esc	This is the Escape key. It is used mainly to back out of whatever you're doing at the moment. When you press the Escape key, First Choice usually returns to the menu that took you to whatever you're doing at that moment.
PgUp and PgDn	These two keys, located on the right-hand side of the keyboard, are used to scroll up and down the screen display.
Function keys	The ten keys labeled F1 through F10 are called function keys. Each is used for a special purpose by First Choice, and we'll encounter them as we introduce various topics.
Help	Pressing the F1 key will call up First Choice's Help system. You'll learn more about the Help system later in this chapter.

SELECTING A MENU ITEM

You can select an item from a menu by any of the following methods:

- Move the cursor to the item by using the ↑ and ↓ keys. Then select the item by pressing ←┘.

- Press the number corresponding to the item of choice. For example, if you want to create a report from the Main menu, press the key labeled "3" at the top of the keyboard. (You can use the numbered keys at the right-hand side of the keyboard only if you press the Num Lock key first.)

See "Using a Mouse with First Choice" in Appendix A for information on using this device.

- If you're using a mouse, drag the cursor to the item of choice on the screen. Then click any key on the mouse to select that item.

EXPLORING THE FIRST CHOICE WORD PROCESSING SCREEN

In order for you to gain access to First Choice's word processor, the Main menu must be displayed on the screen. If it isn't, return to it by pressing the Esc key.

Select item 1, *Create a document,* by any of the methods described earlier. The word processing screen shown in Figure 1.2 will appear.

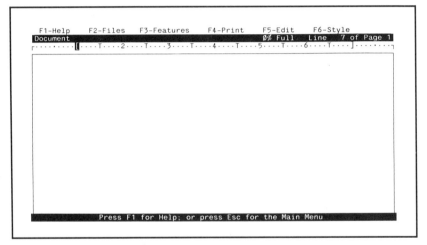

Figure 1.2: Word processing screen

This display contains various elements. Some of these provide you with valuable information, while others are used for specific purposes. We'll explore these below.

THE TEXT CURSOR

This is the blinking line that appears on-screen. Any text you enter will appear exactly where the cursor is positioned on the screen. By the same token, when you want to delete text, you must first move the cursor to the appropriate spot on the screen.

This is *not* the same cursor as the one used to select items from a menu. Normally, we'll refer to the text cursor simply as the *cursor,* unless there's a chance of confusion, in which case we'll use *text cursor.*

THE RULER LINE

This is the third line down from the top of your screen. It displays the following information:

- *Column numbers.* The columns on the screen are numbered from 1 (the leftmost column) to 80 (at the right-hand end of the screen). Each column is indicated by a period on the Ruler line. Column number 20 is indicated by the number "2," column 30 by "3," and so on.

- *Margin settings.* These are indicated by square brackets ([and]) for the left and right margins. Initially the margins are set by First Choice at columns 10 and 70.

- *Tab settings.* Each setting is indicated by the letter "T" on the Ruler line. Several tabs are preset by First Choice.

- *Cursor position.* The current position (expressed as a column number) of the cursor is always indicated by the solid box on the Ruler line. As you move the cursor, the box also moves, so that you always know the cursor's exact column position.

THE INFORMATION LINE

The second line at the top of the screen lists several useful items. This information will be helpful to you as you work with a document:

- *Document.* If you are working with a document that was previously stored on a disk, the name of the document is listed here. (We'll explain how to name a document later on.)

- *% Full.* This indicator tells you how much computer memory is available for your document. Initially, when you have no document, the memory is empty, or 0% full. The total amount of available memory corresponds to approximately 62,000 characters of text (roughly 20 single-spaced pages). If you plan to produce a very long document, you may need to divide it into two or more smaller documents that will fit into First Choice's memory.

• *Line* n *of Page* m. The line and page numbers tell you exactly where the cursor is at any instant. The default for page length is 54 lines. When you start the word processor, the cursor is positioned at column 10 of the first line of the first page. (Note that the information line actually reads *Line 7,* since the first six lines of the page are used for the top margin.)

THE MENU BAR

The same menu bar appears in almost every screen you use in First Choice. Moreover, each of the menu items has approximately the same function. This is one of the reasons that whatever you're doing in First Choice seems familiar.

The top line of the screen is called the *menu bar.* There are six items on the menu bar; to select one, press the corresponding function key, or click on that item with a mouse, and a new set of choices will be presented to you.

Let's practice using the menu bar:

1. Press the F3 key to select *Features* in the menu bar. The Features pull-down menu appears (Figure 1.3). You can select any particular item in this pull-down menu in the same manner you selected it in previous menus (see "Selecting a Menu Item"). Don't make any selections yet; we're just practicing.

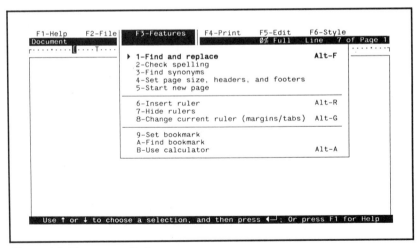

Figure 1.3: Features pull-down menu

2. You can move from one pull-down menu to another simply by pressing one of the function keys (F2 through F6). For example, press the F4 key to select the Print pull-down menu.

3. Move the cursor down to *Print labels*.

4. Press F1 to get help about *Print labels*. The Help screen for this option appears. Use the PgDn and PgUp keys to scroll up and down in this display.

5. Press the Esc key to exit from the Help display.

6. Press → to move to the next pull-down menu in the menu bar. This is another way to move from one menu item to another.

7. Press the Esc key once more to exit from the menu bar.

Because you'll see this same menu bar throughout First Choice, it is a good idea to review the above steps once or twice until you're familiar with them. As you explore the various features of First Choice, you'll become familiar with the different items on the menu bar.

Pressing F1 will give you help on whatever you're doing at any time within First Choice.

GETTING HELP

First Choice's Help system is called *context sensitive* because the help that you get depends on what you're doing at the moment. For example, when you're working with a menu, the Help key (F1) can be used to remind you of the purpose of any particular menu choice.

Let's see how Help works by doing the following exercise:

1. Return to the Main menu by pressing the Esc key.

2. Move the cursor so that it's on the second item of the Main menu, *Create a database*.

3. Now press the F1 key. You'll see a screen of information about what will happen when you select *Create a database* from the Main menu (Figure 1.4).

4. At the bottom of the screen you'll see information about using different keys for various purposes.

5. For example, there's more information available about *Create a database*. To see it, press the PgDn key. This is called *scrolling* down. You can scroll back up by using the PgUp key.

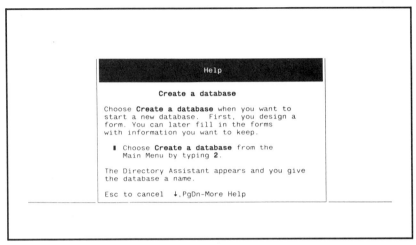

Figure 1.4: Help screen for *Create a database* option

No matter what you're doing within First Choice, you can usually get back to the Main menu by pressing the Esc key.

6. When you've finished reading the Help information, return to the Main menu by pressing the Esc key.

WORD PROCESSING BASICS

The first time that you begin to enter text into a word processor, you may find that strange and unexpected things happen. The following sections will give you some helpful hints.

THE KEYBOARD

Figure 1.5 shows some common keyboard layouts. As you can see, the keyboard layout for letters and numbers is the same as the layout on a standard typewriter. The Shift keys also function like the ones on a typewriter; you press them to get uppercase letters, and to get the special characters on the various keys of the keyboard, including the ten keys at the top numbered 1 through 10.

The Num Lock key controls the keys on the numeric keypad—the 11 keys on the right-hand side of the keyboard. Normally, Num Lock is off, and the keys are used for cursor control. (This is not true for the IBM enhanced keyboard, which has a separate set of cursor-control keys.) When Num Lock is on, the keys are used for the digits 0

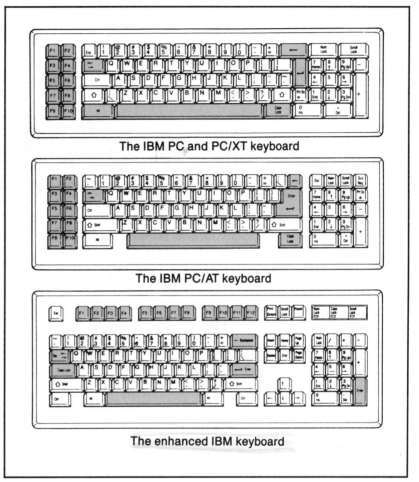

The IBM PC and PC/XT keyboard

The IBM PC/AT keyboard

The enhanced IBM keyboard

Figure 1.5: The IBM PC, PC/AT, and enhanced keyboards

through 9 and the decimal point. The Num Lock key is a *toggle:* press it once to turn Num Lock on; press it again to turn Num Lock off.

The Caps Lock key is another toggle key: press it once and the letter keys are locked into uppercase; press it again to unlock the letters back to lowercase. Only the letter keys are affected by the Caps Lock key: none of the other keys are shifted.

The Ctrl and Alt keys are similar to the Shift key, in that they are used together with other keys. To use either key, you hold it down, then press another key. First Choice uses several combinations of the Ctrl key plus another, or the Alt key plus another, for special purposes.

The Del and Backspace keys are used to delete characters: press the Del key, and the character directly over the cursor is deleted. Or, press the Backspace key and the character to the left of the cursor is deleted.

INSERT AND OVERWRITE MODES

The word processor can operate in either of two modes: *Insert* and *Overwrite*. Every time you begin working on a document, make sure that the word processor is in the Insert mode. Unfortunately, the word processor always starts up in the Overwrite mode. To enter the Insert mode, press the Ins key. You can always tell which mode is in effect by the shape of the cursor. In Overwrite mode the cursor is a blinking line. In Insert mode the cursor is a blinking square. You can use the Ins key to toggle back and forth between the two modes.

Insert is the normal mode to use for text entry and editing of documents. On the other hand, when you use the word processor to enter and edit information in First Choice's other modules, such as the database manager, the Overwrite mode is preferable.

If you accidentally press the Ins key and don't notice that the cursor changes to the Overwrite mode, you'll soon observe that your editing is not doing what you expect. Simply press the Ins key to return to the Insert mode and continue editing.

When new text is entered at the current cursor position, any existing text beyond the cursor (to the right and down) is pushed over to make room for the new text. If text runs over beyond the right margin, First Choice will automatically reformat that line, and any lines after that if necessary, to the end of the paragraph.

When the word processor is in the Overwrite mode, new text overwrites existing text at the cursor position. If you wish to replace existing text, move the cursor to the beginning of the string to be replaced and enter the new text. The new text replaces old, character for character. This method of text editing is useful provided that the new text is exactly the same length as the original. If you play around with this mode, you'll soon discover that it's usually more of a nuisance than a help when editing text.

CREATING A DOCUMENT

Now that you've been introduced to the word processing screen and the keyboard, it's time to begin using the software by creating a simple document. Make sure that your screen looks like the one shown in Figure 1.2 before going on.

As we mentioned earlier, a document is any type of text that you create with the word processor. Creating a document involves these basic steps:

- Select *Create a document* from the Main menu. This accesses the word processor.

- Enter the text at the keyboard, making sure the word processor is in Insert mode.

- Make corrections as needed, using the editing features of the word processor.

- Print out a copy of the document.

- Save a copy of the document on disk.

- Exit from First Choice or make another selection from the Main menu.

Suppose that you want to send a short note to one of your business associates. Also, you want to store a copy of the note on your floppy disk. In the following sections, we'll follow the steps necessary to carry this out. At the same time, we'll learn about some of First Choice's word processing features.

ENTERING TEXT

Now you're ready to enter your first text into First Choice's word processor. If you notice a typing error as soon as it occurs, you can delete a character by pressing the Backspace key.

As you enter text, you do *not* press ⏎ at the end of each line. One of the advantages of using a word processor like First Choice is that it keeps track of lines for you. When a word is too long to fit on a line, First Choice automatically moves the word to the next line. This is called automatic *wordwrap*.

As you enter text, the cursor moves along; it's always exactly at the spot where the next character will appear on the screen.

Enter the following paragraph at the keyboard:

Hi, Tom. I just wanted to let you know that our monthly sales meeting will be held on Monday at the Fish Grotto restaurant. Hope to see you then.

Don't worry about errors that you notice after you've finished; you'll take care of those in the following section.

Any document that you are currently working on with the word processor, such as the one you just typed, is called the *working copy,* which always resides in the computer's memory. If you have just retrieved a document from a disk file, then the working copy is an exact duplicate of that document. If you are creating a new document, then you must take care to protect it; if you accidentally wipe it out, there will be no disk file from which you can recover the original. You'll learn about saving documents to protect your work later in this chapter.

MAKING TEXT CORRECTIONS

After you've entered some text, you'd probably like to make changes or improvements. In this section you'll replace text, add a sentence, split one paragraph into two, and delete text. In order to make these changes, you have to move the cursor around the screen. Let's look at some cursor movement techniques.

MOVING THE CURSOR

The four cursor keys, ↑, ↓, ←, and →, can be used to move the cursor one character at a time in any direction. Let's practice using these keys:

1. Press the ← key several times. Notice how the cursor moves.

2. Continue pressing the ← key until the cursor is at the beginning of the word *Hope*.

3. Now press the ← key once more. Notice how the cursor jumps to the end of the previous line.

4. Hold the ← key down. This is one way to move the cursor rapidly.

5. Practice using the other cursor keys.

6. If you hold the ↓ down, you'll see your text scroll off the top of the screen. You can scroll it back by holding down the ↑ key.

USING A MOUSE FOR CURSOR MOVEMENT If you're using a mouse, remember that it has its own cursor on the screen: a solid, nonblinking bright rectangle. Whenever there's the possibility of confusion in our discussions, we'll refer to the *mouse cursor* and the *text cursor.*

You can use the mouse to position the text cursor. Simply drag the mouse cursor to the desired spot, then click any button on the mouse. The text cursor jumps to that spot.

Though you can use the PgUp and PgDn keys to scroll through a long document, you can use a mouse to quickly scroll in a very convenient way.

To scroll down a document, move the mouse cursor to the bottom line of the screen. Then hold any mouse button down. The text will scroll continuously down until you release the button.

To scroll up a document, position the mouse cursor on the Information line (the second line from the top of the screen). Then hold down any button, and the text will scroll up continuously.

Even though the end of your document is defined as the end of the last word, you can move past this point with any keystroke that moves the cursor down. First Choice is simply displaying "empty space" in the computer's memory.

OTHER WAYS TO MOVE THE CURSOR In addition to the four basic cursor keys, there are several other methods of moving the cursor around the screen. Table 1.1 lists these. You might want to become familiar with the keystrokes in this table; in many of the examples later in this chapter, we'll emphasize the use of these keystrokes.

CHANGING TEXT

In order to make an alteration to a specific part of the text, you must move the cursor to that location. First, be sure the word processor is in Insert mode. In the note you just typed, let's change the

The inside of the cover of this book also lists all the cursor-movement commands.

Table 1.1: Cursor Movement Operations

KEYSTROKE(S)	CURSOR MOVES TO
←	left by one character
→	right by one character
↑	up by one line
↓	down by one line
Ctrl →	beginning of next word
Ctrl ←	beginning of previous word
Tab	next tab setting
Shift-Tab	previous tab setting
Home	beginning of current line
End	end of current line
Home, Home	top of current screen
End, End	bottom of current screen
Ctrl-Home or Home, Home, Home	beginning of current document
Ctrl-End or End, End, End	end of current document
PgDn	beginning of next screen (down)
PgUp	beginning of previous screen (up)

word *Monday* to *Thursday*:

1. Move the cursor to the beginning of the word *Monday*.

2. Using the Del key, remove the entire word.

Did you notice that pressing the Del key deletes the character at the cursor position, and that the remaining text automatically moves left to fill in the space created by the deleted characters?

3. Now enter the word **Thursday**, making sure that there's a space after the word. Notice how the text automatically moves to make room for the new characters.

Now you'll see how the Overwrite mode can be useful.

1. Switch to the Overwrite mode by pressing the Ins key once.

2. Move the cursor to the beginning of the word *Thursday.*

3. Enter the word **Saturday**, watching what happens on the screen.

4. Return to the Insert mode by pressing the Ins key.

5. Move the cursor to the beginning of the word *Saturday.* Using the Delete key, delete *Saturday* and reinsert **Monday**.

CREATING BLANK LINES AND NEW PARAGRAPHS

You can add space to a document by adding blank lines at well-chosen positions. All you do is move the cursor to the end of the line after which a blank line is to be added, then press ←┘ once.

In a similar manner, you can split a single paragraph into two paragraphs, creating what is called a *paragraph break* (the beginning of a new paragraph). Just move the cursor to the position in the original paragraph where you want the break to occur, then press ←┘. If you want a blank line between the two new paragraphs, press ←┘ again. When you press ←┘, a special character called a *hard return* is inserted into the text. The hard return is treated by First Choice as an instruction to begin a new paragraph.

Remember, you can create a new paragraph as described above *only* if you are in the Insert mode. If you are in the Overwrite mode, pressing ←┘ simply moves the cursor to the next line.

The document that you created has one serious flaw: there should be a new paragraph after the opening salutation. Let's fix this.

> First Choice also supplies you with another (and slower) way to insert a new line: item 5 on the Edit menu.

1. Make sure that the Insert mode is on.

2. Move the cursor to the third word in the document (*I*).

3. Press ←┘, creating a paragraph break.

4. Press ←┘ again to create a blank line, and the document should look like the one shown in Figure 1.6.

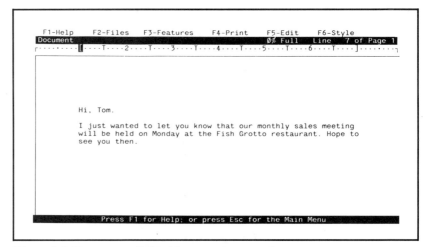

Figure 1.6: Document divided into two paragraphs

COMBINING PARAGRAPHS

You can combine two paragraphs into one by deleting the invisible hard return that separates them. Just position the cursor beyond the last character in the first paragraph, then press the Del key until the second paragraph joins the first one. Each time you press the Del key, you're removing either trailing blanks or an invisible hard return at the end of the paragraph.

ADDING TEXT

You can add text anywhere in your document. Just make sure that the word processor is in the Insert mode. Move the cursor to the desired location in the text, then enter the new text. As you enter text, First Choice automatically makes room for it by moving existing text.

Now add the following sentence after the word *restaurant* in the practice document:

We'll be discussing next year's salary increases.

When you're done, the document should look like the one shown in Figure 1.7. You might want to fix any errors before going on.

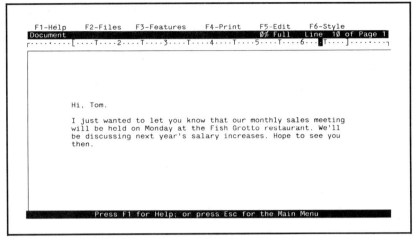

Figure 1.7: Document with an additional sentence

DELETING TEXT

You can use either of two keys for deleting text one character at a time. Pressing the Del key deletes the character at the cursor. Pressing the Backspace key deletes the character to the left of the cursor. This key behaves differently in the Insert and Overwrite modes. You may want to experiment with each to see the difference.

In addition, you can delete entire words, lines, paragraphs, or an arbitrary block of text in one operation. To do this, you'll use the Edit menu, which is described in the next section.

DELETING A WORD   First Choice provides two ways to delete an entire word. With the first method, you move the cursor to any letter of the word to be removed. Select *Edit* from the menu bar by pressing F5. The corresponding pull-down menu will appear (Figure 1.8). Now select item 8, *Erase this word,* in any of the following ways:

- Press the key numbered *8.*
- Use the ↓ key to move the menu cursor down to item 8, then press ⏎ to select the item.
- Use the mouse to select the item.

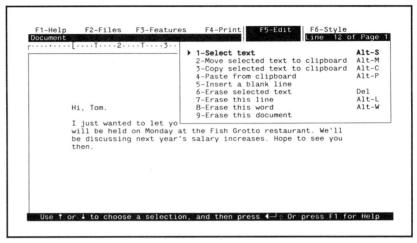

Figure 1.8: Edit pull-down menu

The word is deleted (including a blank space), and the remaining text is reformatted. In fact, you may see the entire paragraph wiggle around as this happens.

If the deleted word is at the beginning of a line, the next word on that line may fit on the previous line. Sometimes First Choice won't notice this, and you'll have to move it up yourself: move the cursor to the end of the previous line, then press the Del key once.

Because deleting a word is such a common operation, First Choice has a second method. This technique involves a *speed key*, which consists of a combination of the Alt key and another key. The speed key for deleting a word is Alt-W (W for *word*). Did you notice *Alt-W* on the Edit menu?

When you want to delete a word, just move the cursor to the word, then press the speed key Alt-W. This is considerably quicker than using the Edit menu, though the menu is handy if you can't remember the correct speed key.

Now let's delete the word *Fish* from the practice document, using the speed key.

1. Move the cursor to any character in the word.

2. Press Alt-W. The word *Fish* disappears, and the remaining text moves over to fill in the space.

First Choice has several speed keys for use in different operations. You'll meet them as you read on; a complete list of the speed keys appears inside the cover of this book.

DELETING A LINE You can delete an entire line at once, using methods similar to those for deleting a word. Move the cursor to any location on the line to be deleted. Next, call up the Edit menu, then select item 7, *Erase this line*. The entire line will disappear.

In some cases, you may need to take up space on the line above the deleted one. To do this, move the cursor to the end of that line, then press the Del key once.

The speed key for deleting a line is Alt-L (L for *line*). To use this speed key, move the cursor to the line to be removed, then press Alt-L. Again, if you forget which speed key to use, you can use the Edit menu to delete a line (the menu also reminds you what the speed key is). You may want to try entering a new line at the bottom of your document, then using the speed key Alt-L to delete the line.

To delete a blank line, you can press either Alt-L or simply the Del key. The latter works because First Choice treats a blank line as a single hard return, which can be deleted just like any other character.

DELETING THE WORKING COPY Once in a while you may decide that what you've done is rubbish, and that you wish to begin again. You can delete your entire working copy by first displaying the Edit menu, then selecting item 9, *Erase this document*. This is such a crucial choice that First Choice asks you if you really want to erase it. At this point, you can change your mind by pressing the Esc key. Be warned that once you've erased the working copy, there is absolutely no way to retrieve it.

If the working copy is a new document, there is no prior version of it on a disk file and you will have lost the document completely.

If your working copy was originally retrieved from a disk file, the disk file remains unchanged when you erase the working copy. This means that you can retrieve a copy of a document into the word processor, work with it for a while, then decide to abandon all of your changes. The original document remains untouched on the disk.

WORKING WITH BLOCKS OF TEXT

You will often find it convenient to work with just a group of characters, like a sentence or paragraph. Such a group is called a *block*. To define a block, you select the beginning and the end of the group of characters (we'll see how shortly). Once you have selected a block, you can do any of the following operations:

- Move the block from one part of a document to another
- Copy the block to a different part of the document
- Create a new document consisting only of the block
- Delete the block
- Print the block
- Boldface, underline, or italicize the block
- Center each line of the block
- Check the spelling of the block

In order to carry out some of the above operations, we'll make use of First Choice's *clipboard*. This is a special area set aside in memory where you can temporarily store any block of text that you wish.

You never actually see the clipboard, but it helps when using block operations for the first few times to visualize it as just that: a place where you temporarily clip a block of text.

HOW TO DEFINE A BLOCK

Before you can do anything with a block of text, you must first select, or define it. Remember: a block can be any group of consecutive characters. This might be just a few words, an entire sentence or paragraph, or even several pages. If a block is too long to fit on the clipboard, you can work with it in smaller parts.

Let's define a block in your practice document.

1. Move the cursor to the beginning of the sentence "We'll be discussing next year's salary increases." (directly under the "W").

2. Choose item 1, *Select text*, from the Edit menu (F5). This defines the start of the block.

You can also use the speed key Alt-S to define the beginning of a block, or to cancel (unselect) a block.

3. Expand the block with the → and ↓ cursor keys until the entire sentence is highlighted. When you're done, your screen should look like the one in Figure 1.9.

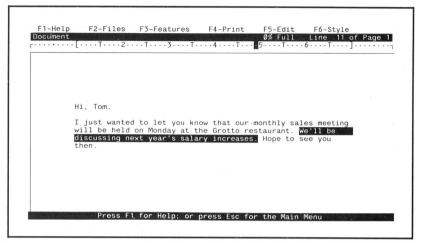

Figure 1.9: Sentence defined as a block of text

After you've defined the beginning of a block, you can use any combination of cursor-moving keystrokes to expand it. You can even make a block smaller by moving "backward" with the cursor keys. If you move the cursor to the left of the beginning of the block, the block expands in that direction. You can define an entire line as a block: move the cursor to any position on the line, then press the speed key Alt-H.

You'll soon learn how to move, copy, and delete blocks of text. All of these operations require the use of the clipboard.

USING THE MOUSE TO SELECT A BLOCK The mouse also can be used to select a block of text. Move the mouse cursor to the beginning of the text. Holding down a mouse button, drag the mouse cursor to the end of the block. If you let up on the mouse button, you'll have to start the whole process over again.

MOVING A TEXT BLOCK

Suppose that you want to move a group of text from one part of a document to another. You would first define the text as a block. Then, using the Edit menu, you'd move the block from its current position in the text to the clipboard. Next, place the cursor at the new position where the block is to be placed, then "paste" the block from the clipboard to the new location.

Using the practice document, let's move the sentence that begins, "We'll be discussing" to the end of the paragraph. If you haven't yet defined this sentence as a block, please do so before going on.

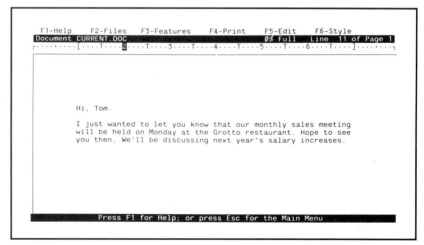

When you move a block of text, you must use the Edit menu three times: (1) to begin the process of selecting the text for the block, (2) to move the block to the clipboard, and (3) to paste the block from the clipboard to the new position in the document.

1. Choose *Move selected text to clipboard* from the Edit menu. Your sentence will be removed from the document. Don't worry: it's stored on First Choice's clipboard.

2. Take up any blank space as necessary by positioning the cursor after the word *restaurant* and pressing the Del key.

3. Move the cursor to the start of the sentence's new location, after the phrase ... *see you then.*

4. Select *Paste from clipboard* from the Edit menu. Your text will appear as the last sentence in the paragraph (Figure 1.10).

First Choice occasionally behaves a little unpredictably when you move or delete a block of text: sometimes the "leftover" blank space will be automatically filled in after the text is moved; other times you'll need to use the Del key to remove one or two spaces and readjust the remaining text.

```
 F1-Help    F2-Files   F3-Features    F4-Print    F5-Edit    F6-Style
Document CURRENT.DOC                            0% Full    Line  11 of Page 1
 r········[····T····2····T····3····T····4····T····5····T····6····T····]·········


        Hi, Tom.

        I just wanted to let you know that our monthly sales meeting
        will be held on Monday at the Grotto restaurant. Hope to see
        you then. We'll be discussing next year's salary increases.




               Press F1 for Help; or press Esc for the Main Menu
```

Figure 1.10: Rearranged text

USING SPEED KEYS WITH TEXT BLOCKS

In order to make working with blocks easier, First Choice offers several speed keys, which can be used instead of the corresponding selections on the Edit menu. Press the F5 key to see the menu so that you can see what the following items refer to:

Speed key	Edit menu choice
Alt-S	Select text
Alt-C	Copy selected text to clipboard
Alt-M	Move selected text to clipboard
Alt-P	Paste from clipboard

Now let's use the speed keys to move the last sentence in the practice document back to its original position:

1. Move the cursor to the beginning of the sentence "We'll be...."

2. Press the speed key Alt-S to begin defining the block.

3. Define the entire block by using the cursor-movement keys.

4. Press Alt-M to move the block to the clipboard.

5. Move the cursor to immediately after the word *restaurant.*

6. Press Alt-P to paste the block to its new location.

When a block is pasted immediately after a period, two extra spaces are inserted as well. You may want to use the Del key to delete one of these.

Try to get into the habit of using speed keys whenever possible; they'll greatly enhance your speed with First Choice. Remember that a list of all speed keys appears inside the cover of this book.

COPYING A TEXT BLOCK

In addition to moving a block of text, you can *copy* a block. The difference between the two operations is that when a block is moved, it's deleted from its original position. When a block is copied, the original text remains in place.

The procedure for copying a block is almost identical to that for moving a block. You first define the block to be copied, either by using the Alt-S speed key or by choosing *Select text* from the Edit menu. Copy the block to the clipboard, using the speed key Alt-C or choosing *Copy selected text to clipboard* from the Edit menu. Move the cursor to the position in the text where the block is to be copied, then paste the block to the new location from the clipboard, either by using the speed key Alt-P or by selecting the Edit menu and choosing *Paste from clipboard.*

Once a block of text is moved to the clipboard, it remains there until another block of text is put on the clipboard either by a copy or move operation.

DELETING A TEXT BLOCK

To delete a group of text, first define it as a block. Then, either select *Erase selected text* from the Edit menu, or press the Del key. Note that when text is deleted in this way, it is not placed on the clipboard: once the text has been deleted, it's gone forever.

A safer way to delete a block of text is to move it to the clipboard using the speed key Alt-M. Then, if you change your mind about the deletion, the text can be pasted back from the clipboard.

The contents of the clipboard are preserved by First Choice, even when you exit back to DOS.

Once a block of text is placed on the clipboard, either by a move or copy operation, it remains there until another block is moved or copied to the clipboard.

SAVING A COPY OF YOUR DOCUMENT

One of the advantages of using a word processor is that you can save your work, turn off the computer, then come back at a later time and pick up where you left off. In addition, because each document is "computerized," it's easy to make changes later.

As you work with a document, it's kept in the computer's main memory. However, if the computer accidentally loses power, or if you make certain types of mistakes, you can easily lose your working copy. You then have to reenter the entire document.

To prevent such disasters, it's a very good idea to copy your document to a disk periodically. How often you do this is a matter of how much of your work you're willing to risk, but the few seconds spent are usually a good investment.

If you plan to store your document on a hard disk, you can skip to the next section "The Directory Assistant." However, if you want to store your document on a floppy disk, *regardless of whether or not your computer has a hard disk,* continue reading.

If you're saving a document for the first time, make sure that the disk is *formatted.* (For instructions on how to format a disk, refer to Appendix A.)

For hard-disk computers:	Insert the floppy disk into drive A. If your computer has two floppy drives, you can use either drive A or drive B.
For floppy-disk computers:	Insert the floppy disk into drive B.

If you're saving a document that was retrieved from a floppy disk, that disk should still be in the same drive as the one used when the document was retrieved. Now you're ready to save your document.

THE DIRECTORY ASSISTANT

To save a document, you begin by selecting the Files menu with the F2 key (Figure 1.11). This menu gives you several options, and you may want to glance over them before going on. We'll come back to this menu later on, but for now let's select item 1, *Save a copy of this document.* When you do, the Directory Assistant of First Choice appears (Figure 1.12). Your display may differ to some extent from that shown in Figure 1.12, depending on whether you have a hard-disk computer, and also depending on which files are on your disk.

The Directory Assistant is one of First Choice's most commonly used features. You'll use it whenever you want to save or retrieve a file of any type. Let's look around the screen.

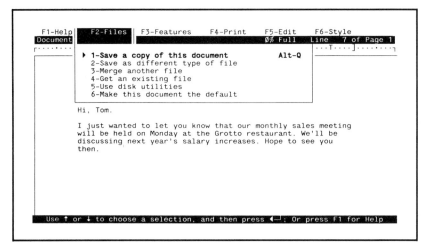

Figure 1.11: Files pull-down menu

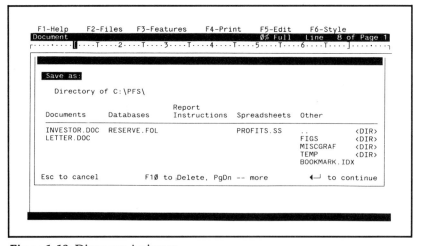

Figure 1.12: Directory Assistant

THE DIRECTORY LINE   The line beginning *Directory of...* provides this information:

- The *current drive,* which is the disk drive currently being accessed by First Choice (for a hard-disk computer, this is usually drive C). In Figure 1.12, the current drive is shown as **C:** (drive C).

- The *current subdirectory* is shown if the current drive is a hard disk. This indicates which subdirectory is currently being accessed by First Choice. For example, in Figure 1.12, the subdirectory \PFS on drive C is being accessed. This subdirectory is where the new file will be saved.

THE FILES DISPLAY   Regardless of what type of information you work with, it's stored in a *file*. There are different types of files: document files hold word-processed documents, spreadsheet files hold spreadsheets, and so on.

Each column on the bottom half of the screen contains the names of a particular type of file. For example, those files listed under the Spreadsheets column are for use in the spreadsheet module of First Choice. Each file listed under the Documents column is a document generated by word processing.

To distinguish each type of file, First Choice assigns unique *file extensions* (the last part of the file name). For example, each word-processed document ends with .DOC, each spreadsheet file ends with .SS, and so on.

Under the Other column, hard-disk users may see one or more entries labeled <DIR>. Each refers either to a subdirectory of the current directory or to its parent directory. The latter is indicated by the entry .. <DIR>.

CREATING A FILE FOR A NEW DOCUMENT

In this section you'll save your document to a file named FIRST. Just follow these steps:

1. If the Directory Assistant display is not showing, call it up from the word processor by choosing item 1 of the Files menu.

2. If either the current drive or the current subdirectory is not correct, enter the correct values:

For floppy-disk computers:	If the Directory line shows that the current drive is *not* B, then type in **B:** and press ←⏎. The Directory line should now show B as the current drive. You don't have to

move the cursor before entering the drive name.

For hard-disk computers: If you wish to use one of the floppy disk drives for storing the document, then enter the name of that drive (either **A:** or **B:**), followed by ⏎. If you wish to specify a different subdirectory from that shown on the Directory line, then enter the name of that subdirectory. For example, you would type in *\PFSFILES* if you want to store your document on that subdirectory. The Directory line will change accordingly.

3. If your working copy is brand new, there should be no name on the line reading *Save as:*. Enter the name **FIRST** for the new file that is to contain the document.

4. Press ⏎, and the document is written to the file named FIRST.DOC. (First Choice automatically adds the extension .DOC to the name of your file.) First Choice then returns to the word processor.

A file name can be up to eight characters long; the first character must be a letter. The name can contain digits, hyphens, underscores, and other special characters such as @. If you choose an illegal character, First Choice will warn you in a message, or it simply will not display the message *Saving....* It's a good idea to pick a file name that has some significance for you, so that you'll be able to recognize the contents of the file from its name.

PRINTING YOUR DOCUMENT

You can print all or part of your working copy at any time. The Print menu offers various options to be used in printing. In many cases, you can use First Choice's standard options.

Before you attempt to do any printing, make sure that the printer is ready to receive what First Choice will try to send to it. Check that:

- There is paper in the printer.

- The printer is attached to the correct port (connector) of the computer.
- The printer is on and the *Ready* or *Select* light is lit.

Now let's print the current working copy:

1. Press F4 for the Print menu (Figure 1.13).

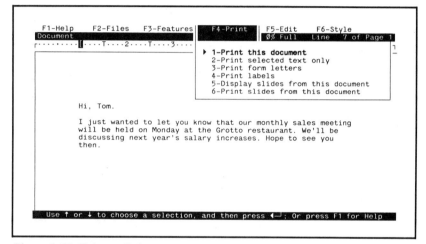

Figure 1.13: Print pull-down menu

2. Choose *Print this document.* The Print Options menu (Figure 1.14) will appear. First Choice comes with standard options preselected in this menu. For now, we'll print the document using these options. The next chapter discusses all of the choices on the Print Options menu.

3. Press ◄─ to accept the standard options and begin printing. You may be prompted here to insert a piece of paper. Press ◄─ again after having done so.

Your entire document should now be printed in *draft-quality* mode, which is the default selection of First Choice. Draft quality is usually the poorest quality print generated by a printer; however, it's also the fastest printing mode. (See the next chapter for a discussion of printing modes.)

Figure 1.14: Print Options menu

If your document fails to print, it could be due to one of the following reasons:

- The printer is not in the *Ready* or *Select* state.

- The printer is not properly connected to the computer.

- The incorrect port or printer type was selected when First Choice was customized for your computer.

HOW TO END A WORD PROCESSING SESSION

The speed key Alt-Q saves the document to the original file.

There are a few steps to take when you're ready to end the current session. First, you must save the current version of the working copy, as described earlier, either to the same file as the earlier version, or to a new file. In the first case, the earlier version is replaced by the working copy. However, if you store the document in a new file, the original version remains unchanged. The next step is to exit from the word processor. Since you've already saved FIRST, let's finish our word processing session and exit.

1. Press the Esc key. If you've made any changes to the working copy since the last time it was saved to a document, First

Choice informs you and gives you a chance to change your mind about exiting.

2. The screen then displays the Main menu, where you can make a new selection within First Choice or exit to DOS.

SUMMARY

You have now been introduced to most of the fundamental features of First Choice's word processor. These features will enable you to generate many different types of documents. Chapter 2 will explore more advanced word processing.

However, you may want to skip Chapter 2 and go on to learn about some of First Choice's other modules. You can then refer to Chapter 2 when you need information about advanced word processing operations.

Chapter

2

Advanced Editing and Formatting

Chapter 1 described how to use the basic word processing operations of First Choice. This chapter describes more advanced word processing features. The main topics that will be covered are

- Retrieving and replacing existing documents
- Enhancing your document with special effects
- Setting margins, page length, and spacing
- Creating headers and footers
- Setting and using tabs and indents
- Using the bookmark feature
- Checking the spelling of a document
- Creating your own dictionary
- Finding synonyms for a word
- Searching a document for selected text
- Finding and replacing text automatically
- Advanced document manipulation features
- Advanced printing features

This chapter can be used either as a reference guide to First Choice's word processor (along with Chapter 1), or as a continuation of the tutorial begun in Chapter 1. If you are reading this chapter as a tutorial, note that we'll continue to use the document FIRST.DOC in the exercises.

Before proceeding with this chapter, make sure that your computer is on and that First Choice is running; the Main menu should be displayed on your screen.

If you plan to use another document while following each topic, retrieve it using the procedure in the next section.

RETRIEVING AN EXISTING DOCUMENT

There will be many times when you will want to retrieve an existing document from a disk. This might be to update the document, or perhaps to print it. In order to do anything with a document, you must first bring it into the computer's memory, so that it becomes First Choice's current working copy. Let's retrieve the document from the file named FIRST.DOC. Here are the steps to follow:

1. Make sure that First Choice is running, and that the Main menu is displayed.

2. Select item 6, *Get an existing file.* The Directory Assistant display will appear, asking you to supply the name of the file to retrieve. (You may want to review the discussion of the Directory Assistant in Chapter 1.)

3. **For floppy-disk computers:** Insert the correct data disk into drive B. Then type **B:** and press ←⏎.

   For hard-disk computers: Type in the name of the subdirectory in which the file is stored. Or, if the file is on a floppy disk, insert the floppy into drive A, then type **A:** and press ←⏎.

4. If there are many files on your disk drive (or on the current subdirectory), the file name that you want may not be visible. Use the PgDn and PgUp keys to scroll through all of the file names until you see the one that you want.

5. Using the cursor keys, move down the list of document files until the correct one is highlighted.

6. Press ◄─┘ to select that file. First Choice retrieves the document in that file, makes it the working copy, and puts you into the word processor.

   Alternatively, you may type in the file name, **FIRST.DOC**, then press ◄─┘. If you do this, you *must* include its extension, .DOC. If you enter the name of a nonexistent file, First Choice issues a message to that effect. You can then try again to enter the correct file name. (Notice that First Choice is demonstrating a bit of intelligence: because the file ends with the extension .DOC, First Choice knows that the file contains a document, and it therefore calls up the word processor.)

 When you retrieve a file from a disk, the current working copy in memory is destroyed. This is a common way of losing a lot of valuable work (and patience). First Choice informs you if you have made any changes since the last time you saved a copy of the current working copy, giving you a chance to save it before retrieving the new document.

REPLACING AN EXISTING DOCUMENT

If you change your mind and decide not to replace the existing copy in the file, you can back out of the process by pressing the Esc key. First Choice will return you to the word processor without replacing the contents of the file.

You will often replace an existing document with an updated version. For example, you may wish to retrieve an old document from a file, update it, and then replace the old version with the new one.

In order to replace the old version, call up the Directory Assistant from the word processor (item 1 of the Files menu). The name of the document containing the original file should appear. Press ◄─┘ to indicate that the current file name is correct. In response to the screen query, press ◄─┘ again to verify that you indeed wish to replace the old version of the document with the new one.

If you want to save the working copy back to the file from which it was originally retrieved, you can use the speed key Alt-Q (for quick save). The current working copy replaces the original version on the file. Be careful when you use this command, because First Choice doesn't give you a chance to change your mind; when you press Alt-Q , the file is immediately updated.

KEEPING SEVERAL VERSIONS

Suppose that you have retrieved an old document, made some changes to it, and want to save the new version, but you also want to retain the original version. You can do so by first calling up the Directory Assistant from the word processor (item 1 of the Files menu). Make sure that the correct disk drive and subdirectory are displayed, as described in Chapter 1. Enter a new file name by overwriting the existing name. (You can most easily do this by selecting the Overwrite mode with the Ins key. The cursor will look like a blinking line in this mode.) Make sure that you overwrite the entire file name, using blank spaces if necessary to get rid of unwanted characters from the old name. Press ← to create the new file. If a file with that name already exists, First Choice will warn you, asking if you wish to replace the contents of that file.

ENHANCING YOUR DOCUMENT WITH SPECIAL EFFECTS

The First Choice word processor allows you to enter text quickly, fix errors, and move blocks around. Several other features let you improve significantly the appearance of a document. This section explains how to use these features, or *styles:*

- Boldfacing
- Underlining
- Italicizing
- Superscripting

- Subscripting
- Double spacing
- Centering

Each of these is available from the Style menu, which you can access by pressing the F6 key. You can specify any of these styles to change the appearance of an existing block of text, or when entering new text.

BOLDFACING EXISTING TEXT

Suppose that you decide to boldface a block of existing text in a document. To illustrate how to do this, we'll boldface the text *Grotto* in your FIRST document. If you haven't retrieved the file, do so now.

1. First define the text to be boldfaced as a block. Move the cursor to the beginning of the string, to the *G* in *Grotto*. Define the beginning of the block, using either the Alt-S speed key or by selecting *Select text* from the Edit menu. Expand the block by using cursor-movement keys to include all of the text to be boldfaced.

2. Press F6 for the Style menu (Figure 2.1). (You can use the speed key Alt-B instead of the Style menu.)

3. Select item 1, *Boldface*.

4. Press Alt-S to deselect the block, and the selected text should appear boldfaced on the screen.

If your screen does not show the boldfacing, try adjusting the contrast and brightness controls of the monitor. If this fails, the monitor may not be working properly.

Text that is boldfaced on the screen will also appear boldfaced when the document is printed out. If it doesn't, the equipment setup process will have to be redone and the proper printer selected (see "Customizing PFS: First Choice for Your Computer" in Appendix A).

Figure 2.1: Style pull-down menu

BOLDFACING TEXT AS YOU TYPE

You also can tell First Choice to enter new text at the beginning of a new paragraph as automatically boldfaced. Make sure that you are in the Insert mode (cursor is a square). Move the cursor to the start of a new blank line and select *Boldface* from the Style menu, or press the speed key Alt-B. Begin typing your text. When you wish to end bold-facing, select *Erase style* from the Style menu, or press the speed key Alt-N. Subsequent text will be entered normally.

If you enter text in the middle of a group of boldfaced characters, the new text will also be boldfaced. Otherwise, you can't enter new text directly as boldfaced in the middle of a document. You must first enter the text normally, then select it as a block and boldface the block.

When entering stylized text as a new paragraph, First Choice inserts a superflu-ous leading blank. You can delete this blank with the Del key.

SELECTING OTHER STYLES

You can use the techniques illustrated above with any of the special styles listed in the Style menu. To change existing text, define the desired text as a block, then choose the desired style from the Style menu. The selected text will be given the chosen style.

Let's add a paragraph to the FIRST document to practice enter-ing new text with a special style. We'll underline the first part of the paragraph, for emphasis.

1. Move the cursor to the end of the document, then press ◄─┘ twice.

2. Choose item 2, *Underline,* from the Style menu, or press the speed key Alt-U.

3. Type

   Nobody at all

   in the desired style. The text should appear underlined on your screen.

4. Turn off underlining by selecting item 6, *Erase style,* from the Style menu, or press the speed key Alt-U.

5. Type in the remainder of the paragraph in normal text style:

   has suggested any new business items, so the meeting should be a shortie. Any last-minute business can be brought up after dessert.

When you select text as a block, then assign it a particular style, such as boldfaced or underlined, the text remains selected. This allows you the option of selecting additional styles for the block. To deselect the block, simply press Esc or Alt-S.

WHAT'S MY STYLE? In First Choice, the following styles cannot be displayed properly on a computer monitor: superscript, subscript, and italic. As a compromise, First Choice displays all of these styles as boldface so that you can tell when a block of text is in a special style. If you're not sure what style or styles have been assigned to a particular character on the screen, you can find out by moving the cursor to that character and pressing F6 for the Style menu. The styles assigned to that character will be preceded by a bullet.

Even though many styles won't show up properly on the screen, they should appear when printed, provided that your printer has the capability to handle them, and that First Choice has been properly installed for your printer.

Nearly all printers can handle boldfacing and underlining, but some of the older ones cannot print the italic, superscript, or subscript styles. If your printer doesn't do what you think it should, you may need to pore over its manual or consult an expert.

If you do not know what kind of printer you have, you may have selected *Unlisted Printer* when you customized First Choice for your computer. In that case, the printer may only boldface and underline text because First Choice is sending incorrect codes for superscript, subscript, and italic.

COMBINING STYLES   Many styles can be combined. You can boldface and underline the same text string, for example, by using the speed key Alt-. There are a few obvious incompatibilities; for instance, it doesn't make sense to assign both superscript and subscript styles to the same text.

UNDOING A STYLE   It is possible to remove a style from a block of text. For example, you may wish to unboldface a word or two. To accomplish this, define the desired text as a block. Then either choose *Erase style* from the Style menu, or use the speed key Alt-N. All special styles will be eliminated from the selected text. You can also use the speed key Alt-N to undo one character at a time.

Before going on, save the current version of the practice document for later use:

1. Make sure that the document looks exactly like the one in Figure 2.2.

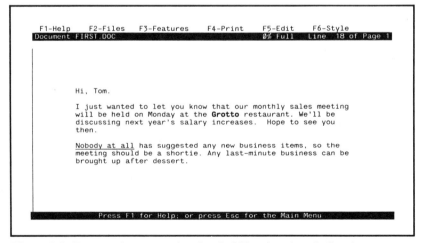

Figure 2.2: Current document showing boldfaced and underlined text

2. Press F2 for the Files menu, then select item 1, *Save a copy of this document.* The Directory Assistant should appear.

3. If the file name FIRST.DOC appears after *Save as:*, press ↵, then verify with another ↵. The current version of your document will replace the old one. If no file name appears, or a different file name appears, type **FIRST.DOC**, overwriting any other file name.

CHANGING PAGE APPEARANCE

There are several ways you can control the way a page looks, both on the screen and when printed. These include margin sizes, line spacing, tabs, and page numbering.

WORKING WITH RULERS

The Ruler line, which is the third line down from the top of the page, controls several layout features of your document, such as left and right margins and tab settings. The left and right margin settings are indicated by the characters [and], which are set at columns 10 and 70. Each tab setting is indicated by the letter T.

If you want to change the margins, tab settings, or the indent in the middle of a document, you can do so by creating a new ruler at that spot in the document and then changing the appropriate settings in that ruler. The ruler shows on the screen but is not printed.

You can insert as many rulers as you like into a document. The margin, tab, and indent settings of each ruler affect all following text, up until a new ruler appears. Its settings, in turn, affect subsequent text.

To insert a ruler into the text, move the cursor to the place that the ruler is to appear. Select *Insert ruler* from the Features menu, or press the speed key Alt-R. The ruler will appear on the screen.

Initially, each new ruler will take on the settings of the ruler immediately above it in the text. You can change any of these settings by selecting *Change current ruler* from the Features menu or by pressing Alt-G. The cursor is placed on the nearest ruler above, and you can then make any desired changes to it.

At any time, you can change margin, tab, or indent settings on a ruler by moving the cursor to it and making any desired alterations.

CH. 2

However, existing text below the ruler is affected only by changes to the margin settings; changes to either tab or indent settings affect only text entered after the new settings are made.

CHANGING THE TOP RULER   Initially, the ruler at the top of the screen contains First Choice's default settings for margins and tabs. You can change these by moving the cursor above all rulers in the document. Press the speed key Alt-G. A duplicate of the top ruler appears at the top of the document with the cursor positioned on it. You can then make any desired changes to the settings on the ruler.

HIDING THE RULERS   While you are working with a document, it's usually a good idea to leave the rulers displayed to help you understand why margins and tabs are appearing as they do. Sometimes, however, you may wish to eliminate the rulers from the screen, so that you can get a clean picture of your document.

To hide the rulers, select *Hide rulers* from the Features menu. Although the rulers disappear from the screen, they're still buried within your document. To redisplay the rulers, select *Show rulers* from the Features menu. The rulers are also redisplayed whenever you insert a new ruler.

ERASING A RULER   You can erase a ruler by moving the cursor onto it, then pressing the speed key Alt-L (or by selecting *Erase this ruler* from the Edit menu). If a ruler is erased, text following it is reformatted to conform to the margin settings of the previous ruler.

CHANGING LEFT AND RIGHT MARGINS

To change the margin settings, first insert a ruler at the desired location. Then, to change each margin, move the cursor to the desired column position and enter the appropriate keystroke.

Either the Insert or Overwrite modes can be used for changing margins.

Let's suppose that we want to add some new text to the end of the current working copy, but with new left and right margins of 20 and 60:

1. Move the cursor to the first blank line at the end of the document.

2. Create a new ruler, either by selecting *Insert ruler* from the Features menu, or by using the speed key Alt-R. The new ruler appears on the line above the current cursor position, which in this case is at the end of the document. Notice that this ruler has the same margin and tab settings as the original ruler at the top of the screen.

3. Move the cursor to column 20 on the new ruler, then enter the character [, which stands for *left margin*. When you do this, the old left margin setting disappears, and the new one appears at column 20.

4. Move the cursor to column 60, then enter the character], which stands for *right margin*. The old right margin setting is replaced by the one at position 60.

5. Press ◄━┘ to move the cursor to the blank line after the new ruler, then enter the following text:

> **This is a demonstration of how to modify margins within a document.**

The margins of text following the new ruler will conform to the margin settings of that ruler.

At any time, you can move the cursor to an existing ruler and change one or both margins. Text following the ruler will be automatically reformatted as soon as you move the cursor off the ruler.

Many printers are capable of printing more than 80 characters per line. For example, in condensed mode many printers can print over 110 characters. To accommodate this fact, the right margin can be set within First Choice to a maximum of 250. However, for lines longer than 79 characters, part of each line will always be off the screen. However, First Choice will continuously adjust the screen so that the text that you're entering is always visible.

CHANGING TAB SETTINGS

Tab settings in the word processor are similar to those used on a typewriter. When you press the Tab key, the cursor moves to the next tab setting. First Choice comes with preselected tab settings, shown on the Ruler line at the top of the screen, but you can change these as needed.

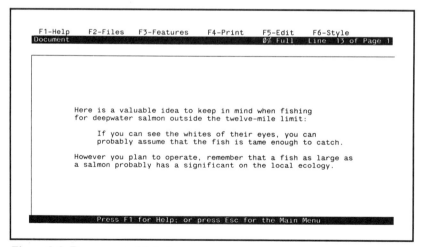

When changing tab settings, you can use either the Insert or Overwrite modes.

To insert one or more new tab settings into a document, you follow basically the same steps you do for changing margins. First, insert a new ruler where the new settings are to take effect. Move the cursor onto the new Ruler line to the desired column and press **T**.

To delete a tab setting, move the cursor to the setting and press the spacebar.

All text typed in below the ruler after the new tab settings are made will conform to those settings. However, existing text is not affected. Note that this is different from changing margin settings on a ruler, which does alter the margins of existing text below the ruler.

You can change the tab position of text that's already been entered as follows:

- Move the cursor to the beginning of the paragraph whose tab position is to be changed.

- Add or delete as many spaces as you wish. The text after these spaces will be automatically reformatted.

CREATING AN INDENT

An *indent* is a temporary left margin. Figure 2.3 shows a document that uses indents. You can create an indent as follows:

```
   F1-Help     F2-Files    F3-Features    F4-Print    F5-Edit    F6-Style
  Document                                    0% Full    Line  13 of Page 1



          Here is a valuable idea to keep in mind when fishing
          for deepwater salmon outside the twelve-mile limit:

                 If you can see the whites of their eyes, you can
                 probably assume that the fish is tame enough to catch.

          However you plan to operate, remember that a fish as large as
          a salmon probably has a significant on the local ecology.




              Press F1 for Help; or press Esc for the Main Menu
```

Figure 2.3: Document with indents

You can use the speed key Alt-I to place the indent marker on the first ruler above the cursor location.

- Move the cursor to the place in the document where indenting is to occur.

- Press the speed key Alt-R to insert a new ruler.

- Move the cursor *on the ruler* to the column where the indenting is to begin.

- Press **I**, and the > symbol will appear on the ruler.

- Move the cursor off the ruler and add the new text.

All new text entered after the ruler will be indented, but existing text is not affected. To end indentation, press the speed key Alt-I, and the indent marker will be erased from the ruler.

You can undo the indenting of existing text, but it's a bit of a nuisance. First, you must make sure that there is no indent currently set. Then, you must delete each space at the beginning of each indented line, using the Del or Backspace keys. Make sure that the Insert mode is turned on (the cursor will be a blinking square).

Similarly, you can't change indented text from one left margin setting to another—you must delete the text and reenter it with a new indent setting. However, you can get around this problem by "simulating" an indent: insert one ruler before the indented text to set the left margin, then insert a second ruler right after the indented text to restore the original margin setting.

SETTING TOP AND BOTTOM MARGINS AND PAGE LENGTH

You can control to a great extent how much information appears on each page by setting the top and bottom margins and the page length. A standard page consists of 66 single-spaced lines. Margins reduce the amount of printed text on a page, but can greatly enhance the page appearance.

First Choice comes with the top and bottom margins preset to 6 lines each. That means that there are six blank lines at the top and bottom of each page. For a standard printer generating 6 lines per inch, this amounts to 1-inch margins.

All margins are shown on the screen. When you come to the end of a page, which is called a *page-break,* you'll see the top and bottom margins between the two pages. The page-break itself is indicated on the screen by a solid double line.

To change either of the margin settings, or to change the total length of each page (for example, legal-size paper has 84 lines per page), follow the steps below, where we'll change the top and bottom margins on our practice document:

1. Press F3 for the Features menu.

2. Select *Set page size, headers, and footers,* which brings up the menu shown in Figure 2.4. This menu contains, among other things, the current settings for the margins and the page length.

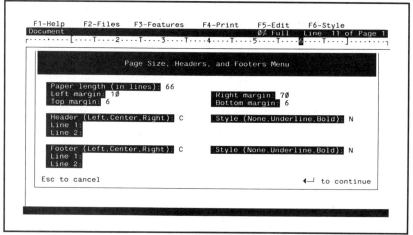

Figure 2.4: Page Size, Headers, and Footers

3. Move to the *Top margin* setting with the Tab key, then type in the new value **10**. (To move back up the menu, use the key combination Shift-Tab.)

4. Move to the *Bottom margin* setting with the Tab key and type in **10**.

5. When you are done making changes, exit back to the document by pressing ←⏎. Notice that the Information line at the

top of the screen now indicates that the first line of the document begins on line 11. Also, the screen displays more blank space (10 lines total) above the first line of text.

6. Before going on, change the top and bottom margins back to six lines each.

A new top or bottom margin setting affects the entire document. That is, you can't change either of these margins in the middle of the document.

When you erase the working copy, the margin and page length settings are returned to their default values. When you save a document to a disk, its margin and page length settings are saved as well. Then, whenever you load an existing document into the word processor, its margin and page length settings become the current ones.

HEADERS AND FOOTERS

You must leave enough room in the top or bottom margin for the header or footer. For example, for a two-line header, the top margin must be at least two lines long.

A *header* is a section of text that appears at the top of each printed page of a document. A *footer* appears at the bottom of each page. It's not necessary for a document to have a header or a footer, but they can often enhance its appearance. If a header or footer exists, it will appear on the screen as well as on the printed output. And, you can have a header or footer in bold or underlined text, with or without page numbers.

We'll create a header for our practice document that reads *My document.* The header will be boldfaced, and will have page numbers starting with page 1.

1. Choose *Set page size, headers, and footers* from the Features menu to display the menu shown in Figure 2.4.

2. Use the Tab key to move the cursor down to the line reading *Header (Left, Center, Right)*. You can specify whether the header is to be positioned to the left (L), centered (C), or to the right (R). We'll place ours to the right, so enter **R**.

3. Press the Tab key once to move the cursor to the Header Style position. Our header is to be boldfaced, so type **B**.

4. Press the Tab key once more to position the cursor at line 1 of the header. Enter the following header text, leaving a few spaces between *document* and **1**:

   My document   *1*

   The *1* indicates that page numbers are to be printed in the header, starting with page 1.

5. Press ◄—◄ to return to the document. The header appears at the top of the document (Figure 2.5).

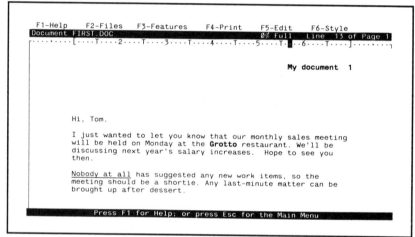

Figure 2.5: FIRST document with a header

To create a footer, repeat the above steps for the footer entries in the Page Size, Headers, and Footers menu.

If you want the document to have a cover page without a page number or header (or footer), type *0* in the header (or footer). Page numbering at 1, along with the header, will begin on the second page. For two or more cover pages, use an appropriate negative number. For example, for two cover pages, type *-1* on the header line.

You can edit a header or footer with any of the keys that you use for ordinary text editing. For example, pressing the End key moves the cursor to the end of a line. Or, you can delete an entire header line with the speed key Alt-L.

LINE SPACING

You can use the Style menu to adjust the line spacing of part or all of a document, either to single or double spacing. Existing text that is single-spaced can be changed to double spacing, and vice versa. New text can be entered either single- or double-spaced.

SPACING OF EXISTING TEXT   To change the spacing of existing text, select the text lines to be double-spaced by moving the cursor to the beginning of the desired text, then pressing the speed key Alt-S to define the beginning of the block. Expand the block to include all of the desired text. Select *Double space* or *Single space* from the Style menu. The text block will be spaced accordingly.

not shown on
Style menu !

SPACING OF NEW TEXT   To enter new text double-spaced, move the cursor to the beginning of the new line where text is to be entered, and select *Double space* from the Style menu. Enter the text. To return to single spacing, select *Single space* from the Style menu. New text will be entered single-spaced, beginning with the current line.

CENTERING TEXT

You can center a block of existing text, or you can create new text that's automatically centered as it's typed in.

To center one or more lines of existing text, first select the text as a block. Then choose *Center* from the Style menu. Each line will be centered between the existing margins, by adding or deleting blanks at the beginning of the line. If you subsequently change the existing margins, lines that were previously centered will have to be recentered.

To center one or more lines as they're being entered, select *Center* from the Style menu, then enter the text. Each line will be centered automatically. This feature is most useful for short title lines, and usually you'll want to make each line a separate paragraph by ending it with a hard return (by pressing ◄┘). To end the centering, select *Stop centering* from the Style menu.

STARTING A NEW PAGE

First Choice begins a new page automatically when the current page has filled up. With the standard settings (six lines each for top and bottom margins and a page length of 66 lines), each page consists of 54 text lines, plus any header or footer.

A page-break is indicated on the screen by a solid double line extending across the entire screen. You can see this by pressing the PgDn key several times. Remember that you can scroll past the end of your document—First Choice shows you the blank space left in memory, as well as each page-break.

If you want to force a new page to begin at a particular spot in the text, move the cursor to the line *above* which the new page is to begin, then select *Start new page* from the Features menu. First Choice will insert the special command *NEW PAGE* into the text, and you'll see the page-break appear. Although this command appears on the screen, it won't be printed.

NOT IN FEATURES MENU

You can also insert the *NEW PAGE* (or simply *N*) command yourself wherever you want a page-break to occur. Note that this command must be at the beginning of a line, and no other text can be on the line.

KEEPING YOUR PLACE WITH BOOKMARKS

If you're working with a long document, you may want to temporarily move to one part of it, then come back to the original position. This is made easy by a nice feature of First Choice: the *bookmark*. You can set a bookmark at the current cursor position, go do something else, and then return directly to that bookmark. Up to nine bookmarks can be in use within First Choice at the same time.

As we'll see later, bookmarks have an even more valuable feature: you can use them to jump instantly from one document to another, or from one First Choice application to another.

You can't set a bookmark on a blank space. Also, two bookmarks can't be set at the same position.

Before you can insert a bookmark into a document (or any other type of First Choice application), the document must have been saved to disk. In other words, you can't place a bookmark into a new working copy for which there is no disk file. The reason for this is that when a bookmark is set, First Choice places it not only in the working copy, but also in the corresponding disk file. This allows rapid movement between bookmarks.

To use a bookmark, move the cursor to the place in the document that you want to remember. Set a bookmark at this position by selecting *Set bookmark* from the Features menu. The Bookmark menu will appear (Figure 2.6). Select any bookmark by typing in a number between one and nine. Press ← to return to the document. The position of the bookmark will be indicated by a highlight.

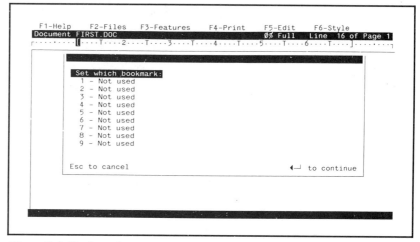

Figure 2.6: Bookmark menu

Now you can continue editing in the document. When you need to return to the location of the bookmark, select *Find bookmark* from the Features menu. The Bookmark menu describes the position of each set bookmark. Type the bookmark number, then press ←.

If you remember the number of the bookmark, you can use a speed key to go directly to it. For example, to go directly to bookmark 1, press Alt-1.

For more information about bookmarks, see Chapter 11.

CHECKING YOUR DOCUMENT FOR SPELLING ERRORS

First Choice's built-in dictionary can be used to check a document (or a block of text) for spelling errors. You can also create a personal dictionary for spell checking that can include unusual words not in First Choice's dictionary. Installation of the dictionary depends on the type of computer you have:

For floppy-disk computers:	The dictionary is on the Dictionary disk. Insert this disk into drive B of the computer.
For hard-disk computers:	The dictionary should be on the hard disk along with the other First Choice programs.

WHAT THE SPELL CHECKER CHECKS

The spell checker actually does more than look for spelling errors. When it examines a document with First Choice's built-in dictionary, it will catch the following:

- Any word that does not appear in either the built-in or personal dictionaries

- Some capitalization errors

- Incorrect punctuation of numbers, such as *35,20.00*

- Any word that's repeated twice in a row

When any of the above errors is detected, First Choice pauses with an error message for you.

If a spelling error is found, First Choice displays likely spelling alternatives (if any) from its dictionary. You're then given the following choices:

- Accept the word as is. (In other words, even though First Choice thinks it's not correct, you do.)

- Fix the error, either by deleting the word or changing its spelling.

- If the "error" is a word not found in the main dictionary, add it to your personal dictionary.

When other types of errors are found, the spell checker gives you similar choices: accept the "error" as is, or fix it.

STARTING THE SPELL CHECKER

Here are the steps for inspecting an entire document with the spell checker. We'll spell-check our FIRST practice document.

1. Move the cursor to the beginning of the document. Spell-checking always begins at the current cursor position.

2. Select *Check spelling* from the Features menu. Spell-checking begins, and you can watch the progress at the bottom of the screen.

3. When First Choice finds a word that does not appear in its dictionary, or when it finds some other type of error, it pauses to give you a message (see Figure 2.7).

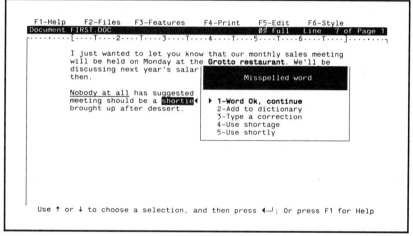

Figure 2.7: The spell checker finds an "error"

4. In the example in Figure 2.7, First Choice indicates that the word *shortie* is not in the main dictionary. Your options are

   a. Accept the word as it is, and continue with the spell-checking.

   b. Add *shortie* to your personal dictionary (you'll learn about this in a moment).

   c. Make corrections to the word before going on.

   d. Replace *shortie* with *shortage*.

   e. Replace *shortie* with *shortly*.

In this example, First Choice has found two words in its dictionary that resemble *shortie* (options 4 and 5). Sometimes First Choice will find no possibilities; other times it may find several.

5. For our document, choose option 1, *Word OK, continue;* the spell-checking continues.

CREATING A PERSONAL DICTIONARY

As in the above example, whenever First Choice encounters a word that's not in its dictionary, it gives you the option of adding the word to your own dictionary. This can be very handy, especially if you do a lot of technical writing.

Your personal dictionary is stored in a file named PERSONAL.FC, and you can add virtually anything to it. There are two ways to do this:

- Select option 2, *Add to dictionary*, when an unknown word is found during spell-checking.

- Enter a list of words directly into the dictionary.

The personal dictionary, PERSONAL.FC, is stored as an ordinary word processed file. You can bring it into the word processor, just as you would any other file, as follows:

- Select *Get an existing file* from the Files menu.

- When the Directory Assistant appears, use the PgDn key to scroll down the list of files in the *Other* column, until PERSONAL.FC appears.

- Use the cursor keys to select PERSONAL.FC, then press ◄─┘.

- The file becomes the working copy, and you can view the current contents of the dictionary.

If no personal dictionary exists (i.e., there is no file with the name PERSONAL.FC), you can create a new document and store it in the file PERSONAL.FC.

Each word in the dictionary must begin on a new line. Also, it's a good idea to keep words in alphabetical order. This can improve the searching speed if the dictionary contains a large number of entries. You can edit the personal dictionary just as you would any other document, by adding new words or by deleting or modifying existing words.

You can create several different personal dictionaries with the word processor, each one for a specific use. To do this, observe the following rules:

- Store each dictionary in a separate file (such as MYDICT1, MYDICT2, etc.).

- When you want to use a specific dictionary to check the spelling of a document, use the disk utilities module to change the name of the file PERSONAL.FC to something else.

- Use the disk utilities module to change the file name of the dictionary that you want to use to PERSONAL.FC.

For details about the disk utilities module, see Chapter 11.

SPELL CHECKING A BLOCK

You can check the spelling of a selected block of text. To do so, select the text as a block. Then choose *Check spelling* from the Features menu. Only the text in the block will be checked.

USING THE THESAURUS

You can use First Choice's built-in thesaurus to find alternatives for a particular word. Moveover, once you've found a group of synonyms for a word, you can continue the process by finding synonyms for any word in the first group of synonyms!

Let's find an alternative for the word *business* in our practice document; we've used it twice, and would like to use another word. (If you're using a floppy-disk computer, first insert the Dictionary disk into drive B of the computer.) Follow these steps:

1. Move the cursor to any letter in the second occurrence of the word *business*.

2. Select *Find synonyms* from the Features menu. First Choice grinds away for a few seconds, then displays the synonyms that it's found (Figure 2.8).

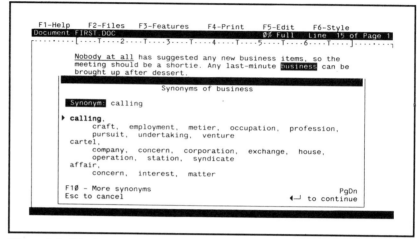

Figure 2.8: Display of synonyms for *business*

3. Often (as in this case), not all of the synonyms that were found will fit on the screen; use the PgDn and PgUp keys to scroll through the entire list.

At this point, you can do one of three things. You can exit from the synonyms display with the Esc key, you can select a word from the list of synonyms and use it to replace the original word in the text, or you can find synonyms for other words on the screen.

To find synonyms for any word on the screen, move the cursor to the desired word, then press the F10 key. The synonyms for the selected word will be displayed. You can continue this process until you run out of either words or patience. Let's replace *business* with *matter.*

1. Use the cursor keys to move the cursor to *matter.*

2. Press ◄─┘, and that word will be substituted in the text.

SEARCHING AND REPLACING WORDS

You can use First Choice features to search for a specific word within a document. This can be useful when you are working with a long document and want to find a particular section. It's also very useful if you want to replace all occurrences of a certain word with another word or phrase. This process is called *Find and Replace*. For example, you might want to replace all instances of *exquisite* within a document with the phrase *very nice*.

REPLACING WORDS

Let's use the Find and Replace feature of First Choice to change *business* to *work* in the text:

1. Move the cursor to the beginning of the document. Searching always begins at the current cursor position.

2. Select *Find and replace* from the Features menu, or press the speed key Alt-F. The display shown in Figure 2.9 will appear. You can use the Tab, Shift-Tab, ↑, and ↓ keys to move back and forth in this display.

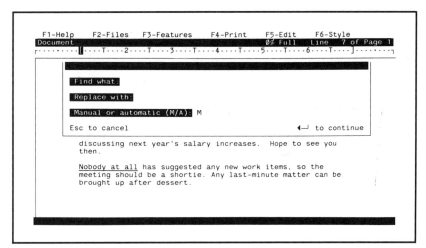

Figure 2.9: Find and Replace display

3. Enter the original word (**business**) on the first line.

4. Enter the new word (**work**) on the second line.

5. Move to the third line in the display. If you enter **A**, all replacements will be made automatically. If you enter **M**, you'll be asked to verify each replacement before it's made.

6. Press ⏎ to begin the Find and Replace operation. When First Choice is finished, it tells you how many words were replaced.

First Choice finds *every* occurrence of the string that you specify, even if it's only part of a larger word. For example, if you specify that you want to find the word *the,* First Choice will stop at words like *these, other,* and so on. Because of this, the M option is preferable. Otherwise, if you select option A, you may get some strange results. For instance, if you chose to replace *the* with *a,* you could wind up with words like *ase* and *oar* (from *these* and *other*) in your text.

Another thing to keep in mind is that First Choice ignores case in finding matches. For instance, if you specify the word *the,* First Choice will stop at *The* and *THE.* However, it will maintain the case of the word it replaces. For example, if you specified that all occurrences of *the* should be replaced with *a,* you'd see these replacements:

Original word	First Choice's replacement
the	a
The	A
THE	A

When a new word replaces an old one, the original style is also maintained. For example, if the original word was boldfaced and underlined, so will be the new one.

FINDING WITHOUT REPLACEMENT

See the preceding section for a description of how First Choice finds matches.

You can use the Find and Replace option to find one or more occurrences of a particular string without replacing them. Move the cursor to the beginning of the document, then select *Find and replace* from the Features menu. Enter the string to be searched for on the first line and press ⏎ to begin the search.

SETTING NEW DEFAULTS

When you begin creating a new document, First Choice automatically sets various defaults for that document. These defaults are for margins, tab settings, and page size. Table 2.1 shows the default values that come preset with First Choice.

Table 2.1: Standard Defaults Supplied by First Choice

Default	Setting
Left margin	10 (1 inch)
Right margin	70 (1 inch)
Top margin	6 lines (1 inch)
Bottom margin	6 lines (1 inch)
Page length	66 lines (10 inch)
Header	None
Footer	None
Tabs	Every 10 spaces, beginning at 15
Indent	None

If you wish, you can choose a different set of default values to tailor First Choice to your needs. After you've chosen a new set of defaults, they will be automatically assigned to every new document that you create. Of course, you can change any of the new default values for any particular document.

In addition to selecting different default values for any of the items listed in Table 2.1, you can also set default text that appears whenever you create a new document. For example, you might want to begin each document with a standard heading that includes your name and address.

To create a new set of default values, select *Create a document* from the Main menu, then select *Set page size, headers, and footers.* Now make any desired changes to the various options displayed on the screen; press ↵ after you've made your selections. Select new margin, tab,

"CREATE A DOCUMENT"
NOT IN MENU

and indent settings by inserting a new ruler into the blank document. Type in any desired default text. Finally, select *Make this document the default* from the Files menu.

Your new default values are recorded by First Choice and will be used whenever you create a new document.

You can always alter any of the current default settings by going through the above steps. Whenever you select a new set of defaults, the previous ones are replaced. If you want to return to First Choice's standard defaults, go through the above steps, supplying the values shown in Table 2.1.

MAKING A BACKUP COPY OF YOUR DOCUMENT

One of the most important qualities that you should cultivate as a computer user is a small degree of paranoia: it's a good idea to be prepared for the unexpected. For example, you can easily wipe out an entire file with the DOS command DEL *filename*. There are also several ways to erase a file from within First choice.

Here's another common type of disastrous error that you can make within First Choice's word processor. Suppose you retrieve a long document from a disk file, making it the working copy (remember that the disk file still contains the original document). You then make so many changes that the working copy no longer resembles the original document. Finally, you replace the original file with the current working copy, using the keystrokes F2 ↵ ↵ ↵.

The result of these last four keystrokes is the elimination of the original document from the file. You may think that you will never let this type of error happen, and of course you won't—intentionally. But whether you intend it or not, it *will* happen to you!

Keep at least one backup of each important file, so that you can gracefully recover from a disastrous error.

What can you do? The answer is to make frequent *backups* of your work. You can do this by using First Choice's disk utilities module. Here's the basic idea: after you've worked with a document for a while (say an hour), you first copy it back to its original file. The quickest way to do this is by pressing the speed key Alt-Q.

You then make a backup copy of the same document to another file with a slightly different name. Just select *Save a copy of this document* from the Files menu. When the Directory Assistant appears, enter a new file name by overwriting the original one shown on the *Save as:* line, then press ◄━┛ to create the new file.

For the backup file, choose a name similar to that of the original file. For example, if the original file is MENU.DOC, you might choose the name MENU2.DOC for the backup file (you must include .DOC in the backup file name).

DELETING A DOCUMENT

In contrast to the situation in which you accidentally remove a document from a disk, there will be many times when you specifically want to get rid of obsolete files. To delete a file, first select *Use disk utilities* from the Files menu. Then select *Erase a file* from the list on the screen. Enter the name of the file, or select it with the cursor keys. If necessary, first enter the appropriate drive name and/or subdirectory on which the file is stored. First Choice asks you to verify that it's all right to erase the file. Press ◄━┛ to allow the file to be erased. (For complete information on using the disk utilities module, refer to Chapter 11.)

You can also delete a file any time that the Directory Assistant is displayed. To do so, enter the file name or select it with the cursor keys. Then press F10 to delete the file. First Choice asks you to verify that you want to delete the file by pressing Y.

Once you've deleted a file, it's gone forever, unless you happen to know a clever hacker or own a software package that can unerase a file. There are several of these on the market.

If you're a serious computer user, it's a very good idea to own an unerase utility. The day comes to all of us when an important file is accidentally erased (this isn't the voice of doom talking—it's the voice of experience).

WORKING WITH OTHER TYPES OF FILES

First Choice allows you to save a document in various formats that are compatible with many different word processors. You can also retrieve documents generated by other word processors: First Choice converts them to its own form, and you can then edit them in any way that you wish. This capability allows you to transfer documents not only between different computers, but also between users of different word processing packages. Here is a list of the word processing formats that can be converted by First Choice:

ASCII

DCA

Microsoft Word (version 3)

Multimate

Professional Write (versions 1 and 2)

Wang PC

WordPerfect (versions 3, 4.1, and 4.2)

WordStar (versions 3 and 4)

SAVING DOCUMENTS IN OTHER FORMATS

If you have been editing a document, and you then wish to save it to a disk file in a format other than First Choice's own, select *Save as a different type of file* from the Files menu. Enter the name of the file to hold the document. This should not be the same as the original file name, unless you wish to destroy its original contents. Select the format for the new file from the list that appears on the screen.

As the file is saved, First Choice converts it to the format that you specify. If the document is long, this conversion process may take some time.

ASCII is a text format that's recognized by nearly every software package that reads and writes text files. ASCII format contains nothing but the text and hard returns; when a document is converted to ASCII format, nearly every special feature is stripped from the data, including margin and tab settings, and boldface, underline, and other special styles.

In order to perform conversions to any form other than ASCII, you'll need to have First Choice's floppy disk labeled *Document Conversion*. (You can obtain this disk from Software Publishing by mailing in your registration card.)

For hard-disk computers:	If you've installed the Document Conversion disk on the hard disk along with the other parts of First Choice, the conversion will proceed automatically.
For floppy-disk computers:	You'll be asked by First Choice to insert the disk into the computer.

When a document is converted to another format, most text styles, such as boldface and underline, are converted satisfactorily. Margins, headers, and footers are also usually converted correctly. However, you should always check the converted document carefully with the word processor for which it's intended, to be sure that it looks the way you want.

RETRIEVING FILES IN OTHER FORMATS

You can retrieve a file into First Choice that's been generated by any of the word processors with formats that can be converted by First Choice—again provided that you have the Document Conversion disk. To retrieve a file, select *Get an existing file,* either from the Main menu or the Files menu. Enter the name of the file. If necessary, enter the name of the drive and/or directory on which the file exists. Select the word processing format of the file.

First Choice recognizes when a document is not in its own format, so it will ask you to specify exactly what the format is. For long documents, the conversion process may take several minutes. Bear in mind that unlike some word processors, First Choice can handle documents of up to approximately 20 pages in length. If you need to convert longer documents, just break them up into shorter pieces, using the word processor that generated the original document. You can then convert each smaller piece individually with First Choice.

COMBINING SEVERAL DOCUMENTS

While you are working with a document in the word processor, it's possible to merge it with a document in another file (see Figure 2.10). The only types of documents that can be merged in are those either in First Choice format or ASCII format. To merge a document with the current one, move the cursor to the position in the working copy where you want the new text to appear, then choose *Merge another file* from the Files menu. Enter the name of the file, or select it with the cursor keys. If necessary, first enter the disk drive and/or directory on which the desired file is stored. If the file is type ASCII, specify whether or not extra carriage returns (such as those for double spacing) are to be preserved or removed.

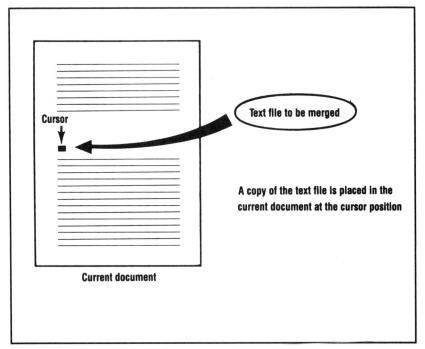

Figure 2.10: Document merging

Once a new document has been merged with the working copy, it literally becomes part of the working copy, and you can edit it in any manner that you wish. The original contents of the file that were merged with the working copy remain unchanged.

The margins of the merged document are changed to those at the cursor position (where the merging occurs). However, if the merged document contains one or more rulers, these are also merged, and they will affect the margins, tab settings, and indents of any text following them.

Make sure that the combined length of the two documents will not exceed the maximum allowed size of a document, which is approximately 20 single-spaced pages.

You now know how to merge word-processed documents. Later in the book you'll see how to merge other types of files generated by First Choice.

WORKING WITH LONG DOCUMENTS

Because First Choice keeps the entire working copy in the computer's main memory, there is an upper limit to the size of a working copy—approximately 20 single-spaced pages (about 65,000 characters). If you are planning to generate a document longer than this, you'll have to create it in sections, each of which is less than the size limit. For convenience, you could name the different files in a similar way, such as REPORT1, REPORT2, REPORT3, and so on.

This may seem like an unnecessary restriction, because some word processors allow you to create documents of almost any size. However, this limitation has a positive side: because the entire working copy is kept in the computer's main memory, you can move the cursor from one end of the document to the other in the blink of an eye (some word processors are very slow by comparison). In addition, many writers find that 20 pages or so is the limit of a working copy for comfortable editing.

PRINTING LONG DOCUMENTS

If you have a long document divided among different files, you may at some point want to print the entire document as a single unit, with consistent page numbering throughout the entire document. First Choice has a simple device for doing this: the *JOIN* command.

Suppose that you have a long document stored in files BOOK1, BOOK2, BOOK3, and BOOK4. Here's how to print them consecutively. Bring the first document, BOOK1, into the word processor as the working copy. Move the cursor to the end of the document. Type the following lines:

```
*JOIN BOOK2*
*JOIN BOOK3*
*JOIN BOOK4*
```

Print the working copy. When First Choice encounters the command *JOIN *filename* (in our example, *JOIN BOOK2*) during printing, it immediately prints the entire document stored in the file named *filename*. Then, in our example printing job, First Choice goes on to print the BOOK3 and BOOK4 files. Page numbers, headers, and footers are printed from the specifications of the working copy. Any page numbering, header, or footer specifications in *filename* are ignored. However, margin and tab settings in *filename* are followed during printing.

A *JOIN* command can be placed anywhere in a document; it doesn't have to be at the very end. This can be a convenient way of merging information from one file into another at print time. As soon as First Choice comes to a *JOIN* command, it prints the named file and then continues printing the working copy.

If the file in a *JOIN* command isn't on the current disk drive or directory, this information must be included as part of the file name in the *JOIN* command. For example, if your working copy is in the subdirectory \MYDOCS and you want to print it out along with the file MORESTUF.DOC in subdirectory \OTHER, you would use the command

     JOIN C:\OTHER\MORESTUF.DOC

If First Choice can't find the named file, it prints out the *JOIN* command instead.

The *JOIN* command affects printing only; the original working copy remains unchanged. That is, the file in the *JOIN* command is not merged with the working copy in the computer's memory.

ADVANCED PRINTING FEATURES

When you print a document, you normally can use First Choice's Style and Print Options menus to take advantage of the following capabilities of your printer:

- Boldface, underlining, and italics
- Draft- and correspondence-quality print

- Subscripts and superscripts
- Compressed type

Let's take a closer look at the Print Options menu, which is accessed from the Print menu.

THE PRINT OPTIONS MENU

In Chapter 1 you used the Print Options menu defaults to print your FIRST document. However, this menu also allows you to select special printing options. You can change any option by moving the cursor to it with the Tab or Shift-Tab keystrokes, then entering a new value. Here is a short description of each option:

FROM PAGE/TO PAGE   These specify the beginning and ending pages to print. For example, if you wish to print only page 5 of a document, type "5" for both options.

NUMBER OF COPIES   If you want to print more than one copy, enter the number here.

DRAFT OR CORRESPONDENCE QUALITY   Many printers can print in either of these modes. *Draft* mode usually refers to the printer's fastest speed and poorest print quality. *Correspondence* mode often refers to the printer's best print quality and slowest speed. If you specified your exact printer during the customization process, First Choice will know how to communicate each of these modes to the printer.

If your printer can't print in correspondence mode, it will print in draft mode no matter what mode you specify.

Right-justified printing is not always the best choice. Often, a lot of space has to be placed between words to make each line the same length. This is distracting to the reader, and increases the time required to read the page.

RIGHT JUSTIFY   Normally, printed output will have the same ragged-right edge that appears on the screen. If you want text right justified, type "Y."

COMPRESSED TYPE   Some printers can print in *Compressed* mode. On a standard $8\frac{1}{2} \times 11$-inch sheet, this can be up to 132 characters per line. If your printer doesn't support this mode, it will ignore whatever you specify for this option.

PAUSE BETWEEN PAGES   If individual sheets are being fed to the printer, choose "Y" for this option. First Choice will give you time to feed each new sheet by asking you to press ◄─┘ when you're ready.

PRINT TO   The standard option is *Printer,* which refers to your printer. If you want to direct the output to a disk file instead of the printer, enter the name of the file here. Supply the drive name and subdirectory if necessary. For example, if you want to print to the file HOLDIT on drive B, type B:HOLDIT.

A file generated in this way can then be sent directly to the printer at any time, using the DOS COPY command. For example, to print the file B:HOLDIT, you would exit from First Choice, then enter the following DOS command (we've assumed that the printer is connected to the port LPT1):

```
COPY B:HOLDIT, LPT1
```

You can also send the output directly to the screen by typing in SCREEN for this option. First Choice will pause between each screenload.

INDENT   If you enter a number here, each line of the output will be shifted to the right by that number of spaces. This can be useful if the built-in left margin of the printer is not exactly what you want.

PRINTING PART OF YOUR DOCUMENT

First Choice also provides two ways in which you can print out selected portions of the text.

PRINTING A SET OF PAGES   You can specify a range of pages, using the *From page/To page* line on the Print Options menu. This option only works when the printout that you want corresponds exactly to a particular set of adjacent pages.

PRINTING SELECTED TEXT   Here's how to print out a block of selected text. Define the block to be printed, then choose *Print selected text only* from the Print menu. Specify any desired options from the Print Options menu, as described earlier. Press ◄┘ to start the printout.

PRINTER CAPABILITIES

For a complete list of printers and their features that are supported by First Choice, see Appendix B.

Many printers have additional capabilities. These include

- A choice of basic character size, usually either 10 or 12 characters per inch
- Double-wide, or elongated, character size
- Letter-quality output
- A combination of one or more of the above options
- A choice of either six or eight lines per inch

These are only a few of the options available with modern printers. They operate by means of special codes that are sent to the printer.

PRINTER CODES   To take advantage of your printer's capabilities, you must obtain its manual, which should contain a detailed description of the printer's features and the code that must be sent to the printer for each one.

Table 2.2 shows some typical printer functions and corresponding codes for several popular dot-matrix printers. These codes are given in *decimal*. Notice that some codes require two numbers. When this is the case, the first of the pair is usually 27, which is the decimal equivalent of Esc (Escape).

The values shown in Table 2.2 are only representative: they may or may not work for your particular printer. You should use your printer's manual to determine the actual codes.

SENDING CODES TO YOUR PRINTER   If you know what some of the special codes are for your printer, you can send them to the printer with the command *Printer *code**. You can also use the abbreviated form, *P *code**. Here, *code* is the decimal code for a particular printer function. For example, if you wanted to select 12 characters per inch, the printer command would be *P 27,77* (based on the information in Table 2.2).

Table 2.2: Typical Dot-Matrix Function Codes

Function	Code
Begin elongated characters	14
End elongated characters	20
Select 10 characters per inch	27,80
Select 12 characters per inch	27,77
Select 8 lines per inch	27,48
Select 6 lines per inch	27,50

You can insert a printer command anywhere in a document. The code within the command will be sent to the printer *as the document is printed.* For example, if the command *P 27,77* is encountered in a document during printing, the code 27,77 will be sent to the printer, which will begin printing 12 characters per inch.

Some printer codes begin a function that continues until another code is sent to end that function.

Be very careful when sending printer codes, or you could wind up with pages and pages of garble. It's a good idea to experiment first with a sample of text.

SUMMARY

This chapter has presented nearly all of First Choice's advanced word processing features not covered in Chapter 1. With the information in these first two chapters, you should be able to carry out just about any type of word processing task. The few remaining specialized features, such as mail merging and generation of slides, are covered in the latter part of this book.

You'll find that you'll be using the principal word processing features presented in these two chapters many times as you learn how to use the other modules of First Choice. In addition, the menu bar that you've been using will appear throughout all of First Choice, so that you always feel like you're on familiar territory.

Chapter
3

Managing Your Database Files

One of the most convenient uses of a computer is to store information. In the last chapters, we saw how First Choice's word processor can be used to create, store, and manipulate documents. Other types of information may be conveniently handled by First Choice's database manager.

A database manager is a convenient tool if you want to store and manipulate information about collections of similar things, such as customers, schedules, events—just about any type of information that you might think of storing on a set of standard index cards.

As you begin to use the database manager, you'll discover some of the advantages of working with an integrated package like First Choice: when you enter information into the database manager, you're actually using First Choice's word processor. Consequently, you already know a great deal about manipulating data with the database manager!

In addition, many of the menus that you'll see here will be familiar. First Choice was designed to make the menu bar as uniform as possible for all modules. As you progress through the various modules of First Choice, you'll appreciate more and more the benefits of integration: a great deal of what you learn for one module carries over to the others, so that your learning time is significantly reduced.

In this chapter you'll explore how to work with common types of data using First Choice's database manager. You'll begin by learning what types of information are handled by the database manager. You'll then be shown how to design and create a database. Next, you'll learn how to add records to the database and how to modify them. The chapter will then explain how to store and retrieve databases, how to modify the design of a database, and how to search a database for selected records. Finally, you'll see how to print the contents of selected records.

As you read the chapter, you'll find several exercises to help you practice using the database manager.

FIRST CHOICE'S COMPUTERIZED FILING SYSTEM

Suppose that you want to create and maintain a mailing list. This might be a list of your clients, or of the people to whom you distribute a weekly newsletter. If you weren't using First Choice, you might decide to keep the list in a 3 × 5 card file, with one card for each person on the list. You'd decide exactly what information about each person you want to save. Then you would write one or two sample cards, and make some changes in the way you lay out the information. Eventually, you'd settle on a nice-looking design, and you'd begin to accumulate cards in the file (Figure 3.1).

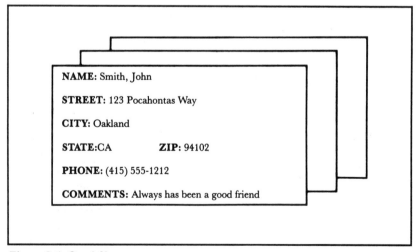

Figure 3.1: Card file

The procedure just described is the mechanical equivalent of designing a computerized data file. Instead of designing the placement of data on a 3 × 5 file card, you design a *form* for a new database on your computer's screen. When you want to add information about a new client, you fill a blank form on the screen, and the data becomes a new *record*—one for each client. Each distinct category within a record is called a *field*.

All of the records are stored in a single *database,* just as all of your 3 × 5 cards might be put in a box. When you create a new database, you also name the file in which it's stored. First Choice can be used to maintain as many different databases as you wish.

To summarize:

- A database holds a collection of records that contain information about a group of people or items, such as customers, orders, recipes, concerts, etc. There is one record per person or item.

- Each record consists of a set of fields. Each field holds one piece of information, such as a name, a date, or a number.

- Every record in a particular database has the same field structure.

Notice that a file can contain either a word processed document, or a database of records. In fact, First Choice stores *all* information in some type of file: word processed information is stored in document files, and groups of records are stored in database files. Later on, we'll describe other types of files as well, such as those used to hold spreadsheets.

ADVANTAGES OF COMPUTERIZED DATA

There are several advantages to maintaining data in computerized form, rather than on 3 × 5 cards or sheets of paper.

First, you can quickly search through hundreds or even thousands of records, isolating those of interest to you at the moment. For example, you might want to inspect the records of all customers living in San Francisco, or of all customers who owe you more than $500. The First Choice database manager lends itself quite well to this type of search.

Next, it's very easy to update computerized information, as you saw in the case of word processing documents. Moreover, you can change the design of a computerized database without reentering the information already in the computer.

Another benefit of a database manager is that it can easily generate many different types of reports. For example, you might want one report showing your entire data file, while another report might describe only clients living in California. In fact, it could be argued that the end-product of a database manager is the reports it can generate, because computerized data is of no value if it can't be seen! Generating reports is a strong feature of First Choice.

Finally, a database manager can check data as it's being input, verifying that the data conforms to a set of rules that you have specified. First Choice allows you to designate just about any conditions on incoming data. This check helps to ensure that the information is as accurate as possible.

HOW TO CREATE A DATABASE

Later in this chapter you will create a database for a selected body of information. However, you must first decide what information is to be included in the computerized file. You also must design the database form that will be used for entering data for each record. It's usually best to work out the design with pencil and paper before entering it into First Choice.

As an illustration, let's suppose that you have a business involving many clients. You want to use First Choice to create and maintain a computerized file of data on these clients. The following sections will describe the procedure in detail.

SELECTING THE INFORMATION TO STORE

To get started, you must decide exactly what information you want to keep in your computerized file. For example, if you have a group of clients, you might want to record for each of them the information listed in Table 3.1.

Table 3.1: Sample Set of Data Items

- First and last name
- Address, including street, city, state, and zip code
- Telephone number (perhaps more than one)
- Customer status (preferred or ordinary)
- Amount of money owed to you
- Date of last payment to you
- General comments about the client

Be selective about the information to be retained, because there's no point in cluttering up your screen and data disks with unimportant data. If you won't need the information on a regular basis, it probably doesn't have to be computerized.

TYPES OF DATA   Each data item that you select to be included in the computerized file is called a field. When you decide on a particular field, you must also decide on the type of information it will contain. A database can store several types of information:

- *Numeric.* Examples of numerical values are *Balance Due* and *Age.* Numeric fields are handy because you can do various types of arithmetic with them.

- *Alphanumeric* or *string.* This is the most common type of information, consisting of garden-variety characters that you find on your keyboard. Examples of alphanumeric fields are names, addresses, and comments.

- *Date.* A field can be defined to hold only date-type information. This can be quite useful, because you can enter dates in a variety of formats that First Choice can understand. You can then perform operations on date-type fields, such as sorting and simple arithmetic operations. For example, you can calculate the number of days between two dates.

- *Time.* A field can be specified to hold only time-type values. Again, First Choice understands a variety of time formats.

Like date information, time data can be used for sorting or arithmetic operations.

- *Yes/No.* A field can be defined to hold only yes/no (true/false)-type information. For example, you might define a field named ADULT, which would be used to indicate the age status of each individual in a database.

Every record that you enter into a particular database will have exactly the same fields. For example, if one record has the fields *Name, Age,* and *Address,* then all records will have these same fields. Of course, each record will contain different data in these fields.

If you want to store records with different *types* of information, you'll need to design a separate database for each. Thus, you might wind up with one database for clients, another for stock on hand, and still another for orders that you've filled.

OTHER CONSIDERATIONS   Deciding what data items to include in each record depends to some extent on what you plan to do with the data. Here are some examples.

With the help of First Choice's word processor, you can generate form letters and mailing labels, using data from one or more fields in a database. If you plan to do either of these, the fields should be designed accordingly. For instance, if you expect to generate form letters beginning with a salutation such as *Dear John,* where the value *John* would come from the database, then you would create a field to contain first names.

Similarly, if you plan to generate mailing labels, you would create separate fields for the street, city, state, and zip code.

You can do *record sorting* with the help of the database manager. For example, you might plan to generate reports in which the records are sorted by client name. If so, you would need to design separate fields for the first and last names.

Note that you can include as many different fields as you like in the design of a database.

CHOOSING A KEY   Usually, it's convenient to have one or two fields that can uniquely identify each record in a database. This is called the *key* of the database. The idea is that when you want to find a

First Choice doesn't make the provisions for a key. It's up to you to make sure that there is a field or group of fields that uniquely identify each record in a database.

particular record, you can do so by specifying the *key value* for that record, and First Choice can then directly retrieve it for you.

Frequently, a personal-name field is used as a key. This is fine, provided that you always know exactly how to spell a particular name, and that the same conventions are always used when entering names into a database.

For example, suppose that for a particular record you enter a person's name as *John Peter Longfellow*. Also suppose that at some later time you want to retrieve that record. To do so, you tell First Choice to find the record for *John P. Longfellow*. Because you didn't spell the name the same way, First Choice will be unable to locate the record. Try to select a key that will be easy and reliable to use.

DESIGNING A DATABASE FORM

Figure 3.2 shows a typical database form on the screen, which you will reproduce later in this chapter. The field names are the highlighted items. Each field name describes a field and shows where the value for that field is to be entered. Data is entered—one value for each field—in the empty spaces following the fields.

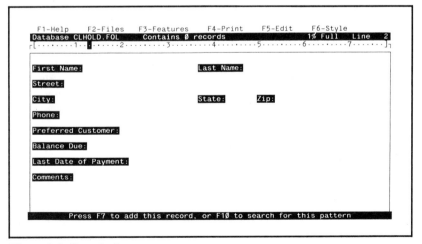

Figure 3.2: Sample form

Figure 3.3 shows the same form, but with data added for a record. Note that, in contrast to field names, this data is not highlighted.

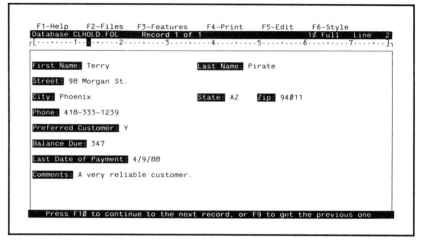

```
    F1-Help    F2-Files   F3-Features    F4-Print   F5-Edit    F6-Style
  Database CLHOLD.FOL       Record 1 of 1                    1% Full    Line   2
  ┌[·······1···█·····2·········3········4·········5········6········7······]┐

  First Name: Terry                       Last Name: Pirate

  Street: 98 Morgan St.

  City: Phoenix                    State: AZ     Zip: 94011

  Phone: 418-333-1239

  Preferred Customer: Y

  Balance Due: 347

  Last Date of Payment: 4/9/88

  Comments: A very reliable customer.



       Press F10 to continue to the next record, or F9 to get the previous one
```

Figure 3.3: Filled-in form

When you are ready to enter a new record, First Choice will display a blank form on the screen, consisting of the highlighted field names. You can then enter data next to any or all of the field names. When you're done, First Choice stores the data as a new record and then displays another blank form.

PLANNING THE FORM LAYOUT   After you've decided on the fields to include in the database, you need to design the physical layout of the form that will appear on the screen (such as Figure 3.2). It's a good idea to do a preliminary design with pencil and paper before you build the form on the computer.

As you design the form, keep in mind the following:

- A field name should be long and plain enough to clearly indicate what information is to follow. Although a field name can be as long as an entire line, in actual practice a few words are usually enough to identify the information.

- A field name can contain any character except the asterisk (*), colon (:), or two consecutive spaces. However, single spaces can be included, which means that typical field names might be *Customer Name, Date of Departure,* and so on.

- No two field names can be identical. Because First Choice differentiates between uppercase and lowercase, the two fields *First Name* and *First name* are not considered the same.
- Each field name must end with a colon.
- A form can be as long as you like (within practical limits to be described below).

You can enhance the design of a form by inserting background text between some fields. For example, in the form shown in Figure 3.2, a title like "Financial Data" might be inserted before the BALANCE DUE field. A line of background text might simply consist of a set of solid or broken dashes, inserted to give style to the form.

ESTIMATING SPACE FOR FIELD VALUES As you design a form, place each field name so that there is room for the value of the previous field. For example, suppose that the following line represents a line on the form, on which data for the fields *Firstname* and *Lastname* are to be entered:

FIRSTNAME: LASTNAME:

The idea is to place *Lastname* far enough over to the right to accommodate the longest value that you expect to insert for *Firstname*.

With some fields, you just can't predict how long the largest value might be. A good example of this is a *Comments* field: in one record you might only enter a few words, but for another you'll want to enter several paragraphs. For reasons that become clear as you begin to enter data, this type of field should be placed at the end of a form.

Another example of this type of field is *Telephones:* for some records, there may be only one value (i.e., one telephone number); another record may have several numbers stored in this field, perhaps one number per line for legibility.

SIZE RESTRICTIONS As you design a folder, keep in mind that there are size limitations. Each field name is limited to a single line. The total size of each record (field name *plus* data) is limited to approximately 16,000 characters. This implies that a single record may occupy several screenloads (each screenload can contain approximately 1500 characters).

There is a maximum number of records that can be kept in a single database, depending on how big each record is, and the type of disk used for data storage. There is no firm formula for determining exactly how many records of a particular type will fit in a single database, but here are some guidelines:

- If you're using a low-density (360K) 5¼-inch floppy disk, plan on no more than 2,800 records per database, provided that the disk is used entirely for the database.

- For low-density (700K) 3½-inch floppies, the upper limit is approximately 5,600 records.

- For a hard disk, the upper limit will be significantly higher than the above numbers, on the order of 64,000 records maximum.

Bear in mind, however, that if a database holds too many records, the time required to search through it may become too long for comfort. If this becomes a problem, consider dividing your data up into two or more smaller databases.

CREATING THE DATABASE FORM

Before you proceed, First Choice should be running and the Main menu should be displayed (Figure 3.4). If you're using a floppy-disk computer, the disk to hold any new databases should be in drive B.

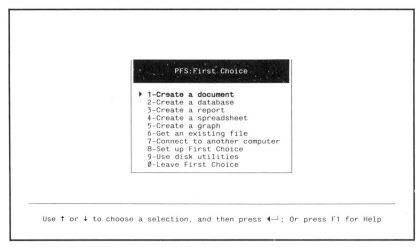

Figure 3.4: Main menu

In order to create a new form, you must begin by creating the file folder itself. You'll be constructing the form shown in Figure 3.2, which corresponds to the fields listed in Table 3.1.

For a complete discussion of this screen display, refer to "The Directory Assistant" in Chapter 1.

1. Select *Create a database* from the Main menu. The Directory Assistant will appear on the screen.

   For floppy-disk computers: The Directory line should show that the current drive is B. If not, type in **B:** and press ⏎. The Directory line should now show **B:** as the current drive.

   For Hard-disk computers: If you wish to use one of the floppy disk drives for storing data, enter the name of that drive (either **A:** or **B:**), and press ⏎. If you wish to specify a different directory from that shown on the Directory line, enter its name, then press ⏎.

2. Enter the name of the file in which the database will be stored: for the current example, let's use **CLIENTS**. When you invent a file name, it must be different from any others listed in the Databases column. When First Choice creates this file, it will append the extension .FOL to it; all database files must have this extension.

THE FORMS DESIGN DISPLAY   After you've entered the file name, First Choice enters the *Forms Design* display shown in Figure 3.5. In many ways, this display is similar to the opening screen of First Choice's word processor. In fact, as we mentioned earlier, you'll be using the word processor to create the form.

Before you begin to enter the new form into the computer, take a quick look around this display:

The *menu bar* at the top of the screen should look familiar now that you've used First Choice's word processor. In fact, the six menus have the same basic functions as those in the word processor. However, because you're using the database manager, some of the options that were used in word processing don't apply here, and won't appear in the menus. By the same token, the database manager has its own requirements, for which there are corresponding options in the menus.

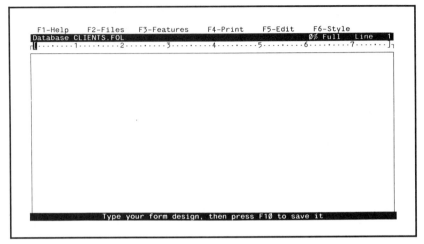

Figure 3.5: Forms Design display

The *Information line,* right under the menu bar, tells you the name of the database you're working with. It also tells you which line the cursor is on. The *% Full* indicator is used when entering data in a record; it tells you how much space is left in the current record (16,000 characters maximum).

The third line from the top is the *Ruler line,* which shows only the current column position of the cursor: tabs and indents are not available, and the margins can't be reset from their values of 1 and 78.

ENTERING FIELD NAMES   You're now ready to begin creating the database form by "painting" the field names on the screen. You can use all of the standard word processing features when entering and editing the field names and background text. This includes all of the cursor-movement keys and editing features. However, special styles such as underlining, boldface, and italics will not be displayed. Notice that the cursor is a blinking *line,* meaning that First Choice is in the Overwrite mode. (Use the Ins key to switch modes.) For convenience, you might want to change to the Insert mode while building the form.

As you enter the field names, keep the following in mind:

- Leave enough space after each field name to accommodate the longest value you expect to enter.

Background text at the top of the form sometimes causes problems within First Choice.

- Insert background text anywhere you like on the screen. A block of background text can be up to 20 lines long. To end background text, either press ◄─┘ or enter two or more spaces. This allows First Choice to distinguish background text from field names.

- Place fields whose length can't be predicted at the bottom of the form. (Later you'll learn to change the position of a field, if you need to.)

- A colon must be used as the last character of each field name, and nowhere else within a field name.

Don't press the F10 key until you're entirely finished, because that will terminate the design process. If you do accidentally press F10, start over again by pressing the Esc key twice to exit back to the Main menu. Select item 2, *Create a database,* then reenter the original file name. When First Choice asks you if you want to replace the existing file, press ◄─┘ to indicate yes.

Now enter the field names as shown in Figure 3.2.

1. Move the cursor to the top of the form.

2. Enter the field name **First Name:** (make sure to include the colon).

3. Move the cursor over, then enter the field name **Last Name:**.

4. Continue entering field names, ending each with a colon.

First Choice's spelling checker can search your form for spelling errors. Position the cursor at the top of the form, press F3 for the Features menu, then select the *Check spelling* option. (See Chapter 2 for a complete description of the spelling checker.)

FIXING ERRORS As you enter field names, you can make corrections exactly as you would in the word processor. You can use either the Overwrite or Insert modes (switching back and forth with the Ins key). Remember that at this point you're simply "painting" the form onto the screen, using the word processor as your pencil and eraser.

If you make a lot of mistakes and would rather start over again, press F5 for the Edit menu, and select *Erase this record.* Everything that you've done will be deleted, and you can begin again.

SAVING YOUR DATABASE FORM When you're satisfied with the design of your form, you can tell First Choice to go on by pressing the F10 key. The structure of the form will be saved in the file that you named earlier.

ABANDONING THE FORM CREATION At any time, you can abort the form-creation process and return to First Choice's Main menu by pressing the Esc key once or twice. If you haven't saved the new form structure that you've been developing, First Choice issues a warning message, telling you that you are about to lose your work. You can either proceed by pressing ◄─┘, or you can go back into the database manager by pressing the Esc key.

However, even if you abort the process, First Choice still creates the file that you originally named for this database. This file is empty. You can then either delete the file using First Choice's disk utilities module, or reuse the file to create another database.

SELECTING FIELD TYPES

After you press the F10 key to save the database form, First Choice gives you the option to assign data types to each field. You may specify types for any or none of the fields. You can specify that each field be one of the following types:

    N: Numeric data

    D: Date values

    T: Time values

    Y: Yes/No values

If a field is not specified to be one of the above types, it automatically becomes a *string* or *character* field type.

There are several reasons for selecting a field to be a particular type. Date, time, or numeric fields can be sorted according to their values. For instance, you could sort the records in a file by date, according to the values in a field called BIRTHDAY.

Similar field values also can be compared. For instance, two dates can be compared to determine which is later in time. Also, various types of arithmetic calculations can be performed on data in numeric fields.

One of the most significant advantages of using field types is the ability to do input data checking. If you attempt to enter a value for a field that's in conflict with the field's assigned data type, then First Choice issues a warning message. For example, suppose that you specify a particular field to be numeric. If you then try to enter a string of characters into this field, a warning will appear on the screen. You can then either correct the data or allow it into the record.

FORMATS FOR FIELD TYPES First Choice accepts several different formats for each of the four field types. Table 3.2 shows examples of each of the acceptable formats for each.

Table 3.2: Valid Formats for Different Data Types

NUMERIC	DATE	TIME	YES/NO
125	11-25-89	9:04 (assumes a.m.)	Y
125.	11-02-89	9:04 am	y
125.12	11-02-1989	9:04am	Yes
+125	11.25.89	9:04AM	YES
−125	11.25.1989	9:04pm	N
$125	11/25/89	21:04	n
0.001	11/25/1989	9:04:25 (seconds)	NO
	11 25 89		
	11 25 1989		
	89-11-25		
	1898-11-25		

Make a backup of your database before making any changes to its design.

CHANGING FIELD TYPES You can alter the type of one or more fields at any time. Here are the steps:

1. Retrieve the database.

2. Select *Change form design* from the Features menu, then verify the process by pressing ⏎. The Change Form Design menu will appear on the screen.

3. Select *Change field types*. The databases form will appear, along with the type of each field.

4. Reassign field types by moving the cursor to each field, then entering the new field type—either N, D, T, Y, or a blank.

5. Press the F10 key when you've finished.

When you change the type of a field, First Choice doesn't do any data checking to determine whether any existing data conflicts with the new type. Consequently, if there are any such conflicts, that data may present problems later on if you attempt to do any sorting or comparisons based on the values of that field.

Enter the following field types to the CLIENTS file:

1. Move the cursor with the Tab or Shift-Tab keys to the Preferred Customer field, then enter **Y**.

2. Move to the Balance Due field and enter **N**.

3. Move to the Last Date of Payment field and enter **D**.

4. When you've finished assigning field types, press the F10 key.

You can abandon the assignment of field types at any time by pressing the Esc key. In either case, First Choice will then put you into the Data Entry mode, and you can, if you wish, begin to enter records (see "Adding Records to a Database" below). Otherwise, you can return to the Main menu by pressing the Esc key.

ADDING RECORDS TO A DATABASE

See Appendix C for details on writing programs to streamline the operation of a database.

You can add records to a database in one of two ways. First, you can retrieve an existing database (see "Retrieving an Existing Database from a Disk"). Or, after you have finished defining the structure of a new database, First Choice will assume that you want to start entering records, and will automatically place you into the Data Entry mode.

Once you have retrieved a database, an empty form like the one in Figure 3.2 will appear. This form contains the names of each field. If the form is quite long, many of these field names may not be displayed on the screen. In that case, you can scroll up and down the entire form with the PgDn and PgUp keys.

EFFECTIVE DATA ENTRY

Data is added to one record at a time. To add data for a new record, make sure that First Choice is in the Overwrite mode (cursor is a blinking line). Move the cursor to the first field, by using either the Tab or Shift-Tab keys, then enter the value for the first field. Use the standard editing keys to fix up any errors. Add data for all of the fields. After you've finished, press the F7 key. The data is recorded in the file as a new record. When a new blank form appears, you can either add a new record or return to the Main menu by pressing the Esc key.

Values for the various fields can be entered in any order that you wish. In addition, you can move the cursor back and forth between fields by pressing Tab or Shift-Tab. Data can be edited with the standard word processing commands. However, do not use the Del key to delete errors; you'll see why in the next section. Overwrite the errors with the correct data. Field names are protected; you can't overwrite them.

Let's add a few records to the CLIENTS database, using the data shown in Table 3.3.

1. Using the Tab or Shift-Tab keystrokes as needed, move the cursor to the field *First Name.*

2. Enter **Terry**.

3. Move the cursor to the *Last Name* field with the Tab key.

4. Enter **Pirate**.

5. Continue entering values for all of the fields. After you've finished, and you're sure that all of the data that you've entered is correct, press the F7 key. The record is stored in the database, and a new blank form is displayed on the screen.

If you wish, enter the records for all of the data shown in Table 3.3. This will give you more practice; also, what is shown in the various figures in this chapter will correspond with what you see on the screen.

REPOSITIONING FIELD NAMES IN A RECORD

It is not a good idea to move field names around on the screen as you enter data unless it's absolutely necessary. Otherwise, when you

Table 3.3: Sample Data for CLIENTS Database. (P indicates preferred customer; Balance indicates the balance due; Date indicates last date of payment.)

FIRST NAME	LAST NAME	STREET	CITY	STATE	ZIP	PHONE	P	BALANCE	DATE	COMMENTS
Terry	Pirate	98 Morgan St.	Phoenix	AZ	94011	418-333-1239	Y	347	4-9-88	A very reliable customer
Janice	Peters	111 Acker St.	Oakland	CA	94155	415-999-1234	N	805.11	3-2-88	Always late with payments
Ruby	Gold	35 Everett Ave.	Phoenix	AZ	42001	901-444-1233	N	750.25	4-25-88	Never pays on time
Howard	Duck	123 92nd Ave.	Oakland	CA	97102	418-998-1234	Y	750	1-19-88	Eats a lot of crackers
Harry	Peters	137 Jackson Dr.	Berkeley	CA	94707	415-666-1836	Y	874.02	6-30-88	Runs up large bills
Sarah	Lo	1327 Mylvia St.	Alameda	CA	94511	415-531-9854	N	429.39	2-18-87	Can't be depended on to pay up
Mary	Smith	3827 1st St.	Oakland	CA	94611	415-654-8688	Y	125.46	3-7-88	Call on Mondays only
Pete	Lick	14 Fine Ave.	Oakland	CA	94602	415-666-1254	Y	0	7-2-88	Never around during the week
Sam	Drew	3 Ada St.	Phoenix	AZ	52001	212-531-5432	Y	25.27	6-19-88	A fine worker, and very reliable

If a field name is moved from its original location on the form, it doesn't affect any of the field values for that record. In addition, it doesn't affect the position of field names for any other records.

view the records at a later time, corresponding fields for different records will be in different screen locations.

You can accidentally move a field in two ways. First, if you enter the Insert mode by pressing the Ins key, everything to the right of the cursor will be pushed over when you begin typing, including field names. Or, if you use the Del key to remove characters, any field names to the right of the cursor will be dragged to the left. If a field name does get moved for any reason (see "Adding Space for Data to a Record"), you can reposition it by entering Insert mode, moving the cursor to the immediate left of the field name, and then using the spacebar and Del keys.

ADDING SPACE FOR LONG DATA

In some cases, you may need to enter a value that's longer than the available space on the screen. You can deliberately make additional room by moving the next field name over (and, if necessary, down). To do this, change to the Insert mode by pressing the Ins key once. The cursor will take on a square shape. Continue entering the data for this item. If necessary, create a new line using the ←┘ key. Make sure to return to the Overwrite mode when you're done.

ENTERING DATA IN A RECORD WITH STYLE

As you enter data, you can use the various styles available on the Style menu. First, make sure that the Insert mode is on. Press F6 for the Style menu and select the desired style, then enter the data. Make sure that you turn off the style when you're done, by entering the Style menu again and selecting *Erase style*. You also can assign a style to data that you've already entered. Just select the text block to be stylized, then press F6 for the Style menu and choose the desired style.

Some styles, such as superscript and subscript, don't display on the screen. Instead, First Choice boldfaces text assigned these styles.

THE DITTO FEATURE: A DATA-ENTRY SHORTCUT

If you are entering several records for which part of the data is the same, you can use First Choice's *ditto* feature to save yourself some keystrokes. Suppose that you're entering a new record, and you know that the value for a particular field is the same as for the previous record added. When you get to that field, simply press the speed key Alt-D (for *ditto*), or select *Ditto field* from the Edit menu. The previous value for that field will be automatically entered into the current record.

If you want to duplicate an entire record, press Alt-E (or select *Ditto entire record* from the Edit menu); the entire contents of the previous record are copied to the new record. This is a valuable feature even if you only need to copy most of the previous record: copy the entire record, then overwrite the fields that aren't the same.

ERASING A RECORD IN PROGRESS

If you want to erase the record you've been working on, select the Edit menu, then choose *Erase this record*. First Choice gives you a chance to change your mind, then proceeds if you press ←┘. The current contents of the form on the screen are erased.

SAVING A RECORD

When you've finished entering data for a record, press the F7 key. The record will be saved in the database on the disk, and a new blank form will be presented on the screen.

Note that every time that you press the F7 key, a new record is added to the database. This includes blank records, which are counted as real records because they take up real space on the disk. It's a nuisance to have blank records in the database, so be careful with the F7 key.

When you are done entering records, press the Esc key to return to First Choice's Main menu. If you haven't yet saved the current record with the F7 key, First Choice issues a warning to that effect.

When you leave a database and return to the Main menu, you don't have to do anything special to make sure that any new data that you've added is safely stored. This is because as each new record is added with the F7 key, it immediately becomes part of the database on the disk file. Note how this is in contrast to leaving First Choice's word processor, where you must first save the current document to a disk file if you want to use it later.

RETRIEVING AN EXISTING DATABASE FROM A DISK

Over a period of time, you may accumulate many databases containing different types of information. In order to use the data in a database, you must first retrieve it from the file in which it's stored. Note that when First Choice retrieves a database, it doesn't bring all of the records into the computer's memory. What's actually happening is that First Choice opens the database file, so that you can then work with its records. No records are actually copied from the file into the computer's memory until you perform some type of database search.

Let's retrieve the CLIENTS database that you created in the previous section. You'll use it to learn about copying databases and modifying database forms.

1. Select *Get an existing file,* either from First Choice's Main menu, or from the Files menu within a module (such as the word processor or the database manager). The Directory Assistant will appear, asking you for a file name.

2. If necessary, specify the disk drive and/or subdirectory on which your database file is stored.

3. Specify the CLIENTS database by either of the following methods:

   a. Use the cursor keys and the PgDn and PgUp keys to select the file, then press ◄─┘; *or*

   b. Enter **CLIENTS.FOL** (be sure to include the .FOL extension), then press ◄─┘.

After First Choice retrieves your database, a blank database form is displayed. You can then add, modify, or delete records, or search through the database for any records that you wish to review.

If the desired database is not on the current disk drive or directory, you'll need to include the drive and directory names when you enter the file name (step 2 above). For example, suppose that the Directory Assistant is displaying the directory for drive A, but you want to retrieve the file MYJUNQUE in the \MYSTUFF subdirectory of drive C. You would enter the name C:\MYSTUFF\MYJUNQUE.FOL.

If the Directory Assistant can't locate the file that you specify, it displays a message to that effect at the bottom of the screen.

CHANGING THE DESIGN OF A DATABASE

From time to time, you may decide to make changes to the design of an existing database. You may want to improve the design by changing the location of one or more fields, or by changing their names. Or, you may decide to add or delete fields to make better use of the database. In this section you'll learn how to make these design changes, as well as others.

MAKING A BACKUP OF A DATABASE

You can accomplish any combination of the above modifications to an existing database. However, before attempting to do so, you should first make an exact copy of the entire database. The reason for this is that it's easy to make a mistake when modifying the database form, resulting in the *permanent* loss of data. However, if you have a backup copy, you can recover from any type of error that destroys your data.

You can easily make a backup by using First Choice's disk utilities module.

For more information on the disk utilities module, see Chapter 11.

- At the Main menu, select *Use disk utilities.* The Disk Utilities menu will appear.

- Select *Copy a file,* and the Directory Assistant will be displayed.

- Enter the name of the database file to be copied, or select it with the cursor keys, then press ←┘.

- Enter the name of the new file, which will become a duplicate of the original. After the copy operation has been completed, the Disk Utilities reappears.

- Select *Return to Main Menu.*

When you type in the name of the new file, you don't need to include an .FOL extension. In fact, you might want to name the new file the same as the original one, except for a different extension. For example, you might copy MYFILE.FOL to the file MYFILE.BAK. If you subsequently retrieve MYFILE.BAK, First Choice will recognize it as a database file (even though it doesn't have the .FOL extension) and treat it accordingly.

First Choice enables you to make several types of changes to a database through the Change Form Design menu (Figure 3.6). You can add or delete fields, change a field name, or move a field to another location on the form. You can also modify background text and change the type of one or more fields. Finally, you can write a program to perform data checking on your database.

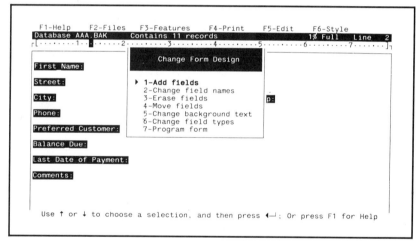

Figure 3.6: Change Form Design menu

If you plan to make several changes to your database, you'll need to do so in stages. For instance, you can't add a new field and at the same time delete or move another one. Here's the safest order to follow. First delete unwanted fields. Then move existing fields to new locations. Next, add new fields. Finally, you can modify or add background text to enhance the new design on the screen.

In order to make any design changes to a database, you must first retrieve it, either from the Main menu or, if you're within one of First Choice's applications, from the Files menu. Next, select *Change form design* from the Features menu. A warning will appear onscreen advising you to make a backup before making changes. If you have done so, press ↵ to continue. The Change Form Design menu will appear on the screen. After you select an option, a blank database form will be displayed, and you can proceed with your changes.

In the following sections, we'll describe each type of modification and the pitfalls you may encounter.

DELETING FIELDS   Be warned that the data from deleted fields is permanently gone! Think carefully before carrying out deletions. However, if you were careful to make a backup of your database, you can change your mind later and recover the lost data.

Let's delete the Preferred Customer field from the database:

1. Select *Change form design* from the Features menu. A warning appears that you should back up your data. Press ↵ to verify that you want to proceed. The next menu appears.

2. Select *Erase fields*. A blank form will appear, with instructions at the bottom of the screen.

3. Move the cursor to the Preferred Customer field.

4. Type **ERASE** (or just **E**).

5. Press the F10 key. First Choice will go through the entire database, rebuilding each record.

Database rebuilding can be a long process. If you have a very large database, bring a book to read. When the rebuilding process is done, the new database form will appear on the screen.

You can delete several fields at the same time. If their absence leaves holes in the form, you might want to then move around one or more of the remaining fields.

MOVING FIELDS   This step isn't as risky as deleting fields, because First Choice is very good about not losing data as it rebuilds a database. Let's move the Last Date of Payment field:

1. Select *Change form design* from the Features menu. The next menu appears.

2. Select *Move fields*. A blank form will appear, with instructions at the bottom of the screen.

3. Using the Tab or Shift-Tab key, move the cursor to the blank line *above* the Balance Due field.

4. Enter the field name **Last Date of Payment:** (remember to include the colon).

5. Delete any extra blank lines on the form by moving to each line, then pressing the speed key Alt-L.

6. Press the F10 key. First Choice will readjust the form design and then process all of the records in the database, re-arranging the field positions.

When you type a field name in its new position, the name must appear exactly the same as the original. If you simply want to move a field by a few spaces one way or the other on the same line, and if the field name is not on the far left of the line, you can do so by using the Ins key to enter the Insert mode (square cursor). Position the cursor to the immediate left of the field name. To move the field to the right, press the spacebar as many spaces as you wish. To move the field to the left, press the Backspace key.

If you move fields in this manner, every field to the right of the cursor will move, as well as the one that you want. You can reposition those fields the same way.

If you need to add a new line to the form to accommodate your changes, enter the Insert mode by pressing the Ins key. Position the cursor at the end of the line below which a new line is to be inserted. Press ◄─┘; a new line will appear.

You may find that you can't conveniently make all of your field moves at one time. If so, move as many as you can, press F10 to process the database, then go back and move the remaining fields. This procedure may seem clumsy, but it's well worth it for the flexibility that it provides.

ADDING FIELDS You can add one or more fields to an existing database. To illustrate the process, we'll add back the Preferred Customer field that we deleted earlier.

1. Select *Change form design* from the Features menu. The next menu appears.

2. Select *Add fields*. A blank form will appear, with instructions at the bottom of the screen.

3. Move the cursor to the end of the line containing the Phone field.

4. Make sure that you're in the Insert mode (the cursor is a blinking square).

5. Press ⏎ twice to insert two blank lines.

6. Press the Ins key to return to the Overwrite mode.

7. Type in the field name **Preferred Customer**, followed by a colon.

8. Press the F10 key. First Choice readjusts the design of the form, then processes all of the records by adding a new blank Preferred Customer field to each.

If you want to put a new field where there isn't enough room for it, you can make space by moving existing fields around and inserting extra lines. In this way, you can add several new fields at the same time.

After you've made enough space for the new fields, enter each new field name in the desired location, ending each name with a colon. Finish up by pressing the F10 key.

CHANGING FIELD NAMES You can change the names of existing fields. We'll illustrate the process by changing the field Last Date of Payment to Last Payment Date.

1. Select *Change form design* from the Features menu. The next menu appears.

2. Select *Change field names*. A blank form will appear, with an informative message at the bottom of the screen.

3. Make sure that you are in the Overwrite mode. If you're in the Insert mode, you may accidentally move fields around.

4. Move the cursor to the right of the Last Date of Payment field.

5. Enter the new name **Last Payment Date:**, ending with a colon.

6. When you are done, press the F10 key and all of the records will be processed.

Note that the original data is preserved by First Choice as a field name is changed.

If necessary, you can use the Insert mode to move fields to the right in order to make room for the new name.

CHANGING BACKGROUND TEXT   Background text is used simply to enhance the physical appearance of a database form. To change existing background text, or add new text, select *Change form design* from the Features menu. Select *Change background text,* then add new background text anywhere on the form, or alter existing text.

You can add new lines for additional background text by positioning the cursor at the end of the desired line, making sure that you're in the Insert mode, then pressing ← once for each new blank line you want to add.

Remember that you must end a block of background text either by pressing ← or by entering two or more spaces at the end of the text.

You can place background text on the same line with a field, but this might introduce some confusion between field names and background text. The safest rule is not to mix the two on the same line.

POLISHING THE FORM   After you've added all of the new fields and deleted the unwanted ones, you may want to spruce up the final appearance of your form. Here are a couple of hints.

Add blank lines for appearance by positioning the cursor at the end of a line and then pressing ←. Everything below the cursor will move down one line. (First Choice must be in the Insert mode.)

Delete excess lines by moving the cursor to the offending line, then removing it with the speed key Alt-L. For either of these changes, you would select *Move fields* from the Change Forms Design menu.

WORKING WITH THE INFORMATION IN A DATABASE

After you have accumulated a few records in a database, you probably would like to make use of them. First Choice lets you browse through a database, displaying one record at a time. Or you can browse through specific groups of records by supplying First Choice with *search instructions*. You can also edit or delete one or more records, print one or more records, and convert records to documents that can be handled by the word processor.

BROWSING THROUGH RECORDS

The best way to use this section is to practice each command at your screen with an actual database containing at least a few records. If possible, use First Choice to retrieve an existing database before going on. If you need to review how to retrieve a database, see the earlier section, "Retrieving an Existing Database from a Disk."

As each record is displayed on the screen, you can do one of several things with it:

- Look it over, but leave it alone.
- Use any of the word processor features to make changes to the information displayed on the screen. These changes are permanently recorded in the database.
- Print the record.
- Transform the record's information into document format, so that it can be read and manipulated by First Choice's word processor.
- Set a bookmark anywhere within the record.

When a database is first retrieved, an empty form is displayed, giving you a chance to review the database structure. You can then begin displaying one record after another on the screen.

To begin browsing, press the F10 key. The first record in the database will be displayed. The Information line (second from the top) displays the current *record number*. This number helps you keep track of where you are in the database. You can move around within the database, using the following keys:

F10	Displays the next record
F9	Displays the previous record

Shift-F10   Displays the last record in the database

Shift-F9   Displays the first record in the database

To terminate the browsing, press the Esc key. This returns the blank form to the screen.

When all of the records have been displayed, First Choice gives the total record count. You can then press the Esc key twice to return to a blank form display.

EDITING A RECORD

Use the Overwrite mode when editing records.

When a record is displayed on the screen, you can edit any part of it that you wish, replacing old information with more recent data. All of First Choice's standard editing commands can be used. However, the Overwrite mode should normally be used; otherwise the field names will be moved on the screen. If you need to move a field name to make room for a long field entry, then use the Insert mode. The adjacent field names will be moved for the current record only. Make sure to return to the Overwrite mode before going on.

You can use the *Find and replace, Check spelling,* or *Find synonyms* selections of the Features menu. Each of these options works only within the current record.

If you want to completely replace the data in the record, erase the record's contents by choosing *Erase this record* from the Edit menu. Then enter the new information.

DELETING A RECORD

You can remove more than one record from a folder at a time. See "Removing Selected Records" in Chapter 4.

You can remove a record completely from the database. To do so, the record must be displayed on the screen. Then select *Remove this record* from the Features menu. (Note the difference between *Erase this record,* which only erases the contents of the current record, and *Remove this record,* which completely deletes the record from the database.)

When a record is deleted from a database, many of the records in the folder are renumbered by First Choice (the record numbers appear near the top of the screen). For example, suppose you delete record 5. The following record, Record 6, will then be renumbered Record 5, and so on for the remaining records in the database. Consequently, the record numbers assigned by First Choice can't be used as a means of record identification. If you want to assign unique numbers to each record, you should create a field for that purpose. You can even write a *form program* to automatically assign unique record numbers. For a discussion of form programs, see Appendix C.

PRINTING A RECORD

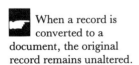
You can print more than one record at a time. See "Printing Selected Records" in this chapter.

You can print the entire record currently displayed on the screen by selecting *Print this record* from the Print menu. For a description of the print options, see the section "The Print Options Menu" in Chapter 2. After you've made your selections, press ◄┘ and the record will be printed out—field names as well as field values.

PRINTING PART OF A RECORD

You can print a selected part of a record. To see how this works, let's print only the first two fields of the current record:

1. Using the Shift-Tab key, move the cursor to just before the beginning of the first field name.

2. Press the speed key Alt-S to indicate the beginning of block to be printed.

3. Enlarge the block by moving the cursor to include both the first and second fields (both field names and values).

4. Select the Print menu.

5. Choose *Print selected text only.*

6. Fill in the options on the Print Options menu, then press ◄┘.

Note that whatever is included in the selected block will be printed, field names as well as values.

CONVERTING A RECORD TO A DOCUMENT

When a record is converted to a document, the original record remains unaltered.

A record can be converted from its database form into a document that can be accessed by First Choice's word processor. Let's see how to do this by converting the record shown in Figure 3.7 (this is the first record in our CLIENTS database).

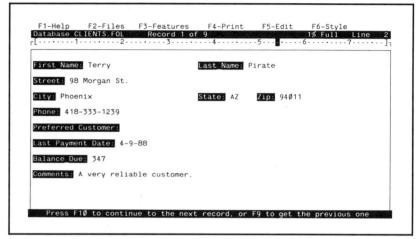

```
    F1-Help    F2-Files    F3-Features    F4-Print    F5-Edit    F6-Style
   Database CLIENTS.FOL        Record 1 of 9                1% Full   Line   2
  r[·········1·········2·········3·········4·········5···|·····6·········7······]¬

    First Name: Terry                    Last Name: Pirate

    Street: 98 Morgan St.

    City: Phoenix                State: AZ    Zip: 94011

    Phone: 418-333-1239

    Preferred Customer:

    Last Payment Date: 4-9-88

    Balance Due: 347

    Comments: A very reliable customer.



       Press F10 to continue to the next record, or F9 to get the previous one
```

Figure 3.7: A database record

1. Display the desired record on the screen.
2. Press F2 for the Files menu.
3. Select *Save a copy of this record.* The Directory Assistant will appear and ask you to supply a file name.
4. Enter a file name. If necessary, enter the name of the disk and/or directory where the file is to be written.
5. Press ◄─┘. The record will be saved as a document in the file that you specified. First Choice will attach the extension .DOC to the file name.

If you now retrieve this document, it will appear as shown in Figure 3.8. Notice that the field names are boldfaced, and the field values appear as ordinary text.

GENERATING TABLES

Up to now, the methods that we've seen for manipulating database information involve the display of one record at a time. This is

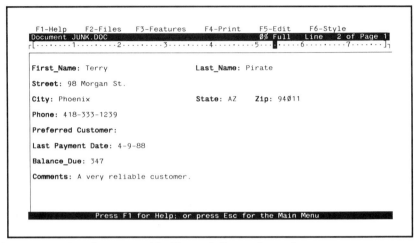

Figure 3.8: Database record in Figure 3.7 stored as a document

quite convenient, especially if you're editing existing records or add-ing new ones. However, it's often useful to be able to view a group of records in table form, so that data from several records is visible at the same time. First Choice provides you with this capability. When records are displayed as a table, each record occupies one line of the table, and each field is displayed as a single column.

You can view all of the records in a database at once, or selected groups of records. In addition, you can sort a table of records. You can choose which fields from the records are to be displayed, and you can determine the displayed width of each field. Up to 250 char-acters can be shown on each line. A table of database information can be output to the printer, to a disk file, or to a spreadsheet. If the out-put is sent to a disk file, it can subsequently be edited by First Choice's word processor.

Although you can't edit records when they appear in tabular form, you can quickly jump from the displayed table to any particular record in its usual form, where it can then be edited.

DISPLAYING A TABLE

To display all of the records in a database in tabular form, retrieve the database; a blank database form appears on the screen. Next, select *Show table view* from the Features menu, or simply press the speed key Alt-T (T for table). The entire database will appear as a table, with the default values set by First Choice.

The first time that you display a table view of a database, First Choice's standard options are chosen: all fields are displayed, and each field is given a display width of ten spaces.

If your database contains many records, not all of them will appear at once on the screen. However, you can scroll through the database, using the PgUp and PgDn keys. Also, many of the fields may have part of their values cut off, because of First Choice's default display width. If a value is too long to be displayed on the screen, the ">" symbol appears at the end of the value. If each line is longer than the display width of your screen (79 characters), you can scroll right and left with the Tab and Shift-Tab keys. Table 3.4 lists the keystrokes for moving around within a table.

Table 3.4: Keystrokes for Moving Cursor within a Table

KEYSTROKE	CURSOR MOVES TO
PgUp	Previous screen or top of current screen
PgDn	Next screen or bottom of current screen
Home	Beginning of current row
End	End of current row
Ctrl-Home	Upper left-hand corner of table
Ctrl-End	Lower right-hand corner of table
Tab	Start of next column
Shift-Tab	Start of previous column
Arrow keys	One character or line in any direction

You can move between the tabular display and the ordinary display of any particular record in the database. To do so, move the cursor to the desired record in the table. Then press the speed key Alt-T (or select *Show this record* from the Features menu). The record will appear on the screen, and you can edit it in any way that you wish.

To return to the tabular view of the database, press Alt-T again.

CUSTOMIZING YOUR TABLES

You can tailor a table so that it displays just the data that you want to see. Here are the steps for altering the default table settings:

1. Display the table.

2. Select *Define table view* from the Features menu. A blank database form will appear on the screen. At this point, you can choose which fields are to appear in the tabular output, as well as the displayed width in the table of each field.

3. Enter a digit (from 1 to 9999) next to each field to be displayed in the table. After the digit, enter **W***nn*, where *nn* is the number of spaces to be used for displaying values of this field.

4. After you've chosen all of the fields to be output, press the F10 key, and the customized table will appear.

The fields will be displayed in the table in the order dictated by the digits entered for each field.

Make sure that the total number of characters that you specify for all fields is less than 250.

CHANGING A TABLE DESIGN   Although you can define only one table view for a given database, you can alter the table design at any time and in any manner that you wish: first press Alt-T to display the table view of the database, then select *Define table view* from the Features menu. You can then assign new numbers and widths to different fields.

PRINTING A TABLE

You can output all or part of a table, either to the printer or a disk file. To print the entire table, select *Print this table view* from the Print menu. When the Print Options menu appears, choose any options that you wish from this menu. When you've finished, press ←, and the table will be printed.

To print only part of a table, move the cursor to the upper left-hand corner of the part to be printed, then press Alt-S. Select the table section to be printed by expanding the block with the cursor keys. Select *Print selected text only* from the Print menu, then choose any desired print options. Press ← to print the table.

OUTPUTTING A TABLE TO A DISK FILE To output part or all of a table to a disk file, follow the above procedure, with the following exception: when the Print Options menu appears, select the name of a file for the *Print to* option. The output will be directed to this file.

COPYING A TABLE TO A SPREADSHEET

You can copy all or part of a table either to a new or existing spreadsheet by using First Choice's clipboard. Here are the steps:

1. Select the part of the table to be copied (move the cursor to the start of the block, press Alt-S, then use the cursor keys to expand the block).

2. Copy the selected portion to the clipboard by pressing Alt-C (or by selecting *Copy selected text to clipboard* from the Edit menu).

3. Retrieve the desired spreadsheet, or create a new one.

4. Move the cursor to the upper left-hand corner, where the data is to be transferred.

5. Press Alt-P (or select *Paste from clipboard* from the Edit menu) to paste the data from the clipboard to the spreadsheet.

Each value copied from the table to the clipboard will be pasted to an individual cell in the spreadsheet. Any data pasted into the cells will overwrite any data already in those cells.

COPYING A TABLE TO A DOCUMENT

All or part of a table can be copied to a new or existing document. It can then be edited in any way that you wish. For example, you might want to enhance the title at the top, or improve on the column headings.

To copy a table to a document, first copy to the clipboard the part of the table to be transferred, as described above. Then retrieve the desired document, or create a new one. Finally, move the cursor to the desired position in the document and press Alt-P to paste the values from the clipboard to the document.

If the margin settings of the document are less than the length of each line of the selected part of the table, each line will wrap around when the right margin is reached. You can then fix this by changing the right margin of the document.

FINDING SELECTED RECORDS IN A DATABASE

The database manager can be used to locate and display selected records. You specify which record or records are to be displayed by entering a set of *search instructions*. A search instruction is a single value entered for a field. Several search instructions may be specified at the same time. The database manager then displays (one at a time) those records that satisfy the search instructions.

HOW TO USE SEARCH INSTRUCTIONS

Search instructions are entered by using the "query by example" method. Easy to use, this method is also powerful and fast. Here are some examples.

Let's use the CLIENTS form shown in Figure 3.2. Suppose that we want to display only those records for which the value of the *City* field is *Berkeley*. We'll do so by entering appropriate instructions to First Choice.

Begin by retrieving the CLIENTS database. When the form appears on the screen, take the following steps:

1. Using the Tab key, move the cursor to the *City* field.

2. Enter the value **Berkeley**. *Berkeley* is a search instruction; it tells First Choice what records to display on the screen. The form now looks like the one shown in Figure 3.9.

3. Press the F10 key.

When you press F10, First Choice searches through the database for the first record that has a value of *Berkeley* for the *City* field. If a record is found, it's displayed on the screen. You can find additional matching records by pressing F10 again.

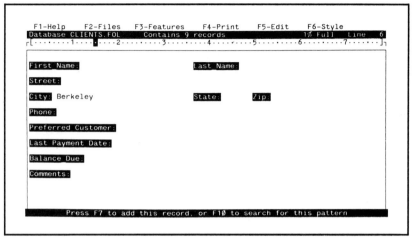

Figure 3.9: Form with a single search instruction

After you've entered the search instructions, instead of pressing F10 to display one record at a time, you can display all of the records that match the search instruction in table format by pressing the speed key Alt-T. For a complete discussion of generating tabular views, see "Generating Tables."

After you have entered all of your search instructions, the following keystrokes can be used for record searching:

F10	Displays the next record satisfying the instructions
F9	Displays the previous record satisfying the instructions
Shift-F9	Displays the first record satisfying the instructions
Shift-F10	Displays the last record satisfying the instructions
Esc	Abandons the search

Here's another example, again using the form shown in Figure 3.2. This time you'll use a set of search instructions consisting of values for more than one field. Suppose that you want to locate and display the record for a client named Ruby Gold, who lives in Phoenix. Here are the steps to follow:

1. Display a blank form on the screen.

2. Fill in the blanks as follows:

   City: Phoenix
   First Name: Ruby
   Last Name: Gold

3. Press the F10 key.

The complete set of search instructions is shown in Figure 3.10.

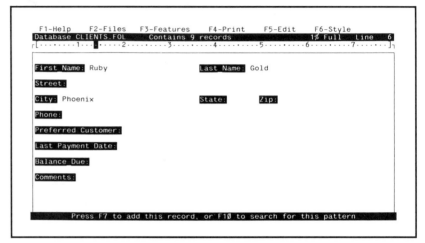

Figure 3.10: Set of search instructions

You can use search instructions in as many fields as you wish, provided that the total number of characters in all of the search instructions is less than 600.

First Choice begins examining each record in the database. The first record that satisfies all of the search instructions will be displayed on the screen. You can check if any other records satisfy the same search instructions by pressing the F10 key again, and First Choice will continue examining records.

When no more records can be found that satisfy the search instructions, First Choice displays a message to that effect on the screen. You can then return to a blank database form by pressing the Esc key twice.

If you press F10 without entering any search instructions, First Choice will display every record in the database. This is because a blank field is interpreted in a special way. It does *not* mean "no value;" instead, it means "any value." This is a handy way of letting you specify only those fields that you want.

TYPES OF SEARCH INSTRUCTIONS

A search instruction can be given for any field, regardless of the type of data it contains: alphanumeric, numeric, and so on. In addition, there are several ways in which you can write search instructions. We'll describe each of these in detail below.

EXACT MATCHES   With this type of search instruction, you specify the exact value of a certain field (this is the type of search we used in the examples above). For instance, to find all of the records for clients living in the area bounded by the zip code 12345, you would type **12345** into the *Zip* field on the screen. A search of the database by First Choice would then display only records matching this zip code.

There are several exceptions to this "exact matching." Uppercase and lowercase letters are not distinguished during a search. For example, if you enter *OAKLAND,* the following values would be found as matches:

OAKLAND
Oakland
oakland

Also, leading and trailing blank spaces are ignored. For example, if you specify " *Berkeley* " as the value in the *City* field, the value would be converted to *"Berkeley"* before the search begins. Likewise, leading and trailing blanks in values stored in fields are ignored during a search.

If you are searching for a particular value for a date-type field, you can enter the date in any date format that First Choice recognizes. For instance, suppose that for a particular record, the value of the field Last Payment Date is stored as 3-4-87. If you entered a search instruction for this field as 3/4/87, First Choice would consider that record to match the search condition. In other words, the values 3-4-87 and 3/4/87 are considered equivalent. The same would be true for other forms of the same date, such as 3 4 87 or 1987 3 4.

This also applies to other types of fields—numeric, time, and yes/no. For instance, if a record contained the value 3.00 for a numeric field, and you entered the search instruction **3** for that field, First Choice would consider that record to match the search condition.

If you enter a search instruction for a field in a format that's inconsistent with the data type assigned to that field, First Choice will display a warning on the screen. If you press ◄┘ to proceed anyway, First Choice will perform a search by considering both the search instruction and values for that field as strings of characters. For example, if you enter **R** as a search instruction for a yes/no-type field, First Choice will search for those records with a value of R in that field.

PARTIAL MATCHES   Often, you may wish to specify only part of the value of a field. For example, you may want to display all of the customers whose last name begins with *Sm.* Or, you may not know exactly how to spell a particular entry and have to guess at part of the spelling.

You can specify partial matches by using the string .. as part of a search instruction to match any group of characters, or by using the character ? as part of a search instruction to match any single character. Each of these is called a *wild card,* because it can represent a number of possibilities. Both types of wild cards may appear any number of times in a single search instruction.

Several examples of how wild cards can be used are shown in Table 3.5. Each entry in the left-hand column is a value entered as a search instruction. The corresponding entries in the right-hand column are typical values that would be found, or matched, during a search.

When used by itself, .. finds only nonblank values. This is a good way to distinguish between *no value* and *any value.* You may recall that if you leave a blank search instruction in a field, *any value* (which includes *no value*) will be found as a match. On the other hand, when attached to one or more additional characters, .. matches either *no characters* or *any characters* (see the fourth and seventh examples in Table 3.3, for instance). By contrast, the ? wild card always matches exactly one character.

Now let's suppose that you want to find the record for a client who is known to live in Oakland, but you can't remember her last name, although you think that her first name starts with an M. You could try to locate the record by entering the search instruction

    M..

in the *First Name* field and

    Oakland

in the *City* field.

Table 3.5: Using Wild Cards in Search Instructions

SEARCH INSTRUCTION	CORRESPONDING VALUES THAT WOULD MATCH
S..	S, Smith, s, 2.smith
Sm..	Sm, Smith, Smyth
..nes	Jones, stones, IBM clones
..z..	azure, zero, fuzz
95..	95, 95121
..	*{any nonblank value}*
Sm..th..	Smith, Smythe
?aft	daft, waft, raft
??aft	draft, craft
????	*{any nonblank value four characters in length}*
?at?	fate, bath
Sm?th	Smith, Smyth
Sm?th?	Smythe

On the other hand, suppose that you can't remember her first name, but you know that her last name is something like *Smith* or *Smythe*. You could try entering

    Sm..th..

in the *Last Name* field and

    Oakland

in the *City* field.

These examples illustrate an important point about search instructions: Individual search instructions can be combined to include exact as well as partial matches.

Search instructions using wild cards can be used only with strings of characters. If you enter a partial-match search instruction for any other type of field, First Choice will only make comparisons by treating the data in that field as strings of characters.

For example, suppose that you enter the following search instruction for a date-type field called MYDATE:

3/..

First Choice will match only those records whose value of MYDATE begins with the precise characters 3/. A record with a value of 3- would not be considered as a match. In other words, when you use partial-match searches, you lose First Choice's ability to recognize various date formats as equivalent. The same is also true for numeric, time, and Yes/No fields.

RELATIVE MATCHES   Often, you may wish to find values that are either less than or greater than a specific number. For example, you may want to find all CLIENTS records for which the client owes you more than $500. You can perform this type of search using relative match search instructions.

Here are the symbols that you use for specifying relative matches:

SYMBOL	MEANING
=	Equal to
>	Greater than
<	Less than
> =	Greater than or equal to
< =	Less than or equal to

Relative matching works best for numeric, date, and time fields.

Again using the CLIENTS database, suppose that you want to find all of the records for clients who owe you $500 or more. To do so, enter

> = 500

as the search instruction in the *Balance Due* field. When you press F10, First Choice searches the database until it finds a record for which the value of the balance due is greater than 500. The matching record, if any, is displayed on the screen. When you're ready to go on, press the

F10 key again, and First Choice looks for the next matching record. If one is found, it is then displayed.

The = (is equal to) instruction is not particularly useful for numeric fields, because you usually don't know exact values.

If you want to display records for clients who haven't made a payment since June 1, 1988, you could enter the following search instruction in the *Last Payment Date* field:

> 6/1/88

Table 3.6 gives some examples of relative matching. In this table, a value in the left-hand column refers to the search instruction you type for a particular field. The corresponding value in the middle column indicates the contents of a field for a particular record. The entry in the last column indicates whether that record would be considered a match for the search instruction.

Table 3.6 illustrates that relative matching can be used with character fields. You should study the last few examples carefully, because they illustrate the rules that are used when comparing two strings for equality or inequality:

- Upper- and lowercase are ignored.

- Two strings are equal only if there is a complete character-by-character match.

- Strings are compared character by character. The first unequal character determines which string is the "larger." For instance, the string *ac* is "greater than" the string *abcdefghijklmnop.*

As with exact matching, if you enter a relative-match search instruction for a field that's incompatible with the data type specified for that field, First Choice will treat all values in that field as character strings when making comparisons.

NONMATCHES You can tell First Choice to find all records that do *not* match a particular search instruction. To do this, you begin a search instruction with the slash (/) character. Table 3.7 lists a few examples of nonmatching search instructions.

Table 3.6: Examples of Relative Matching

SEARCH INSTRUCTION	FIELD CONTENTS	MATCHES RECORD? (Y/N)
= 10	10	Y
	10.0	Y
	0.99999	N
>10	10	N
	10.0001	Y
> = 10	9.999	N
	10.000	Y
	10.00001	Y
> −5	0	Y
> −5	−4	Y
> −5	−6	N
< 6/1/88	5/1/88	Y
< 6/1/88	5-1-88	Y
< 6/1/88	6-2-88	N
< = 6/1/88	6-1-88	Y
= Bob	Bob	Y
= bob	Bob	Y
> bob	boob	Y
< boob	bob	Y
= bob	bobo	N
> bob	bobo	Y
< bob	boaaaaaaaaaaaa	Y

RANGE MATCHES   A search instruction can specify a range of acceptable values for a field. For instance, you might want to find records whose value of the *Balance Due* field is between zero and $500. The search instruction for this would be written as

   0 -> 500

Table 3.7: Using Nonmatching Search Instructions

RECORDS TO FIND	SEARCH INSTRUCTION
Those for cities other than Oakland	/Oakland
Those for all zip codes except 54321	/ = 54321
Those for last names not beginning with "S"	/S..

(The two characters between the two numbers are the dash and the greater-than character.)

In general, a range search instruction is written as

first value - > last value

Spaces between "->" and the two values are optional.

Range search instructions can be used for any type of field except yes/no. If a search instruction contains an illegal range, First Choice treats it—as well as all values for that field—as a character string.

With a range type of search instruction, the second value must be greater than the first one. Otherwise, no records will be found.

Suppose that you want to display all records in the CLIENTS database for clients whose last names begin with the letters a–g. Here's the search instruction to use:

a->g

PRINTING SELECTED RECORDS

You can print one or more records in a database by entering suitable search instructions. Only those records satisfying the instructions will be printed. Here are the steps to take:

1. Make sure that the printer is properly connected and that the Ready or Select light is on.

2. Retrieve the appropriate database.

3. When the blank database form appears, choose *Print records* from the Print menu.

4. When the Print Options menu appears, enter any changes to the standard options shown on the screen. (See "The Print Options Menu" in Chapter 2.) Finish by pressing ←.

5. Enter the appropriate search instructions on the blank form that appears. Only records that satisfy these options will be printed.

6. Press ← to begin printing.

PREVIEWING THE PRINTOUT

You can get an on-screen preview of what will be printed, to see if what is being generated is what you really want. This could save you a good deal of print time. To do this, enter *SCREEN* for the *Print to* option in step 4 above. When you press ← at the end of step 4, the output will be generated on your screen, rather than at the printer.

When you are satisfied that the output is what you intended, repeat the above process. This time, in step 4, change *SCREEN* to *PRINTER* in the Print Options menu. The output will then be sent to the printer.

SAVING PAPER

Normally, one record is printed per page, and the format of the printed record duplicates the database form that appears on the screen. However, you may be able to print two or more short records per page by using the following trick. In the Print Options menu, select a value for *Lines per page* that's consistent with the number of records that will fit on a single page. The following table shows some typical values to use:

TOTAL LINES PER RECORD	VALUE TO USE FOR LINES PER PAGE
34-66	66
23-33	33
17-22	22
14-16	16

You may need to experiment to determine the optimum number of records that you can fit onto a single page.

SUMMARY

In this chapter, you've been presented with the main features of First Choice's database manager. You should now be able to use it for many different types of database processing. However, there are several other features that may be of use as you become more familiar with databases. These will be covered in Chapter 4.

Chapter
4

Advanced Database Features

In this chapter, we'll present First Choice's advanced database manager features. We'll discuss how to copy records from one file to another, remove selected groups of records, and sort records. We'll also make use of bookmarks and the calculator, and employ special text-editing aids. We'll then see how to transform data files for use with other software packages, as well as input data files from other software packages.

MAKING COPIES OF RECORDS

It's often useful to be able to copy selected records from one database to another, which we'll call the *target* database. This target may be empty, or it may already contain records.

Suppose that you're going to copy one or more records from Database A into Database B. First Choice first copies the value of the first field of record in A into the first field of the new record in B. No matter how big this value is, room is made for it in the new record. The value of the second field of the record in A is then copied into the second field of the new record in B. The process continues until all fields have been copied.

This means that Database B must already exist. In addition, the fields of B must correspond in *order* and *type* to the fields in A. We can then say that B has the *same form* as A. A field of Database B may have a different name from its corresponding field in Database A, provided that it's in the same relative position in the database.

Database B may be empty, or it may already contain records. If B is not empty, the new records are added to the existing ones.

MAKING A COPY OF A DATABASE FORM

Anytime records are to be copied from one database into another (the target database), the target must already exist. If it doesn't, then it must first be created as an empty database with the same form as the original one.

Let's create an empty database (we'll call it CLTEMP) with the same form as the CLIENTS database shown in Chapter 3, Figure 3.2 and Table 3.2.

1. Select the CLIENTS database. Choose *Get an existing file* from either the Main menu or the Files menu. When the Directory Assistant appears, select the database either with the cursor keys or by entering the database name. (If necessary, first enter the name of the appropriate disk drive and/or subdirectory.)

2. Select *Copy form design* from the Files menu. The Directory Assistant will appear again.

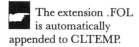
The extension .FOL is automatically appended to CLTEMP.

3. Enter the name of the new file—**CLTEMP**. First Choice creates a file with this name and copies the form design into it. Press ◄┘ to return to the database manager.

The new database contains a form, but no records. In the next section you will copy records into it from the CLIENTS database. You could also copy records into it from any other database with the same form.

COPYING GROUPS OF RECORDS

When copying records from a database, you can choose to copy every record. Alternatively, you can select a particular group of records to copy by supplying the appropriate search instructions; only those records that satisfy the instructions will be copied. For a discussion of search instructions, refer to Chapter 3.

Now let's copy into CLTEMP all the records from CLIENTS except records of people living in Oakland.

1. Retrieve the CLIENTS database by choosing *Get an existing file* from either the Main menu or the Files menu. When the Directory Assistant appears, select CLIENTS either with the cursor keys or by entering the name. (If necessary, first enter the name of the disk drive and/or subdirectory where CLIENTS is stored.)

2. Select *Copy records* from the Files menu. Again, the Directory Assistant appears.

3. Select the name of the target database—**CLTEMP**—and press ◄┘. You don't have to supply the .FOL extension, because First Choice assumes that the file must contain a database.

4. Enter the following search instructions in the *City* field:

   /Oakland

   These instructions specify all records except those with the value of *Oakland* in the *City* field. (If all records are to be copied, then no search instructions should be entered.)

5. Press F10 to begin the copying. To interrupt the copy process, press the Esc key. You then have the choice of quitting

the process or continuing. If you choose to abandon the copying, the records copied up to the moment of interruption will remain in the new file.

When it's finished, First Choice will give you a count of how many records were copied.

REMOVING SELECTED RECORDS

In Chapter 3, we described how to remove a single record from a database. In this section, we'll show how to remove selected groups of records. Remember, when records are removed, they are permanently deleted from the database. Once a record has been removed, there is no way to retrieve it. Consequently, it's a good idea to make a backup (an exact copy) of a database before removing any records from it. Then, if you later decide that you've made a mistake, you can recover the original records from the backup. This is particularly important when removing large numbers of records. To make an exact duplicate of a database, you can use First Choice's disk utilities module. For details, see Chapter 3 and Chapter 11.

A large group of records can be removed quickly, provided that these records can be specified with a set of search instructions. However, because First Choice can only directly remove one record at a time, you have to use tricky methods to remove groups of records. An outline of the necessary steps is shown in Figure 4.1.

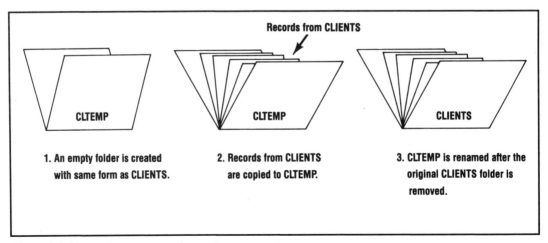

1. An empty folder is created with same form as CLIENTS.
2. Records from CLIENTS are copied to CLTEMP.
3. CLTEMP is renamed after the original CLIENTS folder is removed.

Figure 4.1: Removing a group of records

Suppose that you want to delete all CLIENTS records for which the value of the *City* field is *Berkeley.* Here are the steps:

1. Create a new folder called CLTEMP, with the same structure as CLIENTS.

2. Bring up a blank database form to the screen for CLIENTS.

3. Choose *Copy records* from the Files menu.

4. When the Directory Assistant appears, enter the name of the target file, which is **CLTEMP.FOL.**

5. When the blank CLIENTS form appears on the screen, enter the following search instruction for the *City* field: **/Berkeley.**

6. Press the F10 key. All records except those for which the value of the *City* field is *Berkeley* will be copied.

7. Select *Use Disk Utilities* from the Files menu.

8. Delete the original CLIENTS database.

9. Rename CLTEMP.FOL to CLIENTS.FOL.

10. Exit from the disk utilities module.

The new database named CLIENTS.FOL contains all records except those that you deleted.

The reason for this indirect method of deletion is that First Choice can remove only one record at a time, but it can copy many records at once from one database to another.

The trick to this method of deletion lies in using an appropriate search instruction: to specify *everything but,* we used the nonmatching search instruction: **/Berkeley.**

Now suppose that you want to remove from the CLIENTS database all records for customers who owe $1000 or more. The same method is used as in the previous exercise, but you would copy only records for which the value of the *Balance Due* field is *less than* 1000. The search instruction to use is **<1000.**

Or suppose that you want to remove all records for clients living either in Oakland or Berkeley. In this case, we use the same method we used in deleting records for Oakland clients, but the method has to be applied twice:

1. Create a new database (CLTEMP) with the same structure as CLIENTS.

2. From CLIENTS, copy into CLTEMP all records for which the value of the *City* field is not *Berkeley*: use the search instruction **/Berkeley** in the *City* field.

When the copy process ends, CLTEMP contains all records *except* those for which the value in the *City* field is *Berkeley*. Now we use the same procedure again, this time starting with the folder CLTEMP.

3. Create another new database, CL2, again with the same structure as CLTEMP.

4. Retrieve the CLTEMP database.

5. From CLTEMP, copy into CL2 all records except those for which the value in the *City* field is *Oakland*. Use the search instruction **/Oakland** in the *City* field.

The database CL2 now contains all records from the original CLIENTS database except those for which the value in the *City* field is either *Berkeley* or *Oakland*, and this is what we are after.

6. To finish up, we must delete both the CLIENTS and CLTEMP files, then rename CL2 to CLIENTS. The disk utilities can be used for this.

DELETING A DATABASE

Once a file has been deleted, it's gone forever, so be very careful about using this operation.

You can delete an entire database from a disk. You might want to do this when the database information has become out-of-date or otherwise of no use. When a database is deleted, the entire file is erased from the disk, including both the form and all of the records.

To delete a database, make sure that the database is *not* currently in First Choice's memory. If it is, return to the Main menu by pressing the Esc key. Next, select *Use disk utilities* from the Main menu. When the Directory Assistant appears, enter the name of the file to be deleted, or select it with the cursor keys, then press ◄─┘. Verify that you really want to erase the file by pressing ◄─┘ again.

SORTING RECORDS

In Chapter 3, as well as the first part of this chapter, we described many ways of working with a database. These all had one thing in common: when you search through a database, the records always appear in the same order.

Many times, however, you may want to work with records in a different order. For example, if a database contains a *Name* field, you may want to view the records alphabetically according to the values in this field. Or if a database contains a *Balance Due* field, you may want to list the records according to the values in this field, either in ascending or descending order.

Records can be sorted according to values in either one or two fields. For instance, you could sort a group of records first by the values in the *State* field, then by the values in the *City* field.

Records can be sorted for many different purposes, such as:

- Browsing through a collection of records displayed in a particular order. You might want to browse through an entire database, or through a group of records specified by a set of search instructions.

- Printing all or part of a database.

- Copying all or part of a database to another one or to another type of file.

Don't confuse the sorting described in this section with the type used to create reports (Chapter 5). The two techniques are entirely different, including the instructions to First Choice for controlling the sorting.

Any type of field can be used for sorting. For numeric fields, numeric sorting is automatically carried out. For date and time fields, sorting is done in a "time" sense. That is, earlier dates or times are considered "less than" later dates or times. For instance, the date 4-5-87 is less than 5-1-87. For date fields, all valid date formats are treated equally during sorting. Thus, the dates 5-1-85 and 5/1/85 are considered equal. The same applies for all valid time formats.

If sorting is done on a Yes/No field, a value of Y (or any of its equivalents) is treated as greater than a value of N (or any of its equivalents).

When sorting is done on character fields, the rules in Table 4.1 apply.

Table 4.1: Examples of Character Sorting

VALUE1		VALUE2
A	is less than	B
B	is less than	C
a	is equal to	A
AA	is less than	AB
AC	is greater than	ABCDEFGHIJKLMNOP
1	is less than	2
0	is less than	9
9	is less than	A

SPECIFYING SORT INSTRUCTIONS

To illustrate how to use sort instructions, we'll continue to use the CLIENTS database.

Suppose that you want to browse through the entire database, with the records appearing in alphabetical order according to the values in the *City* field. Here's how to do it:

1. Display a blank database form on the screen: If you've just retrieved the database, the form automatically appears; if a record is displayed on the screen, press Esc once or twice.

2. Enter the following sort instruction next to the *City* field name: **[1]** (see Figure 4.2).

The sort instruction [1] in the *City* field tells First Choice to sort according to values of that field. Table 4.2 lists examples of sort instructions.

3. Press the F10 key to begin the search. As you press the F10 key, the records will appear alphabetically by city.

4. Press F10 to search record by record through the database.

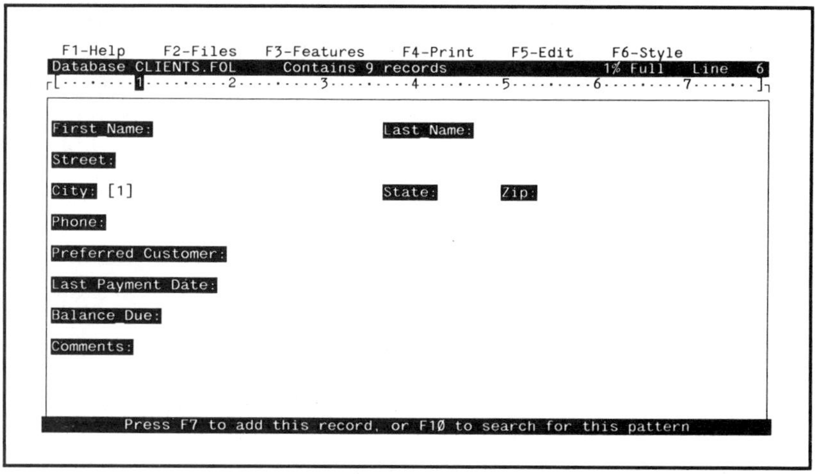

```
       F1-Help    F2-Files    F3-Features    F4-Print    F5-Edit    F6-Style
Database CLIENTS.FOL        Contains 9 records              1% Full   Line   6
r[·······1·········2·········3·········4·········5·········6·········7·······]n

First Name:                              Last Name:
Street:
City: [1]                                State:      Zip:
Phone:
Preferred Customer:
Last Payment Date:
Balance Due:
Comments:



          Press F7 to add this record, or F10 to search for this pattern
```

Figure 4.2: Simple sort instruction

Instead of display-ing the sorted records one at a time, you can display them all at once as a table by press-ing the speed key Alt-T instead of the F10 key. See "Generating Tables" in Chapter 3.

Table 4.2: Sort Instructions

INSTRUCTION	MEANING
[1]	Sort first on this field
[2]	Sort next on this field
[1A]	Sort first on this field, in ascending order
[1D]	Sort first on this field, in descending order
[1N]	Sort first on this field, using a numerical sort (used for character fields containing numbers)
[1ND]	Sort first on this field in descending order, using a numerical sort

Sort instructions must be enclosed in square brackets ([ ]). Each sort instruction must contain the number 1 or 2. These determine which field is used for the primary sort and which for the secondary sort (if any). Sort instructions may be combined, as shown in several examples in Table 4.2. The order in which they are combined is irrelevant, that is, [1A] is the same as [A1]. Default sorting is in ascending order. If you want records sorted in descending order, include "D" in the sort instruction.

Suppose that you want to sort the records in the CLIENTS database in descending order by *Last Name*. To do so, you would insert the sort instruction [1D] next to the *Last Name* field.

As another example, suppose that you want to sort the CLIENTS records first by city in descending order, and then by last name in ascending order. In other words, all records would be sorted by *City* field values in reverse alphabetical order. Then the records for each city would be sorted alphabetically by values in the *Last Name* field. Figure 4.3 shows the sort instructions to use.

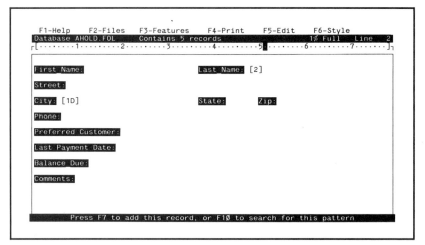

Figure 4.3: Pair of sort instructions

SORTING WITH SEARCH INSTRUCTIONS

Sort instructions can be combined with search instructions in a single operation. For example, you might want to display all records for the city of Oakland. In addition, you might like to display these records alphabetically according to the *Last Name* field. You could do this by combining the appropriate search and sort instructions on a blank form, as shown in Figure 4.4.

Both sort and search instructions can be combined in the same field. For example, suppose that you want to list records for which the balance due is greater than $100, and you also want the records to be displayed in ascending order based on the values in this field. Figure 4.5 shows the combined instructions.

> When combining sort and search instructions in the same field, the sort instructions must be written first.

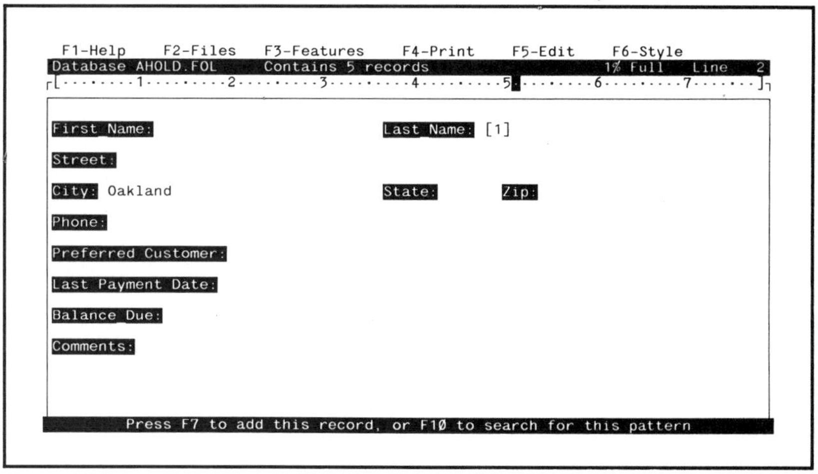

```
    F1-Help    F2-Files    F3-Features    F4-Print    F5-Edit    F6-Style
  Database AHOLD.FOL        Contains 5 records                1% Full   Line   2
  ┌[·····1······2·······3·······4······5·······6·······7·····]┐

  First Name:                         Last Name: [1]

  Street:

  City: Oakland                       State:        Zip:

  Phone:

  Preferred Customer:

  Last Payment Date:

  Balance Due:

  Comments:



          Press F7 to add this record, or F10 to search for this pattern
```

Figure 4.4: Combination of sort and search instructions

```
    F1-Help    F2-Files    F3-Features    F4-Print    F5-Edit    F6-Style
  Database CLIENTS.FOL     Contains 9 records                1% Full   Line  14
  ┌[·····1······2·······3·······4······5·······6·······7·····]┐

  First Name:                         Last Name:

  Street:

  City:                               State:        Zip:

  Phone:

  Preferred Customer:

  Last Payment Date:

  Balance Due: [1] >100

  Comments:



          Press F7 to add this record, or F10 to search for this pattern
```

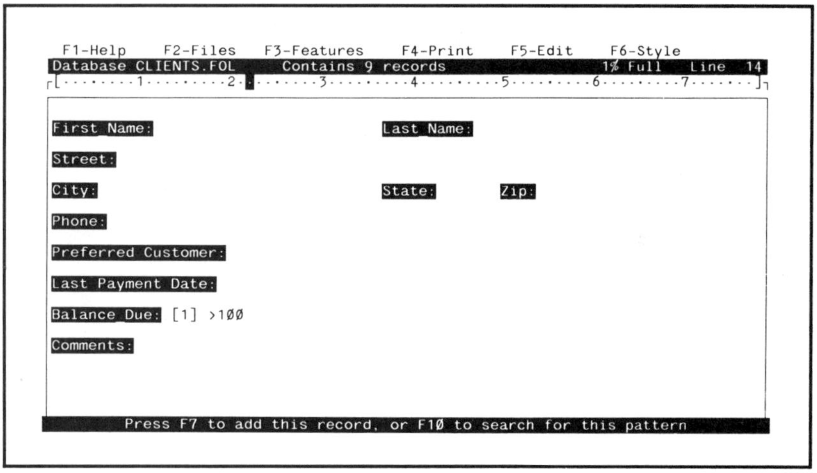

Figure 4.5: Sort and search instructions in the same field

Now suppose that you want to list all records for clients who do not live in Oakland. Also, you want the records to be displayed alphabetically by the value in the *City* field. In addition, within each city, you want the records listed alphabetically by last name. Figure 4.6 shows the combination of search and sort instructions that will list the records in this sequence.

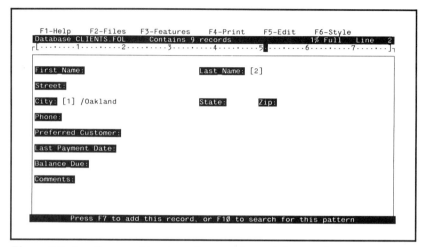

Figure 4.6: Another combination of sort and search instructions

PRINTING SORTED RECORDS

Records from a database can be printed in sorted order. All of the records can be printed, or only a group of records specified by a set of search instructions. Refer to Chapter 3 for details on printing records.

To illustrate this process, let's print the records from the CLIENTS database, sorted by values of the *Last Name* field.

1. Retrieve the CLIENTS file.

2. Choose *Print records* from the Print menu. The Print Options menu will appear.

3. Specify any desired options from the Print Options menu.

4. When you're done, press ←⏎, and a blank form for the CLIENTS database will appear.

5. Enter the sort instruction [1] next to the *Last Name* field.

6. Press the F10 key to begin the printing.

If you enter a set of search instructions, as well as sort instructions, then only the records specified by those instructions will be printed, and they will be in the order specified by the sort instructions. If no search instructions are entered, all records will be printed.

COPYING SORTED RECORDS

In a previous section, you learned how to copy a group of records from one database to another. Now you'll see how the records can be copied in sorted order.

All of the records in a database can be copied, or only a group of them specified by a set of search instructions. Before reading on, you may wish to review the earlier section in this chapter, "Making Copies of Records."

To copy a database of records in sorted order to another database (the target), select the database to be copied from the Directory Assistant. Choose *Copy records* from the Files menu, and enter the name of the target database. Now type the sort instructions into the blank form. If you want to limit the copying to a particular group of records, type the appropriate search instructions as well. Press F10 to begin the copying process.

Only the records specified by the search instructions will be copied to the new database, and those will be in the order specified by the sort instructions. If no search instructions are entered, all records in the database will be copied.

USING BOOKMARKS

You can place one or more bookmarks anywhere you wish within a database. Then, no matter what you are doing, you can return instantly to a bookmark. Several bookmarks can be placed within a single record, or one bookmark in each of several records.

For other details concerning the use of bookmarks, refer to Chapter 11.

For example, you might be working on a particular record, but for some reason you need to see data located somewhere else. You could set a bookmark where you are working, then go exploring for the other data, which can even be located in another database! When you're ready, you can instantly jump back to the original spot where the bookmark was placed.

PLACING A BOOKMARK

To set a bookmark anywhere within a record, first move the cursor to the desired spot. Select *Set bookmark* from the Features menu, and choose any bookmark that isn't already in use.

JUMPING TO A BOOKMARK

You can jump to any previously set bookmark by selecting *Find bookmark* from the Features menu. You can also use a speed key as a shortcut. Press the speed key Alt-*m*, where *m* is the number of the bookmark.

USING THE CALCULATOR

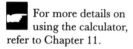 For more details on using the calculator, refer to Chapter 11.

You can use First Choice's pop-up calculator to perform computations, no matter what you're doing in a database. If desired, you can transfer the result of a calculation directly to a field. Move the cursor to the desired location within a record. Select *Use calculator* from the Features menu. Enter the calculation and press ←. If you press F10, the result of the calculation will appear at the current cursor position.

TEXT-EDITING YOUR DATABASE

These features work only with the data within a record; the field names are ignored.

Most of the editing aids available with First Choice's word processor can be used with database information. For instance, an entire record can be checked for spelling errors, or the thesaurus can be used to find possible synonyms for any word in a record. The search-and-replace feature can be used to find specific text strings and optionally replace them with other strings.

For a complete discussion of these features, refer to Chapters 1 and 2.

USING THE SPELL CHECKER AND THESAURUS

You can check the spelling of all or part of the data within a particular record. Position the cursor at the place in the record where spell-checking is to begin. Pick *Check spelling* from the Features menu. All of the field values from the cursor position to the end of the record will be checked for spelling.

To use the thesaurus, position the cursor at the desired word. Select *Find synonyms* from the Features menu. First Choice will present you with any possible synonyms that it finds in its dictionary.

USING THE SEARCH-AND-REPLACE FEATURE

This feature can be used to find a specific text string—either a whole word, part of a word, or several words. It can also be used to replace each instance of a text string with another string. First, position the cursor at the place in the record from which the searching is to begin. Next, select *Find and Replace* from the Features menu. You must now indicate what you want to look for; whether you want to replace it with anything else; and whether you want each replacement to be made automatically or with your approval.

First Choice searches from the cursor position to the end of the record, pausing at each item found.

COMMUNICATING WITH OTHER SYSTEMS: ASCII FILES

It is possible to transform data in a First Choice database so that it can be read by many different software packages. Similarly, First Choice can import information from other packages.

The two industry-standard formats that First Choice uses for importing and exporting files are *delimited ASCII* and *fixed-length ASCII* files. In a delimited ASCII file, each field value is enclosed by a special character called a *quote character*; fields are separated by another special character called a *delimiter*.

In a fixed-length ASCII file, all records are the same length. Indeed, for each field, every value is the same length. For instance, if the records in the CLIENTS database were output as a fixed-length ASCII file, every *First Name* value would be the same length, every *Last Name* value would also be the same length, and so on. You can picture all of the records in a fixed-length ASCII file as a table of rows and columns.

As an example, suppose that you want to import (bring into First Choice) a file of records stored in dBASE III PLUS. You can do so by first having the dBASE software output these records in the form of a delimited ASCII file. Then, First Choice can read this file and create its own database, which will contain all of the records originally in the dBASE file.

Similarly, First Choice can transform a group of records into a delimited ASCII file, which can then be read by dBASE III PLUS or other database systems. This same file can also be read by most word processors.

CREATING A DELIMITED ASCII FILE

In previous exercises you created the CLIENTS database, which contains the records shown in Table 3.2. If you ask First Choice to transform these records into a delimited ASCII file, you'll get the result shown in Figure 4.7.

If you compare Figure 4.7 with Table 3.2, you'll see that both contain the same data, but the records in the delimited ASCII file are in a special format:

- The value of each field is enclosed in double quotation marks (the *quote character*).

- Each field terminates with a comma, called a *delimiter* (hence the term *delimited* file).

- Each record ends with a *hard return* character (←┘), but you can't see these in the figure.

- Only field values appear in the file; field names do not.

Although not obvious from Figure 4.7, the data itself is coded in ASCII form, which is an industry standard—most software packages know how to read and write files of text in ASCII format.

Here are the steps to follow for creating a delimited ASCII file from a First Choice database:

1. Select *Get an existing file,* either from the Main menu or the Files menu. The Directory Assistant will appear.

2. Choose the database to be copied, either by typing its name (including the .FOL extension) or by using the cursor keys.

3. Pick *Save ASCII data* from the Files menu. The Directory Assistant display will again appear.

4. Enter a name for the file to hold the output data. You may, if you wish, include a file name extension.

```
"","Terry","Pirate","98 Morgan St.","Phoenix","AZ","94011","418-333-1239","y","4-9-88",347,"A very reliable customer."
"","Janice","Peters","111 Acker St.","Oakland","CA","94155","415-999-1234","n","3-2-88",805.11,"Always late with payments"
"","Ruby","Gold","35 Everett Ave.","Phoenix","AZ","42001","901-444-1233","n","4-25-88",750.25,"Never pays on time."
"","Howard","Duck","123 92nd Ave.","Oakland","CA","97102","418-998-1234","y","1-19-88",750,"Eats a lot of crackers."
"","Harry","Peters","137 Jackson Dr.","Berkeley","CA","94707","415-666-1836","n","6-30-88",874.02,"Runs up large bills"
"","Sarah","Lo","1327 Mylvia St.","Alameda","CA","94511","415-531-9854","n","2-18-87",429.39,"Can't be depended on to pay up."
"","Mary","Smith","3827 1st St.","Oakland","CA","94611","415-654-8688","y","3-7-88",125.46,"Call on Mondays only."
"","Pete","Lick","14 Fine Ave.","Oakland","CA","94602","415-666-1254","y","7-2-88",0,"Never around during the week."
"","Sam","Drew","3 Ada St.","Phoenix","AZ","52001","212-531-5432","y","6-19-88",25.27,"A fine worker, and very reliable."
```

Figure 4.7: Delimited ASCII file

Numeric fields are
not enclosed with
quote characters.

5. First Choice then presents you with a screen (Figure 4.8) for
selecting the quote character that encloses each field (the
default choice is the double quote) and the delimiter character that marks the end of each field (the default choice is the
comma).

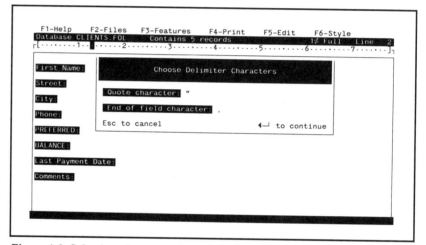

Figure 4.8: Selecting characters for a delimited ASCII file

You can select any non-blank character for either of these, if you
don't like the defaults. This may be necessary if you plan to read the
ASCII file with a program that expects characters other than the double quote and comma (see additional comments below). To go on,
press ◄┘.

6. If you want to copy only selected records, enter the search
instructions on the blank form. To copy all records, don't
enter anything.

7. If you want the copied records to be sorted, enter the sort
instructions.

8. Begin copying by pressing F10.

All records specified by the search instructions are copied to the
new file in delimited ASCII form. If sort instructions are included,
the records will be sorted.

If you plan to read the delimited ASCII file with another software package, you must match the form of this file to the requirements of the software package. For example, if the package uses particular quote and end-of-field characters, these must appear in the file.

Some software packages (dBASE III PLUS, for example) use a quote character to enclose only character information; numeric or other special types of fields are not enclosed by any special character. Each software package has its own requirements.

In most cases, it will be possible to edit the ASCII file so that it can be read by any particular software package. Read the file into First Choice's word processor as an ASCII file. You can then make the changes required by the other software, hopefully with the aid of the search-and-replace feature.

READING A DELIMITED ASCII FILE

If a delimited ASCII file has been generated from a file of records managed by another software package, First Choice can read that file into an existing database. The database can be empty, or it can contain records. The new records are added to any already in the database.

In order to read records from a delimited ASCII file into an existing database, these requirements must be met:

- The target database must already exist.

- The form, or structure, of this database must correspond to the data in the ASCII file, item-by-item. That is, the first field of the database must correspond to the first data item of each record in the ASCII file, and so on.

- You must know the exact form of the data in the delimited ASCII file. If each data item is enclosed by quote characters and ends with a delimiter, then you can read the file directly into a database.

- If the ASCII file has an unusual format, you may need to edit it with First Choice's word processor before reading it into a database.

After these requirements have been met, the ASCII file can be read into a database:

- Retrieve the database.

- Select *Get ASCII data* from the Files menu.

- Choose **D** (for delimited ASCII file).

- When the Directory Assistant appears, enter the name of the delimited ASCII file.

- Select the quote character and delimiter that are used in the ASCII file, then press ◄─┘.

The data from the ASCII file will be converted into records and stored in the First Choice database.

Note that when First Choice creates a delimited ASCII file, it does *not* enclose values from numeric fields in quote characters. However, when First Choice reads in data from a delimited ASCII file, values going into a numeric field may be enclosed in quote characters.

As an ASCII file is being read in, the copy process can be interrupted by pressing the Esc key. You can then choose to go on or to cancel the process. Any records already copied to the database will remain there.

CREATING A FIXED-LENGTH ASCII FILE

This type of file can be read in by many types of software, including database managers and spreadsheet programs. To create a fixed length ASCII file, you must first create a table view that contains all of the data that you wish to transfer, then build the ASCII file from that table. Here are the steps:

- Retrieve the database.

- Create the table view that includes all of the fields that are to be transferred. You can select widths for each field in the table, but remember that the maximum width for the table is 250 characters. For details on building tables, see "Generating Tables" in Chapter 3.

- After the table appears as you want it, select *Save table as an ASCII file* from the Files menu.

- When the Directory Assistant appears, enter the name of the file to hold the fixed-length ASCII data.

You can retrieve a fixed-length ASCII file into First Choice's word processor. You might want to do this to examine the file's contents, just to make sure that it contains what you expected. This is particularly important if you plan to read in the file with another software package.

READING A FIXED-LENGTH ASCII FILE

This type of file is generated by many different types of software packages, including database managers and spreadsheet programs. Data in this type of file is written as a series of records, with each record ending with a hard return character. The data can be thought of as a series of rows and columns: each row represents one record, and each column contains data for a single field.

Before attempting to read a file of this type into a First Choice database, make absolutely sure that you know the exact form of the file. If there's any doubt, retrieve the file as an ASCII file into the word processor. You can then examine its structure. For instance, if you know that the file contains records, each of which consists of ten fields, you'll need to know the exact length of each field, and how many columns—if any—separate one field from the next. You'll also need to know which type of data appears in each field on the file: character, numeric, date, time, or yes/no.

The database into which you plan to read data from a fixed-length ASCII file must conform to the structure of the file on a field-by-field basis. You may need to create a new database that has the correct structure.

To read in the file:

- Retrieve the database into which the file is to be read.

- Select *Get ASCII data* from the Files menu.

- Specify **F** for "fixed length file."

- When the Directory Assistant appears, enter the name of the ASCII file containing the data.

- A blank database form will appear. For each field, enter the starting and ending column numbers that contain the data for that field. Separate the two numbers with a space or a comma. For example, if the first field in the ASCII file occupies the first 15 columns, enter 1,15 for the first field on the database form.

- After you've entered the column numbers for every field, press F10 to read the data into the database.

DIALING A TELEPHONE NUMBER IN A DATABASE

You can have First Choice dial a telephone number for you, if that number is contained in a record within a database. For example, suppose you have a list of names and telephone numbers stored in a First Choice database: you can search the database for the record of a particular person, then have First Choice dial that person's number.

To use this feature you must have a telephone plugged into your modem. This is not usually a problem, since most modems have a standard connection for just this purpose. If you selected either *Unlisted modem* or *Acoustic modem* when you installed First Choice, then you can't use this auto-dial feature.

To dial a number:

With some modems, you'll need to pick up the telephone as soon as you hear the phone ringing (through the speaker in the modem). This is because First Choice sometimes disconnects abruptly after the first ring.

1. Locate the record with the phone number you want to dial. An easy way to do this is to enter a personal name as a search instruction and let First Choice find the record for you.

2. When the record appears, move the cursor to any part of the telephone number, which can be anywhere in the record.

3. Select *Dial this number* from the Features menu. The number will then be dialed for you. If the number is busy, First Choice automatically hangs up after a few seconds.

SUMMARY

First Choice's advanced database manager features enable you to rearrange database records so that you can get optimum use of your information. By copying records from one file to another, for example, you can save yourself the work of entering new records. Or, you can easily keep your database up to date by deleting selected groups of records. These features are made more useful with the help of the Calculator and Bookmark features. You can even use First Choice's data files with other software programs, and bring in files from those programs into First Choice. In the next chapter, you'll learn to transform and organize the information in your databases to create reports.

Chapter
5

Creating
Reports

A report is any type of output containing information from the records in a database. Generally, a report presents data in a rearranged format, making it as presentable as possible. A report may consist of the entire contents of a database, or it may contain data from a few records.

Most often, a report is sent to a printer so that hard copy can be obtained. First Choice's report writer can also output to the screen. This is a handy way of inspecting a good deal of information quickly. For example, you could condense the data within a database into columnar format, so that many records would appear on the screen at the same time. First Choice can also send a report to a disk file, where it can later be edited or improved with the word processor.

In this chapter we'll cover how to create and save a set of report instructions. You'll also be shown how to create a report from an existing set of report instructions, and how to generate a summary report. Finally, you'll learn techniques for enhancing the appearance of a report.

AN OVERVIEW OF REPORT GENERATION

First Choice's report writer provides a great deal of flexibility in the way that information in a database is presented. Data can be rearranged, sorted, condensed, and used in calculations, all of which becomes the basis of a report. In this section, we'll outline the characteristics of the report writer.

MAIN FEATURES OF A REPORT

A typical report generated by First Choice is shown in Figure 5.1. Here are some of the features illustrated in this report:

- *Content:* The entire contents of a report comes from a single First Choice database. Except for headings, totals, and so on, each line of a report contains data from a single record.

- *Columnar output:* Most reports consist of one or more columns. Usually, each column contains data from a single field.

- *Column headings:* Often, each column is given a heading, which may or may not be the name of the corresponding field.

- *Title:* The top line of the report contains a title, supplied by the user.

- *Ordering:* The rows of data are arranged alphabetically according to the *City* values in the first column. Notice also that where there are several rows corresponding to the same city (such as Oakland), the name of the city is not repeated.

- *Averages and totals:* Both the average value and the total value of the data in the Balance Due column are printed.

- *Page numbering:* Pages in a report are automatically numbered.

Another sample report is shown in Figure 5.2. It illustrates additional features that can be included in report generation:

- *Subtotals:* This report shows customers from two cities; at the end of the list for each city, the subtotal of the Balance Due column is printed.

```
    City          First Name      Last Name       Balance Due     Last Payment Date
  --------        ----------      ---------       -----------     -----------------
  Alameda         Sarah           Lo                   429.39     2-18-87
  Berkeley        Harry           Peters               874.02     6-30-88
  Oakland         Howard          Duck                 750.00     1-19-88
                  Janice          Peters               805.11     3-2-88
                  Mary            Smith                125.46     3-7-88
                  Pete            Lick                   0.00     7-2-88
  Phoenix         Ruby            Gold                 750.25     4-25-88
                  Sam             Drew                  25.27     6-19-88
                  Terry           Pirate               347.00     4-9-88

                                             -------------------
                                  Average:          456.28
                                  Total:          4,106.50
                                             -------------------
```

Figure 5.1: Report generated by First Choice

```
              SECONDARY REPORT ON ACCOUNTS RECEIVABLE

    City       First Name   Last Name    Balance Due    Penalty Due
 ---------     ----------   ----------   -----------    -----------

 Oakland       Howard       Duck            750.00          75.00
               Janice       Peters          805.11          80.51
               Mary         Smith           125.46          12.55
               Pete         Lick              0.00           0.00

                                 Total:    1,680.57

 Phoenix       Ruby         Gold            750.25          75.03
               Sam          Drew             25.27           2.53
               Terry        Pirate          347.00          34.70

                                 Total:    1,122.52

                                          -------------------
                                 Total:    4,106.50
                                          -------------------

                            Page 1
```

Figure 5.2: Report with subtotals and a derived column

- *Derived column:* Each entry in the Penalty Due column contains the 10% penalty levied on each customer. The derived column does not represent data actually in the records; the values are calculated from other data in the report.

In the rest of this chapter, we'll describe how to create each of the elements shown in Figures 5.1 and 5.2.

THE ELEMENTS OF REPORT GENERATION

Several steps are involved in the creation of a report. To begin, you must create a set of *report instructions*. These give First Choice the information that it needs to generate the report. The instructions contain the following information:

- The name of the database to be used in generating the report.

- Details concerning print options, such as number and length of lines on each page, whether or not headings should be printed on each page, and so on. Also, you must specify whether the output is to be directed to the printer, the screen, or a disk file.

- The contents and layout of the report. You must specify the names of the fields to be included in the output, and the order in which they're to be printed. You may also specify one or more derived columns, which contain values based on the contents of other fields in the report. You can control column widths, wraparound of long lines, and pagination. Finally, you may specify that one or more fields be *invisible,* which means that its contents are not displayed on the report. This type of field is used either for sorting the output or for inputting values for a derived column.

- Calculations, if any, to be performed on each field in the report. For numerical fields, these can include totals, subtotals, averages, and subaverages. The number of items appearing in a column can also be output.

- Search instructions, for defining which records are to be included in the report. If a report is to include every record in a database, then no search instructions are necessary.

After you have entered all of the above report instructions you can, if you wish, save them in a file. This file can then be used at any time to generate additional reports of the same type; the instructions can be modified as needed.

Finally, you can instruct First Choice to generate the report, using the report instructions as a guide. Depending on what you have selected in the instructions, the output will go either to the printer, the screen, or a disk file.

Learning how to create a report is equivalent to following a recipe: Certain things have to be entered, and in the correct order. The next section, "Creating a Set of Report Instructions," describes each step necessary for creating a "standard" type of report. In later sections, we'll describe other aspects of report generation.

CREATING A SET OF REPORT INSTRUCTIONS

In this section, we'll describe in detail the steps needed to create report instructions for the report shown in Figure 5.1. During each step, we'll also describe the options available to you.

The report in Figure 5.1 is based on the same CLIENTS database used in previous chapters. For convenience, this database form is shown in Figure 5.3.

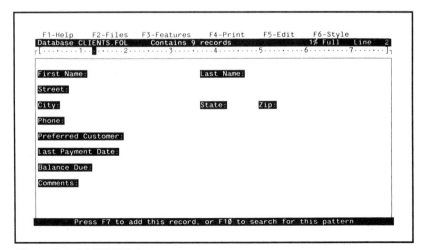

Figure 5.3: CLIENTS form

In the following discussion, we'll assume that you're using the CLIENTS database. If you have your own database, you can duplicate the procedure on your computer, selecting options appropriate to that database.

Note that to create a report, First Choice must be in the Overwrite mode (the cursor is a blinking line). Press the Ins key once or twice to make sure that the correct mode is on.

GETTING STARTED

You can abandon the report generation process at any time by pressing the Esc key.

To begin the process of creating a new set of report instructions, you must tell First Choice that you want to do so, then specify the database that contains the records to be used in the report.

Here are the preliminary steps:

1. Return to First Choice's Main menu. If you're working within one of First Choice's modules, you can get back to the Main menu by pressing the Esc key once or twice. Otherwise, when you first start up First Choice, the Main menu is automatically displayed.

2. Select *Create a report*. The Directory Assistant will appear.

3. Select the database to be used (CLIENTS.FOL or your own database) by typing in the name or by using the cursor keys. If necessary, first type in the drive name and/or subdirectory where the file is stored. If First Choice can't find the database that you specify, a warning message appears near the bottom of the screen.

After First Choice locates the database that you specify, the Print Options display appears (Figure 5.4). Let's look at each option.

SELECTING PRINT OPTIONS

For each option shown on the Print Options screen, a standard value also appears. If you want to change one or more of these, press Tab or Shift-Tab to move to the desired option, then enter the desired value.

If you have an ordinary dot-matrix printer, the standard options shown on the Print Options screen will suffice to generate a report

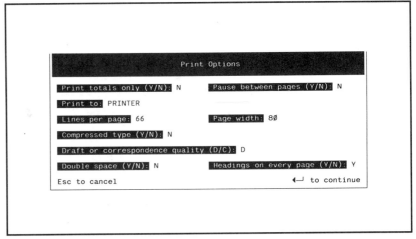

Figure 5.4: Print Options display

from your database. To select these, simply press ◄┘. This section describes each of the options in detail.

PRINT TOTALS ONLY (Y/N)   If your report includes one or more numeric columns, you can choose to print a summary report, which contains only totals for the numeric columns. If so, enter "Y" for this option.

PAUSE BETWEEN PAGES (Y/N)   If you are using single hand-fed sheets in your printer, select "Y" for this option. First Choice will pause at the end of each page to give you time to insert a new page.

PRINT TO   The report can be directed to a number of different output devices. If the report is to be printed, the correct choice is PRINTER. If you want to preview the report on the screen before sending it to the printer, enter the value SCREEN. This is generally a good procedure to follow when creating a new report; you can quickly glance at the output, then make any necessary changes to the report instructions, thereby saving time and paper.

If the report is to be written to a disk file, enter the name of the file. If the file is not on the current disk drive and/or subdirectory, enter the appropriate names along with the file name. For example,

If the report is written to a file, you can later edit it with the word processor. It can then be copied to the printer (see the later section, "Improving the Appearance of a Report").

to write a report to the file MYREPORT on the subdirectory \MYSTUFF of drive C, you would enter the name C:\MYSTUFF\ MYREPORT. The file that you specify can be a new or existing one. If the file exists, First Choice will later ask you to confirm that it's all right to overwrite the file.

LINES PER PAGE A standard page has room for 66 lines. (Some laser printers require a value of 60.) If you are using an unusual page size, enter the total number of lines that fit on each page. For example, legal documents are 14 inches long and hold 84 lines per page.

See Appendix B for information about specific printers.

PAGE WIDTH This value specifies the number of characters that fit on each line. You can enter any value between 1 and 255.

Ordinary printers print up to 80 characters per line in normal Draft mode. Some printers can fit 96 characters on a line in Elite mode, and up to 132 per line in Compressed mode (printers with wide carriages can print up to 255 characters per line in Compressed mode). Consult your printer's manual to find out what its capabilities are. If the manual is not available, you can always resort to trial-and-error.

If you're outputting to either the screen or a disk file, you can use a page width from 1 to 255 characters. However, if you plan to eventually output the report to the printer, be guided by the printer's limitations.

COMPRESSED TYPE (Y/N) If you plan to print in Compressed mode, enter "Y" for this option. For this feature to work properly, you may need to specify the exact printer when customizing First Choice for your hardware. Also, some printers may not print in Compressed mode at all.

DRAFT OR CORRESPONDENCE QUALITY (D/C) Again, you may need to use trial-and-error to determine what your printer does for each of these choices. If the correct printer has not been specified during the customization process, you may not be able to obtain correspondence quality from the printer.

DOUBLE SPACE (Y/N) Typing "Y" generates a double-spaced report.

HEADINGS ON EVERY PAGE (Y/N) If you select "Y," any heading that you specify (later on) will be printed at the top of each page. If you want the heading to appear only on the first page of the report, enter "N."

When you have finished selecting options, press ← to go on. The options will be remembered by First Choice and kept as part of the report instructions.

USING FIELDS IN YOUR REPORT

You can't back up to the previous display (Print Options). If you realize that you've made an error in entering data on that screen, you'll have to abort the entire process with the Esc key and begin over.

After you have finished entering the print options, the Column Selection display (Figure 5.5) appears. You use this display to specify which fields are to appear in the report, and the order in which the fields are to appear.

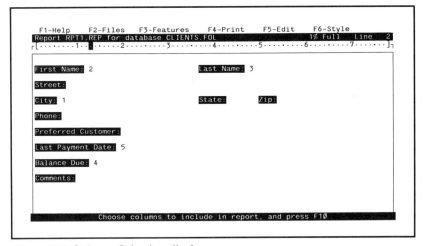

Figure 5.5: Column Selection display

However, before selecting the fields for a report, you must understand how the information in a report is sorted, because that will help you decide how to choose the order of the fields.

HOW DATA IN A REPORT IS SORTED The rows of a report are always sorted according to the values in the first column. In addition, if the values in the first column are the same for two or more rows, then they are sorted according to the values in the second column.

The way in which sorting is done depends on the type of data in the first or second column. If the data consists of text, rows are sorted alphabetically. Table 5.1 illustrates how sorting works.

Table 5.1: Sorting Examples

This entry	comes before	this entry
$		1
1		2
1		11
1		A
1 3		12
A		B
A		AA
A B		AA
AAAAA		AB
A B		A$B
a	no!	A
A	no!	a

All special characters come before either digits or letters.
No distinction is made between uppercase and lowercase.

When First Choice compares two characters, it uses the following sorting order:

1. Blank space

2. Special characters

3. Digits (1-9)

4. Letters (a-z)

In other words, any special character ($, %, etc.) is "less than" any digit or letter; and any digit is "less than" any letter. In fact, the special characters have their own sorting order as well, but we won't go into that.

When First Choice compares two strings, it makes a character-by-character comparison. As soon as a mismatch is found between two corresponding characters, the above sorting order determines which of the two strings comes first.

There are several other things you should keep in mind about sorting order. First, no distinction is made between uppercase and lowercase. Also, before a comparison is made between two strings, any leading blanks are stripped off. Finally, it's quite possible for a very long string (*AAAAAAAAAAAAAA,* for example) to come before a short string (*AB,* for example).

Digits are treated as ordinary characters when involved in an alphabetic sort, and this can lead to problems. For example, the value "12" comes before the value "2" when they are treated alphabetically. If you plan to sort on a series of numeric values, it's best to keep them in a numeric field, if possible.

When First Choice examines a number in a character field for sorting purposes, it ignores all characters except those that are normally part of a number:

digits (0 thru 9)

decimal point (.)

minus sign (−)

A number is taken to be negative if a minus sign appears either before or after the number.

Date and *Time* fields are sorted from earlier to later time.

A report can contain up to 20 columns, including any derived ones.

CHOOSING FIELDS AND THEIR ORDER   To select a field, enter a number after the field name. The value of the number indicates the position of the field in the report.

Follow these steps to select the fields to appear in the report shown in Figure 5.1:

1. Move the cursor to the *First Name* field, using the Tab key.

2. Enter the number **2**. This indicates that this field will appear in the second column of the report.

3. Using the Tab and Shift-Tab keys, move to the following fields, entering the appropriate column numbers for each:

Field	Column Number
Last Name	3
City	1
Last Payment Date	5
Balance Due	4

4. After you've finished entering the column numbers, your screen should look like that shown in Figure 5.5. Press the F10 key, and the Headings and Calculations display (Figure 5.6) will appear.

Figure 5.6: Headings and Calculation display

When choosing the order of fields, remember that the values in the first two columns determine the sorting order of the final report. If you don't want the report data to be sorted, start numbering columns with 3 rather than 1. In this case, however, the report can contain a maximum of 18 columns (rather than 20).

The entries in Figure 5.5 correspond to the report shown in Figure 5.1. You might want to verify that the records in this report are sorted as you would expect.

CHOOSING HEADINGS
AND SPECIFYING CALCULATIONS

The Headings and Calculations display is used to specify any of the following:

- Report title

- Headings and widths for each column

- The manner in which information is sorted

- Calculations to be performed on numeric columns

- Derived columns that are to appear in the report

- Columns that are to be invisible (that are not to appear in the report)

- Page control

To enter a value for an item, move to that item with the Tab and Shift-Tab keystrokes, then enter the desired value. The entire Headings and Calculations display may not fit on a single screen. You can use the PgUp and PgDn keys to scroll through the display.

REPORT TITLE At your option, you can enter a title to appear at the top of the report (or on each page, depending on your previous choice from the Print Options display). A title can occupy only one line, and it can be as long as the width of the report, which was specified in the Print Options display.

SORTING ORDER Data in a report is always sorted, according to the values in the first column (and the second column when two or more values are the same in the first column). Sorting can be either in ascending (A) or descending (D) order.

COLUMN HEADINGS For each field that you have selected to be in the report, a column heading line is shown on the screen. The default column heading is the field name. You can replace this default value by moving the cursor to the heading and entering a new value. You can also eliminate a column heading by using the spacebar to blank out the heading on the screen.

One reason for changing a column heading is to conserve space on the report. If you let First Choice choose each column width, it is determined by either the column heading or the longest data entry for that column. If the heading is longer than the longest entry, space will probably be wasted on the report. To avoid this situation, you may want to select column widths yourself (described later).

You can enhance column headings with any of First Choice's styles, such as boldfacing, italics, or underlining. Move the cursor to the beginning of a heading line on the screen. Enter the new heading, then select the heading by moving the cursor to the beginning of the heading, pressing Alt-S, then moving the cursor keys to include the entire heading. Choose the desired style from the Style menu.

CALCULATIONS   Each report column has a line on the Headings and Calculations screen labeled *Calculation*. You can enter one or more options for each column; each option controls how that particular column is treated when the report is generated. As an example, in Figure 5.6 the options "T" and "A" are entered for the fourth column.

Let's look closer at these options.

T (Total)	The total of all values for the column is printed at the end of the report. This option should be used only with numeric fields.
A (Average)	The average value of all entries in the column is printed at the end of the report.
C (Count)	The number of entries for the column is printed at the end of the report. This option can be used for any type of data.
ST (Subtotal)	A subtotal is printed in the column each time the value in the *first* column changes. In addition, a grand total is printed at the end of the report. An example is shown in Figure 5.2: Each time the value changes in the City column, a subtotal is printed for the

Balance Due column. We say that a *control break* occurs each time the value in the first column changes. Note that each subtotal is labeled *Total:*, even though it's really a subtotal. Also, each subtotal refers only to those values printed since the last control break. For example, in Figure 5.2, the total of 1,122.52 refers only to the entries for Phoenix.

SA (Subaverage)   This is another control-break option. An average value is printed each time the value in the first column changes. In addition, a final average is printed at the end of the report.

SC (Subcount)   A subcount is printed at each control break.

I (Invisible)   The column is not printed. The I option is selected if the values of the column are to be used in generating the report (such as in the calculation of a derived column), but the actual field values are not wanted in the final output. An invisible column can be made the first column of the report. The rows in the report will be sorted based on the values in the first column, even though this column itself is not printed.

P (New Page)   A new page will be started each time the value in the first column changes.

R (Repeat)   Normally, if the value in the first column is the same for two or more rows, it is printed only for the first row (see Figure 5.1, for example). The R option causes the value in the first column to print in each row. This applies as well to the second column, but not to any of the others.

W*nn* (Width)	Assigns a width of *nn* characters to a column. You can select any width up to 255. If you don't use this option, First Choice automatically selects a width to accommodate the longest value in the column, or up to 40 characters. Values longer than the assigned width for the column wrap to the next line, unless the L option is selected (see below).
L (Line)	A long value is truncated to a single line, rather than wrapping around. Normally, a value that's longer than the assigned column width wraps around to the next line.
D*d* (Decimals)	Assigns *d* decimal places to each number placed in this column. The value of *d* can be from zero to 15. If this option is not selected, then the number of decimal places output is determined by whichever value in the column has the maximum number of decimal places.
N (Numeric)	The column contains numeric data. This option can be used for alphanumeric fields that contain numeric data. This is valuable if you want to store numeric values along with alphabetic descriptors, such as *2500 dollars,* or *$7500 credit.* These kinds of data can't be used in a numeric-type field, because they're not legal numeric values. However, if you select the N option for an alphanumeric field, then First Choice will do its best to sort out the actual numbers from any other non-numeric information. To do this, First Choice uses the following rules when it examines a string to see if it

First Choice automatically assigns "N" to numeric fields.

contains a number:

- All characters are ignored except those that are normally part of a number: digits (0 through 9), the decimal point (.), and the minus sign (−).

- If there is more than one decimal point or minus sign, only the first one is not ignored.

- A number is taken to be negative if a minus sign appears either before or after the number. Internal minus signs are ignored.

- All spaces and other characters within a number are ignored. Thus, the values *333, 3 33,* and *33Z3* are all considered equal.

When a field is assigned the N option, any numeric values will be printed in the report, and any non-numeric parts will be ignored. A field assigned the N option can also be used for sorting a report, by making it the first column.

If you select any of the numeric-type options for a column, such as "T," "ST," "A," and so on, First Choice treats that field as though you'd also assigned the N option.

The N option isn't needed for a field that was assigned as a numeric type when the database was built. However, for this type of field, only valid numbers can be input in the first place. For example, a value such as *500 dollars* couldn't be input.

More than one option can be selected for a column (see Figure 5.6, for example). They can be entered in any order with no separating spaces. However, regardless of this order, the order in which calculations are printed is always the same: averages first, then totals, and finally counts.

When outputting a column of numbers, First Choice nicely lines them up on decimal points and inserts commas as needed.

If First Choice cannot do a calculation for any reason (division by zero, for example), then ** is printed to indicate that a problem exists.

The last part of the Headings and Calculations display is used to specify any derived columns. We'll return to this topic later in the chapter.

Here are the steps for filling in the Headings and Calculations display for the report shown in Figure 5.1:

1. Using the Tab or Shift-Tab key, move the cursor to the line labeled *Report title:*. Type in the title **ACCOUNTS RECEIVABLE SUMMARY** (or, if you're using another database, any suitable title).

2. Move the cursor to the Column 4 Calculation line. Enter the values **TA** (for Total and Average).

3. Press the F10 key, and the Search Instructions display will appear (Figure 5.7).

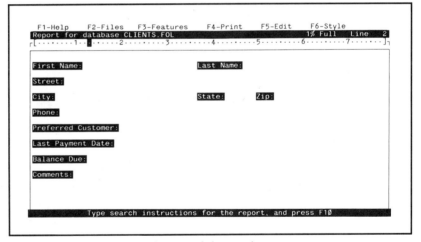

Figure 5.7: Screen for entering search instructions

When you are done entering values for options on the screen, press F10. The values are saved as part of the report instructions.

ENTERING SEARCH AND SORT INSTRUCTIONS

When the Search Instructions display appears, you can enter the specifications for records to appear in the report. If all of the records in the database are to be printed, then no search instructions should be entered. If you want the records to appear in a particular order, enter the appropriate sort instructions. For a complete discussion of search instructions, see Chapter 3.

SAVING THE REPORT INSTRUCTIONS

After you have finished entering any search or sort instructions, you can, if you wish, save the report instructions that you have generated up to this point, so that they can later be used for other reports. To do this, select the Files menu and choose *Save this report*. The Directory Assistant will appear. Enter the name of the file in which the report instructions are to be saved. If the file is to be stored on a disk drive or subdirectory other than the current ones, they should be entered as part of the file name. For example, to save the instructions in the file MYINS in the directory \MYSTUFF of drive C, enter the file name C:\MYSTUFF\MYINS.

First Choice automatically appends the extension .REP to the file name.

GENERATING THE REPORT

When you are done entering search instructions, and after you've saved the report instructions, you are ready to produce the actual report. If the report is to be sent to the printer, make sure that it's on and ready. The report in Figure 5.1 includes all of the records in the CLIENTS database. To duplicate this report, no search instructions should be entered.

1. After the Search Instructions display (Figure 5.7) appears, press the F10 key to print the report.

2. First Choice issues a warning message that you haven't yet saved all of the report instructions that you've painstakingly entered. If you don't want to save the report instructions, press ←. Otherwise, press the Esc key, then select *Save this report* from the Files menu.

3. When the Directory Assistant appears, enter the name **MYREPORT** ←. If necessary, first enter the name of the

disk drive and/or directory where the file is to be stored. A copy of the report instructions will be saved in this file.

4. When the Search Instructions display reappears, press F10; this time, the report will be printed.

The file MYREPORT.REP contains all of the report instructions that you've generated. You can recall them at any time, modify them as needed, then generate a new report.

SENDING THE REPORT TO A DISK FILE

Instead of sending a report to the printer, you can have First Choice write it to a disk file. To create this file, enter a name for it on the Print Options display (the first display when you start creating a report), next to the *Print to* option. If necessary, include the drive name and subdirectory as part of the file name. For example, to send the report to a file called HOLDME on drive A, enter the name A:HOLDME.

You can add a three-letter extension (such as .DOC) to the file name to help you remember what the file contains. If the extension .DOC is used, the file will be listed in the Documents column on the Directory Assistant.

After you have finished building the report instructions and saved them to a disk file, the report is generated as usual, except that now it goes to the disk file specified in the Print Options display.

VIEWING THE REPORT ON A DISK FILE

Now that you know how to send a report to a disk file, you'll find that this comes in handy when you want to view a report that has more columns than your printer can accommodate. (Most printers can't print more than about 130 characters per line, even in Compressed mode.) The word processor can handle lines up to 255 characters long.

To create a report and view it on-screen,

1. Begin creating the report instructions for your file.

2. From the Print Options menu, select a value of 255 for the

page width. Then select the name of a disk file to hold the report.

3. On the Column Selection display, select as many fields as you want to see displayed on the report.

4. Finish creating the report instructions, then save them.

5. Generate the report, which is written to the file that you selected.

6. Enter the Directory Assistant, and select the file containing the report.

7. Select *ASCII - Preserve carriage returns*.

8. Using the cursor keys, you can scan the report up, down, left, and right. The keystrokes Ctrl ← and Ctrl → move the cursor a *word* at a time, which in this case will often be a column at a time.

CREATING A REPORT WITH DERIVED COLUMNS

A *derived* column is one that contains data not actually in the database. Instead, this data is derived from calculations involving other columns containing numerical data.

This section will describe the ins and outs of creating derived columns. The derived column in the report shown in Figure 5.2 will be used as an example.

SPECIFYING DERIVED COLUMNS

This type of column is defined in the Headings and Calculations display. Figure 5.8 shows this display filled in for the report shown in Figure 5.2. In this report, the derived column is *Penalty Due*. For each row, the value in this column indicates the 10% penalty charged to each client with an outstanding balance.

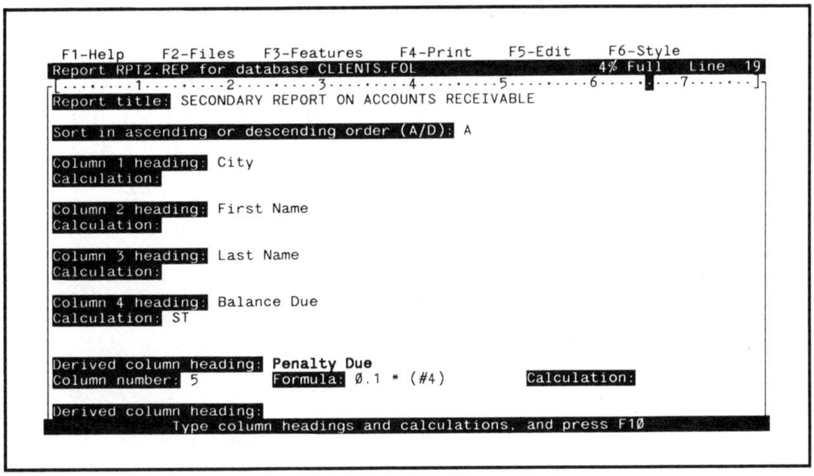

Figure 5.8: Headings and Calculations display with derived column

The entries for this derived column are shown at the bottom of the screen. Notice that since there is no actual field in the database for this column, there is initially no heading, and you must supply one. In Figure 5.8, the heading *Penalty Due* has been entered. Notice that the heading has been boldfaced for emphasis.

Each derived column must also be given a number, to indicate its position in the report. This is true even if a derived column is to be invisible. A derived column may be made column 1, in which case data is sorted based on the values of this column. A derived column can also be made both column 1 and invisible. This means that the report is sorted according to the values in this column, but that they themselves don't appear in the report.

Any of the calculation options described earlier may be entered in the space labeled *Calculation*. For example, if option T is entered, then a grand total for all values in this column will be printed.

DERIVED COLUMN FORMULAS

This is the heart of the derived column. The contents of this entry determine the final contents of the column. The entry in Figure 5.8 is a simple example of a formula: 0.1*(#4). This translates as follows: For each row, the value of the entry in the derived column consists of the entry in column 4 multiplied by 0.1.

A formula can contain column numbers, arithmetic operators, and one or more ordinary numbers such as 1, 1.5, and – 10. A column number is written as # n, where n is the number of the column; it refers to the value of that column for the current row.

You can do any of the standard arithmetic operations within a formula, using the following symbols:

*   Multiplication

/   Division

+   Addition

-     Subtraction

^   Exponentiation

( )   Parentheses, to clarify meanings

When First Choice evaluates a formula, it follows these rules:

- Multiplication and division are done first.

- Addition and subtraction are done next.

- Subject to the above two rules, calculations are done from left to right.

- Anything inside a set of parentheses is done before anything outside parentheses. Within each set of parentheses, the above three rules are followed.

- Blank spaces within a calculation are ignored. You can insert blanks liberally to improve readability.

When you enter a formula, you can make space as needed for a long formula by using the Insert mode. Press the Ins key once to enter this mode, once again to go back to the Overwrite mode. You can use all of the standard editing features to correct anything you enter.

These rules may seem a bit confusing, but in practice it's usually simple to write a formula correctly. A good rule of thumb is to use parentheses to clarify any calculations. For example, consider this formula:

#2 * (#1 – #3)

This means to first subtract #3 from #1, then multiply the result by #2.

Suppose you wrote this formula without parentheses:

#2 * #1 – #3

First of all, it wouldn't look very clear, and worse yet it would be evaluated differently, according to the above rules: the multiplication would be done first. The use of parentheses not only helps clarify what you mean, but also makes First Choice do the calculation correctly.

Table 5.2 shows some examples of formulas.

Table 5.2: Sample Formulas for Defining Derived Columns

Formula	Meaning
#1 + #2	Add the values of columns 1 and 2.
#3 − #4	Subtract the value of column 4 from the value of column 3.
2*(#3 + #5)	Add the values of columns 3 and 5, then multiply the result by 2.
#1/#2	Divide the value of column 1 by the value of column 2.
#1 + #2*#3	Multiply the values of columns 2 and 3. Add the value of column 1 to the result.

WORKING WITH DERIVED COLUMNS

Up to three derived columns can be included in a single report: three sets of entries are included at the bottom of the Headings and Calculations display. To define an entry, you must enter a column number and a formula.

Every derived column is assumed by First Choice to be numeric. If an ordinary column is used in the calculation of a derived column, it's also assumed to be numeric.

A derived column can refer to a *previous* derived column (one with a lower column number), but not to a later one. This is because of the order in which First Choice performs its calculations.

USING AN EXISTING SET OF REPORT INSTRUCTIONS

If a set of report instructions has been saved on a disk, it can be used repeatedly for many reports. For example, you might want to

It's a good idea to do periodic housekeeping on your files. If you're in First Choice, you can delete a file containing obsolete search instructions by using the disk utilities module.

generate a standard report on a regular basis. To do this, you would define the report instructions once and save them. Then, whenever necessary, you could use these to generate a report based on the data in the current database.

You can use an existing set of instructions exactly as they were last stored in a file, or you can modify the instructions before using them to generate a new report.

To use an existing set of instructions, first retrieve them by using the Directory Assistant. You then go through the same steps as you did when you first created the instructions. As each display appears on the screen, the options that you chose for these report instructions will appear. You can either leave them alone or modify them as you wish. To make a modification, use the Tab and Shift-Tab keys to move to the desired option, then overwrite the old value with the new one. When the last screen appears (the Search Instructions display), you can save the modified report instructions either to the original file or to a new one. If you don't save the modifications, the original instructions will remain unchanged in the file. You can then print the new report.

Let's use the set of report instructions generated in earlier exercises and stored in the file MYREPORT.REP to create a new report on the records in the CLIENTS database. We'll make the following modifications to the original report instructions:

- Information will be printed only for clients living in Oakland and who owe more than $500.

- Each client's first name will be deleted from the report.

- The client's telephone number will be added.

When you select a file containing report instructions, First Choice automatically selects the corresponding database, namely the one that was specified when the instructions were created.

Here are the steps to follow:

1. Select *Get an existing file,* either from the Main menu or from the Files menu. The Directory Assistant will appear. (If necessary, enter the name of the drive and/or subdirectory on which the file MYREPORT.REP is stored.)

2. Select the file MYREPORT.REP, either with the cursor keys or by typing in the name (including the .REP extension). The file name should be listed in the Report Instructions

column. You can use the PgUp and PgDn keys to scroll through the file names.

3. The Print Options menu will appear. Because no changes are needed here, just press ◄—.

4. When the Column Selection display appears, make the following changes by moving the cursor to each field with the Tab and Shift-Tab keys:

Field	Original Value	New Value
First Name	2	—
Last Name	3	2
Phone	—	3

5. After you've made these changes, press F10 to go on to the Headings and Calculations display. No changes are needed for this display, so press F10 again to continue.

6. When the Search Instructions screen appears, enter the search instruction **Oakland** for the *City* field, then enter the search instruction **>500** for the *Balance Due* field.

7. Save the modified report instructions by selecting *Save this report* from the Files menu. When the Directory Assistant appears, enter the file name **RPT2**. The instructions will be copied to this file for later use.

8. When the Search Instructions screen reappears, press the F10 key to print the report.

To print the report using the current report instructions, press F10. First Choice will warn you if you've made any modifications to the report instructions but haven't saved them. Press ◄— to proceed with the printing.

USING INSTRUCTIONS WITH DIFFERENT DATABASES

A set of report instructions is designed to be used only for the database for which it was created. It can't be used directly with another database. However, with a little ingenuity you can get around this restriction.

Suppose that a set of report instructions has been defined for Database A, which is stored in the file DBA.FOL. You have another database, B, stored in the file DBB.FOL. Database B has the same form as Database A, but with different data. To use the report instructions to output the data from Database B, select *Use disk utilities* either from the Main menu or the Files menu. (For details on using the disk utilities module, see Chapter 11.) Rename the file DBA.FOL to something else (TEMP.FOL, for example), then rename DBB.FOL to DBA.FOL. First Choice will now think that the file DBB.FOL is the file DBA.FOL, because it's been renamed.

Reenter First Choice. You can now use the report instructions on Database B, because it's in a file named DBA.FOL, and First Choice will use that file to supply data for the report. When you have finished generating the report, you can use the disk utilities module to change the files back to their original names.

This technique only works if Database B has exactly the same form as Database A. For a discussion of what constitutes the "same form," refer to "Making Copies of Records" in Chapter 4.

GENERATING A SUMMARY REPORT

This type of report does not contain data from individual records. Instead, it gives you overall totals, averages, and counts, if any. To create a set of report instructions for a summary, follow the procedure described earlier for an ordinary report, with the following difference. In the Print Options display, enter "Y" for the *Print totals only* option.

Figure 5.9 illustrates a summary report corresponding to the full report shown in Figure 5.1. Note that the total and average refer specifically to the Balance Due column. (A better version of this report would eliminate the unused columns.)

IMPROVING THE APPEARANCE OF A REPORT

As with many built-in report writers, First Choice's is easy to use, but at the expense of flexibility. For example, there is only one line for a title, and one line for each column heading. You can't control

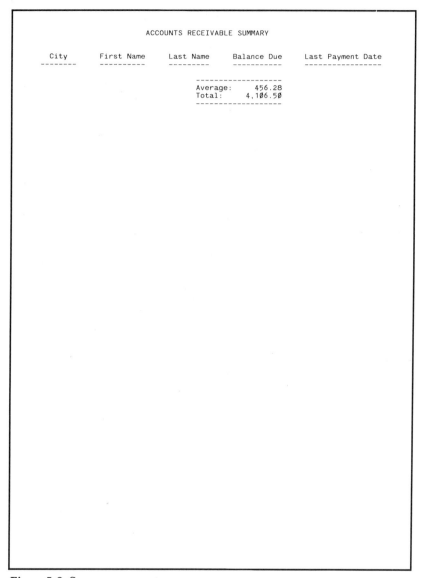

```
                    ACCOUNTS RECEIVABLE SUMMARY

    City       First Name    Last Name    Balance Due    Last Payment Date
   --------    ----------    ---------    -----------    -----------------

                                        --------------------
                                        Average:    456.28
                                        Total:    4,106.50
                                        --------------------
```

Figure 5.9: Summary report

CH. 5

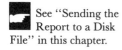 See "Sending the Report to a Disk File" in this chapter.

where the totals appear on the screen, and you have no control over how they are labeled.

If you want to improve the appearance of a report, but you can't do so within the limits of the report writer, you can use First Choice's word processor. You must first send the report to a disk file; after that you can edit and improve the file with the word processor.

EDITING THE REPORT

When a report is sent to a disk file, it is in the form of ordinary text. Consequently, the file can be treated as a document by First Choice's word processor.

First Choice assumes that any file is a document unless it has one of the special extensions (.FOL, .REP, or .SS).

To retrieve the report for editing, select the option *Get an existing file* either from the Main menu or the Files menu. From the Directory Assistant, choose the file that contains the report. If you didn't include a .DOC extension, the file name will appear in the Other column. First Choice may ask you to specify the type of file that you're retrieving. Select *ASCII-Preserve carriage returns*.

You can now edit the report in any way that you wish. You can move text around, add extra lines for the title and for column headings, make enhancements with special styles, and so on.

PRINTER ENHANCEMENTS

If you have the manual for your printer, you may be able to use many of its special features to spruce up your report even further. For example, you may be able to select an extra-wide font for titles and headings, or one or more condensed fonts. For more information about printer features, see "Advanced Printing Features" in Chapter 2, and also Appendix B.

PRINTING THE ENHANCED REPORT

When you are finished modifying the report, you can save it by selecting *Save a copy of this document* from the Files menu. You can either replace the existing copy of the report, or choose a new file for the updated version. In the latter case, the original copy of the report is not altered.

Finally, you can print the report by selecting *Print this document* from the Print menu.

CHANGING THE DATABASE FORM

If you change the form of a database, and if a set of report instructions exists for that database, those instructions may or may not work with the new form. Here are some guidelines to follow:

- You can change a field name, provided that the field remains in the same relative position in the database. Note that the column heading for the report instructions will remain the same, even if it is the same as the original field name.

- If you delete a field, or if you move a field to a different relative position on the form (for example, moving the second field so that it becomes the fourth), then any existing report instructions for that file may no longer work properly.

- If you add a new field to the database form, existing report instructions may no longer work, unless the new field is added at the end of the form.

If you make any changes to the form that invalidates existing report instructions, you'll need to redesign the instructions. First select the report instructions from the Directory Assistant. Go through the screens, making any necessary changes. The instructions most likely to need updating will be in the Column Selection display. When all changes have been made to the Search Instructions display, save the updated instructions by selecting *Save this report* from the Files menu. Either generate a report by pressing F10, or exit to the Main menu with the Esc key.

SAMPLE APPLICATIONS

In this section, we'll give several examples of how information can be output with the report writer. We'll use the CLIENTS form shown in Figure 5.3, and the data shown in Figure 5.1. In each of the examples, only those features that differ from the normal procedure will be discussed.

Our first example is an either-or report. Suppose that you want a report for all clients living either in Berkeley or Oakland. This is a complicated example, because you can't directly use an "either-or" type of condition as part of a search instruction. You must first create a temporary file with the same form as CLIENTS, then copy the desired records in two steps. Here is an outline of these steps:

1. Retrieve the CLIENTS database.

2. Create a duplicate of the CLIENTS form, using *Copy form design* from the Files menu. Name the new database CLTEMP.

The next step is to copy records whose value for the *City* field is *Berkeley* into the database CLTEMP.

3. Select *Copy records* from the Files menu. Choose CLTEMP as the database to receive the records.

4. Enter the search instruction **Berkeley** into the *City* field.

5. Press the F10 key to begin the copy operation.

6. Copy records for the *City* field value *Oakland* into the database CLTEMP, using the procedure described in step 3 above. The database CLTEMP now contains records for all clients living either in Berkeley or Oakland.

7. Create a set of report instructions for the database CLTEMP, then generate the report.

8. When you are done, delete the database CLTEMP by using the disk utilities module.

The next example uses invisible columns. Suppose that you want a report listing the following items for each client (and in the order shown):

- Last Name
- First Name
- Balance Due
- A 10% penalty on all balances due

You want the first column to contain the client names, and you'd like the records to be sorted according to the values of the balance due.

There's a problem with this: the records are automatically sorted according to the values of the first column of the report, but we want the first column to contain the client's name! The way out of this dilemma is to let the first column be the Balance Due field, and make it invisible as well. The records will then be sorted according to values of this field.

But we haven't finished, because we want the value of Balance Due to appear in the third field. We can do this by making the third field a derived column, whose values are simply equal to those of the first column.

Figure 5.10 shows the Column Selection display filled in for this example. Note that only three columns have been specified, because the other one will be a derived column.

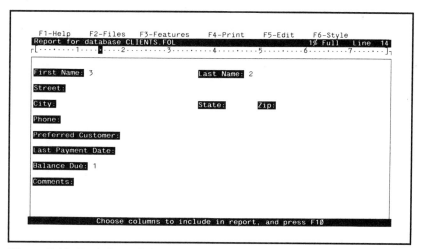

Figure 5.10: Completed Column Selection display

Figure 5.11 shows the Headings and Calculations display filled in for this example. Note that the heading for column 1 has been blanked out. This isn't really necessary, but it's a helpful reminder that the column is not going to display. In addition, the entry in the Calculations for this column (I) specifies that the column is to be invisible.

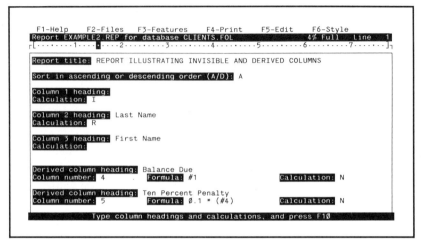

Figure 5.11: Completed Headings and Calculations display

For the second column (Last Name), we've specified the option R. This ensures that if two successive entries in this column have the same value, they will both be printed.

The first derived column is labeled *Balance Due*. Its formula is simply #1, namely the values of the Balance Due field.

The fifth and last column of the report is also derived. The formula computes 10% of the balance due. Notice that we've used another derived column (#4) in the calculation.

Figure 5.12 shows the printed report. Note that there are only four columns printed, because the first one is invisible. Note also that the data is sorted by the values in the Balance Due column, even though it's in the third column position.

SUMMARY

First Choice's report writer is a convenient way to generate structured reports for any First Choice database. Once built, a set of report instructions can be saved and used repeatedly for creating different reports, simply by modifying the report instructions before they are used. Although the reports are easy to build, their structure is limited. To a large extent, this can be circumvented by outputting a report to a disk file, then editing it with First Choice's word processor.

```
           REPORT ILLUSTRATING INVISIBLE AND DERIVED COLUMNS

      Last Name      First Name      Balance Due     Ten Percent Penalty
      ---------      ----------      -----------     -------------------
      Lick           Pete                   0.00                    0.00
      Drew           Sam                   25.27                    2.53
      Smith          Mary                 125.46                   12.55
      Pirate         Terry                347.00                   34.70
      Lo             Sarah                429.39                   42.94
      Duck           Howard               750.00                   75.00
      Gold           Ruby                 750.25                   75.03
      Peters         Janice               805.11                   80.51
      Peters         Harry                874.02                   87.40
```

Figure 5.12: Printed report

Many different sets of report instructions can be created and saved for use with the same database, with each set of instructions containing a different set of output specifications.

A single set of report instructions can be used for several databases, as long as they all have the same form.

Chapter
6

Getting Started with Spreadsheets

A spreadsheet is an electronic tool used when working with rows and columns of information. It has become an indispensable aid in accounting, financial analysis and planning, and many other areas of business and personal use.

As you begin working with First Choice spreadsheets, remember that the word processor is waiting in the background. It's used for data entry and editing, so you already know a lot about working with spreadsheets!

In this chapter, you'll learn how to create a spreadsheet. You'll erase, copy, and move spreadsheet data, and learn how to control its appearance. You'll also see how to save and retrieve spreadsheets, and print spreadsheet data.

SPREADSHEET FUNDAMENTALS

In this section you'll get your first look at a spreadsheet and its parts. Some of these parts, such as the menu bar, Information line, and edit cursor, will be familiar to you from other modules. Others won't; you'll be introduced to rows, columns, cells, and the cell cursor. You'll also learn how to move the cursor around the spreadsheet by using cursor-control keystrokes and the speed key.

THE BASIC SPREADSHEET DISPLAY

Figure 6.1 shows an empty First Choice spreadsheet. The main part of the display is the spreadsheet itself, which consists of a series of rows and columns. The rows are named R1, R2, and so on, and the columns are named C1, C2, etc.

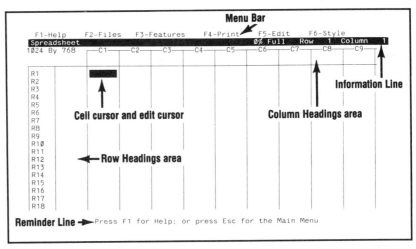

Figure 6.1: An empty spreadsheet

The intersection of a row and a column is called a *cell*. Each cell can contain a single piece of information—a *number*, a *label* (group of characters), or a *formula*. Each cell is identified by its *coordinates*—its row and column numbers. For example, the cell at the intersection of row 1 and column 1 is called R1C1. In addition, you can give a cell a name to help identify its contents.

The maximum size of a spreadsheet is determined by two factors: the total amount of main memory in your computer, and the size of the information in the individual cells that constitute the spreadsheet. If your computer has the maximum of 640K main memory, then the maximum size of a spreadsheet is 1024 rows and 768 columns. If your computer has 512K of main memory (the minimum needed by First Choice), then the maximum size is 768 rows and 512 columns.

These are theoretical upper limits; in practice, the contents of the cells that make up a spreadsheet will determine how many cells will actually fit into the computer's memory.

The spreadsheet display shown in Figure 6.1 also contains a few other items of interest, described below.

HEADINGS AREAS   At the top of the spreadsheet are the column numbers (C1,C2,etc.). Immediately under these numbers is the *Column Headings* area, in which you can insert headings for each column. This area is called *row 0*.

The leftmost column of the spreadsheet is reserved for the row numbers (R1, R2, etc.). Immediately to the right of these is the *Row Headings* area, into which you can enter headings for each row. This area is called *column 0*.

CELL CURSOR   This is the bright rectangle located under the column number C1 that appears when a spreadsheet is first displayed on the screen. You use the cell cursor to select a specific cell by moving it to that cell. Normally, we'll refer to the cell cursor simply as the *cursor*.

MENU BAR   As usual, this is located at the top of the screen and consists of six entries. Each menu contains choices that you've seen in previous modules. However, some of the choices are specific to spreadsheets.

INFORMATION LINE   This is the second line from the top of the screen. At the right end of the line, the *position indicator* indicates the current location of the cursor (row and column numbers). To its left is the *memory indicator*, showing how much memory is left for entering data into the current spreadsheet. Initially, this indicator shows an empty memory (0%). As your spreadsheet grows, the value of the indicator will grow towards the limit of 100%.

If the current spreadsheet was retrieved from an existing file, the name of that file will appear at the left end of the Information Line.

EDIT CURSOR   The blinking line that appears within the cell cursor is the same cursor you've seen in First Choice's word processor, and it's used in the same way. Text is edited at the exact position of this cursor (which always appears within the cell cursor). This cursor will be referred to as the *edit cursor*.

REMINDER LINE   The bottom of the display reminds you that the F1 key is your gateway to online help.

HOW TO MOVE AROUND THE SPREADSHEET

In order to add new data to a cell or update its current contents, the cursor must be moved to that cell. You can move the cursor by using the cursor-control keystrokes or a special speed key. The method that you choose will depend on the situation: cursor-control keystrokes will usually be more convenient.

Table 6.1 shows the complete repertoire of keystrokes at your disposal for moving the cursor. Many of these will look familiar from other First Choice modules. Some, however, are not the same.

Note that there are two ways to move the cursor up or down by one row: if you press the ←┘ key or Ctrl ←┘, the cursor moves down or up, and the edit cursor moves to the beginning of the cell cursor. On the other hand, if you press ↓ or ↑, the cursor moves down or up, but the edit cursor remains in the same relative position within the cell cursor.

You can move the cursor to a specific cell location by using the speed key Alt-G (G for *go*). You can then enter the row and column locations directly.

Because of the limitations of the screen size, you may build a spreadsheet that's much larger than what you can see on the screen.

Table 6.1: Cursor-Control Keystrokes

CURSOR MOVEMENT	KEYSTROKE
Down one row	← (edit cursor moves to beginning of cell cursor) ↓ (edit cursor remains in same position within the cell cursor)
Up one row	Ctrl ← (edit cursor moves to beginning of cell cursor) ↑ (edit cursor remains in same position within the cell cursor)
Right one column	Tab (or → if the text cursor is at the right end of the cell cursor)
Left one column	Shift-Tab (or ← if the text cursor is at the left end of the cell cursor)
To the top of the current column	Ctrl-PgUp
To the bottom of the current column	Ctrl-PgDn
To the beginning (the row heading) of the current row	Home
To the end of the current row	End
To the beginning of the spreadsheet (R1C1)	Ctrl-Home
To the end (lower right corner) of the spreadsheet	Ctrl-End
Up one screen	PgUp
Down one screen	PgDn
Right one screen	Ctrl →
Left one screen	Ctrl ←

You can think of the screen as a small window that sees only a portion of a spreadsheet. However, you can scroll the spreadsheet in any direction to make any part of it visible on the screen by using the cursor movement keys.

CREATING A SPREADSHEET

You're now ready to create a spreadsheet. You'll begin by entering row and column headings. Then you'll enter data onto the spreadsheet. Finally, you'll learn how to edit both headings and data.

Figure 6.2 shows the monthly sales and expenditures figures for the XYZ Company over a 12-month period. In this section, we'll go through the step-by-step process of creating this spreadsheet. You can either follow the steps below, or enter the data on your own.

```
       F1-Help    F2-Files   F3-Features   F4-Print    F5-Edit    F6-Style
      Spreadsheet                                  4% Full   Row  14   Column    1
      400 By 200         —C1—          —C2—      —C3——C4——C5——C6——C7—
                     Monthly Sales Monthly Expenses

      R1     Jan       25,000.00        13,000.00
      R2     Feb       23,000.00        14,500.00
      R3     Mar       21,000.00        12,500.00
      R4     Apr       22,500.00        13,000.00
      R5     May       23,000.00        13,000.00
      R6     Jun       23,500.00        12,500.00
      R7     Jul       21,000.00        11,500.00
      R8     Aug       21,500.00        14,000.00
      R9     Sep       22,500.00        14,500.00
      R10    Oct       24,000.00        15,000.00
      R11    Nov       25,000.00        16,000.00
      R12    Dec       26,000.00        16,500.00
      R13
      R14           ---------------------------------
      R15
      R16
      R17
      R18

             Press F1 for Help; or press Esc for the Main Menu
```

Figure 6.2: Sample spreadsheet

ENTERING COLUMN AND ROW HEADINGS

Either the Insert or Overwrite mode can be used; Overwrite is usually more convenient.

To enter a column heading, move the cursor to the desired location, then enter the heading. Initially, each column width is automatically set to six characters. If you enter a column heading longer than six characters, the column width automatically increases, up to a maximum of 20. Beyond that, data wraps around to the next line, up to a maximum of five lines. Enter the column heading for your sample spreadsheet.

1. Move the cursor to the heading area for the first column (just below the column number C1) with Ctrl-Home, Ctrl ◄—┘. Enter the first column heading, **Monthly Sales**. Notice how the column width expands as needed.

2. Using the Tab key, move the cursor to the next column.

3. Enter the second heading, **Monthly Expenses**.

Entering a row heading works the same way. The column will expand as necessary up to a maximum width of 20, and then the heading will wrap around to a maximum of five lines. Let's enter row headings for the spreadsheet:

1. Move the cursor to the heading area for the first row (just to the right of the row number R1) with Ctrl-Home, Shift-Tab.

2. Enter the first row heading, **Jan**.

3. Using the ◄—┘ key, move the cursor down to the second row.

4. Continue entering all of the row headings through **Dec**.

HOW TO CREATE MULTILINE HEADINGS Suppose that you want the column heading *Monthly Sales* to be a two-line heading. Normally, if you enter *Monthly Sales,* First Choice will fit the entire heading on a single line, and the resulting column will be 13 characters wide. You can shorten it by breaking the heading into two lines as follows. First, enter the heading normally. Then put the editor into Insert mode by pressing the Ins key. Move the edit cursor to the beginning of the heading, over the letter "M." Press the spacebar several times. Eventually, the additional spaces will push the word *Sales* to the second line. Now move the cell cursor to another cell. When you do, both of the words *Monthly* and *Sales* will be centered, and the column will be only ten characters wide.

You can use a variation on this method for entering multi-line row headings. For example, to enter *First Title* as two lines in a row heading, first enter the word *First*. Then press the space bar until the text cursor drops to the next line and type in *Title*.

ENTERING DATA

Each cell can contain a number, a label (a string of characters), or a formula. In this section, we'll enter numbers.

To enter a number, move the cursor to the desired cell, then type in the value. Each number is limited to a maximum of 20 characters, including commas and decimal point. If you enter too many digits, the value ★★★★ appears in the cell. You'll need to reenter the number with fewer digits or change its style (see ''Changing the Global Style'' later in this chapter).

To enter a label, move the cursor to the desired cell, then type in the label. If the label is wider than the cell, it continues into the adjacent cell. The maximum width of a label is 240 characters. If a label extends into a cell that already contains a label, that cell's contents are overwritten with the new label. However, First Choice won't let you overwrite a cell containing a value or a formula.

Now enter the numbers for the spreadsheet.

1. Move the cursor to cell R1C1. (Try using the speed key Alt-G for this move.)

2. Enter **25000** (no comma or decimal point).

3. Press ⏎ to move down to the second row. Note what happened to the value you just entered.

4. Continue entering values for all of the rows in this column.

5. Move the cursor to cell R1C2 by pressing Ctrl-PgUp, Tab.

6. Enter values for each cell in this column.

Now enter the separator line at the bottom of the columns of numbers:

7. Move the cursor to cell R13C1.

8. Press the minus key (at the top of the keyboard) several times, watching how it displays on the screen. Continue until the line extends across column 2.

When you are done, your spreadsheet should look like the one in Figure 6.2.

EDITING HEADINGS AND DATA   When you're entering headings and data, the editor should be in the Overwrite mode. If you make a mistake, you can use any of the standard editing features to correct it. In addition, you can delete an entire entry with the speed key Alt-W.

Values for the various cells and headings can be entered in any order you wish. You can also go back and change a heading or data value; move the cursor to the desired cell and overwrite the old value with the new one.

THE QUICK ENTRY FEATURE

This is a special feature that can help you enter groups of values rapidly. You can use quick entry to enter groups of related headings, or to enter the same number or formula into a collection of cells.

ENTERING ROW AND COLUMN HEADINGS

Quick entry works in any direction. However, if you change the direction of the cursor movement, quick entry ends.

If you are entering headings containing the names of months or days, in either rows or columns, quick entry can help you. For example, here are the steps for entering the names of months as column headings (Figure 6.3):

- Move the cursor to the heading area for column 1.

- Enter *January* for the heading.

- Begin quick entry, either by pressing the speed key Alt-Q or by choosing *Start quick entry* from the Features menu.

- Press Tab to move the cursor to the next column heading. The heading *February* is automatically entered, in the same combination of uppercase and lowercase used for the first entry.

- Continue pressing Tab until all headings have been entered. To end quick entry, press Esc or Alt-Q, or select *Stop quick entry* from the Features menu.

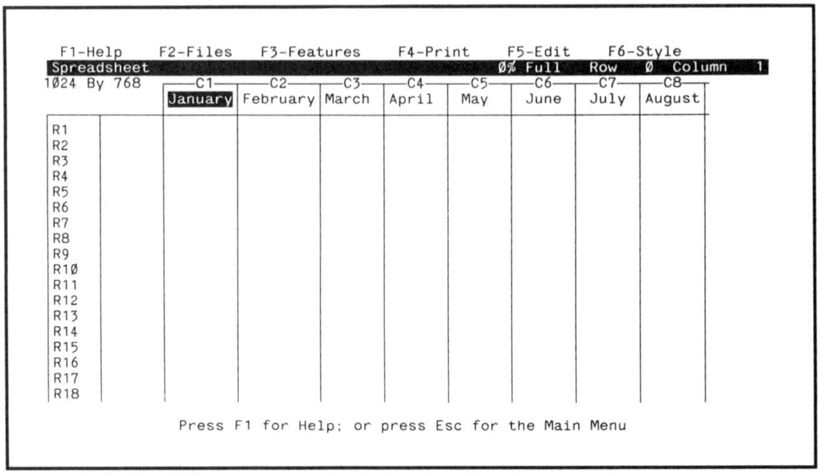

```
     F1-Help    F2-Files    F3-Features    F4-Print    F5-Edit    F6-Style
    Spreadsheet                                 Ø% Full    Row   Ø  Column   1
    1Ø24 By 768  ──C1──────C2──────C3──────C4──────C5──────C6──────C7──────C8──
                  January  February March  April  May    June   July  August

     R1
     R2
     R3
     R4
     R5
     R6
     R7
     R8
     R9
     R1Ø
     R11
     R12
     R13
     R14
     R15
     R16
     R17
     R18

               Press F1 for Help; or press Esc for the Main Menu
```

Figure 6.3: Months as column headings

Quick entry also works for the days of the week. The standard three-letter abbreviations for months and days (Mon, Tue, etc.) work as well as full names. However, periods cannot be added after an abbreviation.

You do not have to start at the beginning of a sequence. For example, you can start row or column headings with April or Thursday. Also, you can start in any row or column. Regardless of where you start, quick entry advances each heading after the first one by a month or a day. For example, if you enter *Jan 86,* then quick entry will enter *Feb 86, Mar 86,* and so on for successive entries.

Quick entry can also be used for headings ending in successive numbers. The entire heading is duplicated, except that the ending number is increased by one. This does not apply to headings containing day or month names.

Table 6.2 lists the various types of headings that can be entered with quick entry.

Table 6.2: Using Quick Entry for Headings

FIRST ENTRY	SUCCESSIVE ENTRIES
January	February, March...
JAN	FEB, MAR...
Monday	Tuesday, Wednesday...
Mon	Tue, Wed...
Jan 1988	Feb 1988, Mar 1988...
1988	1989, 1990...
Day 1	Day 2, Day 3...

COPYING A SINGLE VALUE TO A RANGE OF CELLS

This procedure works only for numerical values. Labels can't be copied with quick entry. To copy a label to a group of other cells, see "Copying a Group of Cells" and "Copying One Cell to a Range" in this chapter. Quick entry can also be used to copy formulas. For details, see Chapter 7.

If you want to copy the value of a particular cell into a group of adjacent cells, quick entry can be very helpful. Move the cursor to the cell whose value is to be copied. Start quick entry, either with Alt-Q or from the Features menu. To begin copying the value, move to the next cell by pressing the appropriate cursor-movement keystroke. For example, to copy into cells to the right, press Tab once for each cell to receive the value. End quick entry by pressing Ctrl-Q or Esc, or by changing the direction of the cursor movement.

USING FORMULAS

A cell can contain only one formula.

A formula is a particular type of cell entry. A formula can consist of references to other cells, numbers, and one or more of First Choice's built-in functions. You write a formula in a cell to tell First Choice to perform a particular calculation and then assign the resulting value to that cell. Formulas are one of the keystones of using spreadsheets. As you learn how to use them, you'll begin to see how much flexibility and power they offer. In this section, you'll learn the basics of using formulas; Chapter 7 will explain them in more depth.

EXAMPLES OF FORMULAS

Formulas can be simple or complex. Here are some examples of simple formulas:

FORMULA	MEANING
R1C1-R2C2	Subtract the value of cell R2C2 from the value of cell R1C1.
2*(R1C1-R2C2)	Multiply the value of (R1C1-R2C2) by 2.
@TOTAL (R1C1..R12C1)	Add up the values of the cells R1C1, R2C1, R3C1...R12C1.

Each of these formulas would be entered into a separate cell exactly as shown.

In the first example, the formula calculates the difference between the values of two other cells. For example, if the values in cells R1C1 and R2C2 were 5 and 3, the cell containing the formula would be given the value 2.

The second example is a bit more complex: the difference between the values in R1C1 and R2C2 is computed, then the result is multiplied by 2.

The third example uses one of First Choice's many built-in *functions*: @TOTAL. A function has two parts:

- Its *name,* in this case @TOTAL.
- Its *argument,* which is what the function operates on. The argument is everything inside the parentheses.

The function name denotes the purpose of the function. In this case, the purpose of @TOTAL is to add up groups of values.

The argument of @TOTAL supplies those items to be added up. In our example, the argument is R1C1..R12C1, which means "all cells from R1C1 to R12C1." Therefore, @TOTAL(R1C1..R12C1) tells First Choice to add up the 12 cells running from R1C1 to R12C1.

HOW TO ENTER A FORMULA INTO A CELL

In the following exercise, we'll add these items to the spreadsheet created earlier (Figure 6.2):

- A total for each of the two columns. Each total will be computed by a formula.

- A cell showing the net profit (total sales minus total expenses). This also will be calculated with a formula.

- Identifying labels for each of the above items.

- A long comment at the bottom of the spreadsheet.

The spreadsheet will look like the one shown in Figure 6.4.

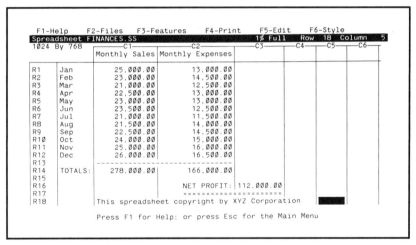

Figure 6.4: Modified spreadsheet

Here are some general rules for entering formulas:

- To enter a formula into a cell, you use the *Formula Box* for that cell, which is displayed by pressing Alt-F.

- A formula can be up to 240 characters long, including spaces. It wraps around within the Formula Box as necessary.

- If you want to abandon the formula, press the Esc key to exit the Formula Box.

- If you made an error while entering a formula, an error message will appear on the screen when you try to exit from the Formula Box.

- While you're in the Formula Box, you can enter a simple number instead of a formula. When you do this, First Choice issues a warning message, but it accepts the number.

ADDING FORMULAS FOR COLUMN TOTALS We'll first add formulas to compute the total monthly sales for the year. This is the sum of the entries in column C1. To do this:

1. Move the cursor to cell R14C1.

2. Display the Formula Box for that cell (Figure 6.5) by pressing Alt-F or by using the Features menu.

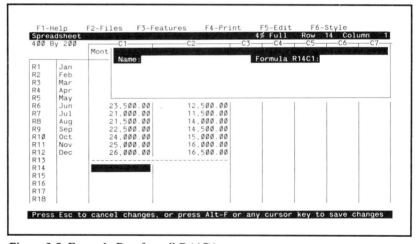

Figure 6.5: Formula Box for cell R14C1

3. Enter the following formula: **@TOTAL(R1C1..R12C1)**. This formula computes the sum of the 12 cells from R1C1 to R12C1 and assigns the sum to cell R14C1.

4. Press the Tab key to move the cursor to the next column in the same row. You should see the sum appear on the spreadsheet. The Formula Box for this cell also appears.

You can't tell if a cell contains a formula by looking at the spreadsheet, because only the *value* of a cell appears on the screen. To see what a cell actually contains, move the cursor to that cell, then press Alt-F to display its Formula Box.

5. Enter the following formula to compute the sum of the monthly expenses: **@TOTAL(R1C2..R12C2)**.

6. Exit from the Formula Box by pressing Alt-F. Notice that the value 166,000.00 appears in R14C2. This is the *result* of the formula calculation.

Usually, cells with formulas display particularly important results, and these may need to be labeled for clarity. In this case, you can define the values in R14C1 and R14C2 by entering the label *TOTALS:* in cell R14CO, as shown in Figure 6.4.

ADDING A FORMULA FOR THE NET PROFIT Now let's add a formula to have the spreadsheet calculate the net profit, namely the difference between the total sales and the total expenses:

1. Move to cell R16C2 and type in the identifying label **NET PROFIT:**.

2. Move to cell R16C3 and display the Formula Box.

3. Enter the formula **R14C1-R14C2**.

4. Exit the Formula Box.

5. Move to cell R17C2.

6. Press the key labeled " = " several times to underscore the values for cells R16C2 and R16C3, as shown in Figure 6.4. Notice how the underscore moves across the cell boundary into the next cell.

Note that the formula for the net profit consists of the names of two other cells, which themselves contain formulas!

To complete the spreadsheet, let's add a comment at the bottom:

7. Move the cursor to cell R18C1.

8. Enter the label:

This spreadsheet copyright by XYZ Corporation

Your spreadsheet should now look like the example in Figure 6.4. Keep it on the screen; in a moment you'll learn to save it.

CHANGING A CELL FORMULA

If you change the value of a cell referred to by a formula, First Choice automatically recalculates the formula. In this way, First Choice keeps the value of the formula updated with the current data in the spreadsheet.

At any time, the existing formula of a cell can be deleted or changed. To delete a formula, move the cursor to the desired cell. Press the speed key Alt-W, or select *Erase this cell* from the Edit menu. The formula is erased and the value of the cell is made blank.

To edit a formula, move the cursor to the desired cell. Display the Formula Box, either by pressing Alt-F or by using the Features menu. Make any desired changes to the formula, using the standard editing keys. Exit from the Formula Box by pressing Alt-F.

ASSIGNING NAMES TO CELLS

It is often convenient to assign a name to a cell. Then, when writing formulas involving that cell, you can refer to the cell by its name, rather than by its label. This technique can greatly simplify writing and reading long formulas.

As an example, consider the spreadsheet in Figure 6.4. As we discussed earlier, the contents of the three cells containing formulas are as follows:

CELL	FORMULA
R14C1	@TOTAL(R1C1..R12C1)
R14C2	@TOTAL(R1C2..R12C2)
R16C3	R14C1-R14C2

Suppose we name the cells R14C1 and R14C2 *TotalSales* and *TotalExpenses*. We could then rewrite the formula for R16C3 as TotalSales minus TotalExpenses.

To name a cell, move the cursor to the cell to be named. Display the Formula Box by using Alt-F or the Features menu. Press the ↑ key to move the cursor to the *Name* selection. Now enter a name for the cell. If a formula is also being entered for the cell, you can move back to that part of the Formula Box with the ↓ key. Exit the Formula Box with Alt-F. First Choice will associate the specified name with the selected cell.

GUIDELINES FOR NAMING CELLS   A name can be as long as 13 characters. It can consist of letters, digits, and the underscore character, and must begin with a letter. Any combination of upper-case and lowercase letters can be used.

No two cells in a single spreadsheet can have the same name. For this purpose, no distinction is made between case. For instance, the names *TOTALSALES* and *TotalSales* are equivalent. Also, a cell can't have the same name as any of First Choice's built-in functions.

A cell name can be erased or changed by using the Formula Box. You can also erase a name by pressing the speed key Alt-W when the cursor is on that cell, but this also erases the cell's contents.

If a cell name is erased or changed, any formulas using the name will become invalid, because they will still contain the original name.

STORING YOUR SPREADSHEET IN A FILE

At some point you will want to store your spreadsheet so you can return to it later. In this section, we'll describe the steps for storing and retrieving spreadsheets.

SAVING THE SPREADSHEET

The steps for saving a spreadsheet to disk are nearly identical to those for saving documents and folders. Follow these steps to save a spreadsheet.

1. Select *Save a copy of this spreadsheet* from the Files menu. The Directory Assistant will appear on the screen.

2. The current disk drive is shown on the Directory line. If this is not the drive that you want to use, type in the name of the correct drive (A:, B:, etc.).

   Hard-disk users: If the correct subdirectory name does not appear on the Directory line, type it in. For example, if the Directory line reads **A:**, you could type in **C:\MYSTUFF** to make it the current subdirectory.

3. Enter the name of the file into which the spreadsheet will be saved. This can be either a new file or an existing one. Note

that if you write onto an existing file, the old contents are gone forever.

When a new spreadsheet file is created, First Choice automatically adds the extension .SS to the file name.

After the file has been written to disk, your spreadsheet reappears on the screen, and you can continue working.

RETRIEVING THE SPREADSHEET

There are two ways to retrieve a spreadsheet from a disk file. You can choose *Get an existing file* from the Main menu, or you can choose *Get an existing file* from the Files menu, which is accessed from within most of First Choice's modules. With either method, the Directory Assistant is brought to the screen, and you can select the file to be used.

If necessary, enter the name of the disk drive where the file is located. If you are using a hard-disk computer, enter the name of the desired subdirectory, if it isn't already showing on the Directory line. Now select the file by using the cursor keys or by typing in the name of the file (including the .SS extension). If First Choice can't find the file that you specify, an error message appears at the bottom of the screen. When the file is found, the spreadsheet module of First Choice is loaded, and the spreadsheet is read into memory.

MANIPULATING SPREADSHEET DATA

Working with spreadsheet data is similar in many ways to working with an ordinary document. Here are some ways in which you can manage spreadsheet information:

- Delete a cell or group of cells

- Copy or move a group of cells from one location to another

- Insert and delete entire rows or columns

- Change the style of a cell or group of cells

In many of these operations, First Choice makes use of its clipboard, in exactly the same way it did for documents. In fact, as we'll see in a later chapter, you can use the clipboard to transfer data between a spreadsheet and other First Choice modules.

SELECTING A RANGE OF CELLS

Any group of neighboring cells is referred to as a *range*. A range can be a group of adjacent cells in a row or in a column. Another type of range is a rectangular block of neighboring cells. As an example, if we want to refer to the first ten cells in the first row (R1), we would write the range as R1C1..R1C10. On the other hand, the range of cells consisting of the first two columns of the first ten rows would be written as R1C1..R10C2. A range can even be a single cell, such as R5C5..R5C5.

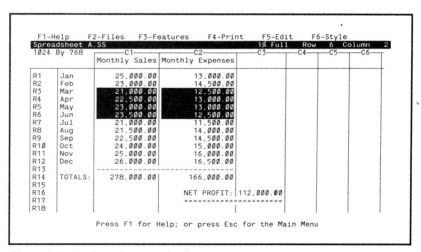 When the Select mode is on, the blinking edit cursor within the cell cursor disappears.

In order to do anything to a range of cells (copy, delete, etc.), you must first select the range. To do this, move the cursor to the upper left-hand corner of the desired range. Define this cell as the beginning of the range to be selected, either with Alt-S or from the Edit menu. Move the cursor to the right and/or down. As you do, you'll see the range expand (each cell in the range is highlighted). Stop when all desired cells are included in the range. Figure 6.6 shows the selection of range R3C1..R6C2.

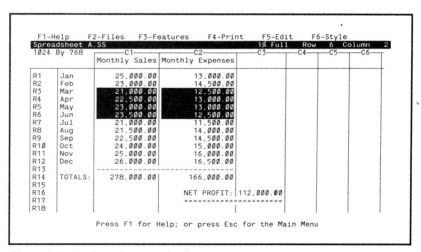

Figure 6.6: A selected range of cells

Be careful not to move the cursor either above or to the left of the first cell you select, or the selection process will be canceled. To deliberately cancel the selection process, press either Alt-S or Esc.

In some circumstances, you may want to define an entire spreadsheet as the range, including the row and column headings. To do this, move the cursor to the cell R0C0, immediately under the left end of the third line from the top (Figure 6.7). Move there by pressing Ctrl-Home, Ctrl←, Shift-Tab.

```
     F1-Help      F2-Files   F3-Features    F4-Print    F5-Edit     F6-Style
    Spreadsheet A.SS                            1% Full    Row   0  Column   0
    1024 By 768        —C1————————C2————————C3————C4————C5————C6———
                      │Monthly Sales│Monthly Expenses│

    R1  │Jan    │    25,000.00│    13,000.00│
    R2  │Feb    │    23,000.00│    14,500.00│
    R3  │Mar    │    21,000.00│    12,500.00│
    R4  │Apr    │    22,500.00│    13,000.00│
    R5  │May    │    23,000.00│    13,000.00│
    R6  │Jun    │    23,500.00│    12,500.00│
    R7  │Jul    │    21,000.00│    11,500.00│
    R8  │Aug    │    21,500.00│    14,000.00│
    R9  │Sep    │    22,500.00│    14,500.00│
    R10 │Oct    │    24,000.00│    15,000.00│
    R11 │Nov    │    25,000.00│    16,000.00│
    R12 │Dec    │    26,000.00│    16,500.00│
    R13 │       │-----------------------------│
    R14 │TOTALS:│   278,000.00│   166,000.00│
    R15 │       │             │             │
    R16 │       │             │NET PROFIT:│112,000.00│
    R17 │       │             │=======================│
    R18 │       │             │             │

            Press F1 for Help; or press Esc for the Main Menu
```

Figure 6.7: Cursor in the area R0C0

Now begin selecting the range by pressing Alt-S. Press Ctrl-End to move the cursor to the end of the spreadsheet. The entire spreadsheet is now selected. This is a handy technique for copying the full spreadsheet to the clipboard, including the row and column headings (see Figure 6.8 for an example).

ERASING CELLS

To erase a single cell, move the cursor to the cell. Press the speed key Alt-W (W for *word*). Alternatively, you can select *Erase this cell* from the Edit menu. In either case, the contents of the cell are erased from the spreadsheet.

To erase a range of cells, first select the range of cells. Press the speed key Alt-M, or select *Move selected cells to clipboard* from the Edit

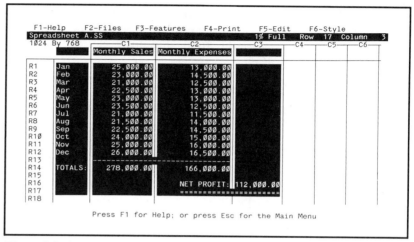

Figure 6.8: An entire spreadsheet defined as a range

menu. The cells are erased, and the values are copied to the clip-board. Notice that after you press Alt-M, the blinking edit cursor returns to the cell cursor, indicating that the Select mode is off.

DELETING A ROW OR COLUMN   You can use the following shortcut if you want to delete an entire row or column. This is a risky procedure, and you should be very sure of what you are doing before using it. When an entire row or column is deleted using this method, the values are gone forever; they are not stored on the clipboard. To delete a row or column:

- Move the cursor to any position on the desired row or column.

- Select *Cut out row/column* from the Edit menu.

- Enter "R" for a row, or "C" for a column.

- Press the Tab key; then enter the number of rows or columns to be deleted. Rows are counted down from the current one; columns are counted to the right of the current one.

- Press ⬅ to go on.

When you use the clipboard to remove a group of cells, they remain on the clipboard until something else is copied or moved to it. This can be handy if you erase a group of cells, then change your mind; they may still be on the clipboard.

If you delete a row or column containing a cell that's referenced by a formula anywhere in the spreadsheet, that formula will no longer be valid. When you attempt to do this, a warning message is issued on the screen.

If a column is deleted, any remaining columns to the right of it are shifted over to the left. For example, if you delete column 3, all of the values in column 4 become the new values in column 3. Figures 6.9 and 6.10 illustrate this.

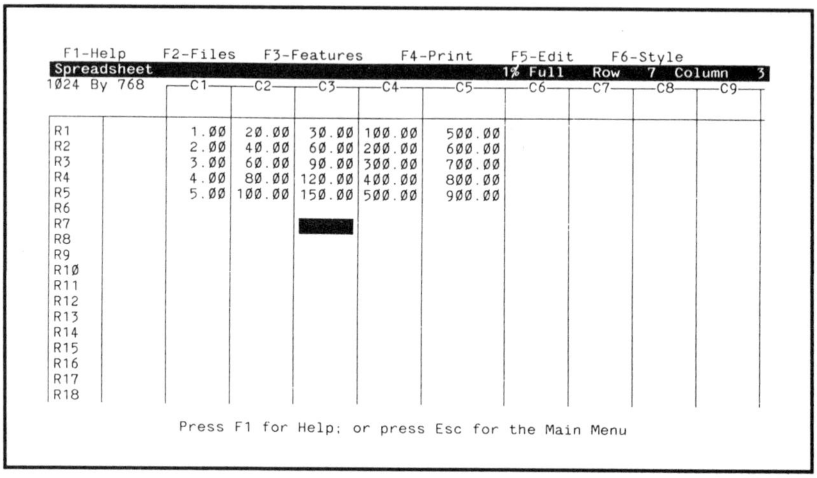

Figure 6.9: Spreadsheet before deletion

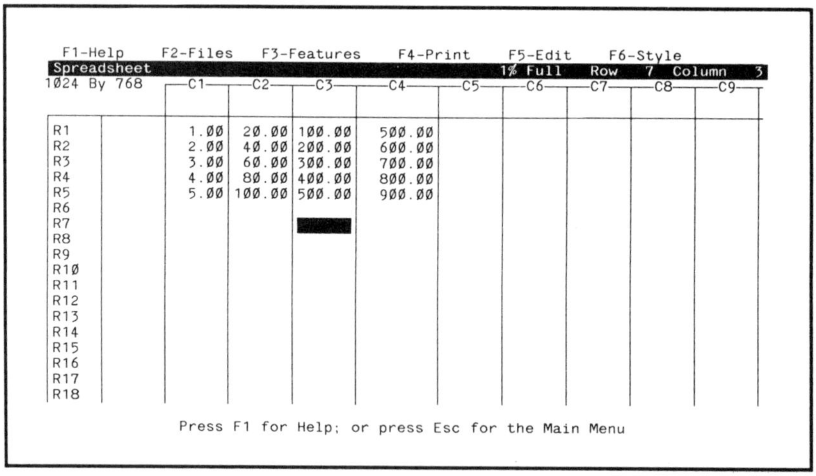

Figure 6.10: Spreadsheet after deletion

If a cell in a shifted column is referenced by a formula somewhere in the spreadsheet, that formula is automatically updated to reflect the new location of the original cell. As an example, suppose that a cell on the spreadsheet in Figure 6.9 contains the formula @ABS(R1C3). If column 2 is deleted, this formula will be changed to @ABS(R1C2), because the value in cell R1C3 has been shifted over to cell R1C2.

If you delete a row or column containing a cell referenced as part of a range by a formula, that formula changes automatically to adjust for the new limits on the range. On the other hand, if you delete a row or column containing a cell that's either the beginning or the end of a range referenced by a formula, you get an error message from First Choice telling you that the formula is about to become incorrect. See "Automatic Formula Adjustment" in Chapter 7 for details and examples.

ERASING THE SPREADSHEET   You can erase the spreadsheet currently in the computer's memory (called the working copy). To do this, select *Erase this spreadsheet* from the Edit menu.

MOVING A GROUP OF CELLS

You can move a group of cells from one place in a spreadsheet to another. When you "move" cells you actually erase the values in selected cells and paste them into others. To move a range of cells, select the range of cells to be moved (this can be either a single cell or a group of cells). Move the selected values to the clipboard, either with Alt-M or by selecting *Move selected cells* from the Edit menu. Remember that the selected cells are erased. Move the cursor to the upper left corner of the new range into which the cells are to be written. Paste the cells from the clipboard to the new location, either by pressing the speed key Alt-P (P for paste), or by selecting *Paste from clipboard* from the Edit menu.

When you paste the contents of the clipboard onto a spreadsheet, the values remain on the clipboard until something else is copied or moved to it. Any existing values in the target cells (the cells being written to) are replaced by the pasted values.

When a spreadsheet is erased, the contents of the clipboard remain untouched. This is a handy way of starting a new spreadsheet with selected parts of the old one.

If a moved cell is referred to by a formula somewhere, that formula is automatically updated to reflect the new value of the original cell (zero).

Sometimes a single long label may occupy several cells. To move the label to another location, you need only select the first cell of the label, then move it to the new location, as described above.

COPYING A GROUP OF CELLS

Copying a group of cells differs from moving them: when cells are copied, the original cells retain their values. To copy a range of cells:

- Select the range of cells. This can be either a single cell or a group of cells.

- Copy the cells to the clipboard, either by using the speed key Alt-C, or by choosing *Copy selected cells to clipboard* from the Edit menu.

- Move the cursor to the new upper left-hand corner of the range into which the cells are to be copied.

- Paste the cells from the clipboard with the speed key Alt-P.

Remember that when a group of values are pasted onto the spreadsheet, any values in the target cells are replaced by the values being pasted.

COPYING ONE CELL TO A RANGE

Follow these steps to copy the contents of a single cell into a range of cells, which we'll call the target range:

- Move the cursor to the cell to be copied.

- Select that cell either with Alt-S or from the Edit menu.

- Copy that cell's contents to the clipboard, either by pressing Alt-C or by using the Edit menu.

- Move the cursor to the first cell of the target range, i.e., the cell in the upper left-hand corner.

- Begin selecting cells by pressing Alt-S.

- Using the cursor keys, expand the target range to include all desired cells.
- Paste the contents of the clipboard into each of the selected cells, either by pressing Alt-P or by using the Edit menu.

This same technique can be used to copy any number of cells to another group of cells of a different size. For instance, you could copy the contents of two adjacent cells into any number of other cells. The copying is done first down, then across the range of the selected target cells.

SPEED KEY REVIEW Here's a review of the speed keys you can use when working with ranges of cells:

Alt-S   Begin selecting a range of cells. The current cursor position becomes the upper left-hand corner of the range to be selected.

Alt-C   Copy the values of the currently selected cells to the clipboard.

Alt-M   Move the values of the currently selected cells to the clipboard, erasing values from the selected cells.

Alt-P   Paste the values on the clipboard onto the spreadsheet, beginning at the current position of the cursor.

INSERTING ROWS AND COLUMNS

You can insert one or more blank rows or columns anywhere in a spreadsheet. You might want to do this, for instance, if you decide to add data between existing rows or columns and you don't feel like doing a lot of copying or moving of ranges. To add rows or columns:

- Move the cursor to the appropriate row or column. New rows will be inserted above the cursor position; new columns will be inserted to the left of the cursor.
- Select *Insert row/column* from the Edit menu.
- Specify either row ("R") or column ("C").

- Specify how many rows or columns are to be inserted.
- Press ◀━┘, and the insertions will take place.

If you add a row or column containing a cell referenced as part of a range by a formula, that formula changes automatically to adjust for the new limits on the range. See "Automatic Formula Adjustment" in Chapter 7 for details and examples.

CHANGING CELL STYLES

When a number or a formula is entered into a cell, the cell's value is displayed on the screen with a certain *style*. (Cell styles apply only to cells containing numbers or formulas; cells with labels do not have styles.) The style of a particular number includes the following:

- Which currency symbol, if any, is displayed with the number
- Whether or not a percent sign is written
- Whether or not commas are inserted as necessary
- The number of decimal places displayed to the right of the decimal point
- The minimum allowable width for a column
- The way in which date and time data is displayed

The style in which a cell's value is displayed is determined by either the global style then in effect, or by the style assigned to that individual cell. The latter takes precedence over the former. The *global style* determines how values are displayed throughout the spreadsheet, except for those individual cells to which you have assigned other styles.

Initially, First Choice assigns the following global style to a spreadsheet:

- No currency symbol or percent sign displayed with a number
- Commas inserted as necessary (to the left of the decimal point only)

- Two decimal places displayed to the right of the decimal point
✓ • A minimum column width of six characters
- Date and time values displayed as special numbers generated by First Choice

CHANGING THE GLOBAL STYLE

At any time, you can change one or more settings that make up the global style. When you change the global style, it affects the display of every number entered after the style is changed; cells that already contain data are not changed. If you want to change the style of existing cells, you must do so on a cell-by-cell or range-by-range basis.

To select the global style, choose *Set global style* from the Style menu. The options available to you are then displayed on the screen (Figure 6.11). You can change any of the displayed default values by first moving to it with the Tab and Shift-Tab keys, then overwriting the old value with the new one. When you're finished, press ← to exit from the display. Let's take a look at the options on the Global Style display.

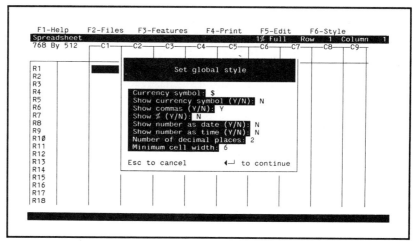

Figure 6.11: Global Style display

Currency symbol

This is the symbol that will precede each number if you opt to have the currency symbol displayed. The default symbol is the dollar sign, but you can choose any symbol from the list shown in Table 6.3.

Table 6.3: Legal Currency Symbols

CURRENCY VALUE	SYMBOL
Dollar (American)	$
Franc	F
Franc (Belgian)	BF
Franc (French)	FF
Franc (Swiss)	SFr
Krone (Swedish)	Kr
Lire	L
Lire (Italian)	Lit
Mark (German)	DM
Peseta (Spanish)	Pts
Peso	P
Pound (British)	£ (press Alt-156)
Rand or ruble	R
Schilling	S
Schilling (Austrian)	oS̈ (press Alt-148)
Yen (Japanese)	Y

Show currency symbol (Y/N)	If you want the selected currency symbol to precede each number on the screen, enter "Y." If "Y" is selected, then "N" must be chosen for the *Show %* option.
Show commas (Y/N)	If you select "Y" (the default), commas are inserted as required. Commas only appear to the left of the decimal point.
Show % (Y/N)	If "Y" is selected, each number that's entered is displayed as a percent. The actual number is stored correctly in memory; only the displayed value is multiplied by 100.

See Chapter 7 for details about date and time functions.

Show number as date (Y/N)	Several of First Choice's built-in functions can be used to generate dates. These are stored internally as special numbers, in a form that probably won't mean much to you. You can display these numbers in regular date form by selecting "Y" for this option.
Show number as time (Y/N)	Several of First Choice's built-in functions can be used to generate time values. As with date values, these are stored internally as special numbers. To display these in an ordinary time format (hours, minutes, seconds), select "Y."

Number of decimal places	The default setting is two places to the right of the decimal point. You can change this to any number from zero to 15.
Minimum cell width	This determines the minimum allowable width for any column. Subject to this restriction, First Choice automatically adjusts the width of each column according to the widest value stored in that column, up to a maximum width of 20. This entry does not affect the area in which row headings are displayed on the screen.

HOW NUMBERS ARE STORED   To understand how the settings for the global style affect the display of numbers, you need to know something about the way First Choice stores numbers.

Numbers are maintained in memory to an accuracy of up to 16 digits. You can enter up to 20 digits for a number, but the last four (the least significant digits) are not stored in memory.

No matter how a number is displayed on the screen, its value remains the same in memory.

If you enter a number that is less than 20 digits, it still may not fit on the screen because of other characters, such as commas and currency symbols. For example, the number 2,000,000,000,000,000 won't fit. When this happens, First Choice displays a row of asterisks instead of the number to indicate that the number plus other characters is too wide. However, the value of the number is still stored in memory correctly, and it can be used for calculations.

If a number contains fewer decimal digits than specified by the global style, the remaining decimal digits are displayed as zeros on the screen.

If you're working with very large numbers, you may find it necessary to delete the display of commas, the currency symbol, and decimal places so that the numbers can fit within the cell on the screen.

When a cell contains a formula, it's the formula—not the value—that's stored in memory. The value of the cell is obtained for display or printing purposes by computing the formula each time.

SETTING INDIVIDUAL CELL STYLES

You can change the style of an existing cell at any time. The new style will override whatever global style is in effect. To change the style of a cell, move the cursor to the desired cell. Select *Set cell style* from the Style menu. The Set Cell Style display (similar to the display in Figure 6.11) appears. Make any desired changes, then exit by pressing ◄─┘.

Only the selected cell is affected by these changes. If you want to set the same style for a group of cells, they must be done on a cell-by-cell basis, unless the cells are adjacent. If they are, they can all be changed at once (see the following section).

A cell must contain a number or formula before its style can be selected in this manner. In other words, you can't set the style of an individual cell "in advance."

If you erase the contents of a cell, its style reverts to the current global style.

You can also affect the style of a particular cell by entering a number in the appropriate style. For example, suppose that the global style specifies no decimal places and no commas. If you enter the value 9,999.00 into a cell, the style of that cell changes to: (1) two decimal places, and (2) commas entered as needed. However, you can't use this method to *reduce* the number of decimal places in the style for that cell, or to eliminate commas or currency symbols.

SETTING THE STYLE OF GROUPS OF CELLS

You can set the style of a group of adjacent cells if they can be defined as a range. Select the cells whose style is to be altered by moving the cursor to the upper left-hand corner of the range of cells. Define this cell as the beginning of the range, either by pressing the speed key Alt-S, or by choosing *Select cells* from the Edit menu. Move the cursor to include the entire group of cells in the range.

Now select *Set cell style* from the Style menu. The Set Cell Style display (similar to the display in Figure 6.11) appears. Make any desired changes, then exit with the ◄━┛ key.

The style of each cell in the selected range will be changed, provided that each cell contains a value or a formula. The style of any blank cells in the range will not be affected; they will keep the global style.

OUTPUTTING A SPREADSHEET

All or part of a spreadsheet can be output, according to the option you select. The output can be directed to the printer, the screen, or a disk file. When you use a printer, the same basic print options as the ones used to print documents and records are available to you.

PRINTING YOUR SPREADSHEET

The "entire" spreadsheet consists of all row and column headings plus all nonblank entries. The vertical lines appearing on the spreadsheet display on the screen are not printed, nor are the row and column labels (C1, C2, etc.).

To print an entire spreadsheet,

- Select the Print menu.

- Choose *Print this spreadsheet*. The Print Options display appears (Figure 6.12).

- Change any of the displayed default values, using Tab and Shift-Tab to move from one option to another. These options are discussed below. (For a description of the options for compressed type and draft or correspondence quality, refer to "The Print Options Menu" in Chapter 2.)

- Press ◄━┛ when done. First Choice will print the spreadsheet, after giving you time to insert paper into the printer.

Figure 6.13 shows a printout of the spreadsheet shown in Figure 6.4, using the print options shown in Figure 6.12. Notice that because the vertical and horizontal lines that show on the screen are not printed, the spreadsheet looks very much like an ordinary report!

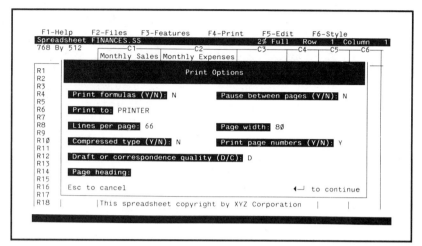

Figure 6.12: Print Options display

```
              Monthly Sales Monthly Expenses
       Jan      25,000.00       13,000.00
       Feb      23,000.00       14,500.00
       Mar      21,000.00       12,500.00
       Apr      22,500.00       13,000.00
       May      23,000.00       13,000.00
       Jun      23,500.00       12,500.00
       Jul      21,000.00       11,500.00
       Aug      21,500.00       14,000.00
       Sep      22,500.00       14,500.00
       Oct      24,000.00       15,000.00
       Nov      25,000.00       16,000.00
       Dec      26,000.00       16,500.00
                ---------------------------
       TOTALS:  278,000.00      166,000.00

                        NET PROFIT: 112,000.00
                        ======================
           This spreadsheet copyright by XYZ Corporation
```

Figure 6.13: Printed spreadsheet

PRINT FORMULAS (Y/N) Normally, when one or more cells contain formulas, it's the values of the formulas that are printed. You can have the formulas themselves printed by selecting "Y" for this option.

PAUSE BETWEEN PAGES If you are printing single sheets rather than continuous form paper, select "Y" for this option. First Choice will pause after each page, to give you time to load the next one.

PRINT TO If the output is going to the printer, enter PRINTER for this option. If you want the output to go to the screen instead of the printer, enter SCREEN. It's a good idea to use SCREEN when you first output a spreadsheet, to see how the final output will appear on the printer. You may want to make some adjustments to the output before you're satisfied with its appearance.

You can also direct the output to a disk file by entering the name of the file here. This can be either a new file or an existing one.

The resulting disk file can be loaded into the word processor for editing, or it can be merged with another document. It can then be sent to the printer directly from the word processor (see "Improving the Spreadsheet's Appearance").

For some laser printers, use a value of 60. See Appendix B for printer details.

LINES PER PAGE If you are using pages of an unusual size, such as legal-sized sheets, enter the size here. Normally, six lines per inch are printed.

PAGE WIDTH The standard width is 80 characters per line, but some printers can print up to 132 characters per line in Compressed mode. Wide-carriage printers may print up to 255 characters per line in Compressed mode. You can select any number up to 255 for the Page Width option.

PAGE HEADING This option allows you to print a one-line heading, which will be centered at the top of the outputted spreadsheet.

IMPROVING THE SPREADSHEET'S APPEARANCE

You can use First Choice's word processor to modify the outputted spreadsheet in any way that you wish. Multiple-line titles and column headings can be added, column positions can be adjusted, text can be boldfaced, and so on. This editing is possible because when a spreadsheet is output to a disk file, that file can be treated as a document by First Choice.

Let's load a "printed" spreadsheet into the word processor and make some improvements to its appearance:

1. Retrieve the spreadsheet you created earlier in this chapter (see "Retrieving the Spreadsheet").

2. Begin the print process by selecting *Print this spreadsheet* from the Print menu.

3. In the Print Options display, select the name of a disk file for the *Print to* option. The output will then go to this file.

4. Press ◄┘ and the output will go to the file you named in step 3.

5. Now choose *Get an existing file* from either the Main menu or the Files menu. Select the file that you named above. The spreadsheet output will be loaded into the word processor.

6. Use any of First Choice's editing commands to make the headings less crowded and to center the bottom line.

7. When you've finished editing, select *Print this document* from the Print menu.

8. Select any desired options from the Print Options display, then press ◄┘, and the revised spreadsheet will be printed.

PRINTING A WIDE SPREADSHEET

If a spreadsheet is too wide to fit within the limits of your printer, First Choice prints it in parts, sectioning the spreadsheet as neatly as possible.

Several software packages are available for printing spreadsheets sideways. If you use one of these packages in combination with the Condensed mode of a printer, a lot of information can be conveniently printed out. To use one of these packages, select a disk file for the *Print to* option on the Print Options display. This disk file can then be used as input to the software package for sideways printing.

PRINTING PART OF A SPREADSHEET

You can choose to print only a certain part of a spreadsheet, including row and/or column headings:

- Select the cells to be printed by moving the cursor to the upper left-hand corner of the range of cells. If you want to include both row and column headings, this should be location R0C0. Define the selected cell as the beginning of the range, either by pressing Alt-S, or by choosing *Select cells* from the Edit menu. Move the cursor to include the entire group of cells in the range.

- Choose *Print selected cells only* from the Print menu.

- Make any desired selections from the Print Options display, then press ◄─┘. The selected part of the spreadsheet will be printed.

OUTPUTTING A SPREADSHEET IN 1-2-3 FORMAT

A spreadsheet can be transformed into Lotus 1-2-3 format, often called WKS format. It can then be read by 1-2-3 or other programs that know how to handle this type of file structure. The process isn't 100 percent accurate because of inherent differences between the spreadsheet programs of First Choice and Lotus.

To convert a First Choice spreadsheet into WKS format, select *Save as Professional Plan/1-2-3 WKS file* from the Files menu. When the Directory Assistant appears, choose the name of the file to hold the converted spreadsheet. First Choice automatically appends the extension .WKS to the file name.

During the conversion process, some information is lost, and other data is transformed. Here are the main features concerning conversion:

- Many First Choice formulas will not work in 1-2-3 (see the next chapter for a complete discussion of formulas), primarily because 1-2-3 doesn't recognize some of First Choice's functions. If a First Choice formula won't work, its current value is placed in the converted cell.

- 1-2-3 has no special areas reserved for row and column headings. Consequently, row headings are converted to a column of left-justified labels, and column headings are converted to a row of centered labels.

- All cell values, both labels and numbers, are saved during conversion.

- All cell names are saved as single-cell range names (in 1-2-3, a range can be assigned a name, but a single cell cannot).

- The global style and individual cell styles are also saved, as are the global minimum column width and the individual column widths.

When you transform a spreadsheet from one format to another, study the resulting spreadsheet very carefully. If the spreadsheet is large and complex, this may be a tedious job, but it's absolutely necessary. As an extra precaution, keep a copy of the original spreadsheet file.

INPUTTING A SPREADSHEET IN 1-2-3 FORMAT

You can have First Choice input a spreadsheet in 1-2-3 (WKS) format, subject to the same types of conditions discussed in the last section. To read this type of file, select *Get an existing file* from the Main menu or the Files menu. The file must have the extension .WKS. When First Choice sees the .WKS extension, it automatically converts the spreadsheet to its own format. Here's what occurs during conversion:

- When possible, cell formulas are converted; otherwise, cell values are inserted instead. This results from the fact that 1-2-3 has many formulas not recognized by First Choice.

- The global style is also converted as much as possible; 1-2-3 has many style options not available in First Choice. Those that can't be converted are ignored.

- Labels are converted, but not all long labels will convert properly. Numbers are also converted, but 1-2-3 can handle much larger numbers than First Choice can. As a result, many large numbers won't display properly on the screen. When this happens, First Choice displays a row of asterisks.

A 1-2-3 spreadsheet can be very large. If you are converting one that's too big for First Choice, you can break it up into smaller parts within 1-2-3, then send the individual parts to First Choice.

MERGING AN ASCII FILE INTO A SPREADSHEET

You can enter the contents of an ASCII file into a spreadsheet—either a new one or one already containing data. In order to do this, the data in the file has to be separated in a way that First Choice can recognize. When the data from the file is merged into a spreadsheet, values are copied into successive cells, beginning with the cell at which the cursor is positioned, and proceeding from left to right in that row. When a hard return is encountered, the values following it are copied into the next spreadsheet row, starting at the column in which the first value was copied.

Values in an ASCII file can be separated by any of the following:

- Comma

- Semicolon

- Two or more adjacent blanks

- Double quotation marks

To merge an ASCII file into a spreadsheet, retrieve the spreadsheet (or create a new one). Select *Merge ASCII data* from the Files menu. When the Directory Assistant appears, select the name of the file containing the ASCII data. If necessary, first enter the name of the disk drive and/or directory on which the file is located. The data will be copied to the spreadsheet in the order described above.

SUMMARY

In this chapter, we've explored many of the features of First Choice's spreadsheet module. With this information, you should be able to create a spreadsheet and enter both numeric and textual data, as well as row and column headings. You should also be familiar with saving and printing a spreadsheet, as well as with importing and exporting files compatible with the Lotus 1-2-3 format.

In the next chapter, we'll discuss the more advanced spreadsheet features, including the use of First Choice's large assortment of built-in functions.

Chapter
7

Using Formulas

Chapter 6 introduced the basics of using formulas. We saw how to use the Formula Box to enter formulas, and how to delete and modify formulas. We also saw how to name cells in order to simplify the use of formulas. In this chapter, we'll describe in detail how First Choice works with formulas. We'll then look at functions that can be used in spreadsheets.

Formulas give spreadsheets much of their power and flexibility. A formula represents not just a single number, but a wide range of possible values. Because of this, spreadsheets can be used not only to make calculations based on a current situation, but also to explore "what if" possibilities.

Another reason formulas are so powerful is that they can incorporate a wide range of functions (sometimes called *keywords*). Each of First Choice's built-in functions represents a particular type of calculation, such as using an interest rate to find the amount of a monthly payment.

PERFORMING ARITHMETIC WITHIN FORMULAS

Note that two asterisks next to each other denote exponentiation, not multiplication twice.

Any of the standard arithmetic operations can be used within a formula. Here are the symbols used:

+	Addition
–	Subtraction
*	Multiplication
/	Division
^ or **	Exponentiation

We use these symbols in combination with cell values, functions, and numbers to build formulas. Here are some examples of simple formulas:

R1 + R2

(R1 + R2)

Fudge_Factor*(Salary + Bonus)

5**3

3*@ABS(AMOUNT)

The first example adds the values of cells R1 and R2. The second example is the same formula as the first, but parentheses have been added for clarity. In the third example, the value of the cell named Fudge_Factor is multiplied by the sum of the cells named Salary and Bonus. The fourth formula raises 5 to the third power (5^3); the result is 125. The last formula uses one of First Choice's built-in functions, @ABS, which in this case computes the absolute value of the cell named AMOUNT. The result of this calculation is then multiplied by 3.

Notice that in the above examples, we've included some extra spaces between various items. First Choice ignores all spaces in formulas, so you can use them freely to improve readability. However, no spaces can appear between the two asterisks in the exponentiation symbol (**).

HOW FIRST CHOICE EVALUATES A FORMULA

When you type in a formula to a cell, First Choice reads and interprets it, displaying the result on the screen. Here are the rules that First Choice follows in interpreting a formula:

- Functions are evaluated first.

- Exponentiations are done next.

- Multiplications and divisions follow.

- Finally, additions and subtractions are performed.

- Within each set of parentheses, the above order is followed.

- Anything written inside a pair of parentheses is evaluated before anything outside the parentheses.

For each of the above steps, evaluation proceeds from left to right.

Several sets of parentheses can be used in a single formula, and you can even enclose one pair of parentheses within another. Parentheses are often needed to force the evaluation of a formula in a particular way. For example, consider the following formula involving a cost-of-living factor applied to a salary and overtime:

Use parentheses to ensure that calculations are done in the correct order.

CostOfLiving * Salary + OverTime

According to the order of operations listed above, the multiplication will be evaluated first, then the addition. If you want the cost of living to apply both to the salary and overtime, the formula must be written

CostOfLiving * (Salary + OverTime)

The rules insist that the part of the formula inside the parentheses is evaluated first, so that the value of CostOfLiving will be multiplied by the sum of Salary and OverTime.

Here are some samples of formulas with only numbers, along with the result that First Choice would calculate. Remember that blank spaces don't affect the results.

FORMULA	*CALCULATED RESULT*
3*4 + 5	17
3*(4 + 5)	27
(1 + 3)*(4/2)	8
(2*(1 + 3)) – (4/2)	6
2*3**3	54
2**3*2	16
2**(3*2)	64

COPYING AND MOVING FORMULAS

Often, it is convenient to copy a formula from one location to another. For example, you may want your spreadsheet to have several columns of numbers, with a formula for calculating the total at the bottom of each column. Instead of writing the formula separately for each column, you can write the formula for one cell, then copy it to the other locations.

This feature is useful because when a formula is copied to a new location, it is adjusted to reflect that location. As an example, consider the spreadsheet shown in Figure 7.1, and in particular the formula in cell R7C1, which totals up the values of the cells in column 1. This formula is shown in the Formula Box in the figure.

Suppose that we want to use a similar formula to calculate the total of the values in column 2. We can do so by copying the formula in R7C1 to cell R7C2 using the following steps:

- Move the cursor to R7C1.

- Select that cell, either with Alt-S or from the Edit menu.

- Press Alt-C to copy the cell's contents to the clipboard.

- Move the cursor to R7C2, and press Alt-P to paste the value from the clipboard into this cell.

The result is shown in Figure 7.2: the formula in R7C2 has been altered to reflect the cells in the second column.

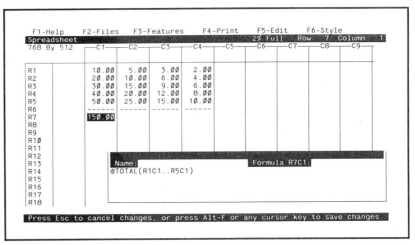

Figure 7.1: Spreadsheet with a formula in cell R7C1

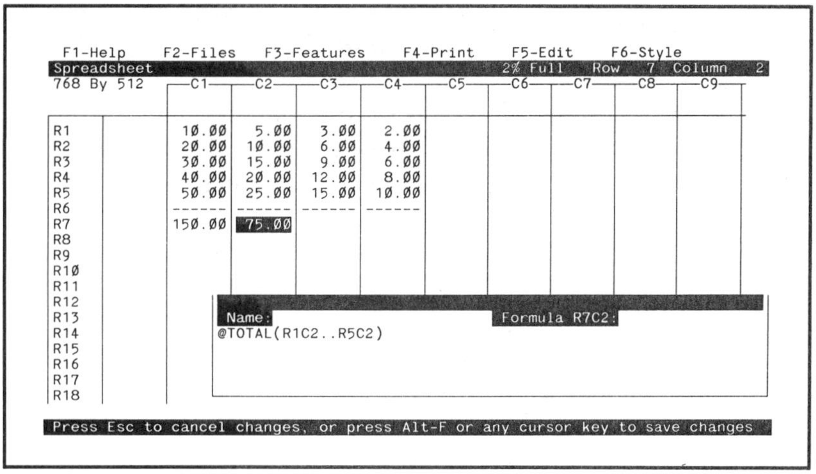

Figure 7.2: Formula in cell R7C1 copied to R7C2

> When a formula is moved, the original cell's contents are blanked out.

A formula can also be moved from one cell to another. The procedure is similar to that described above, except that you move the formula (using Alt-M) to the clipboard instead of copying it. When a formula is moved, its contents are adjusted in the same way as though it had been copied.

HOW FORMULAS CHANGE WHEN COPIED

First Choice determines whether a formula needs to change when you copy or move it from one cell to another by using the following rules:

- If a formula is copied or moved one column to the right, any column number in the formula is increased by one. If the formula is moved one column to the left, column numbers in the formula are decreased by one.

- If a formula is copied or moved down one row, any row number in the formula is increased by one. If the formula is moved up one row, row numbers in the formula are decreased by one.

MAINTAINING A CONSTANT CELL

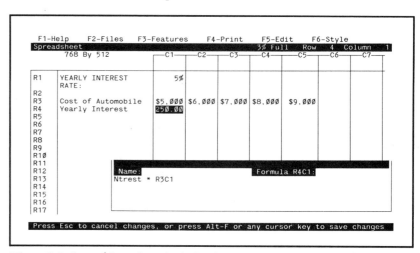

When a formula is copied, named cells remain unchanged.

If you want to refer to the *same cell* in a group of formulas generated by a copy, you can do so by giving that cell a name, then using that name in the original formula.

For example, consider the spreadsheet in Figure 7.3. The number in row R1 shows the prevailing interest rate for new car loans. The values in row R3 show different new car purchase prices. We would like to know approximately how much the yearly interest will amount to for each of these prices, based on the prevailing interest rate. We can have these values computed and stored in row R4.

Figure 7.3: Spreadsheet for calculating interest costs

The approximate yearly cost in interest is equal to the interest rate times the purchase price. We've inserted the appropriate formula in R4C1: Ntrest * R3C1, where Ntrest is the name that we've given to cell R1C1. This formula is shown in the Formula Box.

Referring to Figure 7.3, we can copy the illustrated formula to the remaining cells in row R4, using the copy technique described in Chapter 6:

- Move the cursor to cell R4C1.

- Select that cell, either with Alt-S or from the Edit menu.

- Copy that cell to the clipboard, either with Alt-C or from the Edit menu.

- Define the range of cells into which the value on the clipboard is to be copied by moving the cursor to R4C2, the first cell in the range. Select that cell as the beginning of the range, either with Alt-S or from the Edit menu. Expand the range to include cells R4C3 through R4C5, using cursor-movement keys.

- Paste the formula from the clipboard to each cell in the range, either with Alt-P or from the Edit menu.

Figure 7.4 shows the final spreadsheet, with the formula for cell R4C5 shown in the Formula Box. Note that the column number has

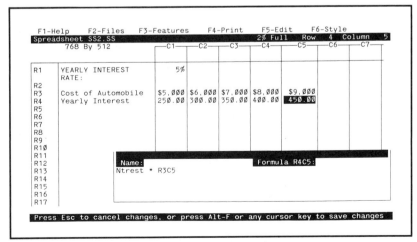

Figure 7.4: Formula in R4C1 copied to other cells

been changed (automatically) to C5, but the named cell, Ntrest, remains the same.

When a formula referencing the cell named Ntrest is evaluated, the current value of Ntrest is used. If you change the value of that cell, it will affect any formulas referencing it (see "Automatic and Manual Recalculation" below).

COPYING FORMULAS WITH QUICK ENTRY

First Choice's quick entry feature can be used to copy a formula to a group of adjacent cells. Here are the steps:

- Move the cursor to the cell containing the formula to be copied.

- Press Alt-Q to begin quick entry, or select *Start quick entry* from the Features menu. The Formula Box for that cell automatically appears on the screen.

- To begin copying the formula, move the cursor to the next cell. As the cursor moves to each new cell, the adjusted formula appears in the Formula Box, but the calculated value doesn't appear in the cell until you do one of the following: Press Alt-F to hide the Formula Box, press Alt-R to force the recalculation of the cell, or move the cursor to another cell.

If manual recalculation has been set, the new formulas are copied but not calculated, so that zero values appear in the cells. To force the recalculation of the cells, press Alt-R (see "Automatic and Manual Recalculation" in this chapter).

To end quick entry, press Alt-Q, Alt-F, or Esc, or change the direction of cursor movement.

After you move the cursor to a new cell, you can modify the formula generated by quick entry, then continue moving the cursor. The modified formula will then propagate under quick entry.

As the formula is copied, it is adjusted for each new cell (see "How Formulas Change When Copied" in this chapter).

AUTOMATIC AND MANUAL RECALCULATION

Whenever you enter a new value for a cell, and that cell is referenced by a formula in another cell, the formula must be recalculated. You can choose between two modes of recalculation. In the automatic mode, whenever a cell's value is changed, any affected formulas are immediately recalculated automatically. In the manual mode, no recalculation is done until you issue an instruction to First Choice to do so.

The advantage of automatic recalculation is just that: it's automatic, so you can always be sure that what you see on the screen reflects the latest values input to the spreadsheet. The disadvantage is that for large spreadsheets, a recalculation can take a considerable amount of time. If you're doing a good deal of updating to a large spreadsheet, it would be more efficient to use the manual mode, so that you don't have to wait for each recalculation; after you've made a series of changes, you can instruct First Choice to do a recalculation by selecting *Recalculate* from the Features menu.

The speed key that instructs First Choice to a do a recalculation is Alt-R.

Initially, First Choice puts each spreadsheet into the automatic mode. To change to the manual mode, select *Set manual recalculation* from the Features menu.

AUTOMATIC FORMULA ADJUSTMENT

If you add or delete a row or column containing a cell referenced as part of a range by a formula, that formula changes automatically to adjust for the new limits on the range. For example, consider the spreadsheet in Figure 7.5. The formula in cell R6C1 calculates the sum of values in cells R1C1 through R4C1.

Now suppose that we add a new row between rows R2 and R3, by selecting *Insert row/column* from the Edit menu. The changed spreadsheet is shown in Figure 7.6. Notice that the formula in cell R7C1 has been changed automatically by First Choice to accommodate the fact that the last cell in the range is now R5C1 instead of R4C1.

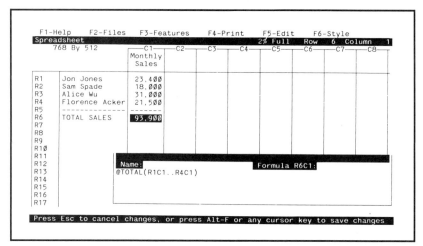

Figure 7.5: Spreadsheet with a formula

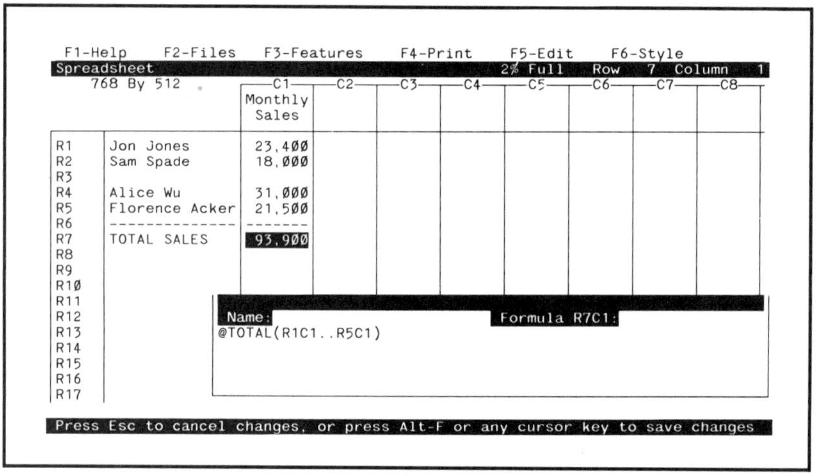

Figure 7.6: Spreadsheet from Figure 7.5 with adjusted formula

The above only applies if the referenced cell is not the beginning or end of a range. If you delete a row or column containing a cell that's either the beginning or the end of a range referenced by a formula, you get an error message telling you that the formula is about to become incorrect. For example, in Figure 7.5, an error results if you try to delete either rows R1 or R4.

WORKING WITH FUNCTIONS

A *function* supplies a built-in prescription for doing a particular operation within a formula. It is a part of a formula that is written into a cell. A function can even be the entire formula. For example, the function @TOTAL(R1C1..R5C1) calculates the sum of the values in the first five cells in column C1. On the other hand, the function @AVERAGE(R1C1..R5C1) calculates the average value of the five cells.

Each function has two parts, a name and a value. The *function name* specifies the operation to be carried out. Normally, function names begin with the character @. Although this character is actually optional, it's a good idea to always include it, to help you distinguish between cell names and functions. A function also includes the *value* or values that are involved in the calculation. These are sometimes called *arguments*.

A complete list of functions and their meanings is found inside the cover of this book.

The following sections describe each of the functions available in First Choice. Each section discusses one of the major groups of functions—arithmetic, financial, string, time, date, and logical. Within each group, discussions are arranged alphabetically by function names. Examples of each function are also given.

As you read about the functions, keep the following points in mind. When a cell contains a formula, the *value* of the cell appears on the screen—not the formula. For example, if a cell contains the formula @ABS(– 5), the screen displays 5.00 for that cell.

When a function is calculated, the result is incorporated into the overall formula. For example, suppose that a formula for a cell is 2*@SQRT(R1C1), and further suppose that cell R1C1 contains the value 9.0. The value of the formula is 6.00, and this is the result that appears on the screen for that cell.

The value ERROR is a special numerical value that's returned when a function can't be calculated. For example, suppose that cell R1C1 contains the formula @SQRT(R5C5), and that cell R5C5 has a value of – 1. Because @SQRT can't calculate the square root of a negative number, it returns a value of ERROR, which is displayed for cell R1C1.

If a function references a cell that contains a label rather than a numerical value, the value of that cell is taken to be zero. This can lead to problems, because you might not realize that a cell is being incorrectly used. For example, suppose the cells R5C10 and R10C10 contain the values 25.00 and *My laundry list.* Also suppose that in some other cell, you accidentally enter the formula @SQRT(R10C10) instead of the correct formula—@SQRT(R5C10). The screen will display a value of zero for that cell, and it might be a long time before you discover the error.

ARITHMETIC FUNCTIONS

These functions perform standard mathematical calculations. They are written in the form FUNCTION_NAME(*value*). *Value* can be a number, a single cell, a range of cells, or another function name. Table 7.1 shows examples of each. The cell or cells represented by *value* must contain numeric quantities.

Table 7.1: Examples of Arithmetic Functions

FUNCTION	MEANING
@ABS(− 5)	Calculates the absolute value of (− 5), which is 5
@ABS(R1C5)	Calculates the absolute value of the contents of cell R1C5
@TOTAL(R1C1..R5C1)	Calculates the sum of the values in cells R1C1 through R5C1
@SIN(ABS(R5C5))	First calculates the absolute value of the quantity in cell R5C5, then calculates the sine of the result

In the examples in the remainder of this chapter, all values are shown with two decimal digits or less. The actual number of decimal digits appearing on the screen for a particular cell depends on the style set for that cell.

@ABS(value)   This function calculates the absolute value of *value.*

FORMULA EXAMPLE	SCREEN DISPLAY
@ABS(15.5)	15.50
@ABS(− 15.5)	15.50
@ABS(R1C1)	10.00 (assuming the value of R1C1 is − 10.00)

FORMULA EXAMPLE	*SCREEN DISPLAY*
@ABS(R2C2)	0.00 (assuming the value of R2C2 is *My laundry list*)
@ABS(@SIN(2))	0.91

The fourth item in the list above, @ABS(R2C2), is a reminder that a label is treated as a numerical value of zero. The last item, @ABS(@SIN(2)), illustrates how one function can operate on the result of another. Here, the function @SIN(−2) is first calculated. Its result (−0.91) is then used as input to the @ABS function. The function @SIN is discussed later.

@ACOS(value) This calculates the angle (in radians) whose cosine is *value*. The value returned is always between zero and π (3.1415...). @ACOS is the inverse of the function @COS. The *value* for this function must be between −1 and +1. Otherwise, the value of the function is ERROR.

FORMULA EXAMPLE	*SCREEN DISPLAY*
@ACOS(1)	0.00
@ACOS(0.1)	1.47
@ACOS(2)	ERROR
@ACOS(0.5)*180/3.1416	60.00 (result in degrees)
@ACOS(@COS(2))	2.00
@ACOS(THETA)	0.00 (assuming the value of the cell named THETA is 1.00)

Note that the numbers returned by @ACOS are angles measured in radians. To convert to degrees, multiply the result by 180/π.

@ASIN(value) Calculates the angle (in radians) whose sine is *value*. The value returned is always between −π/2 and +π/2. @ASIN is the inverse of the function @SIN. *Value* must be between −1 and +1. Otherwise, the value returned is ERROR.

FORMULA EXAMPLE	*SCREEN DISPLAY*
@ASIN(0)	0.00
@ASIN(– 1)	– 1.57
@ASIN(2.00)	ERROR
@ASIN(@SIN(1.23))	1.23

@ATAN(value)   Calculates the angle (in radians) whose tangent is *value*. The returned value is always between $-\pi/2$ and $+\pi/2$. @ATAN is the inverse of the function @TAN.

FORMULA EXAMPLE	*SCREEN DISPLAY*
@ATAN(0)	0.00
@ATAN(100)	1.56
@ATAN(1000)*180/@PI	89.40

@AVERAGE(range) OR @AVG(range)   Calculates the average of the values in the cells specified by *range*. If any cells within *range* contain text or blank values, they are excluded from the calculation. However, a cell containing a value of zero is included.

FORMULA EXAMPLE

@AVERAGE(R1C1..R5C5)

@AVERAGE(BEGIN..END)

@AVG(BEGIN..END)

@COS(angle)   Calculates the cosine of *angle*. The angle must be specified in radians (there are approximately 57.3 degrees per radian). The value returned is always between – 1 and + 1. @COS is the inverse of the function @ACOS.

FORMULA EXAMPLE	*SCREEN DISPLAY*
@COS(0)	1.00
@COS(3.1416/2)	0.00
@COS(90/57.3)	0.00
@COS(@ACOS(0.86))	0.86

@COUNT(range)   Counts the number of numeric entries in the cells defined by *range*. Only cells containing valid numbers, including zero, are counted; cells with labels or blanks are not counted. *Range* must specify both a beginning and an end cell.

FORMULA EXAMPLE	SCREEN DISPLAY
@COUNT(R1C1..R5C2)	10.00, provided that all cells in the range contain numbers
@COUNT(R1C1..R1C1)	1.00, if R1C1 contains a number; otherwise, 0.00
@COUNT(R1C1)	An error message saying that this is an illegal formula

@ERROR   This is a function whose only value is a special number that's called ERROR (confusing, isn't it?). If the formula for a cell is the function @ERROR, then its value is ERROR. If a formula for a cell references a cell whose value is ERROR, then the value of the first cell is also ERROR.

FORMULA EXAMPLE	SCREEN DISPLAY
@ERROR	ERROR
@ABS(@ERROR)	ERROR
@ABS(R1C1)	ERROR (assuming that the value of R1C1 is ERROR)

The value of ERROR propagates: if a function references a cell whose value is ERROR, then the function also returns a value of ERROR. For instance, in the above example, a cell containing the formula ABS(R1C1) would also display ERROR. This property of propagation can be useful for tracing complex paths of interrelated formulas: Set the formula for a cell to @ERROR and see what other cells then display the value ERROR.

@EXP(value)   Calculates **e** raised to the power *value*. The value of **e** is taken to be 2.718281828459045. The inverse of @EXP(*value*) is the function @LN(*value*).

FORMULA EXAMPLE	SCREEN DISPLAY
@EXP(0)	1.00
@EXP(1)	2.72
@EXP(– 1)	0.37
@EXP(SIN(3.1416/2))	2.72
@EXP(@LN(3.45))	3.45

@FRACT(value)   Calculates the decimal, or fractional, part of *value*.

FORMULA EXAMPLE	SCREEN DISPLAY
@FRACT(3.14)	0.14
@FRACT(3.146)	0.15
@FRACT(0)	0.00
@FRACT(150)	0.00
@FRACT(R1C1)	0.10 (where the value of R1C1 is 5.10)
@FRACT(– 5.15)	– 0.15

@INTEGER(value) OR @INT(value)   For positive values of *value*, this function computes the nearest integer less than or equal to *value*. For negative values of *value*, the result is the nearest integer greater than or equal to *value*.

FORMULA EXAMPLE	SCREEN DISPLAY
@INTEGER(1.5)	1.00
@INTEGER(– 1.99)	– 1.00
@INT(0.5)	0.00
@INT(SIN(@PI/2))	1.00

@LN(value)   Calculates the natural logarithm (to the base **e**) of *value*. This is the inverse of the function **@EXP(value)**. *Value* must be greater than 0.

FORMULA EXAMPLE	*SCREEN DISPLAY*
@LN(1.0)	0.00
@LN(2.718)	1.00
@LN(– 1.0)	ERROR
@LN(@EXP(1.24))	1.24

@LOG(value) Calculates the common logarithm (to the base 10) of *value*. The inverse of @LOG(*value*) is (10)**value. *Value* must be greater than 0. Otherwise, the value of the function is ERROR.

FORMULA EXAMPLE	*SCREEN DISPLAY*
@LOG(1.0)	0.00
@LOG(10.0)	1.00
@LOG(–1)	ERROR
@LOG(0.1)	– 1.00
@LOG(@SIN(@PI/2))	0.00
@LOG(10**8.73)	8.73

@MAXIMUM(range) OR @MAX(range) The computed number is the maximum of the cell values in the specified *range*.

FORMULA EXAMPLE

@MAX(R1C1..R5C10)

@MAXIMUM (R1C1..R1C1)

@MINIMUM(range) OR @MIN(range) The result is the minimum of the cell values in the specified *range*.

FORMULA EXAMPLE

@MIN(R1C1..R5C10)

@MINIMUM (R1C1..R1C1)

@MOD(value1, value2)   Returns the remainder, or *modulus*, from the division of *value1* by *value2*. *Value2* must be nonzero. If not, the value returned is ERROR.

FORMULA EXAMPLE	SCREEN DISPLAY
@MOD(5,2)	1.00
@MOD(4,2)	0.00
@MOD(– 10,3)	– 1.00
@MOD(10,0)	ERROR

@PI   Returns the constant value of 3.141592653589793. This is a convenient tool when doing calculations involving trigonometric functions. Note that this is one of the few functions that doesn't require values to work with.

FORMULA EXAMPLE	SCREEN DISPLAY
2*@PI	6.28
@COS(@PI)	– 1.00

@RANDOM OR @RAND   Returns a random number between the values of 0.00 and 1.00. Each time the function is used, a different value is returned. Note that this function doesn't require a value.

FORMULA EXAMPLE	SCREEN DISPLAY
@RANDOM	A value between 0 and 1
100*@RANDOM	A value between 0 and 100
10 + 100*@RANDOM	A value between 10 and 110

@ROUND(value) TO(places)   *Value* is rounded to the number of decimal places specified by *places*. If this number is negative, the digit zero is substituted for one or more significant digits to the left of the decimal point. If TO (*places*) is not included, *value* is rounded to the nearest integer. *Places* must be between – 14 and + 14.

FORMULA EXAMPLE	SCREEN DISPLAY
@ROUND(1.123) TO(1)	1.10
@ROUND(1.153) TO(1)	1.20
@ROUND(– 1.666) TO(2)	– 1.67
@ROUND(227) TO(– 1)	230.00
@ROUND(5.6)	6.00
@ROUND(5.7981) TO (3)	5.80

Rounding deter-mines the number of significant digits of the stored number, not the value displayed on the screen.

Note that the number of places displayed on the screen is controlled by the style set for the cell containing the formula—not by the rounding process. As a result, the display may show zeros to the right of the decimal point that are not valid (as in the first two examples above). On the other hand, a displayed number may not show the complete effect of rounding. This is illustrated by the last example above, where the result is displayed only to two decimal places, whereas the actual number is stored with three decimal places.

Rounding affects the cell containing the @ROUND function only—not the data being rounded. For example, suppose that cell R1C1 contains the value 1.513, and cell R9C9 contains the formula @ROUND(R1C1). The value of R9C9 will be 1, but the value in R1C1 remains 1.513.

@SIN(angle)   Calculates the sine of the specified angle (in radians). The value of @SIN is always between – 1 and + 1.

FORMULA EXAMPLE	SCREEN DISPLAY
@SIN(0.0)	0.00
@SIN(@PI/2)	1.00
@SIN(@ASIN(0.86))	0.86

@SQRT(value)   Returns the square root of *value*. *Value* must be greater than or equal to zero. Otherwise, the value returned is ERROR.

FORMULA EXAMPLE	*SCREEN DISPLAY*
@SQRT(5)	2.24
@SQRT(– 5)	ERROR
@SQRT(@ABS(– 5))	2.24
@SQRT(@ROUND(4.49))	2.00

@STDEV(range) OR @STD(range)   Calculates the standard deviation of the cell values in the specified range. @STDEV(*range*) is the square root of the function @VARIANCE(*range*).

FORMULA EXAMPLE

@STDEV(R1C1..R5C15)

@STDEV(START..STOP)

@TAN(angle)   Calculates the tangent of *angle* (in radians). This function is the inverse of the function @ATAN.

FORMULA EXAMPLE	*SCREEN DISPLAY*
@TAN(0)	0.00
@TAN(– @PI/1.9)	12.07
@TAN(@PI/2.00001)	127,324.59
@TAN(@PI/2)	****** (result is too large to calculate)
@TAN(@ATAN(543))	543.00

@TOTAL(range) OR @TOT(range)   Calculates the sum of the cell values in the specified range.

FORMULA EXAMPLE

@TOTAL(R1C1..R5C1)

@TOT(R1C1..R5C10)

@VARIANCE(range) OR @VAR(range)   This calculates the variance of the cell values in the specified range. @VAR(*range*) is the square of @STDEV(*range*).

FORMULA EXAMPLE

@VARIANCE(R5C1..R5C5)

@VAR(BEGIN..END)

FINANCIAL FUNCTIONS

In this section, we'll describe the functions that perform financially-oriented computations.

@CTERM AT (interest) TO (final value) FROM (present value)   This function computes the number of terms needed to generate a value of *final value*, when the amount (*present value*) is invested at an interest rate (*interest*) per term.

Suppose you have the following values:

Initial investment: $1,000

Yearly interest rate: 0.08

Desired final value: $5,000

Using the formula

@CTERM AT 0.08 TO 5000 FROM 1000

you would find a value of 20.91 years. In other words, assuming that interest is compounded yearly, it will take nearly 21 years to quintuple the original investment.

If an annual interest rate of I_o is compounded monthly, and you want the required time to be expressed in years, enter $I_o/12$ for *interest*, then divide the final result by 12.

@DDB(cost, salvage, lifetime, period)   This function calculates the depreciation allowance that can be taken on an asset during a time period, *period*, based on the double declining balance method. The

Commas can be included as part of a number, but a currency sign cannot. Also, unlike arithmetic functions, financial functions allow the optional use of parentheses around the supplied values.

price paid for the asset is *cost*, and the salvage value, *salvage*, will be reached after *lifetime* periods. Usually, *period* and *lifetime* are measured in years. With this method, depreciation ends when the book value of the asset equals the salvage value.

For example, suppose that your company purchases a sailboat for $500,000. You estimate that the boat will be worn out after 7 years, when its market value will have dropped to $50,000. You would like to calculate the depreciation allowance that can be claimed during the first year of ownership of the boat. Using the formula

@DDB(500000,50000,7,1)

a value of approximately $142,857 would be calculated.

Note that in this function, numbers can't include commas as part of the arguments, because the arguments themselves are separated by commas.

@FV ON *(amount)* AT *(interest)* OVER *(periods)* This is the Future Values function. It calculates the expected value from making a group of equal payments of *amount*, over a number of equally spaced time periods (*periods*), and with an interest rate per period of *interest*.

Suppose that you invest $200 per month at a fixed annual interest rate of 8% compounded monthly. You want to know how much will have accumulated after 20 years. Using the formula

@FV ON (200) AT (0.08/12) OVER (20*12)

the calculated return value is $117,804.08.

@INTEREST ON *(amount)* AT *(interest)* OVER *(periods)* FOR *(period)* This function computes the amount of interest to be paid at a particular period (*period*) during the life of a loan. The initial loan value is *amount*, taken at a fixed interest of *interest* per period, and over a total number of periods equal to *periods*.

Let's say you have borrowed $75,000 for a sailboat loan at a yearly interest rate of 12% compounded monthly, with a total loan period of

15 years. You want to know how much of your monthly payment will go to interest halfway through the life of the loan. The formula

@INTEREST ON 75,000 AT (0.12/12) OVER (15*12) FOR 91

will give you the returned value of $532.52. The value of 91 is based on a loan period of $15*12 = 180$ months: after one-half of this has expired, the next month will be the 91st.

@NPV AT (rate) OF (range)   This function calculates the net present value of a range of values, which represent inflows and out-flows of a particular investment, excluding the initial outlay for the investment. *Rate* is the discount or interest rate, and *range* is the range of inflow and outflow values, one for each period.

For example, you have a chance to purchase a small apartment building for $150,000. You expect the first year's income to be $30,000, growing each year by 7 percent, with a discount rate of 10 percent. Let's assume that you have a spreadsheet containing the first five years of projected income in column C1:

	C1
R1	30,000
R2	32,100
R3	34,347
R4	36,751
R5	39,324

Using the formula @NPV AT 0.10 OF R1C1..R5C1, the result would be $130,835. Since this is less than your initial investment, the building is probably not a reasonable investment.

@PAYMENT ON (amount) AT (interest) OVER (periods)   This function calculates the periodic payment due on a loan of *amount* dollars, with a fixed interest rate of *interest* per period, paid off over a total number of periods equal to *periods*.

If you want to borrow $200,000 for a deepsea trawler, and you want to find out if you can afford to pay the loan back in 15 years at a yearly interest rate of 11% compounded quarterly, use the formula

@PAYMENT ON 200,000 AT (0.11/12) OVER (15*12)

to calculate the value, which is $2,273.19.

@PV ON (amount) AT (interest) OVER (periods)   This is the Present Value function. It calculates the present value of a number (*periods*) of equal payments to be made. Each payment is in the amount of *amount*; the discounted interest rate is *interest*.

Suppose an annuity is purchased for $10,000. It pays $2,000 a year for 15 years, at a discounted interest rate of 12%. To calculate the present value of the annuity, use the formula

@PV ON 2,000 AT .12 OVER 15

to calculate the value of $13,621.73.

@RATE TO (final value) FROM (present value) OVER (periods)   This function calculates the interest rate necessary to increase an initial investment (*present value*) to *final value*. The number of periods over which the interest is compounded is *periods*.

Let's say you want to turn $10,000 into $25,000 over 10 years, assuming that interest is compounded monthly. The formula to calculate the necessary interest rate is

(@RATE TO 25,000 FROM 10,000 OVER 10*12)*12

The resulting value is 0.09.

Note that because interest is compounded monthly, the number of periods must also be expressed in terms of months. The calculated value for @RATE is then the monthly interest rate, which we have multiplied by 12 to convert into a yearly figure.

@SLN(cost, salvage, lifetime)   Calculates annual depreciation of an asset, using the straight-line method. The original cost of the asset is *cost*, with an assumed useful life of *lifetime*, and with a salvage value of *salvage*. This method of calculating assumes a uniform depreciation rate over the lifetime of the asset.

For example, suppose that you purchase a delivery truck for your company for $15,000. You project a useful life of 5 years, at which time you expect to be able to sell the truck for $3,000. To calculate the annual depreciation allowance for the truck, use the formula @SLN(15000,3000,5). The result is $2,400.

@SYD(cost,salvage,lifetime,period)   Calculates depreciation of an asset during a time period, *period*, using the sum-of-the-years' digits method. The original cost of the asset is *cost*, with an assumed useful life of *lifetime* periods, and with a salvage value of *salvage*. With this method, the depreciation allowance of the asset is calculated by using a fraction, whose value decreases each year. The fraction is equal to the number of years of remaining useful life divided by the sum of the years.

For example, suppose that you purchase a delivery truck for your company for $15,000. You project a useful life of 5 years, at which time you expect to be able to sell the truck for $3,000. You want to calculate the first year's depreciation allowance for the truck. The formula @SYD(15000,3000,5,1) yields a value of $4,000.

@TERM ON (payment) AT (interest) TO (final value)   This function calculates the number of payments (each of the amount *payment*) needed to increase to *final value*, with an interest rate of *interest*.

If you want to know how long it will take for a monthly investment of $200, compounded at 8% monthly, to grow to $20,000, calculate this using the formula

(@TERM ON 200 AT (0.08/12) TO 20,000)/12

The resulting value is 6.41. Because the interest is compounded monthly, the calculated result is the number of months. Therefore, @TERM is divided by 12 to convert to years.

DATE FUNCTIONS

These functions are used for manipulating date information within a spreadsheet. A date value can be stored in a cell, just like any other type of data. However, before First Choice can manipulate a date stored in a cell, it must be converted into a *date number*. To convert a date to a date number, you use either the @DATE or @DATEVAL function.

Date numbers, which range in value from 1 to 73109, can also be stored in cells. You can choose to have a date number in a cell displayed as its actual value, or as an ordinary date. Because date numbers are primarily for First Choice's internal use, their values generally are not useful to you. Therefore, you probably will want to display a date number as its corresponding date. For instance, the date number for 01/05/88 is 32147. If this date number is stored in a cell, you can have it displayed as 01/05/88 by setting the style for that cell: select *Set cell style* from the Style menu, then choose **Y** for the option *Show number as date (Y/N)*.

To illustrate the usefulness of date functions, let's look at the following example of spreadsheet cells:

CELL	CELL CONTENTS	CELL DISPLAY
R1C1	01/05/88	01/05/88
R2C1	02/05/88	02/05/88
R3C1	@DATEVAL(R1C1)	32147 or 01/05/88
R4C1	@DATEVAL(R2C1)	32178 or 02/05/88
R5C1	R4C1 – R3C1	31

Cell R1C1 contains the date 01/05/88. Cell R3C1 contains the formula @DATEVAL(R1C1) which, as we'll see later on, converts the contents of R1C1 into a date number—32147. You can have R2C1 displayed as a date number, or as the corresponding date.

The formula in cell R5C1 computes the difference between the two date numbers. The result, 31, is the number of days between the two dates. In general, the difference between any two date numbers is the number of days separating the two corresponding dates.

You can enter dates into a spreadsheet in a variety of formats that can then be converted into internal date numbers. Here are examples of the valid date formats:

01/25/89

1/25/89

1-25-89

1.25.89

1.25.1989

89/1/25

1989-1-25

89-1-25

Notice that all of these formats follow either the format *month*, *day*, *year*, or *year*, *month*, *day*.

For each of the date functions described below, the various examples assume a cell style of zero decimal places and no commas.

@DATE(year,month,day)   Calculates the date number for the values *year*, *month*, and *day*. Any date can be used that falls in the range from March 1, 1900 to February 28, 2100. If a date is used that's out of this range, or if an incorrect month-day combination is used, ERROR is displayed as the contents of the cell using this function.

FORMULA EXAMPLE	SCREEN DISPLAY
@DATE(88,1,25)	32167
@DATE(1988,1,25)	32167
@DATE(1988,25,1)	ERROR
@DATE(R1C1,R1C2,R1C3)	32167 (The three referenced cells are assumed to contain the values 88, 1, and 25.)

@DATEVAL(date)   Calculates the date number for *date*. *Date* can be a valid date surrounded by double quote marks, or it can be a reference to a cell containing a valid date. Look at the following examples to see how @DATEVAL differs from @DATE.

FORMULA EXAMPLE	SCREEN DISPLAY
@DATEVAL("1/25/88")	32167
@DATEVAL("1988-1-25")	32167
@DATEVAL(R1C1)	32167 (R1C1 is assumed to contain the string *1/25/88*.)

@DAY(date number)   Returns the day of the month corresponding to *date number*. The calculated value is between 1 and 31. *Date number* can be obtained from either the @DATEVAL, @DATE, or @NOW functions, or from a cell containing a date number.

FORMULA EXAMPLE	SCREEN DISPLAY
@DAY(@DATEVAL("1-25-88"))	25
@DAY(@DATE(88,1,25))	25
@DAY(R1C1)	25 (assuming that R1C1 contains the date number corresponding to 1-25-88)
@DAY(@NOW)	25 (assuming that today is the 25th of the month)
@DAY(32167)	25
@DAY(32167.500)	25

The fourth example uses the @NOW function, which is discussed later in this section. The last example illustrates that only the integer part of a date number is evaluated when calculating date information; any fractional part of the number is ignored.

@MONTH(date number)   Returns the month corresponding to *date number*. The calculated value is between 1 and 12. *Date number* can be obtained from the @DATEVAL, @NOW, or @DATE functions, or from a cell containing a date number.

FORMULA EXAMPLE	SCREEN DISPLAY
@MONTH(@DATEVAL("1-25-88"))	1
@MONTH(@DATE(88,1,25))	1
@MONTH(R1C1)	1 (assuming that R1C1 contains the date number corresponding to 1-25-88)
@MONTH(@NOW)	1 (assuming that the current month is January)
@MONTH(32167)	1

The last example simply illustrates how @MONTH works: you'll probably never actually use @MONTH in this way.

If your computer has a built-in clock, the time and date are always kept current. Otherwise, you can set the correct time and date on the computer by using the DOS commands TIME and DATE.

@NOW Reads the current date and time from DOS and returns them as a single number. The integer part of this number is the date number, and the fractional part is the time number. Since the current time is constantly changing, it may be important to periodically update the value of a cell containing the @NOW function by pressing Alt-R. This forces First Choice to recalculate the spreadsheet, including the value of @NOW.

FORMULA EXAMPLE	SCREEN DISPLAY
@NOW	32438.5000 (assuming that it's October 22, 1988 at approximately 12:00 noon)

@YEAR(date number) Returns the year corresponding to *date number*. The calculated value will be between 1900 and 2100. *Date number* can be obtained from the @DATEVAL, @NOW, or @DATE functions, or from a cell containing a date number.

FORMULA EXAMPLE	SCREEN DISPLAY
@YEAR(@DATEVAL ("1-25-89"))	1989
@YEAR(@DATE(89,1,25))	1989
@YEAR(R1C1)	1989 (assuming that R1C1 contains the date number corresponding to 1-25-89)
@YEAR(@NOW)	1989 (assuming that it's 1989)
@YEAR(32167)	1989

TIME FUNCTIONS

These functions are used for manipulating time information within a spreadsheet. Like date functions, a time value can be stored in a cell, and for each second of the day there is a corresponding *time number*, ranging from 0 to 0.9999. The time number for noon is 0.5000.

Before First Choice can manipulate a time stored in a cell, it must be transformed into a time number, which can also be stored in a cell. To convert a time to a time number, you use either the @TIME or @TIMEVAL function.

You can choose to have a time number in a cell displayed as its actual value, or as an ordinary time. Because time numbers are primarily for First Choice's internal use, their values are not particularly useful. You usually would want to display a time number as its corresponding time. For instance, if the time number for noon, 0.5000, is stored in a cell, you can display it as 12:00:00 by setting the style for that cell: select *Set cell style* from the Style menu, then choose **Y** for the option *Show number as time (Y/N)*.

First Choice uses a 24-hour clock when displaying times. Midnight is displayed as 00:00:00, and one second before midnight as 23:59:59. However, you can enter times into a spreadsheet in a variety of formats that can then be converted into internal time numbers.

Here are examples of the valid time formats:

14:15:00

14:15

2:15pm

2:15 pm

2:15 PM

2:15am

2:15

If the hour part of a time is less than twelve, as in the last example above, then A.M. is assumed unless P.M. is specifically written.

For each of the time functions described below, the examples assume a cell style of four decimal places.

@HOUR(time number)   Returns the hour corresponding to *time number*. The calculated value is between 0 (midnight) and 23 (11 P.M.). *Time number* can be obtained from either the @TIMEVAL, @TIME, or @NOW functions, or from a cell containing a time number.

FORMULA EXAMPLE	SCREEN DISPLAY
@HOUR(@TIMEVAL("10:15:30"))	10
@HOUR(@TIME(10,15,30))	10
@HOUR(R1C1)	10 (assuming that R1C1 contains the time 10:15)
@HOUR(@NOW)	10 (assuming that it's now 10:15)
@HOUR(0.43)	10
@HOUR(25000.43)	10

The fourth example uses the @NOW function, which is discussed in the section, "Date Functions." The last example illustrates that only the fractional part of a time number is used when evaluating the number for time purposes; the integer portion is ignored.

MINUTE(*time number*)   Returns the minute corresponding to *time number*. The calculated value is between 0 and 59. *Time number* can be obtained from either the @TIMEVAL, @TIME, or @NOW functions, or from a cell containing a time number.

FORMULA EXAMPLE	*SCREEN DISPLAY*
@MINUTE(@TIMEVAL("10:15:30")	15
@MINUTE(@TIME(10,15,30)	15
@MINUTE(R1C1)	15 (assuming that R1C1 contains the time 10:15)
@MINUTE(@NOW)	15 (assuming that it's now 10:15)
@MINUTE(0.4274)	15

@SECOND(*time number*) OR @SEC(*time number*)   Returns the second corresponding to *time number*. The calculated value is between 0 and 59. *Time number* can be obtained from either the @TIMEVAL, @TIME, or @NOW functions, or from a cell containing a time number.

FORMULA EXAMPLE	*SCREEN DISPLAY*
@SECOND(@TIMEVAL("10:15:30"))	30
@SECOND(@TIME(10,15,30)	30
@SECOND(R1C1)	30 (assuming that R1C1 contains the time 10:15:30)
@SECOND(@NOW)	30 (assuming that it's now 10:15:30)
@SECOND(0.4274)	30

@TIME(*hour,minute,second*)   Calculates the time number for the values *hour*, *minute*, and *second*. If an out-of-range value is used for any of these values, ERROR is displayed as the contents of the cell using this function.

FORMULA EXAMPLE	*SCREEN DISPLAY*
@TIME(20,15,30)	0.8441
@TIME(2,0,15)	0.0835
@TIME(25,10,5)	ERROR
@TIME(R1C1,R1C2,R1C3)	0.8441 (The three referenced cells are assumed to contain the values 20, 15, and 30.)

@TIMEVAL(time)   Calculates the time number for *time*. *Time* can be a valid time surrounded by double quote marks, or it can be a reference to a cell containing a valid time. Look at the following examples to see how @TIMEVAL differs from @TIME.

FORMULA EXAMPLE	*SCREEN DISPLAY*
@TIMEVAL("20:15:30")	0.8441
@TIMEVAL("10:25 pm")	0.9340
@TIMEVAL(R1C1)	0.9340 (R1C1 is assumed to contain the string *10:25 pm*.)
@TIMEVAL("14:25 PM")	ERROR

In the last example, the value ERROR is displayed because *14:25 PM* is not a legal format for a time (it could, however, be either *14:25* or *2:25 PM*).

TABLE FUNCTIONS

These functions are used for working with tables of values. A *table* is any rectangular array of cells within a spreadsheet.

@HLOOKUP(value, range, row-number)   This is a horizontal table-lookup function. Its purpose is to find a particular entry in a table of cells defined by *range*. *Value* is the search value, used for scanning the first row of the table. *Row-number* specifies the row of the table in which the desired cell is located, after the correct column has been found. *Value* can be either a number or a character string. If it's a string, it must be enclosed in double quotes.

To illustrate how this function works, we'll use the spreadsheet shown in Figure 7.7. The table in this figure is defined by the range

R1C1..R8C5. This table represents a feeding schedule for various farm animals. For example, on Mondays, pigs are each fed 7 pounds of food. You can use the @HLOOKUP function to find out how much to feed any animal on any day of the week. Suppose that you want to find out how much to feed turkeys on Thursday, then store the answer in cell R15C1 of the spreadsheet. To accomplish this, you would enter the following formula into that cell:

@HLOOKUP("turkeys",R1C1..R8C5,4)

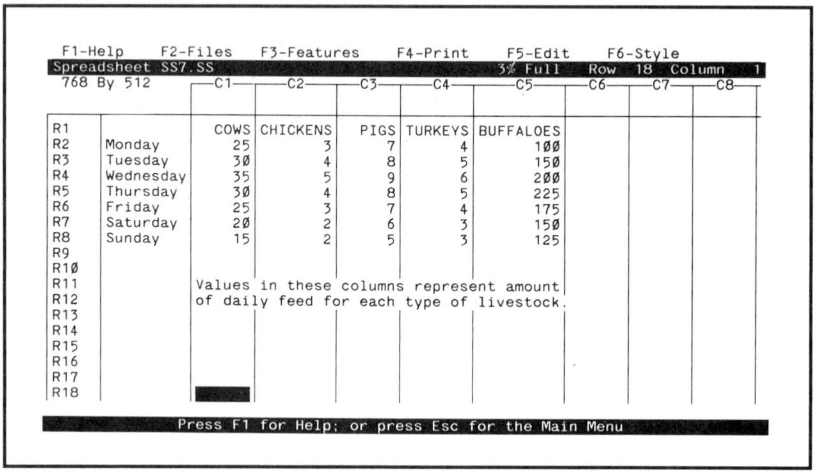

Figure 7.7: Spreadsheet containing an animal feeding schedule

Using this function, First Choice scans the top row of the table defined by the range R1C1..R8C5, starting at the leftmost value and working toward the right, until it finds the first label that exactly matches the search value (except for case)—*turkeys* in this example. This defines the proper column. Using that column, First Choice reads the value of the cell in the row specified by the value of the last argument—*4* in this case. For these purposes, the top row of the table is called row 0, the second is row 1, and so on. The value read from the table in this case is 5, which is returned as the calculated value of @HLOOKUP.

When using @HLOOKUP (*value, range, row-number*), the row of values to be scanned will be the first row of *range*, which is defined as row 0. *Row-number* must be less than the number of rows defined by *range*, or else ERROR will be returned as the value of @HLOOKUP.

If the search value *value* is numeric, then the values in the first row of the table must also be numeric, and they must be arranged sequentially, with the smallest value at the left. The search proceeds from right to left, until the first value is found in the row that's less than or equal to *value*. If *value* is less than the leftmost value in this row, @HLOOKUP returns a value of ERROR.

The first row can even contain formulas that generate numeric or text values. Using this to advantage might be difficult, because for numeric values, you'd need to guarantee that the calculated values were arranged sequentially.

Regardless of the type of values in the first row (either numeric or character), the remaining values in the table can be anything—numeric values, labels, or even formulas.

@VLOOKUP(value, range, col-number)   This is a vertical table-lookup function. It's similar to @HLOOKUP, except that the initial table scan is done on the first column instead of the first row. This function finds a particular entry in a table of cells defined by *range*. *Value* is the search value, used for scanning the first column of the table. *Col-number* specifies the column of the table in which the desired cell is located, after the correct row has been found.

To illustrate how this function works, we'll use the spreadsheet shown in Figure 7.8, using the @VLOOKUP function to search the table defined by the range R1C5..R5C9. The table in Figure 7.8 represents the following portion of an income tax table:

TAXABLE INCOME	SINGLE	MARRIED FILING JOINTLY	MARRIED FILING SEPARATELY	HEAD OF HOUSEHOLD
4,000–4,049	532	484	544	504
4,050–4,099	539	491	551	511
4,100–4,149	547	499	559	519
4,150–4,199	554	506	566	526
4,200–4,249	562	514	574	534

Entries in all columns except the first are values for tax due.

```
       F1-Help      F2-Files    F3-Features    F4-Print    F5-Edit     F6-Style
  Spreadsheet SS7.SS                                     2% Full   Row  16  Column   5
   768 By 512        -C5----C6-----C7------C8------C9----C10---C11----C12-
                               Married  Married
                     Taxable   Filing   Filing    Head of
                     Income   Single Jointly Separately Household

   R1                4.000    532     484      544       504
   R2                4.050    539     491      551       511
   R3                4.100    547     499      559       519
   R4                4.150    554     506      566       526
   R5                4.200    562     514      574       534
   R6
   R7
   R8
   R9
   R10
   R11
   R12
   R13
   R14
   R15
   R16

               Press F1 for Help; or press Esc for the Main Menu
```

Figure 7.8: Spreadsheet containing a tax table

Suppose that your taxable income is $4,075 and you are married, filing jointly. You want to find out how much tax to pay by using the table shown in Figure 7.8, and place the result in cell R10C1. To accomplish this, you would enter the following formula into that cell:

@VLOOKUP(4075,R1C5..R5C9,2)

Using this function, First Choice scans the leftmost column of the table, starting at the bottom and working up, until it finds the first value that's less than or equal to the search value—4075 in this case. This defines the proper row. Using that row, First Choice reads the value of the cell in the column specified by the value of the last argument—2 in this case. For these purposes, the first column of the table is called column 0, the second is column 1, and so on. The value read from the table in this example is 491.

When using @VLOOKUP (*value, range, col-number*), the column of values to be scanned must be the first column of *range*, which is defined as column 0. *Col-number* must be less than the number of columns defined by *range*, or else ERROR will be returned as the value of @VLOOKUP.

The numeric values in the first column of the table must be arranged sequentially, with the smallest value at the top. If *value* is less than the top value in this column, the value returned by @LOOKUP is ERROR.

This function can also be used when *value* is a character string. In this case, *value* must be enclosed in double quotes. In addition, the first column of the table must contain labels (character strings). In that case, the scan of the first column starts at the top, stopping at the first value that exactly matches *value*. If no match is found, then a value of ERROR is returned by @VLOOKUP.

Regardless of the type of values in the first column (either numeric or character), the remaining values in the table can be anything—numeric values, labels, or even formulas.

@INDEX(range, column-number, row-number) This function returns the value of a selected cell from within *range*. The cell is defined by the values *column-number* and *row-number*. Rows and columns are numbered sequentially, starting with zero. As an example of how to use this function, we'll use the table shown in Figure 7.9. Cell R10C4 contains the function @INDEX(R5C4..R8C7,2,3), which returns the value of cell R8C6—namely 80.

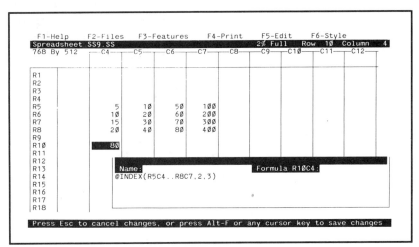

Figure 7.9: Table used by @INDEX function

STRING FUNCTIONS

These functions work with groups of characters, called *strings* or *labels*. A string can be just about any combination of characters—letters, digits, and various special characters such as $ or %. Most of the string functions perform some type of string manipulations. A few of the functions convert between strings and other data types.

Most of these functions take one or more arguments—usually strings. The arguments can usually be a reference to a cell containing a string, another function or calculation that returns a string, or a string enclosed in double quotes.

In general, string operations are insensitive to upper- and lower-case. We'll point out the exceptions as they're encountered.

Strings can be manipulated either by performing some type of operation with a string function, or by combining two strings with the ampersand (&) operator. This operator can also be used to combine two or more string functions.

Some of the functions manipulate parts of a string. In this case, the individual characters within the string are numbered, with the left-most character called position 0, the next character is position 1, and so on.

@CHAR(value) Returns the character whose numeric ASCII value is *value*. Each character in the standard ASCII character set has a unique value between 1 and 255. If *value* is a reference to a cell containing text or only blanks, @CHARACTER returns a value of ERROR. If *value* is larger than 255, then @CHAR returns the character corresponding to (*value*-256).

This function performs the opposite operation from the function @CODE.

FORMULA EXAMPLE	SCREEN DISPLAY
@CHAR(65)	A
@CHAR(R1C1)	A (where R1C1 contains the numerical value 65)
@CHAR(171)	½
@CHAR(R1C1)	ERROR (where R1C1 contains all blanks)
@CHAR(@CODE("abcd"))	a
@CHAR(3)	A
@CHAR(65) & @CHAR(83)	AS

@CODE(string)   Returns the ASCII value of the first character in *string*. This function performs the opposite operation from the function @CHAR. If *string* is a reference to a blank cell, then @CODE returns the value ERROR.

FORMULA EXAMPLE	*SCREEN DISPLAY*
@CODE("A")	65
@CODE("ABCD")	65
@CODE(R1C1)	65 (where R1C1 contains the string *ABCD*)
@CODE("25")	50
@CODE(@CHAR(65))	65
@CODE(R1C1)	ERROR (where R1C1 contains all blanks)

@EXACT(string1,string2)   Returns a value of TRUE if *string1* and *string2* are identical. When a string comparison is made, a blank is considered a valid character. Also, a distinction is made between upper and lower case. If either *string1* or *string2* is a reference to a cell containing either a numerical or a blank value, then @EXACT returns the value ERROR.

FORMULA EXAMPLE	*SCREEN DISPLAY*
@EXACT("abcd","abcd")	TRUE
@EXACT("abcd","Abcd")	FALSE
@EXACT("abcd","abcd")	FALSE
@EXACT("abcd",R1C1)	TRUE (where R1C1 contains the string *abcd*)
@EXACT("abcd",R1C1)	ERROR (where R1C1 contains a numeric value or blank value)

@FIND(test,string,start)   Searches the string *string* for the test string *test*, starting at position number *start* in *string*. If *test* is found within *string*, @FIND returns the starting position within *string*. Otherwise, the value ERROR is returned. If *start* is negative, the value ERROR is returned. This function makes a distinction between upper- and lowercase letters. Here, as with other string functions, the leftmost character of *string* is position 0.

FORMULA EXAMPLE	SCREEN DISPLAY
@FIND("a","cask",0)	1
@FIND("A","cask",0)	ERROR
@FIND("so","reason",0)	3
@FIND("so","reason",1)	3
@FIND("so","reason",4)	ERROR
@FIND(R1C1,R2C2,0)	0 (where both referenced cells contain exactly the same string)

@LEFT(string,m)   Returns the first *m* characters from *string*, beginning with the leftmost character. If *m* is greater than the number of characters in *string*, the entire string is returned. If *m* is negative, the value ERROR is returned.

FORMULA EXAMPLE	SCREEN DISPLAY
@LEFT("reason",3)	rea
@LEFT("reason",15)	reason
@LEFT(R1C1,3)	rea (where R1C1 contains the string *reason*)
@LEFT("abcd",2) & @LEFT("efg",1)	abe

@LENGTH(string)   Returns the total number of characters in *string*. Leading and internal blanks are included in the total character count.

FORMULA EXAMPLE	SCREEN DISPLAY
@LENGTH("abcd")	4
@LENGTH(R1C1)	4 (where R1C1 contains the string *abcd*)
2*@LENGTH("abcd")	8
@LENGTH("ab" & "cd")	4
@LENGTH(R1C1 & R2C2)	4 (where the two cells contain the strings "ab" and "cd")

The last two examples above illustrate an important principle: the argument of a string function can be the combination of two separate strings.

@LOWER(string)   Converts *string* into lowercase letters.

FORMULA EXAMPLE	SCREEN DISPLAY
@LOWER("ABCD")	abcd
@LOWER("ABcd")	abcd
@LOWER(R1C1)	abcd (where R1C1 contains the string *abcd*)
@LOWER("AB" & "CD")	abcd

@MID(string,start,m)   Returns a group of characters from within *string*. The starting position of the returned string is given by *start*, and *m* is the total number of characters returned, including any spaces. If *start* points to beyond the last character, then @MID returns an empty string: "".

Here, as with any string operations (except @LENGTH), the leftmost character of *string* is considered to be at position 0.

FORMULA EXAMPLE	SCREEN DISPLAY
@MID("abcde",1,3)	bcd
@MID(R1C1,1,3)	bcd (where R1C1 contains the string *abcde*)
@MID("The End",1,4)	he E

@PROPER(string)   The first letter of each word in *string* is converted to uppercase, and the remaining letters to lowercase. A new word is considered to be the first character after a blank. If a word begins with a nonalphabetic character, it's skipped, and the first alphabetic character of that word is converted.

FORMULA EXAMPLE	SCREEN DISPLAY
@PROPER(sam spade)	Sam Spade
@PROPER(R1C1)	Sam Spade (where R1C1 contains *sam spade*)
@PROPER(sAM sPADE)	Sam Spade
@PROPER(sam ?spade)	Sam ?Spade
@PROPER(R1C1 & R2C2)	Sam Spade (where the two cells contain "Sam" and "Spade")

@REPEAT(string,m)   This function returns the value of *string* repeated *m* times.

FORMULA EXAMPLE	SCREEN DISPLAY
@REPEAT("abcd",3)	abcdabcdabcd
@REPEAT(R1C1,3)	abcdabcdabcd (where R1C1 contains the string *abc*)

@REPLACE(first string,start,m,final string)   Removes *m* characters from *first string*, starting at position *start*. Then, the text specified by *final string* is inserted starting at position *start*. The first character of *first string* is position 0.

FORMULA EXAMPLE	SCREEN DISPLAY
@REPLACE("hate me",0,4,"love")	love me
@REPLACE("bite it",5,2,"down")	bite down
@REPLACE("Sam",3,0," Spade")	Sam Spade
@REPLACE("Roger Rabbit",0,6,"")	Rabbit

The third example above shows how @REPLACE can be used to combine two different strings. In the last example, we've deleted text from the beginning of the initial string, but we've made *final string* empty, so that no new text is added.

@RIGHT(string,m)   Returns the rightmost *m* characters of *string*. If *m* is greater than the length of *string*, then the entire string is returned.

FORMULA EXAMPLE	SCREEN DISPLAY
@RIGHT("mushroom",4)	room
@RIGHT(R1C1,4)	room (where R1C1 contains the string *mushroom*)
@RIGHT(LEFT("abcdef ",4),2)	cd

@STRING(value,places)   Converts *value* to a string, with *places* positions to the right of the decimal point. The value of *places* must be between -15 and 15. If *places* is less than zero, then it specifies the number of places to be rounded to zero to the left of the decimal point. If *value* contains more decimal places than is specified by *places*, First Choice rounds the result. @STRING performs the opposite operation from the function @VALUE.

FORMULA EXAMPLE	SCREEN DISPLAY
@STRING(25,3)	25.000
@STRING(25.34,0)	25.
@STRING(25.146,2)	25.15
@STRING(2534, -2)	2500
@STRING(@VALUE("25.1"),1)	25.1

@TRIM(string)   This function strips off any leading or trailing blanks from *string*, replaces consecutive internal spaces to a single space, then returns the resulting string.

FORMULA EXAMPLE	SCREEN DISPLAY
@TRIM("my uncle ")	my uncle
@TRIM(" my uncle")	my uncle
@TRIM(R1C1)	my uncle (where R1C1 contains the string " my uncle")
@TRIM("my uncle")	my uncle

@UPPER(*string*)   Converts *string* to all uppercase.

FORMULA EXAMPLE	SCREEN DISPLAY
@UPPER("sam spade")	SAM SPADE
@UPPER(R1C1)	SAM SPADE (where R1C1 contains the string "sam spade")
@UPPER("Sam Spade")	SAM SPADE

@VALUE(*string*)   Converts *string* to its equivalent numeric form. If *string* is an empty string, this function returns a value of 0. If *string* contains anything other than the test equivalent of a valid number, then @VALUE returns the value ERROR. This function performs the opposite operation as @STRING.

In the following examples, the global style is assumed to be two decimal places.

FORMULA EXAMPLE	SCREEN DISPLAY
@VALUE("25.37")	25.37
@VALUE(R1C1)	25.37 (where R1C1 contains the string *25.37*)
@VALUE("abcd")	ERROR
@VALUE(@STRING(25,3))	25.00
@VALUE(3.14E3)	3140.00

The last example illustrates that @VALUE can convert numbers written in scientific notation.

LOGICAL FUNCTIONS

These functions are used for working with yes/no or true/false situations. Most of these functions evaluate some type of *logical condition*, whose value is either TRUE or FALSE. In many cases, a function simply returns a value of TRUE or FALSE.

@FALSE   Returns the value FALSE. Internally, First Choice uses a special number to represent the value FALSE. This function can be used by itself to set the value of a cell to FALSE, or it can be used within other logical functions.

FORMULA EXAMPLE	SCREEN DISPLAY
@FALSE	FALSE

@IF (R1C1 > Ave_Sales)
    THEN @ TRUE
    ELSE @FALSE
	TRUE or FALSE (depending on the value of the expression)

@ISERR(value)   If the value of *value* is ERROR, then this function returns the value TRUE. Otherwise, the value returned is FALSE. ERROR is a special internal number used by First Choice. When a cell has this value, the value ERROR is displayed for the cell. A cell can have a value of ERROR in two ways: (1) it contains the formula @ERROR, which returns the value of ERROR, or (2) it contains a formula that, because of an error condition, returns the value ERROR.

FORMULA EXAMPLE	SCREEN DISPLAY
@ISERR(R1C1/0.0)	TRUE (because division by zero generates an error condition)
@ISERR(R1C1)	TRUE (if the value of R1C1 is ERROR)
	FALSE (if the value of R1C1 is not ERROR)

@ISNUMBER(value)   If *value* is a numerical quantity, then this function returns a value of TRUE. Otherwise, a value of FALSE is returned. If *value* contains all blanks, TRUE is returned.

FORMULA EXAMPLE	SCREEN DISPLAY
@ISNUMBER(5.0)	TRUE
@ISNUMBER("Hi!")	FALSE
@ISNUMBER(R1C1)	TRUE or FALSE (depending on whether or not R1C1 contains a number)
@ISNUMBER (@TRUE)	TRUE (because @TRUE returns the value TRUE, which is a special number used by First Choice)
@ISNUMBER (@ISNUMBER(*anything*))	TRUE (because @ISNUMBER returns either TRUE or FALSE, both of which are special numbers used by First Choice)
@ISNUMBER (@STRING(R1C1))	FALSE (because @STRING returns a string value)

@ISSTRING(value)   If *value* is a string (also called a *label*), this function returns a value of TRUE. Otherwise, a value of FALSE is returned.

FORMULA EXAMPLE	SCREEN DISPLAY
@ISSTRING("abcd")	TRUE
@ISSTRING(25)	FALSE
@ISSTRING(@STRING(R1C1))	TRUE (because @STRING returns a string value)

@TRUE   Returns the value TRUE. Internally, First Choice uses a special number to represent the value TRUE. This function can be used by itself to set the value of a cell to TRUE, or it can be used within other logical functions.

FORMULA EXAMPLE	SCREEN DISPLAY
@TRUE	TRUE
@IF (R1C1 > Ave_Sales) THEN @TRUE ELSE @FALSE	TRUE or FALSE (depending on the value of the logical expression)

@IF (relational expression) THEN (value1) ELSE (value2)   Returns either *value1* or *value2*, depending on whether the expression *relational expression* is true or false. *Value1* and *value2* must be numeric. We'll give two examples, then discuss relational expressions.

For our first example, suppose that a spreadsheet contains a cell (named AGE) that represents the age of an employee. Employees over 21 years of age are entitled to certain benefits, and you want to use the spreadsheet to determine whether or not the particular employee represented by AGE is entitled to these benefits. You would use a separate cell to contain the following formula that displays either the value 1 or 0 for *Yes* or *No*:

@IF AGE > 21 THEN 1 ELSE 0

The value displayed will be either 1 or 0, depending on whether or not the value of AGE is greater than 21.

The @IF function tests the value of AGE: If the value is greater than 21, then the value of the current cell (the one containing the @IF..-THEN..ELSE function) is set equal to 1 (employee gets benefits). Otherwise, the value of the cell is set equal to 0 (no benefits).

In this next example, you want to give all adult employees who earn less than $5,000 a 10% raise. The cell AGE contains an employee's age, and SALARY contains the same employee's current salary. A separate cell will display either 1 for *Yes* or 0 for *No*. The formula you'd use is

@IF (AGE > 21) AND (SALARY < 5,000) THEN 1 ELSE 0

The resulting value will be 1 or 0.

The @IF function examines the two cells AGE and SALARY and looks for the following conditions: the value of AGE is greater than 21, and the value of SALARY is less than 5,000. If both conditions are true, then the value of the current cell is set equal to 1 (employee gets a 10% raise). Otherwise, the value is set equal to 0 (no raise).

In both examples above, a *relational expression* was used to determine whether something was true or false. In the first example, the relational expression was AGE > 21. The symbol > (greater than) is one of six *relational operators*, listed in Table 7.2.

> When a relational expression is evaluated, the result is always either TRUE or FALSE.

Table 7.2: Relational Operators

OPERATOR	MEANING
=	Equal to
< >	Not equal to
>	Greater than
<	Less than
> =	Greater than or equal to
< =	Less than or equal to

When the expression AGE > 21 is evaluated, the value of AGE is compared with the value 21. If AGE is greater than 21, the final value of the expression is TRUE. Otherwise, the value is FALSE.

There are three *logical operators* that can be used to help in writing complicated relational expressions—AND, OR, and NOT. These operators can be used to combine different relational expressions in various ways. For example, here's a pair of relational expressions combined into one larger expression:

IF (AGE > 21) AND (SALARY < 5,000)

If *both* of the expressions are true, then the final value is TRUE. If either of the expressions is false, then the final value is FALSE. (We've used optional pairs of parentheses to separate each logical expression.)

Here's an example that uses the logical operator OR:

@IF (AGE < 21) OR (AGE > 65)

If either of the two expressions is true, then the final value is TRUE. If both expressions are false, then the value of the entire expression is FALSE.

The operator NOT is used to reverse the value of the logical expression that immediately follows it. For example, look at

IF NOT((AGE < 21) OR (AGE > 65))

Because the entire expression has been enclosed in a pair of outer parentheses, it is negated. If either of the expressions is true, then the final value is FALSE. If both expressions are false, then the final value is TRUE.

Suppose that you are building a spreadsheet to contain data about a group of salespersons. As part of this spreadsheet, you want to include a visual indicator for each individual, showing whether he or she is above or below the average performance for all salespersons. Figure 7.10 shows part of this spreadsheet. Column C1 lists the yearly sales for each salesperson. The next column shows the performance index for each person; it has a value of 99999 if the person's sales are above average, otherwise it has a value of zero.

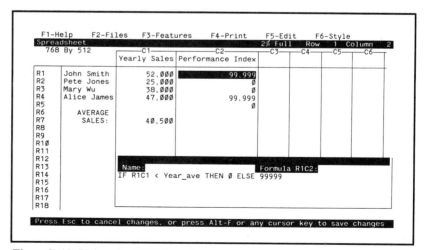

Figure 7.10: Using the @IF function

The performance index is calculated by a formula for each salesperson, and the Formula Box in Figure 7.10 shows this formula for the first salesperson. In these formulas, *Year_Ave* is the name of cell R7C1, which is another formula that calculates the average sales for all of the staff: @AVG(R1C1..R4C1).

The remaining cells in column C2 contain formulas similar to that in R1C2.

SUMMARY

The use of formulas in cells can enhance the usefulness of spreadsheets. Formulas can consist of numerical constants, references to other cells, and built-in functions, all linked with numeric or string operators. Combinations of formulas can also be used to enable spreadsheets to perform complex interconnected calculations. When used in conjunction with First Choice's macro facility, formulas offer the user an especially powerful tool.

Chapter
8

Creating
Graphs

First Choice contains a module that can generate various types of graphs. With the graph module you can create graphs from preexisting data in a First Choice spreadsheet, or you can enter new data directly into the module.

A graph can be produced on a printer, plotter, computer screen, or disk file. It can be generated as a stand-alone item, or incorporated into a printed document.

First Choice allows you to present data in a variety of graphical formats. Once you have entered a set of data into the computer, you can easily experiment with the options, choosing the graph type that best suits your needs.

This chapter presents a survey of the basic graph types and describes how to create a graph. You'll learn how to save and retrieve graphs of different types, and how to print and plot graphs. Then you'll be shown how to generate graphs from spreadsheet data. Finally, you'll get a look at how to incorporate graphs with documents.

INTRODUCING THE GRAPH TYPES

When you want to present a set of data in graphical form, you need to decide on the best type of graph to use. Sometimes, the choice is obvious; in other cases the selection will depend on the intended audience as well as on personal preference. In this section, we'll present an overview of the types of graphs that can be produced by First Choice, and give you suggestions as to which types are best suited to certain situations.

BAR GRAPHS

Figure 8.1 shows a simple bar graph that presents the monthly software sales of the XYZ Corporation for several months. Notice how the bars call attention to the individual values of monthly sales. This is in contrast to line graphs (described later), which indicate general trends rather than individual values.

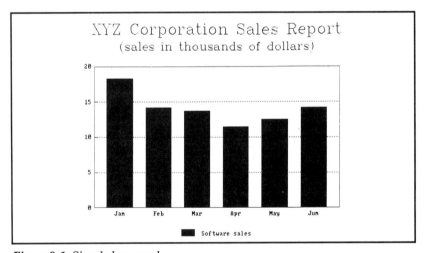

Figure 8.1: Simple bar graph

GRAPH AXES   The graph in Figure 8.1 contains features common to several different types of graphs. The horizontal axis, also called the *x-axis,* is the line at the bottom of the graph. The figure's horizontal axis measures time—in this case months. The vertical axis, also called the *y-axis,* is the line on the left-hand side of the figure. In Figure 8.1, the y-axis measures monthly sales in terms of dollars.

LEGENDS AND GRID LINES   The *legend* of a graph helps define what the graph is showing. In Figure 8.1, the legend indicates that the solid bars represent software sales. Legends are particularly important when more than one set of data is depicted on the same graph.

The horizontal dotted *grid lines* in Figure 8.1 help the eye measure heights of individual bars and compare the bar heights.

DATA SERIES   The set of data represented in Figure 8.1 is referred to as a *data series,* or simply *series.* A data series always consists of two columns of data. One column represents values of something of interest, such as total sales, test grades, etc. The other column indicates when, where, or how the numbers in the first column are measured. Often this second column measures time.

Here is the numerical data that makes up the series in Figure 8.1:

MONTH	SOFTWARE SALES
Jan	18.32
Feb	14.17
Mar	13.71
Apr	11.49
May	12.54
Jun	14.22

COMPLEX BAR GRAPHS   Bar graphs can also be used to show comparisons among different quantities. For example, the *combination bar graph* in Figure 8.2 shows both software and hardware monthly sales for the XYZ Corporation. The legend at the bottom of the figure indicates which bars represent hardware and which represent software. This figure shows that if two (or more) series of data have the same values for the horizontal axis, First Choice can plot them on the same graph.

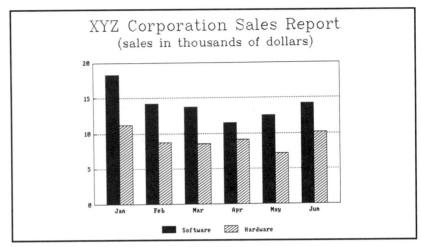

Figure 8.2: Combination bar graph

Here are the two data series plotted in Figure 8.2:

MONTH	SOFTWARE SALES	HARDWARE SALES
Jan	18.32	11.20
Feb	14.17	8.78
Mar	13.71	8.55
Apr	11.49	9.11
May	12.54	7.12
Jun	14.22	10.11

LINE GRAPHS

A line graph is a common way of showing one or more series of data. Figure 8.3 displays a line graph for two series of data. The individual data points are shown as blips on the graph, and the legend at the bottom of the figure shows which blips correspond to each series. The blips for each of the series are connected by straight line segments.

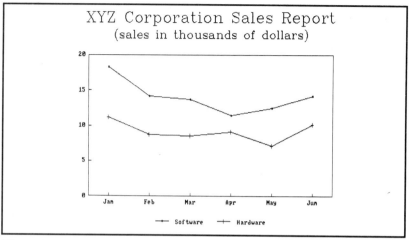

Figure 8.3: Line graph

POINT PLOTS

Another type of graph used to emphasize trends is the *point plot,* also called the *scatter plot.* For example, Figure 8.4 shows a point plot of the same data used in Figure 8.3. The figures are the same, except that in the point plot, the line segments between points have not been plotted. To help in reading the individual data values, horizontal grid lines are frequently used.

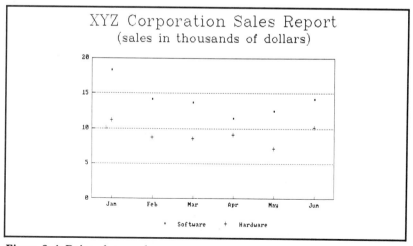

Figure 8.4: Point plot graph

TREND GRAPHS   The point graph in Figure 8.4 may not seem as useful as earlier types of graphs. However, we can do something creative by drawing a *best-fit curve* through the data points, as shown in Figure 8.5. This type of figure is very useful for showing general trends.

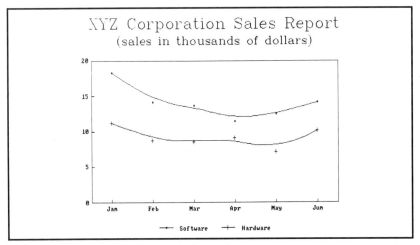

Figure 8.5: Best-fit curve through data points

Another type of trend graph features a best-fit straight line drawn through a point plot of a set of data points. Figure 8.6 shows a point plot for a set of data points. Each data point represents two quantities: the total number of automobiles sold in a particular month, and for that same month, the number of days on which rain fell. In Figure 8.6, a best-fit straight line has been drawn through the data points. This line shows that there is almost a linear relationship between new car sales and the amount of rainfall.

AREA GRAPHS

Another type of graph is an area graph, which combines some of the features of both bar and line graphs. Figure 8.7 shows an area graph of the same data shown in earlier figures.

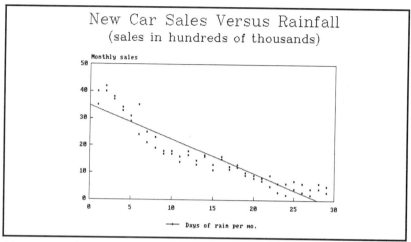

Figure 8.6: Best-fit straight line through scatter plot

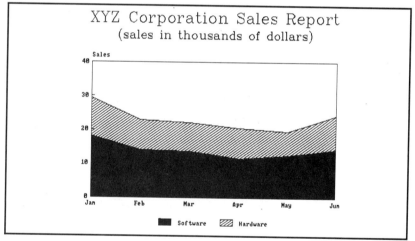

Figure 8.7: Area graph

PIE GRAPHS

The pie graph shown at the left in Figure 8.8 illustrates the components of total yearly sales for a company. For emphasis, one of the pie slices has been "exploded," or set apart, in the figure. A variation of the pie graph, the column pie graph, is illustrated at the right in the same figure.

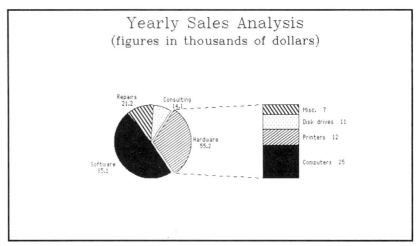

Figure 8.8: Linked pie graphs

As shown, First Choice can draw two pie graphs on the same figure. These can be completely unrelated graphs, or they can be linked. For example, the column pie on the right is a breakdown of one slice of the other pie—namely hardware sales.

HIGH/LOW/CLOSE GRAPHS

This is a specialized type of graph, used primarily to display stock or bond prices over a period of time. Figure 8.9 shows the variation in

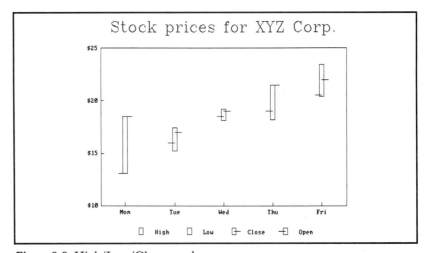

Figure 8.9: High/Low/Close graph

prices for a particular stock over a five-day period. The upper and lower limits of each column show the high and low prices for each day. The horizontal bars protruding from each column indicate the opening and closing prices of the stock.

HOW TO BUILD A NEW GRAPH

This section describes how to generate each of the graph types available with First Choice. First, you'll be given some details that apply to all types of graphs. Then each graph type will be discussed separately.

USING THE GRAPH MODULE

In order to generate a graph from a set of data, First Choice's graph module must be used. There are three ways you can use this module.

- New data can be entered directly into the graph module. The data can then be graphed.

- Existing data in a spreadsheet can be used directly to produce graphs. A graph generated this way is automatically saved as part of the spreadsheet. The advantage of this approach is that the spreadsheet data is directly linked to the graph. In other words, if data in the spreadsheet changes, the graph automatically reflects the changes. Up to eight graphs can be directly linked to a spreadsheet.

- Existing data from a spreadsheet can be copied into the graph module, then graphed. The advantage of this approach is that you may want to edit the data before graphing it, without affecting the original spreadsheet data. When data is copied from a spreadsheet, the new data in the graph module is not linked in any way to the original spreadsheet.

AN OVERVIEW OF THE GRAPHING PROCESS

Some of these steps do not need to be performed in this order.

Begin the graphing process by selecting the graph module from the Main menu. Enter the data to be graphed. This can be one or more data series.

Next, select the type of graph to be generated. (You may wish to try different types of graphs for a given set of data.) Next, choose the graph options. These include titles, labels for the data, and other items that affect the way in which the graph is displayed.

Finally, generate the graph, either on a printer, plotter, or computer screen, and save the graph to a disk file. After a graph has been stored in a file, it can be retrieved later. Modifications to the data and/or the options can be made, and a new graph can then be generated.

ENTERING AND EDITING DATA

To get started, select *Create a graph* from the Main menu. When the Graph Information Form appears, you can begin entering data for one or more series into this form, as shown in Figure 8.10. For example, this figure shows the Graph Information form with the data for the graph in Figure 8.2.

```
  F1-Help      F2-Files    F3-Features    F4-Print    F5-Edit    F6-Style
 Graph                                                  Series B   Value  9
            6Ø By 8                    ┌─C1─             ┌─C2─
                         Legends:        Software          Hardware
            ┌─Labels─
   R1  │ Jan                            18.32              11.2Ø
   R2  │ Feb                            14.17               8.78
   R3  │ Mar                            13.71               8.55
   R4  │ Apr                            11.49               9.11
   R5  │ May                            12.54               7.12
   R6  │ Jun                            14.22              1Ø.11
   R7  │
   R8  │
   R9  │
   R1Ø │
   R11 │
   R12 │
   R13 │
   R14 │
   R15 │
   R16 │
   R17 │
   R18 │
                Press F1 for Help; or press Esc for the Main Menu
```

Figure 8.10: Filled-in Graph Information form

The layout of the Graph Information form is similar to that of a spreadsheet. Rows are labeled R1, R2, etc., and columns are labeled C1, C2, and so on. The intersection of a row and a column is a *cell*, referred to by its row and column numbers. For example, the cell at the intersection of row 1 and column 2 is labeled R1C2.

LABELS The column marked *Labels* contains values that will appear along the horizontal axis of most types of graphs. For pie graphs, this column contains the labels for each slice of the pie.

Values in the Labels column can be either alphanumeric strings or numbers. Each string can contain up to 20 characters. As with other First Choice modules, numbers can contain any of the following characters:

- The digits 0 through 9
- Either a single decimal point or none at all
- A single plus or minus sign before the number (plus signs are optional)
- Optional commas for large numbers

Numbers in the Labels column can also be written in scientific notation. For instance, the number 1000 can be written as 1.0E3.

In general, you should limit the number of characters in each of the values in the Labels column, so that they can all fit along the horizontal axis of whatever graph is generated. If the total number of characters is too large, First Choice truncates as many characters as needed. This is true both for strings and numbers.

You can edit the values in the Labels column as you would any First Choice data. You can even cut and paste labels from one row to another.

If the labels are numeric, check the graph to make sure that significant digits have not been truncated.

LEGENDS The *legend,* or identifier, for each data series appears in the Legends row, which consists of the values at the top of each column. Legends are particularly important because they appear on the final graph. For this reason, you should choose descriptive values for them. Each legend can be up to 20 characters long, but if there are too many characters in too many legends, First Choice truncates characters to accommodate the limitations of the graph size.

The default values for the legends are *Series A, Series B,* and so on, up to *Series H.* You can change these legends simply by overwriting them with other values. Alternatively, you can move the cursor to the desired legend, erase it with Alt-W, then enter the new legend. If you leave a legend blank, it prints on the graph as the default value, such as *Series A.*

Check the legends on the final graph to make sure that they read properly.

You can edit the legends as you would any First Choice data. Legends can be cut and pasted from one column to another.

VALUES FOR THE DATA SERIES Data for the first series is entered into column C1. These must be numbers, conforming to the rules for numbers listed above. For most graphs, these values represent the height of the data points or bars. For pie graphs, these values determine the relative sizes of the pie slices.

Additional series of data can be entered into columns C2, C3, and so on. If an entire row of values is blank, it's ignored when a graph is generated. Up to eight series can be entered into the form, and up to 60 data points can be entered for each series.

Some types of graphs have specific rules regarding the data in the Graph Information form. These rules are discussed in the sections dealing with those graph types.

USING CURSOR AND EDITING KEYSTROKES The keystrokes for moving the cursor are the same as those used within a spreadsheet. You also can use the Alt-G speed key to go directly to a particular cell. Because there are a few variations from other parts of First Choice, we've included the entire repertoire of cursor-movement keystrokes in Table 8.1.

Table 8.1: Keystrokes for Editing Graph Data

CURSOR MOVEMENT	KEYSTROKE
Left and right within a cell	← and →
Down one row	↵ or ↓
Up one row	Shift ↵ or ↑
Right one column	Tab
Left one column	Shift-Tab
To the beginning of a row	Home
To the last value in a row	End
To the top of a column	Ctrl-PgUp

Table 8.1: Keystrokes for Editing Graph Data (continued)

CURSOR MOVEMENT	KEYSTROKE
To the last value in a column	Ctrl-PgDn
To cell R1C1	Ctrl-Home
To the last data row of Series H	Ctrl-End
To the next screen (down)	PgDn
To the previous screen (up)	PgUp
To a specific cell	Alt-G

Most of First Choice's standard editing keystrokes can be used to enter and edit data. Either the Insert or Overwrite modes can be used. In addition, the value of a single cell can be quickly erased by moving the cursor to that cell, then pressing Alt-W. Entire columns or rows of data can be deleted, or the entire graph (all of the data on the Graph Information screen) can be erased, by using the appropriate options from the Edit menu. A new row or column can be inserted between existing ones, again by using selections from the Edit menu.

Data can't be pasted from the regular data area into the Legends row or the Labels column.

Specific groups of cells can be cut and pasted in the usual way. Select the desired group of cells by defining the beginning of the range with the speed key Alt-S, then expanding the range with cursor-movement keys. Use Alt-M (or Alt-C) to move (or copy) the range of values to the clipboard. Using Alt-M is also a handy way to erase a range of values. Use Alt-P to paste values from the clipboard to a new set of cells.

These cut-and-paste operations can be useful for interchanging columns of data. This is sometimes necessary when a particular type of graph requires that certain columns of data appear in a specific order.

The style of a single cell or a group of cells can be specified in the same manner as for spreadsheets (see "Changing Cell Styles" in Chapter 6). However, changing the style of a cell affects only the screen display. There is no effect on the final graph. The style of data in the Labels column can't be changed.

CREATING BAR GRAPHS

A bar graph is one of the most common ways of presenting data. In this section we'll create the bar graph shown in Figure 8.11, using the following data:

MONTH	SALES
Jan	15,000
Feb	19,500
Mar	22,000
Apr	21,500
May	18,000
Jun	15,000

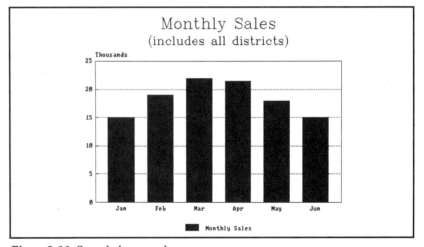

Figure 8.11: Sample bar graph

ENTERING DATA   We'll begin by entering the labels, legend, and data for the graph:

1. Make sure that the Graph Information form is displayed.

2. Move the cursor to the cell in the first row (R1) of the Labels column.

3. Enter **Jan** in the cell.

4. Press Alt-Q to begin quick entry, then press ← several times to enter the remaining labels.

5. Move the cursor to column C1 in the Legends area. To do this, press Ctrl-Home to get to the top of the data area in column C1, then press Ctrl ← to move up into the Legends area.

6. Make sure that you're in the Overwrite mode. Then enter the legend **Sales**, overwriting all of the original legend *Series A*.

7. Move the cursor to cell R1C1, then enter the first value, **15,000**.

8. Move the cursor to cell R2C1 and continue entering the data values, one per cell, using the data listed above.

ENTERING GRAPH TYPE AND TITLES Before you can have First Choice produce a graph, you must select the type of graph to be generated. In addition, you can supply a title, subtitle, and footnote for the graph. You can also choose the font that you want the titles to appear in. Titles always appear centered at the top of the graph. The footnote appears in the lower left-hand corner.

Let's choose the graph type, then enter the title and subtitle for our graph:

1. Select *Set graph options* from the Features menu.

2. When the Graph Options menu appears, select *Set graph type*.

3. From the Graph Type menu, choose *Bar/Line Graph*. Notice how First Choice divides the graph types into four major categories.

4. When the Graph Options menu reappears, choose *Enter titles*. The Graph Titles menu will then appear (Figure 8.12).

5. Begin by entering **Monthly Sales** for the main title.

6. Using the Tab key, move to the *Subtitle* line. Enter the subtitle **(includes all districts)**. This will appear under the main title.

7. Press ← to exit back to the Graph Options menu. (Note that we chose not to enter a footnote or select an alternate font.)

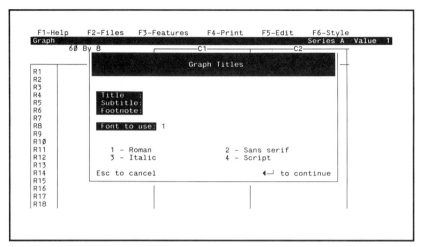

Figure 8.12: Graph Titles menu

DISPLAYING THE GRAPH   You are now ready to display the graph. Make sure that the Graph Options menu is displayed. Select *Draw graph,* and the graph shown in Figure 8.11 should appear. You can also draw the graph when the Graph Information form is displayed: either press the speed key Alt-D, or select *Draw graph* from the Features menu. If your computer doesn't have a graphics board, you can create, edit, save, print, and plot graphs, but you won't be able to display the graph on your screen.

SAVING THE GRAPH   Let's save the graph on a file. In a later section, we'll retrieve this data and practice generating other types of graphs.

1. Select *Save a copy of this graph* from the Files menu.

2. When the Graph File Format appears, select *First Choice Graph.*

3. When the Directory Assistant appears, enter the name **GRAFME** for the file in which the graph will be stored. (If you want to save the file on a disk drive or directory other than the current ones, first enter the appropriate name(s).) Press ←┘, and the graph will be written to the file.

For more information about the different ways in which a graph can be stored, see "Storing and Retrieving Graph Data on Disk Files" in this chapter.

PRINTING THE GRAPH Now let's print the graph (for more details about printing, see "How to Print Graphs"). Make sure that the printer is on and ready to accept data from First Choice.

1. From the Print menu, select *Print graph,* and the Print Graph Options menu will appear.

2. You can change any of the displayed options by using the Tab and Shift-Tab keys to move the cursor to the desired option, then entering a new value.

3. Press ←— and your graph will be printed.

SELECTING SPECIAL OPTIONS FOR BAR GRAPHS In Figure 8.11 you see a graph that was drawn using various standard defaults supplied by First Choice. Many times, you may wish to change one or more of these defaults. In this section we'll describe these various options. Some of these options also apply to line graphs. We'll mention these as they come up.

To change an option, you must first have the Graph Information form displayed. Next, select *Set graph options* from the Features menu. When the Graph Options menu appears, select *Choose options.* The Bar/Line Graph Options display (Figure 8.13) then appears. At first glance, this display appears so complex that you might be tempted to give up computers. However, if you look at it part by part, you'll see that it's actually quite simple (like everything else after you understand it!).

Let's first examine the top part of the display—the table enclosed in a large rectangle. Note that there are eight columns in this table, labeled A through H. Each of these columns corresponds to one of the data series that's to be plotted.

Even though values are on the screen for all eight columns, a column is ignored unless there is data for that series. For example, if you have data only for the first series, the remaining seven columns are ignored, regardless of what's entered in these columns.

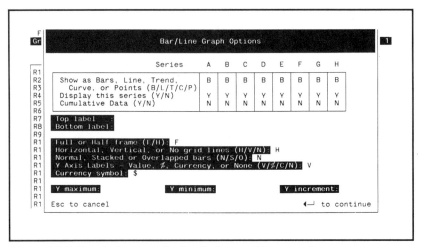

Figure 8.13: Graph Options display for bar and line graphs

Each column contains three options, which control how the data series for that column is to be displayed. The default options are "B," "Y," and "N." You can change these options, depending on how you want each series to be graphed; move the cursor to the desired position and type in the new value.

Show as Bars, Line, Trend, Curve, or Points (B/L/T/C/P) is the most important of the options. With it, you select the type of graph to be drawn for each series by entering the appropriate letter:

B   Bar graph

P   Point graph or scatter plot (data points are drawn alone, with no lines or curves)

L   Line graph (straight line segments connect each pair of data points)

T   Trend line graph (best-fit straight line is drawn through data points)

C   Best-fit curve (First Choice draws the best-fit smooth curve through data points)

Display this series is the next option on the screen. If you enter the value "N" in a column, the series is not plotted, even though you

You can combine different types of graphs. For example, one series might be plotted as a bar graph, another as a line graph, and a third as a point graph. Figure 8.8 gives an example of this type of combination.

have entered data for that series. This means you can enter data for several series, then choose which ones to graph by entering values of "Y" or "N."

Note that even though all series are marked with a default value of "Y," First Choice ignores this for any column that doesn't contain data.

The *Cumulative Data (Y/N)* option allows you to generate a particular type of graph: at each data point the value plotted is the sum of all values up to that point. For example, the data shown in Figure 8.1 can be plotted cumulatively, resulting in the graph in Figure 8.14. The bar for each month represents the total sales up to and including that month.

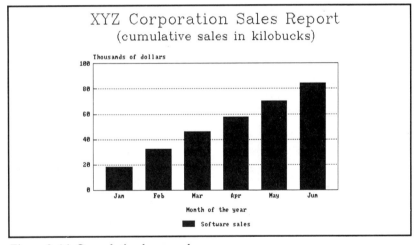

Figure 8.14: Cumulative bar graph

HOW TO MOVE THE CURSOR IN THE GRAPH OPTIONS DISPLAY Before going any further, let's see how to move the cursor in the Graph Options display. You do this a little differently than in other parts of First Choice.

CURSOR MOVEMENT	KEYS
Right or left one column	Tab or Shift-Tab
Up or down one line	↑ or ↓
Leave Graph Options display	↵

SELECTING ADDITIONAL OPTIONS   The bottom part of the Bar/Line Graph Options display contains other options relating to the appearance of the graph. These already have default options assigned, which you can leave alone or replace.

Top label appears at the top of the vertical axis; it can be used to identify the units of this axis. For example, in Figure 8.14 the top label reads *Thousands of dollars*.

Bottom label appears under the horizontal axis and can be used to identify the units of this axis. In Figure 8.14 this label is *Month of the year*.

Full or Half frame (F/H) determines how the graph is framed.

> F   A full rectangle is drawn around the graph, as shown in Figure 8.14.
>
> H   Lines are drawn only at the bottom and at the left-hand side of the graph (i.e., along the two axes).

First Choice cannot plot both horizontal and vertical grid lines on the same figure.

Horizontal, Vertical, or No grid lines (H/V/N) allows you to choose what type of grid lines—if any—to plot along with the graph. You may want to experiment with this option to determine which choice best enhances a particular graph.

> H   Horizontal grid lines are plotted. These can help you read individual values from a graph (see Figure 8.4 for example).
>
> V   Vertical grid lines are plotted. In some situations, these can help you interpret a graph.
>
> N   No grid lines are plotted.

Normal, Stacked, or Overlapped bars (N/S/O) applies only to bar graphs; it selects the type of bar graph to be drawn. Again, you may wish to experiment to find the best type of bar graph for your data.

> N   Normal bar graph (Figures 8.1 and 8.2).
>
> S   Stacked bar graph. If there is more than one series of data, series A is plotted at the bottom, then series B, and so on.

O   Overlapped bar graph. Series A is plotted on the top, then series B beneath A, then series C beneath B, and so on. Usually, this looks best with the largest values on the bottom. If necessary, you can rearrange the series by using the clipboard to cut and paste data.

Suppose you've chosen "O" for this last option, and you want to interchange the data in series A and B, so that the bars for the B series will lie on top of those for the A series. First, move all of the series A data to the clipboard. Paste this data to any blank column (column H, for example). Next, move the series B data to the clipboard. Paste this data to column A. Finally, move and paste the data from column H to column B.

Y-Axis Labels—Value, %, Currency, or None (V/%/C/N) are used for numbers displayed on the vertical axis. These numbers measure the height of bars or data points. You can control how the numbers appear by selecting one of the following values.

V   Numbers are displayed without dollar or percent signs.

%   Each number is followed by a percent sign.

C   Each number is preceded by a currency symbol (see below for selection of the currency symbol).

N   No numbers are plotted along the vertical axis.

Currency symbol lets you decide what currency symbol will be plotted along with each value on the vertical axis. Table 6.3 lists the possible choices for a currency symbol.

Y maximum, Y minimum, Y increment is the option at the bottom of the Bar/Line Graph Options display. You can use this option to override First Choice's selection of values to be displayed on the Y-axis. (This selection is based on the data values being graphed. The axis is divided into equal intervals, with the minimum and maximum values chosen to include all of the data values being graphed.)

If you prefer, you can supply a different set of values for the vertical axis.

Y maximum   Maximum value, placed at the top of the vertical axis.

Y minimum   Minumum value, placed at the bottom of the axis.

Y increment   The axis will be divided into a number of equal intervals, based on this value.

You might want to choose a particular set of values in order to emphasize one aspect of the graph. For example, suppose that the following values are selected:

Y maximum   10

Y minimum   2

Y increment   2

The values appearing on the vertical axis would be 2, 4, 6, 8, and 10.

The minimum and maximum values must include all data values on the graph. For example, if one or more data values is negative, then the value chosen for Y minimum must be negative and also less than or equal to the smallest negative number (remember that -5 is *less* than -4). If you break this rule, First Choice overrides your choices and selects appropriate values.

Also, the values for Y minimum, Y maximum, and Y increment must be chosen carefully for consistency. Otherwise, the intervals on the vertical axis will not all be the same. For example, if the three values chosen are 0, 10, and 3, the values appearing on the axis will be 0, 3, 6, and 9.

In some situations, First Choice forces Y minimum to be zero, regardless of what value you choose. For example, bar graphs are always plotted with a minimum Y-value of zero.

After you have made all of your choices in the Bar/Line Graph Options display, pressing ↵ returns you to the Graph Options menu. You can then make one of the following choices:

- Return to the Graph Information form by pressing the Esc key. You might do this if you decide to add or edit data, or to select an option from one of the other menus.

- Enter or edit the titles for the current graph.

- Select the graph type. You'll do this only if you decide to change the type of graph (see "Choosing the Graph Type" in this chapter). If you change the graph type, you may need to go back to the Graph Options display for that particular type of graph, in order to change some of the options.

- Draw the graph on the screen. When you make this selection, the current graph is displayed on the screen.

CREATING LINE GRAPHS

In the previous section "Creating Bar Graphs," you created a bar graph using the data provided in that section. Here you'll use that same data to generate a line graph. (You also could follow each of the steps using your own graph data.)

Retrieve the graph stored in the file GRAFME by choosing *Get an existing graph* either from the Main menu or the Files menu.

To create a line graph:

1. Select *Set graph options* from the Features menu.

2. When the Graph Options menu appears, select *Set Graph type*.

3. When the Graph Type menu appears, select *Bar/Line Graph*. Notice that this selection doesn't distinguish between bar and line graphs. You'll make that selection in the next menu.

4. When the Graph Options menu reappears, select *Choose options*. The Bar/Line Graph Options menu appears. This is the menu from which you select either a bar or a line graph (among many other options). For a complete discussion of this menu, see "Selecting Special Options for Bar Graphs."

5. The cursor should be positioned on the top line under *Series A*. The letter "B" in this entry indicates that series A is currently selected to be plotted as a bar graph. We want to change this to a line graph, so overwrite the "B" with the letter **L**.

6. Exit from this menu by pressing ←⟂.

You can display a line graph on the screen only if your computer has a graphics board.

DISPLAYING THE GRAPH   You can display the graph in several ways:

- From the Graph Information form, press the speed key Alt-D.
- From the Features menu, select *Draw graph*.
- From the Graph Options menu, select *Draw graph*.

To exit from the graph display on the screen, press any key.

PRINTING THE GRAPH   To print the graph, select *Print graph* from the Print menu. When the Print Graph Options menu appears, select any options you wish, then press ⏎. If the printer has paper and is ready, the graph will print.

SAVING THE GRAPH   You can save the line graph to a disk file for later use. Select *Save a copy of this graph* from the Files menu, then select *First Choice Graph* as the format for saving the graph. Finally, enter the name of the file to hold the graph information. You can choose the same name from which the graph was retrieved, or use a different file name. If you use the same name, the original graph information on the file will be replaced with the new data.

CREATING PIE GRAPHS

A pie graph is well suited to displaying the parts of a whole. When a pie graph is displayed, each value in a column of data (from the Graph Information form) is displayed as a single wedge of the pie. Information in the Labels column becomes identifying information for the wedges. A pie can contain up to 12 wedges; if your series contains more than 12 rows of data, only the first 12 are plotted. For emphasis, one or more wedges can be exploded from the pie.

You can plot two pies on the same figure, but no other type of graph can be plotted along with a pie. Pies come in two shapes: round and columnar, and these can be displayed on the same figure. Figure 8.8 illustrates both types of pies.

Let's create a pie graph.

1. Bring the Graph Information form to the screen. Then enter the data. If this data is stored in a file, simply retrieve that file.

2. Select *Set graph options* from the Features menu. The Graph Options menu will appear.

3. If you want to enter or change a title or subtitle, select *Enter titles,* then enter the new title or subtitle. Press ← when you're finished.

4. From the Graph Options menu, select *Set graph type.*

5. Choose *Pie Graph.*

DISPLAYING THE GRAPH   To display the graph from the Graph Options menu, select *Draw graph.* If the Graph Information form is displayed, press the speed key Alt-D to display the graph.

SELECTING SPECIAL OPTIONS FOR PIE GRAPHS   The pie graph that you displayed above was created using various standard options supplied by First Choice. You can customize a graph in several ways. For example, you can change an ordinary pie to a column pie. Also, you can display two pies on the same figure. Pie wedges can be sorted and exploded, and two pies can be linked together.

To choose one or more of these options, display the Pie Graph Options menu from the Graph Information form by selecting *Set graph options* from the Features menu, then selecting *Choose options.* The Pie Graph Options menu appears (Figure 8.15).

This menu is divided into two parts; we'll discuss each separately.

If two pies are to be graphed together, Pie 1 will appear on the left, and Pie 2 on the right.

SELECTING THE PRINCIPAL OPTIONS   First Choice allows one or two pies to be generated on the same graph. These are represented by the rightmost two columns in the display. The four rows for each of these columns are used to select suitable options for each pie. The default options are "A," "N," "P," and "V." These can be changed by moving the cursor to the appropriate option and overwriting the current value. Here are the options for this part of the display.

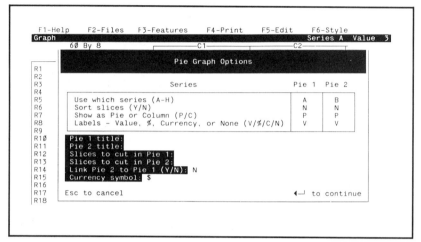

Figure 8.15: Graph Options display for pie graphs

Use which series (A-H) lets you specify which of the data series is to be used for Pie 1 and Pie 2. If you have entered two series of data, enter the series names (usually "A" and "B") in the Pie 1 and Pie 2 columns. If only one data series exists, enter its name in the column for Pie 1; the value listed in the Pie 2 column will be ignored.

If you've entered more than two data series, you must select which of them are to be graphed by entering their names ("A," "B," etc.) in the Pie 1 and Pie 2 columns.

Sort slices (Y/N) is the next option. Normally, when a pie is graphed, the slices are arranged in the order in which the data is entered into the Graph Information form. If you want the slices to be arranged by size, enter "Y" for this option. For column pies, the Y option arranges the slices so that the smallest is on top, the next smallest beneath it, and so on.

Show as Pie or Column (P/C) selects the shape of each displayed pie: "P" for a circular pie, "C" for a column-shaped one. Either option can be selected for either of the two pies. One interesting technique is to show the same data both as a circular pie and as a column pie on the same graph. This gives the data an "extra dimension."

Labels—Value, %, Currency, or None (V/%/C/N) is the final option in this section of the display. When a pie graph is drawn, the values in the Labels column of the Graph Information form are plotted next to the corresponding pie slices. In addition, the numbers in the appropriate series are displayed beside each slice, indicating the proportion of the pie taken up by that slice. You can control how these numbers appear by selecting one of the following values for this option:

V   Numbers are displayed without dollar or percent signs.

%   Each number is followed by a percent sign. When this option is chosen, each number is converted to a percent of the total, so that the sum of all values is approximately 100%.

C   Each number is preceded by a currency symbol (see below for selection of the currency symbol).

N   No numbers are plotted.

SELECTING ADDITIONAL OPTIONS   The bottom half of the Pie Graph Options display contains additional options that control the way the pie graphs appear.

Pie 1 title, Pie 2 title lets you enter a title for either or both pies. Each title can be up to 40 characters in length. However, if both pies have titles, some of each title may be truncated, because they both appear on the same line.

Slices to cut in Pie 1, Slices to cut in Pie 2 is the next option. For emphasis, one or more slices can be cut from either pie. You can select which slices are to be cut by entering the corresponding row numbers from the Graph Information form, separated by commas. For example, to cut Pie 1 slices for data entered in rows R1 and R4, enter 1,4 for the option *Slices to cut in Pie 1.*

Link Pie 2 to Pie 1 (Y/N) allows you to link one of the slices from Pie 1 to Pie 2. (When linking pies, the slice cut from Pie 1 is shown as being linked to Pie 2.) In other words, the data in Pie 2 can show the breakdown of one of the slices of Pie 1. Figure 8.8 shows an example of this; the data in Pie 2 represents a breakdown of the *Hardware* slice of Pie 1. To link two pies, select "Y" for this option.

In order to attach different labels to the two linked pies, data must be staggered on the Graph Information form. For example, Figure 8.16 shows the data plotted in the two pie graphs in Figure 8.8. This

A wedge can't be exploded from a column pie. First Choice ignores any selections for cutting from a column pie, except for purposes of linking pies.

trick can be used as well if you are plotting two completely different pies that each require their own labels.

```
   F1-Help    F2-Files   F3-Features    F4-Print    F5-Edit    F6-Style
  Graph 9P14.GRA                                          Labels  Value 15
          60 By 8                  ─────C1─────         ─────C2─────
                         Legends:     Series A             Series B
              ┌─Labels─┐
         R1   │Software              85
         R2   │Hardware              55
         R3   │Consulting            14
         R4   │Repairs               21
         R5   │
         R6   │Computers                                   25
         R7   │Printers                                    12
         R8   │Disk drives                                 11
         R9   │Misc.                                        7
         R10  │
         R11  │
         R12  │
         R13  │
         R14  │
         R15  │█████████████████
         R16  │
         R17  │
         R18  │

              Press F1 for Help; or press Esc for the Main Menu
```

Figure 8.16: The data plotted in Figure 8.8

When linking two pies, there are certain rules you should know:

- If no slice is cut from Pie 1, then no linking is shown on the graph.

- First Choice draws two straight lines to show a connection between two pies; it has no way of knowing whether or not the data is actually related. It is up to you to make sure that the data displayed by Pie 2 is actually the breakdown of the proper slice of Pie 1.

- When linking two pies, any combination of circular and column pies can be used. Note that if Pie 1 is a column pie, you must select a slice to be cut, even though it isn't shown being cut on the graph.

- If more than one slice is cut from Pie 1, the first slice listed on the Graph Information form is the one linked, unless the slices are sorted. In that case, the largest slice cut is the one linked to Pie 2.

Because of the last two rules above, you may need to move some of the rows of data around, so that the first data row corresponds to the slice that you want to link. You can do this by using First Choice's cut-and-paste feature with the help of the clipboard.

CREATING AREA GRAPHS

To generate this type of graph, follow these steps:

- Return to the Graph Information form by pressing the Esc key once or twice.

- Choose *Set graph options* from the Features menu. The Graph Options menu appears.

- Select *Set graph type* for the Graph Type menu.

- Choose *Area Graph* from this menu.

- When the Graph Options menu reappears, select *Choose options,* and the Area Graph Options display will appear (Figure 8.17).

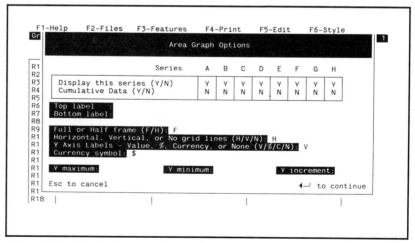

Figure 8.17: Graph Options display for area graphs

The Area Graph Options display is nearly identical to the Bar/Line Graph Options display (Figure 8.13), except that two entries specific to bar and line graphs don't appear here. For a discussion of the various options on this display, refer to the section "Selecting Special Options for Bar Graphs" earlier in this chapter.

Some special rules apply to data being plotted in an area graph. First, all data values must be zero or positive. Also, if two or more series are being plotted on the same graph, every series must have the same number of data points. Finally, an area graph can't be plotted on the same figure with any other type of graph.

When plotting an area graph, you may want to experiment a bit, to see which series looks the best on the bottom, which on top, and so on. As with other graph types, you may find that plotting too many series on the same graph can decrease the clarity of the presentation.

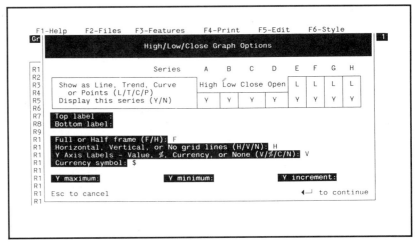

If a series contains one or more negative numbers or blank entries, the series will not be plotted.

CREATING HIGH/LOW/CLOSE GRAPHS

To generate this type of graph, return to the Graph Information form by pressing the Esc key once or twice. Choose *Set graph options* from the Features menu. The Graph Options menu appears. Select *Set graph type* for the Graph Type menu. Select *High/Low/Close Graph* from this menu. When the Graph Options menu reappears, select *Choose options,* and the High/Low/Close Graph Options display will appear (Figure 8.18).

Figure 8.18: Graph Options display for high/low/close graphs

This display is similar to the Bar/Line Graph Options display for bar and line graphs, with one very important difference: The first four data series—A, B, C, and D—are assumed to be values for *High, Low, Close,* and *Open.* For example, Figure 8.19 shows the data that's plotted in Figure 8.9. The first line of data shows the high, low, close, and open figures for Monday. The second line shows the figures for Tuesday, and so on.

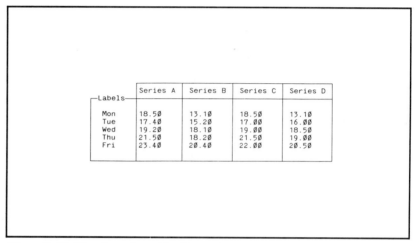

Figure 8.19: The data plotted in Figure 8.9

For each row that contains data, values *must* be supplied for series A and B—the high and low figures. Values for series C and D are optional.

You can plot other types of graphs along with the high/low/close graph. To do so, enter the additional data in the Graph Information form in series E, F, and so on. Then, select the graph type for each of these series on the first line of the Graph Options form.

For a discussion of the remaining options on the High/Low/Close Graph Options display, refer to "Selecting Special Options for Bar Graphs" earlier in this chapter.

CHANGING GRAPH TYPES

Once you have a series of data entered into the Graph Information form, you can easily switch back and forth between various graph types. To select the type of graph, select *Set graph options* from the Features menu, then select *Set graph type*. Choose a graph from the Graph Type menu that appears. To select either a bar, line, trend, curve, or points graph, first select Bar/Line as the graph type, then select *Choose options* from the Graph Options menu. When the Bar/Line Graph Options menu appears, select the type of graph from the top line of the display.

STORING AND RETRIEVING GRAPH DATA ON DISK FILES

When you have entered the raw data in a graph, then filled in the options such as titles, graph type, and so on, you can save this information (which we'll call *graph data*) to a disk file (which we'll call a *graph file*).

Graph data can be written to a graph file in a number of different formats, depending on its intended use. If you want to be able to retrieve the graph data into First Choice's graph module later, it should be written to disk in First Choice Graph format. If the graph data is to be used by some other software package, it should be stored in the appropriate format.

To save graph data to a disk, select *Save a copy of this graph* from the Files menu. The Graph File Format menu will appear (Figure 8.20).

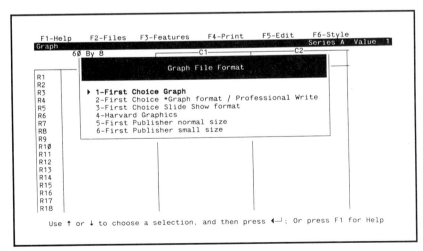

Figure 8.20: Graph File Format menu

Select the appropriate format, depending on which software package will use the graph file. Table 8.2 lists the available formats, along with the software packages that can read each one. Most of these packages are marketed by Software Publishing Corporation.

If graph data is going to be used by PFS: First Publisher, you may need to experiment in order to determine which size to use: normal or small.

Table 8.2: Graph File Formats

FORMAT	SUITABLE FOR
First Choice Graph	PFS: First Choice
First Choice *Graph format	PFS: First Choice and PFS: Professional Write
Harvard Graphics	Harvard Graphics and Harvard Presentation Graphics
First Publisher (normal or small size)	PFS: First Publisher
First Choice Slide Show format	PFS: First Choice

Graph data saved in First Choice Graph format can be retrieved back into First Choice's graph module. However, it cannot be used by any other software or by any other First Choice modules.

Graph data saved in any other format can't be read by First Choice's graph module. However, after graph data has been written to a disk file, the original graph data remains in First Choice's memory. You can continue to work on it, or save it to another type of graph file.

CREATING NEW DEFAULTS

If you plan to create many graphs of the same type, you can set defaults that will simplify the process for you. After you set these defaults, they will automatically be used each time you create a new graph. Virtually everything that you can select for a graph can be made part of the defaults, including graph type, headings, and printer settings. Even data can be made part of the defaults. Here are the steps for creating a set of defaults:

1. Select *Create a graph* from the Main menu.

2. Enter any graph settings that are to become defaults. These include anything that you would normally do to create a new graph.

3. If particular data is to be used for every graph that you plan to create, enter that data into the Graph Information form.

4. After everything has been selected, choose *Make this graph the default* from the Files menu.

You can modify these settings in any way that you wish for the current graph. To change the default settings or to return to First Choice's original settings, you'll have to change each setting, then select *Make this graph the default* from the Files menu.

THE *GRAPH FORMAT

This format is used when the graph data is to be incorporated as a printed graph into a document generated either by PFS: First Choice or PFS: Professional Write. If you select this option, you must also select two other options related to printing, before saving the graph:

*   *Print quality.* You can select from three different qualities: draft (fastest speed, low quality); standard (slower, with better quality); or high (slowest speed, best quality). If your printer has only two different print speeds, you'll need to experiment to see which selection ("S" or "H") generates the best quality.

*   *Print in color.* If you have a color printer, you can select "Y" to generate color printout in up to six colors plus black. First Choice selects these colors, and you have no control over them. If your printer outputs only in black ink, this option is ignored.

When you save graph data in *Graph format, all of the current printer information (chosen when you customized First Choice for your equipment) is saved in the file. If you plan to use a printer other than the one for which First Choice has been customized, you need to go through the following steps *before* saving the graph data in *Graph format.

- Save the data as a First Choice Graph (using the Files menu).
- Exit to the Main menu, and select *Set up equipment.*
- Go through the necessary steps to select the printer that will be used for printing the graph (see "Customizing PFS: First Choice For Your Computer" in Appendix A).
- Return to First Choice's graph module and retrieve the graph data from its file (using the Files menu).
- Save the graph data in *Graph format. Go back to the Main menu, select *Set up equipment* again, and choose the printer normally used by First Choice.

For details on how to incorporate a graph in *Graph format into a document, see Chapter 10.

RETRIEVING EXISTING GRAPH DATA FROM DISK

You can retrieve a set of graph data stored on a disk into the graph module, provided that the data was stored in First Choice Graph format.

Select *Get an existing file,* either from the Main menu or from the Files menu if you are within one of First Choice's modules. The Directory Assistant will appear. If necessary, enter the name of the disk drive and/or hard disk subdirectory containing the file. Specify the name of the file containing the graph, either by entering the file name (including the .GRA extension), or by using the cursor keys to select the file. (Files with .GRA extensions are listed in the *Other* column.)

DISPLAYING A GRAPH ON-SCREEN

After you have entered the data for a graph and chosen options, you can display the graph on the computer screen to see how it looks. Generally, a graph displayed on the screen closely resembles what will be generated on a printer or plotter.

To display a graph, make sure that the Graph Information form is displayed on the screen. Select *Draw graph* from the Features menu. The graph should appear on the screen. To exit from the graph display, press any key, and the Graph Information form will reappear.

If the graph fails to appear, your computer may not have a proper graphics board (called a *display adapter*) installed. This is not likely if you're using a color monitor. However, monochrome monitors can be controlled with various types of internal plug-in boards, some of which can handle only text—not graphics. If you have any doubts, ask your dealer or a computer expert if a graphics display adapter is installed in the computer.

After you have displayed a graph on the screen and verified that it contains all of the features that you want, you should save a copy of the graph data to a disk file. This is a precaution, just in case a disaster during printing or plotting causes your computer to freeze up (and lose your data in memory).

HOW TO PRINT GRAPHS

A graph can be printed in two ways: directly from within the graph module of First Choice, or as part of a document, where the graph has been stored in *Graph format. This latter situation has been discussed in an earlier section and is also explored in Chapter 10.

If you have entered all of the data for a graph and have supplied all of the necessary options (graph type, titles, etc.), you are ready to print. If the graph is stored in a file, retrieve it by selecting *Get an existing file* from the Main menu or the Files menu. You may save a good deal of time by first displaying the graph on the computer screen, just to make sure that everything is where you want it to be. You can then make any necessary changes before printing the graph.

To print the graph, make sure that the printer is on, that it has paper, and that it's ready to print. Make sure that the Graph Information form is displayed. Select *Print graph* from the Print menu. The Print Graph Options menu will appear (Figure 8.21).

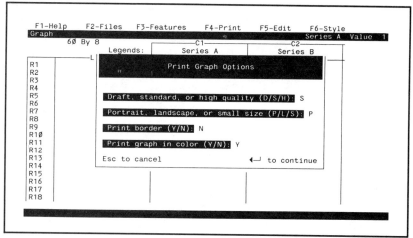

Figure 8.21: Print Graph Options menu

From the Print Graph Options menu, make the following selections.
Draft, standard, or high quality (D/S/H) lets you select the quality of
the printout.

D   Draft, or poorest, print quality (and fastest printing
speed) is useful for taking a quick glance at the
printed graph.

S   Standard, or normal, print quality (modest printing
speed) is the default option.

H   High quality has the best print quality and the
slowest speed.

Many printers have only two different print speeds. If your printer
is one of these, you'll need to experiment to see which selection ("S"
or "H") generates the best-quality output). Surprisingly, in some
cases the "S" selection may generate better quality than "H."

Portrait, landscape, or small size (P/L/S) lets you print the graph in one
of three sizes:

S   The graph prints in the top third of the page. This is the
default option.

P   Larger than the "S" or small size, the graph is centered
in the top half of the page.

L   The largest-size graph, it's printed in the middle of the page and rotated by 90 degrees.

Print border (Y/N) allows you to decide whether or not to have a border drawn around the graph. The standard option is "N" (no border).

Print graph in color (Y/N) allows your graph to print in several colors (chosen by First Choice) if you choose "Y." If your printer outputs in black ink only, the selection of this option has no effect on the printout.

PRINTER CHECKLIST

If your printer fails to print a graph the way you expect, some of the following suggestions may help you locate the trouble source.

CONNECTIONS   Many computers have two or more ports (connectors) on the back of the computer to which a printer cable can be attached. If you've been using your printer with First Choice for other types of output, then the printer cable is undoubtedly connected properly. However, the complete failure of a printer to do anything may be an indication that there's a poor cable connection, or that the cable is connected to the wrong port.

PRINTER SELECTION   When doing graphical printing, it is especially important that First Choice be customized for the correct printer. You may want to review "Customizing PFS: First Choice For Your Computer" in Appendix A, and make absolutely certain that First Choice has been set up for your printer.

If your printer prints text satisfactorily but fails to generate graphical output, First Choice may be sending incorrect commands to the printer, due to incorrect printer selection during customization.

COMMUNICATIONS SETTINGS   If you are using a serial port with your printer, the settings specified during First Choice customization must match those on the printer exactly. On some printers, these are chosen with dip switches. On others, the settings are chosen via a menu selection program that is executed by the printer itself. In either case, you'll need to consult the printer manual for details.

HOW TO PLOT GRAPHS

Before you begin plotting, it's a good idea to carefully check the connections between your plotter and computer. As in the case of printers, there may be several ports (connectors) on the back of your computer to which the plotter may be connected. As part of the customization process, you tell First Choice which port will be used; make sure first that the plotter is in fact connected to this port. This is a particular problem with devices such as plotters, which may share a port with another device.

When disconnecting a device from the computer, it's a good idea to note which physical connector on the computer was used, to avoid later confusion. A good trick is to use a felt-tipped pen to label the various computer connectors ("P1," "P2," and so on).

If you are using a serial port with your plotter, the settings specified during First Choice customization must exactly match those on the plotter. You'll need to consult the plotter manual for details.

Plotters are particularly touchy devices. Pens often dry out or clog up, and poor-quality or dirty paper can cause low-quality output. Worse yet, some pens work only with particular types of paper. Because of these uncertainties, you may find it difficult to decide whether a particular problem is due to the software, cable connections, or pens. Familiarize yourself with the plotter's manual before trying to plot graphs from First Choice.

Before plotting a graph, make sure that you've entered all of the data and chosen values for all of the graph options. In addition, you may save a good deal of time by first displaying the graph on the computer screen (see "Displaying a Graph On-Screen"), just to make sure that everything is where you want it to be. It's a lot quicker to display a graph on the screen than to generate hard copy on the plotter.

Before using a plotter to generate a graph, First Choice must be customized for that particular plotter. See "Customizing PFS: First Choice for Your Computer" in Appendix A for details on how to tell First Choice which plotter you are using.

The *Plot graph* option appears only if you've installed First Choice to use a plotter.

USING THE PLOT GRAPH OPTIONS

To generate a graph on the plotter, select *Plot graph* from the Print menu. The Plot Graph Options menu will appear (Figure 8.22).

You can change the value of any option by moving the cursor to it with Tab or Shift-Tab, then entering the new value. Here are the options.

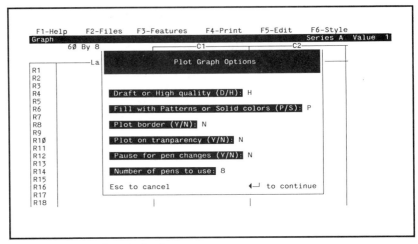

Figure 8.22: Plot Graph Options menu

Draft or High quality (D/H)

D   Draft quality generates fast but crude graphs, suitable for a quick inspection. In the Draft mode, plotters generally don't use alternate fonts.

H   High quality mode takes much longer to plot, but uses the plotter to its best capability.

Fill with Patterns or Solid colors (P/S) is the next option. When First Choice plots graphs such as pies and bars, it uses different fill patterns or solid colors. You can select one or the other with the "P" (fill patterns) or "S" (solid colors) options.

Plot border (Y/N) lets you draw a double-line border around the graph if you select "Y."

Plot on transparency (Y/N) is a convenient way of generating overhead transparencies. If the plotter has the capability, select "Y" for this option to plot on transparency paper.

Pause for pen changes (Y/N), for plotters with two pens, causes First Choice to pause so you can insert a different colored pen.

Number of pens to use tells First Choice how many pens are being used by the plotter. You can specify up to eight pens. First Choice assumes that pen 1 will be used for titles and legends and pen 2 for filling graph segments. Additional pens are used for filling pie slices and bars.

You may need to do a bit of experimenting, to determine exactly how First Choice uses the pens on your plotter. Once you figure this out, you can be creative, using the *Pause for pen changes* option to allow you to choose the colors to use in certain parts of a graph.

GRAPHING SPREADSHEET DATA

You can use First Choice's graph module to generate graphs based on data within an existing spreadsheet. There are two very different ways to accomplish this.

The first way is to transfer the spreadsheet data to First Choice's graph module with the cut-and-paste feature. The graph then can be created as described earlier in this chapter. The strength of this approach is that the data can be edited before graphing, *without affecting the original spreadsheet data.*

By the same token, this type of graph is completely independent from the original spreadsheet. Suppose that you create a graph from existing spreadsheet data and then save the graph data to a file. If you later change the original data in the spreadsheet, the file containing the graph data becomes out-of-date, and you'll have to update it before using it to generate any more graphs.

The second way to generate a graph based on existing spreadsheet data is to create it directly from data in the spreadsheet, without first transferring it to the graph module. This type of graph is automatically saved as part of the spreadsheet when the spreadsheet itself is saved.

The power of this approach is that *the spreadsheet data is directly linked to the graph.* In other words, if data in the spreadsheet is changed, the graph automatically reflects the changes. Up to eight graphs can be directly linked to a spreadsheet.

TRANSFERRING DATA TO THE GRAPH MODULE

If you want to transfer data from an existing spreadsheet to the graph module, here are the steps to follow:

- Load the desired spreadsheet in First Choice.
- Select the range of values to be transferred.

- Copy the range to the clipboard, using either Alt-C or the Edit menu.

- Exit from the spreadsheet back to the Main menu.

- Select *Create a graph* from this menu.

- When the Graph Information form appears, move the cursor to the desired starting cell.

- Paste the data from the clipboard using either Alt-P or the Edit menu.

You can transfer row and column headings from the spreadsheet, as well as the data, by using cell R0C0 as the beginning of the range in the spreadsheet. However, the column headings will become the first row of data in the Graph Information form, and you'll have to do some cleaning up.

For example, after cutting and pasting the entire spreadsheet shown in Figure 8.23, the result is the Graph Information form seen in Figure 8.24. We pasted the data by positioning the cursor in row R1 in the Labels column.

During pasting, the column headings of the spreadsheet were transferred as the first row of data in the Graph Information form. All rows were therefore displaced down by one. For instance, row 1 from the spreadsheet became row 2 of the graph. Row headings from the spreadsheet were transferred to the Labels column of the Graph Information form.

To correct the placement of data in Figure 8.24, you need to move the two column headings up into the Legends area. Unfortunately, First Choice doesn't let you cut and paste from the data area into the Legends areas. Therefore, you must manually copy each heading from row 1 into the Legends heading area. Then delete row 1, using *Remove row/column* from the Edit menu.

Some additional corrections need to be made, namely the deletion of the data in rows R14 through R18 (see Figure 8.24). These contain totals, special labels, and other odds and ends that can't be graphed (we shouldn't have transferred them in the first place). To delete these rows, choose *Remove row/column* from the Edit menu.

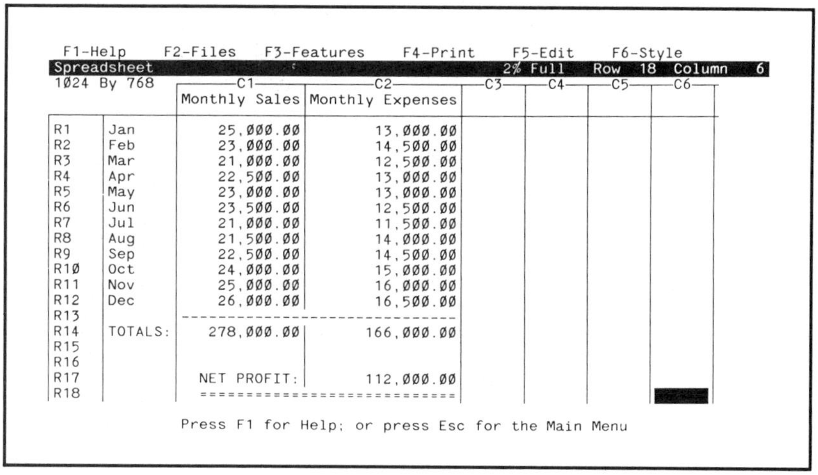

F1-Help F2-Files F3-Features F4-Print F5-Edit F6-Style

Spreadsheet 2% Full Row 18 Column 6

1024 By 768

	C1	C2	C3	C4	C5	C6
	Monthly Sales	Monthly Expenses				
R1 Jan	25,000.00	13,000.00				
R2 Feb	23,000.00	14,500.00				
R3 Mar	21,000.00	12,500.00				
R4 Apr	22,500.00	13,000.00				
R5 May	23,000.00	13,000.00				
R6 Jun	23,500.00	12,500.00				
R7 Jul	21,000.00	11,500.00				
R8 Aug	21,500.00	14,000.00				
R9 Sep	22,500.00	14,500.00				
R10 Oct	24,000.00	15,000.00				
R11 Nov	25,000.00	16,000.00				
R12 Dec	26,000.00	16,500.00				
R13	----------------	----------------				
R14 TOTALS:	278,000.00	166,000.00				
R15						
R16						
R17	NET PROFIT:	112,000.00				
R18	==============	==============				

Press F1 for Help; or press Esc for the Main Menu

Figure 8.23: Simple spreadsheet

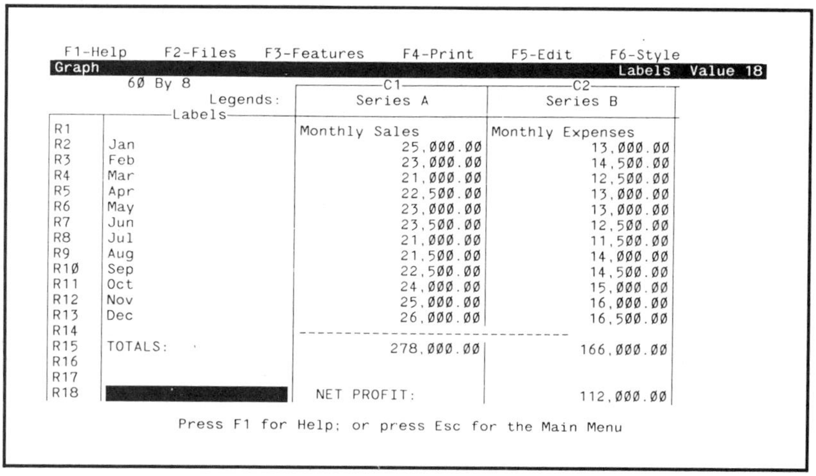

F1-Help F2-Files F3-Features F4-Print F5-Edit F6-Style

Graph Labels Value 18

60 By 8

	Labels	C1 Series A	C2 Series B
	Legends:	Series A	Series B
R1		Monthly Sales	Monthly Expenses
R2	Jan	25,000.00	13,000.00
R3	Feb	23,000.00	14,500.00
R4	Mar	21,000.00	12,500.00
R5	Apr	22,500.00	13,000.00
R6	May	23,000.00	13,000.00
R7	Jun	23,500.00	12,500.00
R8	Jul	21,000.00	11,500.00
R9	Aug	21,500.00	14,000.00
R10	Sep	22,500.00	14,500.00
R11	Oct	24,000.00	15,000.00
R12	Nov	25,000.00	16,000.00
R13	Dec	26,000.00	16,500.00
R14		----------------	----------------
R15	TOTALS:	278,000.00	166,000.00
R16			
R17			
R18		NET PROFIT:	112,000.00

Press F1 for Help; or press Esc for the Main Menu

Figure 8.24: Graph Information form with spreadsheet data from Figure 8.23

GRAPHING DATA DIRECTLY FROM A SPREADSHEET

There are several significant differences between this procedure and the one described in the preceding section. Here, graphs are generated directly from existing data in a spreadsheet. This means that if one or more spreadsheet values change, corresponding changes to the graphs are made automatically. This is a very convenient way to draw several graphs corresponding to variations in a set of spreadsheet data.

Also, when the spreadsheet is saved, the graphs are saved along with it. Up to eight graphs can be linked to a single spreadsheet.

To generate a graph directly from a spreadsheet:

- Load the spreadsheet into First Choice.

- Select *Use graphics* from the Features menu. The Graphics menu (Figure 8.25) appears.

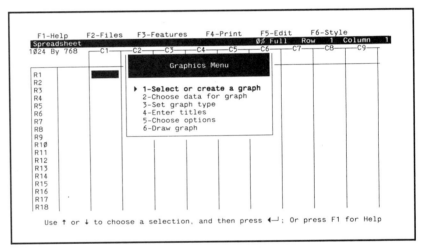

Figure 8.25: Graphics menu

- Assign a name to the graph.

- Select the data to be graphed. Up to eight series of data can be selected for a single graph, with up to 60 data points per series.

- Choose from the options, such as graph title, labels and captions, graph type, and so on.

- Display the graph on-screen, or print or plot it.

Let's look at each step more closely.

Once you've chosen a name for a graph, that graph becomes a permanent part of the spreadsheet. When you save the spreadsheet, the graph is saved as well.

ASSIGNING A NAME TO THE GRAPH The first step in creating a graph must be to assign it a name. To enter a name, choose *Select or create a graph* from the Graphics menu. A name can contain up to eight characters, including letters, digits, and many of the special characters. When you're done, press ◄━┘.

If you create eight graphs (the limit), but still want to create another one, you'll have to sacrifice one of the existing ones. To do this, choose *Select or create a graph* from the Graphics menu. Using the cursor keys, select the graph to be sacrificed. Overwrite all of the choices for the graph: data, titles, and other options. You can't change the graph name.

SELECTING THE DATA TO GRAPH When you are finished selecting a graph name, press ◄━┘ and the Data Selection display (Figure 8.26) appears. Use this display to specify which data is to be plotted. The graph may contain from one to eight series of data, and you must choose the cells to be plotted for each series.

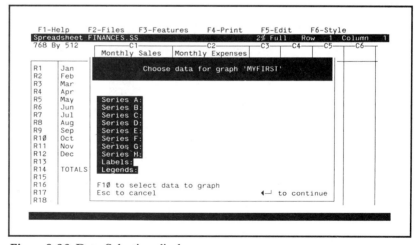

Figure 8.26: Data Selection display

The cells for each series can consist of various combinations of cells from the spreadsheet. Here are several examples of entries for a single series:

1. R1C1..R1C5
2. R1C1..R5C1

3. R2

4. C3

5. R2C3, R8C2, R5C2, R1C3

6. R1C1..R5C1, R1C1..R1C5

7. R4C2, R8C3, R1C1..R5C1

You can specify an entire row (example 3) or column (example 4); part of a row or column (examples 1 and 2); a group of individual cells (example 5); or various combinations of the above separated by commas (examples 6 and 7).

Each data series can consist of several *items* (examples 5, 6, and 7), separated by commas. Each item must be either an individual cell, a row or column, or part of a row or column. If the item is a range, it can't reference more than one row or column.

You can directly write down the cells for a series, or you can do it the easy way:

- Press the F10 key. The Data Selection display temporarily disappears, exposing the entire spreadsheet.

- Select a range of one or more cells to be included for the current series. First move the cursor to the beginning of the range, then press Alt-S to begin selection. Expand the range with the cursor keys. Remember that the range can include either part or all of a *single* row or column. When you're done, press F10 to return to the Data Selection display. The selected range is automatically listed next to the current series.

- Press the F10 key again to select additional cells for the current series.

When First Choice graphs a series of cells, only numeric values are used. If a cell that's part of a series contains any non-numeric information, that cell is ignored during the graphing process.

SELECTING LABELS AND LEGENDS   Labels are the values that appear along the horizontal axis (the x-axis). Legends are the values that appear at the bottom of a graph, helping to identify the individual series of data on the graph. The rules for selecting legends and labels are the same. Both must exist as spreadsheet cells. You can select them by entering their row or column coordinates next to the *Labels* or *Legends* option on the Data Selection display. You can select an entire row or column, or specify a range that's part of a row or column. You can specify R0 for the row of column headings, or C0 for the column of row headings. You can even specify a group of individual cells, separated by commas.

A group of labels or legends can be either alphanumeric strings or numeric values. It's up to you to choose which group of cells to use.

You can decide not to specify any particular cells for labels or legends. In that case, First Choice does its best to select labels for you, by making an intelligent guess. For example:

> If you don't select any cells as the legends, First Choice uses *Series A, Series B,* and so on.

SELECTED CELLS FOR A SERIES	LABELS CHOSEN BY FIRST CHOICE
An entire column	Values in C0
An entire row	Values in R0
Part of a column	Corresponding values in C0
Part of a row	Corresponding values in R0

If you're plotting one or two pies, enter the label coordinates for the options *Pie 1 Labels* and *Pie 2 Labels*. Legends can't be chosen for pie graphs.

CHOOSING THE GRAPH TYPE   As described earlier in this chapter, First Choice divides the graph types into four categories: bar/line, area, high/low/close, and pie. You select the one that you wish by picking *Set graph type* from the Graphics menu.

GRAPH TITLES   To enter titles, subtitles, etc., select *Enter titles* from the Graphics menu. For a discussion of the various types of titles that you can attach to a graph, see ''Entering Graph Titles'' earlier in this chapter.

SELECTING OTHER OPTIONS   Other options must be selected before a graph can be plotted; each type of graph has its own particular set. Select *Choose options* from the Graphics menu (Figure 8.25). For details, refer to the appropriate sections in earlier parts of this chapter. For example, to find out about options for bar graphs, see under "Creating Bar Graphs."

PRINTING AND PLOTTING THE GRAPH   You can output a graph to a printer, plotter, screen or disk file. For details on printing and plotting, refer to "How to Print Graphs" and "How to Plot Graphs," earlier in this chapter.

> To display the graph on the computer screen before printing or plotting, select *Draw graph* from the Graphics menu. After the graph appears, press any key to return to the Graphics menu.

RETRIEVING A GRAPH   To retrieve a spreadsheet graph, choose *Select or create a graph* from the Graphics menu. The list of graphs currently attached to the spreadsheet will appear. Use the cursor keys to select the graph that you want, then press ←. The Data Selection display for that graph will appear, containing data, labels, and legends for that graph.

OUTPUTTING RAW GRAPH DATA

You may want to save the raw data from a graph (for example, the numbers on the Graph Information form) for another use, perhaps to be incorporated into a document or a spreadsheet. You can print the data, send it to a disk, or incorporate it into an existing spreadsheet. Let's look at each option.

PRINTING GRAPH DATA

To send graph data to the printer in columnar format, follow these steps:

1. Select *Print graph data* from the Print menu. The Print Graph Data Options display appears (Figure 8.27).

2. Make any required changes to the displayed options (see "Printing Part of Your Document" in Chapter 2 for a discussion of the options).

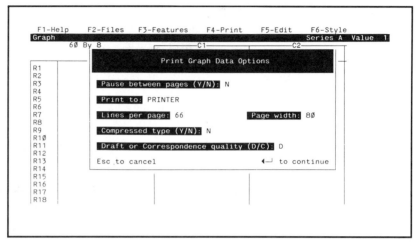

Figure 8.27: Print Graph Data Options display

3. If you want the output directed to a disk file rather than to the printer, enter the name of the file in the *Print to* option. Make sure to include the name of the disk drive and/or subdirectory if they are different from the currently selected ones.

4. Press ◄─┘ to begin outputting the data.

USING THE DATA AS A DOCUMENT

If the data is sent to a disk instead of the printer, the resulting file is in First Choice document format. If you then select *Get an existing file* and specify this file, First Choice loads it in as an ordinary document. You can then edit it as you wish.

This type of file can also be merged with another First Choice document.

MOVING DATA TO A SPREADSHEET

You may want to incorporate graph data into an existing spreadsheet. You can do this by making use of First Choice's cut-and-paste feature:

1. Select the data to be copied from the Graph Information form. Use Alt-S or the Edit menu to define the beginning of the data range, then expand the range with the cursor keys to include all data to be copied.

2. Copy the data to the clipboard using either Alt-C or the Edit menu.

3. Load in the spreadsheet to be used by choosing *Get an existing file,* either from the Files menu or the Main menu.

4. After the spreadsheet has been loaded, move the cursor to the position where the graph data is to be copied.

5. Paste the data from the clipboard, using either Alt-P or the Edit menu.

Alternatively, you can use the graph data to build a new spreadsheet, as follows. Instead of step 3 above, exit to the Main menu, then select *Create a spreadsheet.* When the empty spreadsheet appears, paste the data from the clipboard.

When you select the graph data to be copied to the clipboard, you can include either the column headings or the first column of data. You can't, however, include both, because there's no way to move the cursor to the location on the screen containing the word *Legends.* If you want to copy both the column headings and the first column of data to a spreadsheet, you'll either have to copy something down on paper (heaven forbid!), or transfer the data to the spreadsheet in two steps.

USING SPECIAL FIRST CHOICE FEATURES WITH GRAPHS

When working in the graph module, don't forget that First Choice's bookmark, calculator, and quick entry features can be used here as well as in other modules. Here's how.

BOOKMARKS

You can set bookmarks anywhere on the Graph Information form. Move the cursor to the desired cell. Select *Set bookmark* from the Features menu, and choose a bookmark that's not currently in use.

The bookmark is assigned to a particular cell, but not to any special position within that cell. For more information on bookmarks, refer to Chapter 11.

THE CALCULATOR

Let's transfer the result of a calculation directly to a cell. Move the cursor to the desired cell. Select *Use calculator* from the Features menu. Enter the calculation, and then press F10. The result of the calculation replaces the current contents of the cell.

First Choice's calculator is described in detail in Chapter 11.

QUICK ENTRY

You can use First Choice's quick entry feature to enter a series of related values. For a description of quick entry, see "The Quick Entry Feature" in Chapter 6.

SUMMARY

First Choice's graph module offers flexible ways to generate graph types commonly used to display numerical information. Data for a graph can be entered directly into the graph module, from which the graph can then be generated. Most graph types can display up to eight different series of data, and each series can contain up to 60 data points.

Graphs can be displayed on-screen, printed, plotted, or saved on a disk file. Several output formats are available for saving graphs, some of which allow graphs to be used by other software packages. A graph can also be saved in a format that can be combined with a First Choice document.

Data from within an existing spreadsheet can be directly graphed. A spreadsheet can have up to eight graphs associated with it. These graphs are automatically stored with the spreadsheet, so that when spreadsheet data is altered, the graph data is automatically changed.

Chapter

9

Communicating with Other Computers

With First Choice's communications module, you can establish a connection between your computer and another in a remote location. You may want to connect with any of several commercial information services, such as CompuServe, MCI Mail, or Dow Jones News/Retrieval. These companies offer you a wide variety of services, such as electronic mail, up-to-the-minute stock market quotations, and information on a huge variety of topics.

You can also access any of hundreds of independently operated electronic bulletin boards throughout the country. Each of these serves a particular community of interests, and most are either free or inexpensive. With a bulletin board, you can share information and ideas with both experts and amateurs.

Finally, First Choice's communications module allows you to create an electronic link between your computer and another microcomputer. You can dial up and connect to any PC that is running communications software and is able to receive calls. This software could be First Choice or some other communications package. With a connection established, you can exchange messages and transfer files between the machines.

This chapter will cover connecting to a remote computer, using the word processor as a background aid, communicating with another microcomputer, and sending and receiving files. Finally, it will describe how to automate sign-on procedures.

GETTING STARTED

Establishing connections between First Choice, your modem, and a remote computer can be a touchy and frustrating business, and there are many factors that can prevent a connection from being established. In this section, we'll look at the details you should check over before using the communications module.

USING A MODEM WITH FIRST CHOICE

To use First Choice's communications module, your computer must be connected to either an internal or external modem. Also, you must tailor First Choice for your particular modem. For details on how to do this, see "Customizing PFS: First Choice for Your Computer" in Appendix A.

Verify that your telephone line is properly wired to the modem. Some modems have two external telephone-type connectors, usually on the back. One is for a wire that leads to the telephone wall connection, and the other is used for plugging in a telephone.

Some modems also have several switches that must be properly set. Here are the recommended settings for use with First Choice:

- Follow a carrier detect
- Respond to DTR
- Recognize commands

You might want to check the modem manual or consult your computer dealer to make sure that it's been properly installed.

Make doubly sure that you've specified the correct modem parameters to First Choice. You may want to go back to the Main menu, select *Set up First Choice,* and verify that the correct selections have been made for the type of modem, the name of the communication port (either COM1 or COM2), and the type of telephone line (rotary or touch-tone).

If your modem isn't on the list of modems in the Setup menu, you can select *Unlisted modem.* However, First Choice will work much better if you can find a modem on the list that your modem emulates.

This is not as difficult as it might seem; many clone modems have been designed to imitate the behavior of well-known brands. Rather than choose *Unlisted modem*, select the first modem name from the following list, then see if First Choice communicates properly with a remote computer (following the instructions in this chapter).

Hayes Smartmodem 1200/B (the modem most often imitated)

Hayes Smartmodem 300

Hayes Smartmodem 2400 (only if your modem works at a speed of 2400)

Ven-Tel PC Modem 1200

Ven-Tel PC 1/2 Card

If the modem you've selected doesn't work, try the next one on the list, and continue until you've exhausted either the list or yourself. As a last resort, you can select *Unlisted modem* and follow the special instructions in this chapter for that type of modem.

ACCESSING INFORMATION AND BULLETIN BOARD SERVICES

If you plan to access a commercial information service, such as CompuServe, you may need to establish an account with them first. Usually, you do this by telephone or mail, and you'll be given a password. On the other hand, some information services let you connect to them and then establish an account after you furnish suitable information (including your credit card number).

Most information services charge you according to the amount of time you're connected to them. You might want to investigate these charges carefully; many have off-hour rates that are much less than those for prime time. Also, because these rates are far from trivial, it's a good idea to study any information on how to make the best use of a particular service *before* you try to use it.

By contrast, most electronic bulletin boards charge very little or nothing at all for connect time. These are usually not money-making operations, but are operated by individuals or groups whose prime interest is sharing information on a particular subject. On the other hand, unlike most large commercial information services, electronic bulletin boards seldom have local telephone numbers, so you may wind up paying a bundle for long-distance charges.

The way you connect to electronic bulletin boards will vary; some require prior registration by mail or telephone, while others let anyone sign on.

SETTING UP COMMUNICATIONS OPTIONS WITH THE SERVICE MENU

The first time that you connect to a remote computer, you'll need to supply First Choice with some information about that computer. To begin the process, select *Connect to another computer* from the Main menu. The Service menu will appear (Figure 9.1). When you first use this menu, it will display the names of several commercial information services for which First Choice is already set up. You can choose any of these services, or you can add to the menu the name of any bulletin board, information service, or private individual with a computer.

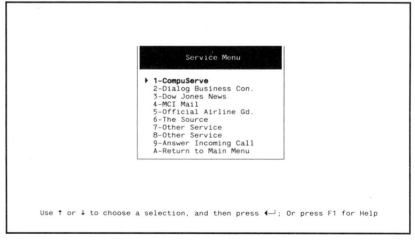

```
                        Service Menu

              ▶ 1-CompuServe
                2-Dialog Business Con.
                3-Dow Jones News
                4-MCI Mail
                5-Official Airline Gd.
                6-The Source
                7-Other Service
                8-Other Service
                9-Answer Incoming Call
                A-Return to Main Menu



    Use ↑ or ↓ to choose a selection, and then press ◀─┘; Or press F1 for Help
```

Figure 9.1: Service menu

USING AN EXISTING ENTRY

After you select the computer that you want to access from the Service menu, the Service Information form for that particular computer will appear, similar to the one shown in Figure 9.2. Most of the options on this form are concerned with *communication parameters*. If you've chosen an information service that was on the original Service menu list, these communication parameters will already be set correctly. This section will explain how to fill in the service name and phone number, and how to set communication speed and other options.

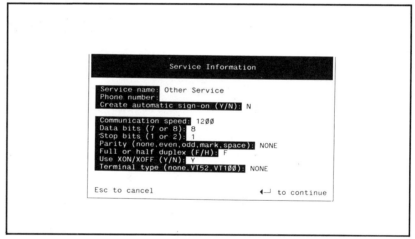

Figure 9.2: Service Information form

ENTERING THE TELEPHONE NUMBER

The first time that you use the Service Information form for a remote computer, you'll need to fill in the entry for *Phone number*. If you're going to connect to a commercial information service, you should consult their published information, which should include a list of telephone numbers. Most of these services have phone numbers for all major U.S. cities.

If you have to dial a special number to get an outside line, include this as part of the *Phone number* entry. After this special number, add as many commas as necessary to simulate the pause before the dial tone is heard; each comma causes a two-second pause. For example, if you need to dial 9 for an outside line, and you generally have to wait up to five seconds for the outside dial tone, enter *9,,,xxx-xxxx*, where *xxx-xxxx* is the telephone number of the remote computer.

When entering a telephone number, you can include any of the characters that are normally part of the number, such as hyphens and parentheses. First Choice ignores these when reading the number, recognizing only the ten digits and the special characters * and #. You can even add a short comment as part of the number, but the entire entry can't be longer than 29 characters.

SELECTING THE COMMUNICATION SPEED

Once you've entered values for the telephone number and communication speed, they are saved by First Choice until you change them. This is true for any of the options on the Service Information form.

The first time that you use the Service Information form for a remote computer, you'll probably want to change the option marked *Communication speed,* which is preset to 1200 baud. This specifies the speed at which characters are transmitted between computers. A value of 1200 baud corresponds to 120 characters per second. Most modems and computers can operate at a speed of 1200 baud, and some can run at 2400. You should find out what is the fastest possible communication speed for the remote computer that you'll be accessing.

If your modem has a manual selection switch for communication speed, set it to match the maximum speed of the remote computer that you're going to access. If your modem can't match this speed, set it to its own maximum speed.

If you have an internal modem (located inside the computer), it probably adjusts automatically to whatever communication speed is specified by First Choice. However, it'll have its own maximum speed (usually 1200 or 2400 baud), and you'll need to find out what it is, either from the modem manual or the dealer from whom the modem was purchased.

If you don't know the maximum speed for your modem, try 2400. If that fails, try 1200, then finally 300 (almost guaranteed to work).

After you've determined the communication speeds for the remote computer and your modem, and after you've adjusted the modem speed (if necessary), set the value for *Communication speed* on the

Service Information form to the *smaller* of the following two values:

- The maximum possible communication speed of the modem
- The maximum possible communication speed of the service

SELECTING THE TERMINAL TYPE

For most remote computers, you can leave the option *Terminal type (none, VT52, VT100)* set at the default value *NONE*. However, in certain situations you'll need to select a different value for this option.

Many remote computers can talk directly to microcomputers, such as your own. However, some remote computers can communicate only with specific types of terminals. To help deal with this situation, First Choice has built-in software that allows your computer to emulate either the DEC VT100 or VT52 terminals—two of the more popular terminal types.

If the remote computer that you plan to access has to talk to either of these two terminal types, fill in the option *Terminal type (none, VT52, VT100)* with the appropriate choice.

ADDING A NEW ENTRY

If you want to connect to a remote computer that's not listed on the Service menu, you can add it to the list by selecting either entry marked *Other service* from the menu. A blank Service Information form will appear (Figure 9.2). You'll need to fill it in as described in the following paragraphs. If there aren't any *Other service* entries on the Service menu, then select from the menu the name of a remote computer that you're not currently using. Then, when the Service Information form appears, replace the existing data with the new values.

You'll need to supply values for the nine options shown on the form. You've already seen how to fill in the phone number, and how to set the communication speed. For *Service name*, enter a name that describes the remote computer (up to 20 characters). The remaining options are communication parameters; they specify the details of computer-to-computer communications. Here are the values most

You don't have to understand the meanings of the various parameters (such as a *stop bit*) in order to enter the correct values.

commonly used for these parameters:

Data bits: 8

Stop bits: 1

Parity: NONE

Full or half duplex: F

Use XON/XOFF: Y

You may save yourself some trouble by trying these values. If First Choice then fails to work properly, you'll have to find out from the operators of the remote computer what settings should be used. This information is usually readily accessible.

Once you've entered the values for the new computer, First Choice stores them permanently, so that you can use them again. Also, the name that you enter for *Service name* will appear on the Service menu whenever it appears on the screen.

CONNECTING TO A REMOTE COMPUTER

To establish a connection with a communication service, electronic bulletin board, or personal computer, select *Connect to another computer* from the Main menu. The Service menu will appear. Select the name of the remote computer that you wish to access. Its Service Information form will appear. If any of the options need to be filled in, see "Setting Up Communications Options with the Service Menu" earlier in this chapter. Next, press ◀─┘. One of two things will happen, depending on the type of modem: First Choice will either automatically dial the number on the Service Information form, or you'll have to dial manually.

AUTOMATIC DIALING

During the customization of First Choice, you had to specify the name of a modem. If you selected either *Unlisted modem* or *Acoustic modem,* skip to the section "Manual Dialing." If you selected any other modem from the list, First Choice will automatically dial the telephone number for you.

If the line is busy, First Choice will redial the number every few seconds, either until a connection is made or until you press Esc to end the process.

As the modem dials the number, you'll probably hear it, along with other strange sounds (most modems have a tiny speaker that squeaks as it works). When the connection has been established, the On-Line screen appears (Figure 9.3), with perhaps an opening message from the remote computer. You're now ready to go on.

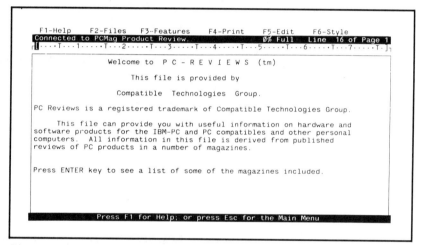

```
   F1-Help    F2-Files   F3-Features    F4-Print    F5-Edit    F6-Style
Connected to PCMag Product Review.              0% Full    Line  16 of Page 1
  [....T...1....T...2....T...3....T...4....T...5....T...6....T...7....T.]

                    Welcome to  P C - R E V I E W S  (tm)

                        This file is provided by

                    Compatible  Technologies  Group.

   PC Reviews is a registered trademark of Compatible Technologies Group.

       This file can provide you with useful information on hardware and
   software products for the IBM-PC and PC compatibles and other personal
   computers.  All information in this file is derived from published
   reviews of PC products in a number of magazines.

   Press ENTER key to see a list of some of the magazines included.



              Press F1 for Help; or press Esc for the Main Menu
```

Figure 9.3: On-Line screen after connection

Note that in Figure 9.3, only the top and bottom part of the display are generated by First Choice. The remainder of the display is produced by the remote computer.

If you selected either VT100 or VT52 as the terminal type, your screen won't look like that shown in Figure 9.3. In this chapter, we'll assume that you're not using either of these terminal types.

If the connection fails, see "Failing to Connect" below.

MANUAL DIALING

If you selected either *Unlisted modem* or *Acoustic modem* during the equipment setup, then you need to dial the number manually. After the Service Information form appears and you've pressed ←, the On-Line screen shown in Figure 9.4 will appear. Note that the erroneous message at the top of the screen indicates that you're connected. Actually, you must now enter the telephone number, preceded by a special modem command that tells the modem to dial the number that you enter. For the majority of modems, this command is ATDT. For example, to have the modem dial the number 555-5555, enter ATDT555-5555. If the code ATDT doesn't work, you'll either have to study your modem manual or consult the dealer who sold you the modem. If the modem works properly, you'll probably hear it dialing, as well as various hisses and screeches.

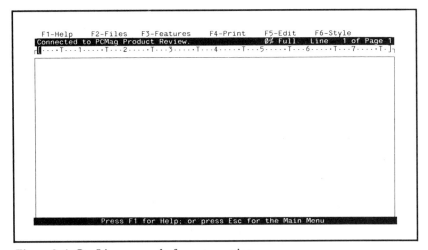

Figure 9.4: On-Line screen before connection

If you're using an acoustic modem, you simply dial the number manually with your telephone. When you hear the high tone from the answering computer, attach the headset to the modem, then press ←.

FAILING TO CONNECT

If your modem fails to establish a connection, you'll probably see a message to that effect on the screen, such as *The telephone line is disconnected.* Before you resort to drastic measures, try once or twice more to connect. Press the Esc key, then follow the instructions on the screen to return to the Main menu. Repeat the process described earlier for establishing a connection. If you can't establish a connection, see "Using a Modem with First Choice" earlier in this chapter.

SIGNING ON TO A REMOTE COMPUTER

After the electronic connection has been made, your computer is ready to "talk" to the remote one. Before the two-way dialog can begin, most remote computers require a *sign-on* procedure. You can automate this signing-on process, using First Choice's automatic sign-on feature. For details, see "Automating the Sign-on Procedure" later in this chapter.

COMMUNICATION SERVICES

To sign on to a communication service, you normally need to supply your name, a password, and possibly other information. In some cases, the instructions on how to do this are displayed on the screen. In other cases, you may need to obtain information from the service first.

Once you've signed on, you are ready to begin the two-way dialog with the service: you send instructions and in return the service provides you with information. The details for carrying on this dialog are specific to each service. Sometimes, these details are supplied in the form of online help provided by the service. However, since you're paying for every minute of connect time, this can be a very expensive way to learn. A more economical procedure is to obtain as much instruction as possible from the communication service before carrying on a session.

ELECTRONIC BULLETIN BOARDS

Using an electronic bulletin board is much easier than using a communication service, because there are far fewer options from which to choose. Signing on to a bulletin board is a fairly straightforward procedure. Usually, you're asked for your name, other details, and sometimes a password.

As with remote communication services, each bulletin board has its own set of commands that allow you to send and receive information. Because they are often run on a shoestring, many bulletin boards do not furnish any written documentation, but instead provide online instructions for using the system. These instructions are often—but unfortunately not always—easy to follow.

PERSONAL COMPUTERS

For more information on connecting with another personal computer, see "PC-to-PC Communication" later in this chapter.

You can dial up and connect to any PC that is running communications software and is in the appropriate mode for receiving telephone calls. This communications software could be PFS: First Choice or any of a large number of commercially available communications packages. In computer jargon, the remote computer is called the *host* and your computer is the *caller*.

There are many different types of communications software, and the way in which you are able to communicate with the host will depend entirely on the nature of this software. For example, some communications packages require that you furnish a password before being allowed access to the host.

USING FIRST CHOICE DURING TWO-WAY COMMUNICATION

The way in which you carry on a two-way dialog with a remote computer is determined by the software at the remote end. Basically you send a message, and the remote computer responds by sending back some information. What you send and what comes back are both displayed on your screen, and as the screen fills up information scrolls off the top.

As you carry on this two-way dialog, First Choice's word processor waits to be used when you need it. In addition to sending messages to the remote computer, you can also send instructions to First Choice. For example, at any time during a session, you can have First Choice generate a printout of everything that has appeared on the screen since the session began.

As you become familiar with the process of using First Choice and communicating with a remote computer at the same time, you'll find this capacity extremely useful.

THE WORKING COPY

Whenever there's a pause in the flow of information from the remote computer, you can perform various routine tasks with the working copy, just as though you were editing an ordinary document.

As information flows back and forth between you and the remote computer, it appears on the screen line by line. Each of these lines is added to the working copy, just as though you were creating an ordinary document with the word processor. In other words, lines that scroll off the top of the screen aren't lost; they're still part of the working copy.

For example, you can scroll back and forth through the entire session, using PgUp, PgDn, and the other cursor keys. You can add, delete, and edit text within the working copy. In fact, you can use nearly all of First Choice's word processing features.

THE TRANSMISSION LINE

You can jump directly to the Transmission line by pressing Ctrl-End.

You can switch back and forth between performing editing and other word processing tasks, and sending instructions to the remote computer. However, when you want to send an instruction, the cursor must be on the Transmission line (the last line of the working copy). In addition, the cursor should be positioned to the right of any existing text on the Transmission line. If you enter any text when the cursor is not on the Transmission line, that text simply becomes part of the working copy.

The Status line, which is the second line from the top of the screen, will display the message ... *but off last line* whenever the cursor is not positioned on the Transmission line.

COMMUNICATING BY SPECIAL KEYS

Some of the instructions that you send to a remote computer may need to include special keys already used by First Choice for other purposes. For example, some computers require that you press Esc for certain purposes. However, First Choice interprets the Esc key as an instruction to end communication. To resolve this conflict, First Choice provides a few special keystrokes, which are listed in Table 9.1.

Table 9.1: Special Communications Keystrokes

KEYSTROKE IN FIRST CHOICE	KEYSTROKE SENT TO REMOTE SERVICE
Alt-F10	Esc
Ctrl-Backspace	Backspace
Ctrl-Break	Ctrl-Break

For example, if the remote service requires that you press Esc, you will instead press Alt-F10. First Choice will send Esc for you.

MONITORING YOUR ONLINE SESSION

Whenever you are connected to a remote computer, you're paying by the minute, either in the form of connect charges to a communication service, time for telephone line usage, or both. Because of this, it's a very good idea to develop habits that help you move efficiently through each online session.

One of the advantages of First Choice's communications package is that it gives you many tools for optimizing the time spent online. The most vital of these tools is the fact that the entire online session is automatically preserved as the working copy. Because of this, you can go rapidly through a session. Then, after you've disconnected from the remote computer, you can review at your leisure the relevant information obtained in the session.

INTERRUPTING DATA TRANSMISSION

Many remote computers transmit a screenload at a time, then pause for you to inspect the screen. A screenload usually consists of

24 or 25 lines, but because the First Choice display occupies four lines, the top few lines of each screenload scroll right off the screen. You can get around this problem with most services by pressing Ctrl-NumLock, which temporarily interrupts transmission. Pressing any other key permits transmission to continue.

Instead of interrupting transmission, a more time-efficient method is to simply wait until there's a normal pause in the transmission from the remote computer. Then you can scroll back to review the information that passed off the screen.

SAVING A COPY OF THE SESSION

At any time during a session, you can save to a file the working copy, which contains everything that's appeared on the screen since you signed on to the remote computer. Wait until the remote computer pauses for input from you. Select *Save a copy of this session* from the Files menu. Then enter a file name in which the session will be stored. You can save just part of a session by selecting the desired block of text, then saving it to a file.

This is a handy way of recording part or all of a session, which you can later review when you're not connected to the remote computer and paying charges.

WATCHING FOR MEMORY OVERFLOW

As the session progresses, the working copy grows, filling up First Choice's memory. Toward the right end of the Status line, the *% Full* message indicates how much of the memory is taken up by the working copy. If the memory completely fills up, First Choice begins to discard the early part of the session from the working copy, in order to make room for new data appearing on the screen. You can counteract this loss by making sure that you periodically save the working copy to different files.

For instance, when the message *95% Full* appears, you could save the entire working copy to a file, say SESS1, then delete most of the earlier part of the session, perhaps everything except the last page or two.

PRINTING THE CONTENTS OF A SESSION

If the remote computer sends you something that you'd like to print on the spot, you can do so:

- Wait for data transmission from the computer to pause.
- Select the information to be printed.
- Choose *Print selected text only* from the Print menu.
- Make any necessary changes to the Print Options menu, then press ◄─┘.

It's helpful to set up the necessary options in the Print Options menu *before* starting a communications session. You can do this by entering the word processor, selecting the Print menu, and making any necessary changes to the Print Options menu. These options will remain in effect until you exit from First Choice.

TRANSMITTING AND RECEIVING FILES

Both computers must be given the appropriate instructions before you can transmit files.

File transfer is one of the great benefits of electronic connection between computers. Many electronic bulletin boards, as well as some communication services, contain large numbers of various types of files—mostly software—that you are free to transfer to your own computer. In addition, a telephone connection between two personal computers is often the quickest way to move files of mutual interest back and forth.

Whether you are communicating with an information service or a bulletin board, you use the same technique for sending a file; this also holds for receiving a file. The steps are described in the following section. For details on sending and receiving files to and from a remote personal computer, see "Transferring Files between PCs."

PREPARING THE REMOTE COMPUTER

Using whatever commands are appropriate to the remote computer, select the file to be sent to your computer (or to be received from your computer) and issue the instructions to begin transmission. Included in these instructions is a specification of the *transmission protocol,* which is the type of coding and error checking that is to take place during the transmission. You must specify to the remote computer that it should use the *XModem protocol* for file transfer, because First Choice always uses that particular protocol.

Usually, all of your instructions are in the form of menu selections, presented to you by the remote computer. For example, you might select *Transmit a file* from one menu, then select *XModem protocol* from another. Most modern communications packages have been well designed, making them fairly easy to use.

After you have finished giving instructions to the remote computer, it prepares to send (or receive) the file. However, it then waits for your computer to initiate the transmission.

PREPARING FIRST CHOICE

You can choose any file name to store the transmitted information; it can be the same as the name of the file at the remote computer, or it can be entirely different.

You must instruct First Choice to begin the process of receiving or transmitting the appropriate file. To receive a file, select *Receive a file (using XModem)* from the Features menu. When the Directory Assistant appears, enter the name of the file on your computer where the data will be written. This can be a new file or an existing one. If the latter, First Choice asks you to verify that it's OK to overwrite the file.

The file from the remote computer will be transmitted and copied into the file that you named. Usually, the remote computer issues messages informing you of the progress of the transmission.

To transmit a file, select *Transmit a file (using XModem)* from the Features menu. When the Directory Assistant appears, enter the name of the file to be transmitted. The file will be transmitted to the remote computer, and First Choice will indicate when it's done.

ENDING A COMMUNICATIONS SESSION

You can end communication in several ways. With a communication service or a bulletin board, the most graceful way is to let the remote computer end the session, by sending it the appropriate instructions. After disconnection, First Choice's On-Line screen will normally remain displayed, and you can then manipulate the working copy at your leisure.

You can also break off communication immediately by selecting *Disconnect* from the Features menu (Figure 9.5), followed by ⏎. This causes your modem to end the connection immediately. The remote computer will eventually sense the disconnect and tidy things up at its end. When you terminate a session in this way, your working copy remains intact, with part of it displayed on the screen. You can then inspect it, save it, print it, or discard it (see "Saving a Copy of the Session").

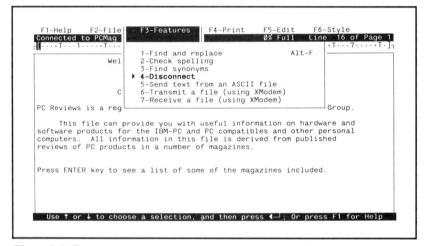

Figure 9.5: Features menu

You can also end communication by pressing the Esc key. First Choice exits to the Main menu after asking you to verify your intention. However, if you use the Esc key to disconnect, the contents of the working copy may be lost.

Most modems will respond to an instruction to disconnect from First Choice. However, some modems may not work this way, and you'll have to issue a special "disconnect" instruction from the keyboard. Your modem manual will probably contain details on this type of instruction.

PC-TO-PC COMMUNICATION

In general, there are three different ways in which you can use First Choice to interact with another personal computer via a telephone connection: person-to-person mode, remote host mode, and local host mode. How you exchange messages and transfer files depends on the mode you are using.

In *person-to-person mode,* a person sits at the host computer, controlling the communications software at that end. Messages can be exchanged between the people at each end, and files can be transmitted from one computer to the other.

In *remote host mode,* the remote computer is unattended. That is, nobody is operating the computer, and your dialog is strictly with the communications software at the host end. The operations that you can perform in this mode are limited by the capabilities of the remote software package. For example, some packages allow you to send and receive files, and perhaps to leave messages for the operator of the host computer.

You can also set up First Choice so that your computer is the host—*local host mode.* That is, a remote computer can dial your computer, and First Choice's communications module will answer the telephone and complete the connection. Once the connection has been established, you would interact with the calling computer in the person-to-person mode, as described above. (See "Making Your Computer the Host" for details on setting your computer to work in this mode.)

EXCHANGING MESSAGES

If you connect to a host computer, messages can be sent back and forth, provided that the host computer can be put into a *chat mode.* Unlike First Choice (which does this automatically), many communications packages must specifically be put into the chat mode by the user (at the remote end) issuing a particular command.

To send a message to the remote computer, you simply type in whatever you wish; First Choice transmits each character as soon as a key is pressed.

In the same way, the user at the other end can send messages to you. However, unlike First Choice, some communications packages require that ◀┘ be pressed before a message is transmitted.

If both users are running First Choice, messages can be sent back and forth quite rapidly; in fact it's easy for the information appearing on the screen to become garbled.

You'll find that the chat mode is best reserved for very brief messages. For extended conversations, a voice connection over the phone lines is much more personal and comfortable, and it costs the same.

TRANSFERRING FILES BETWEEN PCS

You can send a copy of a file to a host microcomputer or have it send a file to you. If the host is in remote host mode (the remote computer is unattended), you control the entire process, as described earlier in "Transmitting and Receiving Files."

If you are running in person-to-person mode, then either sending or receiving a file requires coordination between both parties. To accomplish this, messages can first be sent back and forth in chat mode, in order to agree on who is to send what file to whom.

In the following section, we'll discuss the steps for transferring files when there's a user at each end.

SENDING AND TRANSMITTING FILES   There are two different ways in which a file can be transferred from your computer to the remote one. First Choice calls these two methods sending and transmitting.

When a file is *sent,* the data is moved character by character from the file that you select to the screen and memory of the host computer. The process is exactly the same as if you were entering the characters from the keyboard (you even see the characters on your screen as they're being sent).

In order for this method of sending data to work, the host software must be in the chat mode of operation. If the host is running First Choice, the chat mode is automatically maintained.

Any ordinary ASCII file can be sent this way, including First Choice documents and any other type of file that's been printed to a disk file. This includes graph *data,* but not graphs that have been written to disk.

To send a file, select *Send text from an ASCII file* from the Features menu. When the Directory Assistant appears, enter the name of the file to be sent. As the file is transferred, you'll see the text appear on your screen.

The communications protocol for transmitting files from First Choice is always XModem.

When a file is *transmitted*, it can be any type of file—not just an ASCII file. The file goes directly from your computer to the file named by the user at the host.

To transmit a file, select *Transmit file (using XModem)* from the Features menu. When the Directory Assistant appears, enter the name of the file to be transmitted.

First Choice waits until the host computer is ready to accept data. Normally, the user at that end must enter suitable instructions to his or her communications package. These include the name of the file in which to store the data being transferred, and the communications protocol to be used.

When both computers are ready, data is transmitted in "blocks," and as transmission proceeds, First Choice writes a message on the screen indicating which block is being copied.

Here's a typical scenario of how a file might be transmitted from one computer to another. We'll assume that User 1 is running First Choice, and that he or she is connected with a remote PC at which User 2 is sitting. User 2 could be running either First Choice or some other communications software package. Text in quotes represents messages transmitted from one user to the other:

1. *User 2:* "Will you send me a file using XModem protocol?"

2. *User 1:* "OK. Which one do you want?"

3. *User 2:* "Your file named AUTOEXEC.BAT."

4. *User 1:* "OK. Here it comes."

5. User 1 issues instructions to First Choice to transmit the file named AUTOEXEC.BAT, using XModem protocol; User 2 issues instructions to his or her communications software to receive the file, which is named EXEC.JOE.

6. Both First Choice and the communications package at the remote computer busy themselves with transmitting the file.

RECEIVING FILES FROM A REMOTE COMPUTER   If the remote user is going to *transmit* a file, you need to carry out the following steps. Select *Receive a file (using XModem)* from the Features menu. When the Directory Assistant appears, enter the name of the file on your computer where the data is to be written.

Remember, there's
no need to panic as
the file scrolls off the top of
the screen, because it's
saved in the working copy.

First Choice will wait until the user at the host end has instructed his or her communications software to transmit the file. These instructions must include the name of the file, and the transmission protocol (which must be XModem).

If the remote user is running First Choice, then an ASCII file can be *sent*, rather than transmitted. In this case, you don't have to do anything except watch the file unfold on your screen.

If the remote user is running software other than First Choice, and if the software can transmit a file in ASCII mode, the procedure is the same: You do nothing except watch the file appear on your screen. After transmission has finished, you can then inspect the working copy, print it, save it to a disk file, or discard it.

MAKING YOUR COMPUTER THE HOST

You can set up your computer as the host so that it can automatically answer an incoming call from another computer. Select *Connect to another computer* from the Main menu. When the Service menu appears, select *Answer incoming call*.

First Choice displays the message that it is waiting for another computer to ring up. After a call has been answered and the connection established, you and the user at the calling end can transfer messages and files as described above.

AUTOMATING THE SIGN-ON PROCEDURE

With some remote computers, signing on is a multistep process that can take up a fair amount of time. You must enter a password and perhaps go through other time-consuming steps before you actually begin using the computer.

If you plan to use a particular remote computer frequently, you can automate the entire dialing and sign-on process to that computer, using First Choice's automatic sign-on feature, which is similar to the recording macros of many software packages. Basically, you create an automatic sign-on by recording each step that you make as you sign on to a remote computer. Once this "recording" has been made, you can "play it back" whenever you want to sign on to that particular computer.

You can create a separate automatic sign-on for each computer listed in the Service menu. At any time, you can either erase the automatic sign-on for any particular remote computer or replace it with a new version. This feature can be particularly helpful if you are using a modem that requires you to dial each telephone number manually.

CREATING AN AUTOMATIC SIGN-ON To create an automatic sign-on for a remote computer, select *Connect to another computer* from the Main menu. When the Service menu appears, select the remote computer whose sign-on procedure you wish to automate. When the Service Information form for that computer appears, use the Tab key to move the cursor to the entry *Create automatic sign-on*. Enter Y for this entry, then press ◄┘.

At this point, everything that occurs will be recorded by First Choice—both what you enter and what the remote computer sends back to you. Continue with the normal sign-on procedure for this remote computer, until you are ready to begin using it. When you've completed the sign-on, press F10 (this instruction appears at the bottom of the On-Line screen).

When you press F10, the recording ends, and everything that's been recorded is saved permanently as the automatic sign-on for this remote computer. You can continue using the remote computer as you normally would for the remainder of the current session.

If you plan to use certain commands each time that you sign on to a certain computer, you can include these in the recorded portion. Simply wait until you've entered all of the commands before you press F10.

SIGNING ON AUTOMATICALLY To sign on to a remote computer automatically, the entire sign-on procedure must have been previously recorded. Select the computer from the Service menu. When the Service Information form appears, press ◄┘, and First Choice will take over. As each message is received from the remote computer, First Choice will issue the responses exactly as they were recorded. This will continue until all of the recording has been played back.

You can interrupt the automatic sign-on at any time by pressing the Esc key. If you do this, you'll need to continue signing on manually, or the session will probably be terminated by the remote computer.

An automatic sign-on is saved by First Choice and can be used over and over.

You can choose to sign on manually if you wish. Just press F10 when the Service Information form appears. You might want to do this if the automatic sign-on for a computer contains instructions that you don't want to use for a particular session.

REPLACING OR DELETING AN AUTOMATIC SIGN-ON First Choice expects each sign-on session for a particular computer to be identical to the session that was originally recorded. This means that if any of the remote computer's sign-on messages change, First Choice will probably be unable to continue. You can continue by pressing the Esc key and signing on manually, but the automatic sign-on will have to be replaced with a new recording.

You might also want to replace the automatic sign-on if you decide to alter your initial sign-on responses. For example, you might change your password, or the way in which you enter your name.

To replace an existing automatic sign-on, follow the steps for creating one. Begin by entering "Y" for the option *Create automatic sign-on (Y/N)* on the Services Information form. As you proceed, you'll get a message from First Choice, asking you to confirm that you indeed wish to replace the existing automatic sign-on. If you press ←┘, the replacement continues.

To delete an automatic sign-on, begin as though you were replacing it. As soon as the On-Line screen appears, press F10. Because the new automatic sign-on contains nothing, First Choice deletes it altogether from its memory.

SUMMARY

Not all communications software behaves in the same way. For example, First Choice transmits a character as soon as you strike a key, whereas some software packages transmit only after ←┘ is pressed. Another example: First Choice is basically always in the chat mode, unless you give it a specific instruction to do something special, such as transmit a file. Many communications packages have to be specifically put into chat mode, and some may not even have such a mode.

There is a great deal of variation among the different software packages. The only generalization that can safely be made about their behavior is that it's often difficult to get them to talk to each other. You may need to expend considerable patience and time when trying to get two PCs to communicate.

One of the biggest problems with computer-to-computer communication is that if something fouls up, it could be due to any of the following:

- Something wrong with your computer's hardware

- A bug in your computer's software

- Incorrect installation parameters for First Choice

- Something wrong with the hardware or software at the other end

- Transmission line problems

It may therefore be difficult to know where to begin to track down a problem.

On the other hand, it's almost always possible to get things working right, given enough time and patience. An incredible amount of information is available to you via the telephone lines, and you can reap enormous benefits from computer-to-computer communications.

Chapter
10

Transferring Data between First Choice Modules

First Choice contains many features that make it a truly integrated system, including menu structures and commands for each module, and the all-encompassing editor. Another strong integration feature of First Choice is the ease and flexibility with which it can transfer information from one module to another.

In this chapter, we'll describe the various ways in which information can be shared, or moved, between First Choice's different modules. You'll learn how to use the word processing and database manager modules to generate form letters and print mailing labels. You'll also see how to combine two or more documents. Next, you'll learn how to incorporate information from databases, spreadsheets, and graphs into a document. Finally, you'll discover how to combine various types of data into a spreadsheet.

CREATING PERSONALIZED FORM LETTERS

To generate a group of personalized form letters, you use a basic form letter, written with the word processor, and a group of records in a database containing the information (names, addresses, etc.) to be merged with the form letter.

Suppose that you want to send a group of customers personalized letters similar to the one in Figure 10.1. We'll assume that you have a database called CUSTOMER, which contains information about these customers—one record per customer. The form of the CUSTOMER database is shown in Figure 10.2.

```
                                              June 25, 1988

Mr. Albert Krasnowitch
49 Hampton Way Court
Phoenix, AZ 12343

Dear M. Krasnowith:

We'd like to thank you for your recent business. Please keep
in touch with us, Albert. We'd be happy to mail merchandise
prepaid, even to Phoenix!
                                         Sincerely,


                                         Joe Pringlesbury
```

Figure 10.1: Personalized form letter

BUILDING THE FORM LETTER

Begin by building the form letter shown in Figure 10.3. Note that the letter shown in this figure differs from the one in Figure 10.1, in that specific information has been replaced by items enclosed in asterisks. These represent field names in the CUSTOMER database. For example, the item *FIRST NAME* is the name of a field. When the customized letters are printed, actual field values from the CUSTOMER database will replace the field names in the form letter.

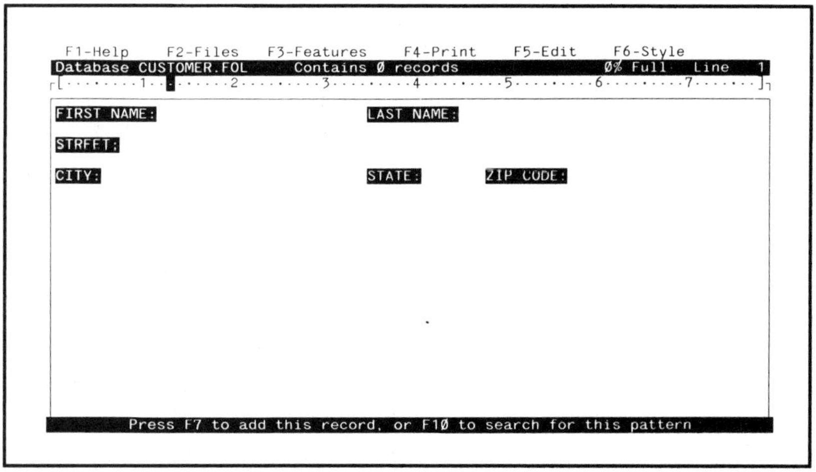

```
     F1-Help     F2-Files    F3-Features    F4-Print    F5-Edit    F6-Style
    Database CUSTOMER.FOL        Contains Ø records             Ø% Full   Line   1
  ┌·······1··┬·······2·········3·········4·········5·········6·········7······┐
    FIRST NAME:                          LAST NAME:
    STREET:
    CITY:                       STATE:        ZIP CODE:




                                      .




          Press F7 to add this record, or F1Ø to search for this pattern
```

Figure 10.2: CUSTOMER database form

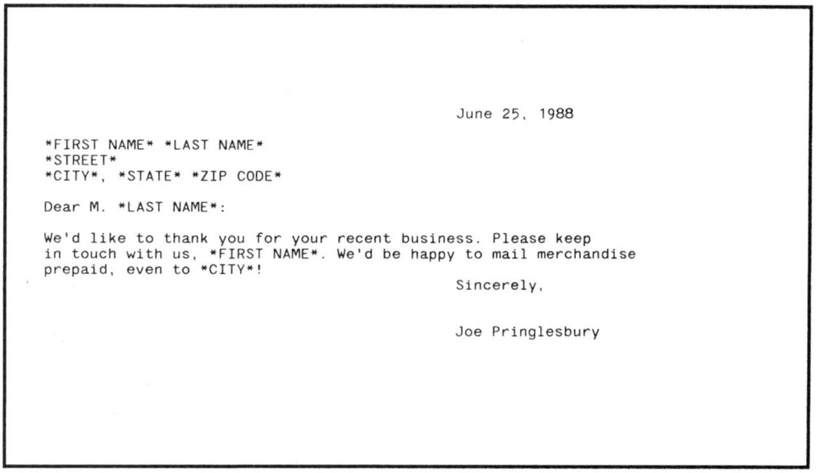

```
                                              June 25, 1988

    *FIRST NAME* *LAST NAME*
    *STREET*
    *CITY*, *STATE* *ZIP CODE*

    Dear M. *LAST NAME*:

    We'd like to thank you for your recent business. Please keep
    in touch with us, *FIRST NAME*. We'd be happy to mail merchandise
    prepaid, even to *CITY*!
                                         Sincerely,


                                         Joe Pringlesbury
```

Figure 10.3: Form letter containing field names

Notice in Figure 10.3 that a space is included between *FIRST NAME* and *LAST NAME*. This is a real space that will separate the first and last names when the letter is printed. Punctuation marks can also be used to separate a field name from ordinary text or other field names. When the value of a field is printed, any trailing blanks are stripped off.

In addition, Figure 10.3 shows that the field name *CITY* has been used twice. A field name can be placed anywhere in a form letter and can appear as many times as desired.

Finally, the field name must be enclosed in asterisks and spelled exactly as it appears in the database, including any spaces; however, you don't have to worry about uppercase and lowercase.

Here are the first steps in building your form letter:

1. Select *Create a document* from the Main menu.

2. Enter the text of the form letter, including any field names.

CHOOSING THE DATABASE AND SPECIFYING PRINT OPTIONS

After you've entered the form letter, you must select various options that control the printing. You also must specify the name of the database containing the information to be merged. Continue working with the form letter, which should be on the screen:

For a discussion of options on the Print menu, refer to "Printing Part of Your Document" in Chapter 2.

1. Select *Print form letters* from the Print menu. The Print Options menu will appear (Figure 10.4).

Figure 10.4: Print Options menu

2. For the option *Database name*, enter the name of the database containing the information to be merged into the form letter (in this case, enter **CUSTOMER**). If the file is not on the current disk drive and/or subdirectory, enter the correct drive name and subdirectory as part of the file name.

3. If you're outputting to the screen or a disk file, make the appropriate entry for the *Print to* option (see "Outputting to Screen or Disk" below).

4. When you have entered the options, press ← and a blank database form will appear. You'll use this form to specify which records from the database are to be merged with the form letter.

SELECTING RECORDS AND PRINTING THE LETTERS

In order to select the records to be merged with your form letter:

1. Enter the search instructions into the database form. If you wish to use all of the records in the database, don't enter any search instructions. For details about search instructions, see "Finding Selected Records in a Database" in Chapter 3.

2. In addition to search instructions, you can enter sort instructions if you'd like to have the letters printed in a certain order. For example, you could print letters sorted by the value of the *City* or *State* fields (or both). For details about sort instructions, see "Sorting Records" in Chapter 4.

3. When you've finished entering search and/or sort instructions, press F10. Printing begins, and First Choice keeps track of its status on the screen.

You can abort the printing at any time by pressing the Esc key.

4. When the printing ends, press ← to return to the form letter.

If you plan to use the same form letter at a later time, save it to a disk file, using the Files menu. It can then be used with the same set of records, or with a different set. These records can be from any database that contains the fields specified in the form letter.

MERGING LONG FIELDS INTO THE TEXT

When a long field is merged into the body of a letter, the resulting letter will sometimes have unwanted breaks at the merging point. This is because First Choice doesn't check for unnecessary line breaks as it performs the merging. You can fix this by writing the field name as follows:

> ... And so, *T,FIRST NAME*, we hope that you'll give serious consideration...

When the letter "T" is added as part of the field name, First Choice will make sure that the resulting merge is handled properly, by deleting any extra blanks.

OUTPUTTING TO SCREEN OR DISK

Instead of printing the letters, you can send the output to the computer screen or to a disk file. You might want to display the output on the screen in order to check how the letters will be printed; their format on the screen is identical to their printed format.

To send the letters to the screen, enter SCREEN for the *Print to* option on the Print menu. When the output begins, First Choice will pause after each screenload so that you can examine the results.

You can send the letters to a disk file by entering the name of the file for the *Print to* option on the Print menu. This file can later be loaded into First Choice's editor. You can then check it over, editing it if necessary, and send it to the printer.

ADDING STYLE TO THE FORM LETTERS

You can enhance the way in which a particular field is printed by selecting a special style for it. For example, in the letter shown in Figure 10.3, you might want to boldface the last name in the heading. You would do this by boldfacing *LAST NAME* (including the asterisks) in the heading. You can use any of the styles in the Style menu.

PRODUCING MAILING LABELS

This process is nearly identical to the one for generating form letters. First you create a master form letter, which consists only of name and address fields. You then specify label sizes and choose the database. Finally, you select the records to be used for generating the labels.

To illustrate how this works, we'll again use the CUSTOMER database (Figure 10.2). Create a mailing label document like the one shown in Figure 10.5. Note that the document consists only of field names.

```
*FIRST NAME* *LAST NAME*
*STREET*
*CITY*, *STATE* *ZIP CODE*
```

Figure 10.5: Mailing label document

SETTING PAGE LENGTH AND MARGINS

To specify the size of the labels being printed, select *Set page size, headers, and footers* from the Features menu. Then use the following guidelines. When you've entered all of the settings, press ← to return to the label document.

PAGE LENGTH   Set this to the total number of lines (usually six) between the tops of two successive labels. You can find the correct value by measuring the label-to-label distance with a ruler (there are six lines per inch).

MARGINS   Initially, set the left margin to 1. Then, set the right margin equal to the number of characters between the start of one label and the start of the next label in the same row (labels usually come one, two, or three per row on a continuous form). You can determine this number by measuring the number of inches between the left edges of the first and second labels in a row. If there's only one label per row, use the width of a single label. Multiply the label-to-label distance by the number of characters per inch, normally 10 or 12. To find out which your printer generates, measure some text that's been printed by First Choice (not in Compressed mode). For example, suppose that your page of labels has three labels per horizontal row, and the horizontal label-to-label distance is 2½ inches. If your printer outputs 10 characters per inch, then you would set the right margin to 25. Finally, set the top and bottom margin values to zero.

SELECTING THE DATABASE AND CHOOSING PRINTER SETTINGS

You're now ready to choose the printer settings for the labels. Also, you'll select the database that will provide the field values for your labels.

1. Select *Print labels* from the Print menu. The mailing labels Print Options menu will appear.

2. Enter the name of the database. If necessary, include the disk drive and subdirectory as part of the name.

3. Enter the number of labels in each row. This will be either **1, 2,** or **3.**

4. Enter the name of the output device. This will be **Printer,** unless you divert the output elsewhere.

5. If necessary, enter the amount by which printing should be indented. You need only do this if the printout is too far to the left. In that case, enter the number of characters by which the printing should be shifted to the right. (You may need to use trial-and-error to determine the correct indent.)

6. When you've finished entering print options, press ◄┘, and a blank database form will appear.

SELECTING RECORDS
AND PRINTING THE LABELS

To select the records used for printing the labels, enter the search instructions. If you wish to use all of the records in the database, don't enter any search instructions. For details on search instructions, see "Finding Selected Records in a Database" in Chapter 3.

In addition to search instructions, you can enter sort instructions. For example, mailing labels are often printed in zip code order. For details about sort instructions, see "Sorting Records" in Chapter 4.

When you've finished entering search and sort instructions, press F10. Printing begins, and First Choice informs you of its progress with on-screen messages.

If you plan to use the same format for labels again, you can save the document to a file. Then, whenever you wish to print a new set of labels, retrieve the document, select the records to use, and start printing.

ADJUSTING PRINTER SETTINGS

You'll probably need to experiment with labels in your printer before you get all of the settings just right; be prepared to waste a few labels.

A good technique is to print only one or two rows of labels after you choose settings (stop the printing with the Esc key). Measure horizontal and vertical distances with a ruler to decide how much to change the margin and page length settings. You can also move the field names around in the document, in order to center the printout on the labels. Once you become familiar with your printer and with how First Choice works, you'll be able to generate a set of labels very quickly.

COMBINING DATA
FROM DIFFERENT FILES

You can use First Choice to merge selected information from nearly any two First Choice files—even files of different types. For example, you might wish to incorporate part of the data from a spreadsheet or database into a quarterly report. You can even combine a graph with a document, provided that the graph has been properly prepared.

TRANSFERRING DATA WITH THE CLIPBOARD

The clipboard can be used to capture and save data from most of First Choice's modules. This is often the quickest way to combine information from one module with that of another.

The clipboard retains data even when you exit from First Choice.

Whatever is placed on the clipboard remains there until something else is put there (the clipboard can hold only one set of data at a time). The clipboard holds only text and numbers; it can hold graph *data*, but not graphs.

The steps for transferring information are basically the same, regardless of the type of data being moved:

- Retrieve the file containing the data to be transferred.

- Select the data to be transferred by defining the beginning of the block with Alt-S, then expanding the block using the cursor keys, until all of the data you want is included.

- Copy the data to the clipboard by pressing Alt-C.

- Retrieve the file into which the data on the clipboard is to be transferred.

- Move the cursor to the place on the screen where the clipboard data is to be pasted.

- Paste the data from the clipboard with Alt-P.

The clipboard can be used in many ways; in fact you can use it to store just about anything displayed on the screen, except graphs and special messages and displays generated by First Choice. You can copy

- A block of text from one document to another document.

- A block of text from a document into the field of a record within a database.

- Columns of text or numbers from a document to a spreadsheet.

- An entire database record into a document, including field names. To do this, display the record on the screen, then copy the entire record to the clipboard. The field names are automatically included.

- A blank database form to a document (you might want to include this as part of the description of a database).

- A database table to a spreadsheet.

- Part of a spreadsheet to a document.

- The data from a graph to a spreadsheet, and vice versa.

- The data from a graph to an existing document.

For very large data transfers, using the clipboard may not be possible; beyond a certain limit, data won't fit on it. Also, using another method of transferring data may be more convenient. We'll describe other methods in the following sections.

MERGING DOCUMENTS

You can combine, or merge, two or more separate documents that have been created with First Choice. Suppose that you want to merge Document B into the middle of Document A:

- Load Document A into First Choice.

- Move the cursor to the position where Document B is to be merged.

- Select *Merge another file* from the Files menu. The Directory Assistant will appear.

- Specify the name of the document to be merged. If necessary, include as part of the file name the drive and subdirectory holding the document.

A copy of Document B will merge with Document A, starting at the original cursor position. Note that the margins of Document B are altered to conform to the current margin settings of Document A, unless Document B contains one or more rulers. In that case, these rulers are merged along with the rest of the document, and they retain their effect in the merged document. For example, the last ruler in Document B can change the margin settings of Document A, from the place in which Document B is merged.

Any file with a .DOC extension can be merged into a document file. Also, any ASCII file can be merged. This includes First Choice reports, spreadsheets, or graphs that have been properly output to a disk file (see the following sections for details). Files that cannot be merged are spreadsheets (.SS or .WKS extension), databases (.FOL extension), and report files (.REP extension).

MERGING DATABASE INFORMATION INTO A DOCUMENT

You can use the clipboard to transfer a single record at a time from a database into a document. However, you may sometimes wish to merge data from several records at once. You can do this by creating a report containing the pertinent data from the database records, then merging this report into an existing document. Alternatively, the clipboard can be used to copy selected parts of the report file into the document. Both methods are described below.

CREATING THE REPORT   If you are creating a new report, start with *Create a report* from the Main menu, and go through the entire report generation procedure. This includes selecting the specific records to appear in the report, entering any sort instructions, and choosing options that affect the report's appearance. If you plan to use an existing set of report instructions, select *Get an existing file* from either the Main menu or the Files menu. When the Directory Assistant appears, select the file containing the report.

It's a good idea to plan the width of the report so that it will conform to the margin settings of the document with which it will be merged. For example, if your document has margins of 10 and 70, but your report is 80 columns wide, there's going to be a problem: if the lines of the report are wider than the lines of your document, the report lines will wrap around, creating unwanted results.

One solution is to change the document margin settings before merging in the report. This will work as long as the report width is not greater than the maximum possible line width of your printer.

Alternatively, you can specify the width of the report on the Print Options menu, but you also need to plan how many fields will comfortably fit across a single line of the report.

When the Print Options menu appears, enter the name of a disk file for the *Print to* option. When the report is output, it will be written to the disk as an ASCII file.

MERGING THE REPORT FILE   The report file that you generated can now be merged with an existing document:

- Choose *Get an existing file* from the Main menu or Files menu to retrieve the document.

- After the document appears, move the cursor to the location where you want the report to be merged.

- Select *Merge another file* from the Files menu.

- When the Directory Assistant appears, specify the name of the file containing the report. You can either enter the file name or select it from the Other column.

- Choose which type of ASCII file, either with or without carriage returns.

The report will be merged where you positioned the cursor. You can now edit the entire document, including the merged report, in any way that you wish. Finally, you can print the document or save it for use at a later time.

COPYING WITH THE CLIPBOARD   As an alternative to the above procedure, you can use the clipboard to copy selected parts of the report file into another document:

- Retrieve the report file into the word processor.

- Edit the report in any way that you wish.

- Select the section of the report to be merged, then use Alt-C to copy it to the clipboard.

- Using *Get an existing file* from the Files menu, retrieve the document of interest.

- Move the cursor to the exact position in this document where you want the report to be merged.

- Press Alt-P to paste the contents of the clipboard into the document.

MERGING A SPREADSHEET INTO A DOCUMENT

You can merge all or any part of a spreadsheet into a document (the *target* document), using either of two different methods. The first method, which involves using the clipboard, is faster and works as long as the amount of data being transferred isn't too large. The second method involves merging the output from a spreadsheet into a document.

USING THE CLIPBOARD   The clipboard can be used effectively when two conditions are met. First, each row of data being transferred must fit comfortably into the line width of the target document. You may need to do some experimenting to determine whether or not the width of the rows being transferred is small enough, because First Choice inserts blank spaces between columns when data is copied to the clipboard.

For details on using the clipboard, see "Tranferring Data with the Clipboard" in this chapter.

Next, the amount of data being transferred must fit on the clipboard. The capacity of the clipboard is hard to predict, because it depends on the contents of the cells being copied. You can generally expect several thousand cells to fit on the clipboard. In any case, First Choice will issue a message if you try to transfer more data to the clipboard than it can hold.

OUTPUTTING THE SPREADSHEET TO A FILE   An alternative method for transferring data from a spreadsheet into a document involves outputting the spreadsheet data to a disk file, then merging that file into the document. This method is similar to the one described in "Merging Database Information into a Document." For very large spreadsheets, or spreadsheets whose width is larger than the line width of the target document, this is the preferred way to transfer spreadsheet data:

- Retrieve the spreadsheet into First Choice's memory by selecting *Get an existing file* either from the Main menu or the Files menu.

- Select the range of cells to be output by moving the cursor to the beginning of the range, then pressing Alt-S or using the Edit menu.

- Using the cursor keys, expand the range to include all of the cells to be output. If you plan to output the entire spreadsheet, you do not have to select a range of cells.

- Select the Print menu and choose either *Print this spreadsheet* or *Print selected cells only,* depending on whether you're going to merge the entire spreadsheet or only selected cells. The Print Options menu will appear.

- For the *Print to* option, enter the name of a disk file into which the spreadsheet data will be output.

- Select a page width compatible with the line width of the target document. First Choice will automatically break up the spreadsheet into sections, each of which fits into the specified width. The minimum page width that First Choice will accept is 29.

- When you've finished entering print options, press ←┘, and the spreadsheet data will be output to the disk as an ASCII file.

- Retrieve the target document into First Choice's word processor, and move the cursor to the spot where the spreadsheet data is to be merged.

- Select *Merge another file* from the Files menu. When the Directory Assistant appears, choose the name of the file containing the spreadsheet data. Remember to include the drive and subdirectory as part of the file name, if necessary.

- Select which kind of ASCII file to merge, either with or without carriage returns.

The spreadsheet data will be merged where the cursor is positioned. You can then edit the entire document in any way that you wish, including the merged spreadsheet data. Finally, you can print the document or save it to a disk file for later use.

COMBINING A GRAPH WITH A DOCUMENT

A document can be enhanced by including one or more graphs with the text. You can do this within First Choice by generating the graph in the appropriate format, then combining it with a document during printing. Here are the key elements:

- Create a graph, using the techniques described in Chapter 8. This graph *must* be saved to a disk file in *Graph format.

- Retrieve the desired document, and move the cursor to the exact spot where the graph is to be inserted.

- Insert the following command directly into the the document where you want the graph to appear:

  *GRAPH *filename******

  where *filename* is the name of the disk file containing the graph in *Graph format. The file extension .PF must be included as part of the name. If the disk drive and/or subdirectory are not the ones currently selected (by the Directory Assistant), include them as part of the file name.

When the document is printed, the graph will be printed at the position occupied by the *GRAPH *filename* command. Each graph occupies approximately 20 lines, and First Choice skips to a new page if a graph won't fit entirely on the current page.

You may want to do some experimenting in order to place the graph in the best possible position on a page. Because printing a high-quality graph can take quite a bit of time, you can speed up the process as follows.

When you save the graph in *Graph format, make two files—one in Draft mode and the other in either Standard or High-quality mode (depending on which gives the best quality on your printer). Then, when you print rough drafts of your document (including the graphs), use the name of the file containing the draft-quality graph in the *GRAPH* command. A draft-quality graph prints much quicker than a high-quality graph. When you've got things just right, change the *GRAPH* command to use the file containing the higher-quality graph.

TRANSFERRING DATA TO A SPREADSHEET

Information from nearly any type of First Choice file can be transferred either to an existing spreadsheet or to a new one. Here are the various forms of data that can be copied:

- An entire ASCII file
- Columns of information from a document
- Information from a database table
- A range of values from a graph or another spreadsheet

When a file of ASCII data is copied into a spreadsheet, the transfer is done directly, without the use of the clipboard.

All but the first item involve using the clipboard: First retrieve the document, database table, graph, or spreadsheet into First Choice. Next, select the block of data to be transferred, and copy it to the clipboard. Finally, retrieve the spreadsheet and paste the data into it from the clipboard.

When data is transferred into a spreadsheet, either from the clipboard or from an ASCII file, First Choice uses certain rules to recognize individual items and rows:

- Each line of data corresponds to a row in the spreadsheet: First Choice recognizes a line ending by a hard return, so if you use the word processor to generate data, end each line by pressing ◄┛.
- The maximum width for a single line is 240 characters.
- Individual items in each row must be separated from one another by one of the following: two or more consecutive spaces (a single space is not a valid separator), a semicolon (;), or a vertical bar (|).

- The double quote character (") can also be used as a valid separator by enclosing text strings. For example, you could write a line of three text items as "Item1""Item2""Item3."

- If an item contains a non-numeric character, or is not a valid number, it's treated as a text string. Otherwise, it's interpreted as a number. For example, *3.5,2* would be treated as a text string.

- The minimum cell width for the spreadsheet must be set at least two characters wider than the longest item being transferred.

To set the cell width, select *Set global style* from the Style menu, then enter the width in the *Minimum cell width* option.

After the transfer from the clipboard has been completed, make sure that the information was copied properly. Also check to see that no blank cells were inserted between data items—this will occur if the minimum cell width is set too narrow.

COPYING DATA FROM A DOCUMENT   Information can be transferred from a document to a spreadsheet, using the clipboard. This information can be a set of numbers, text strings, or a combination of both. Figure 10.6 shows a document consisting of columnar data; Figure 10.7 illustrates that same data after transfer to a spreadsheet.

If you're creating data within a document that will later be transferred, make sure that you use one of the separators mentioned above between data items. Remember: a single space is not a valid separator. For ease in reading, lay out the data in columns, as shown in Figure 10.6. Also, each line must end with a hard return, that is, press ↵ at the end of each line. If you're using an existing file of data, you can guarantee that each line ends with a hard return as follows:

- Move the cursor to the end of the first line to be transferred.

- Press the Del key until the next line (call it Line B) moves up—at least partially—to the current line.

- Press ↵ to force Line B back to the next line.

- Repeat this for each line to be transferred.

To transfer the data, first select the block of items to be transferred, then copy the block to the clipboard by pressing Alt-C. Finally, exit from the document, then retrieve the spreadsheet and paste the data from the clipboard.

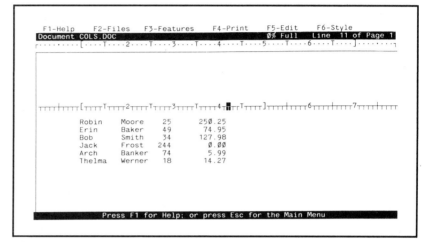

Figure 10.6: Document with columnar data

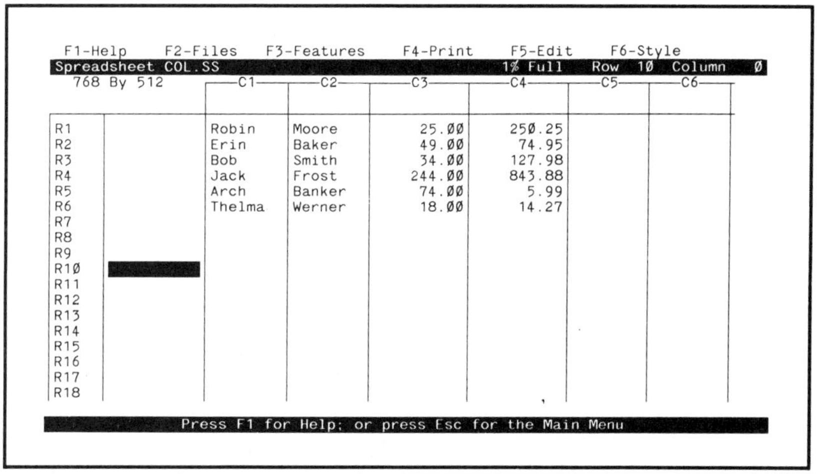

Figure 10.7: Data from Figure 10.6 after transfer to a spreadsheet

COPYING INFORMATION FROM A DATABASE TABLE You can use this technique to copy information from a database into a spreadsheet. Fields from the database become columns in the spreadsheet, and each record becomes a row. This method is particularly easy, because you don't have to worry about supplying separators between items: When a database table is pasted to the clipboard, vertical lines are automatically included as item separators.

To copy database information to a spreadsheet, begin by retrieving the database of interest. Next, define the table view that contains the data to be transferred. Finally, select the part of the table to be transferred, and copy it to the clipboard. You can now retrieve the spreadsheet and paste the data into it from the clipboard.

If your data includes time and date fields, they are transferred in whatever format they were originally entered into the database. YES/NO type of data is transferred as the strings *YES* and *NO*.

COPYING DATA FROM AN ASCII FILE The ASCII file format is a common denominator in the computing industry. Many different types of software packages can generate this type of file—word processors, database managers, spreadsheet programs, and so on. Often, you may generate an ASCII file with First Choice's word processor, then later decide to transfer it to a spreadsheet.

Different separators can be intermixed within the same file.

In order to transfer information from an ASCII file, the data items in the file must be separated with one of the valid separators listed earlier. To transfer the data:

- Retrieve the spreadsheet into which the data is to be transferred, or create a new spreadsheet.

- If necessary, reset the minimum cell width so that it's at least two characters wider than the widest data item to be transferred from the ASCII file.

- Move the cell cursor to the beginning of the range into which the data is to be transferred.

- Select *Merge ASCII data* from the Files menu, and enter the name of the ASCII file. The file then will be merged into the spreadsheet.

SUMMARY

Form letters and mailing labels are easily generated within First Choice, by combining name and address information from a database with a document created in the word processor. Often, the most difficult part of the process is getting the printer to make everything look as nice as possible.

First Choice excels when you want to transfer information from one file type to another. Data can be transferred between nearly all types of First Choice files. Moreover, in most situations, you use exactly the same technique: Copy the data onto the clipboard, then paste it into another application.

Chapter
11

Using the Calculator, Bookmark, Macros, and Disk Utilities Features

First Choice contains special features that can be used from within any module. The built-in calculator provides you with a handy tool for doing arithmetic operations. The results of an operation can even be transferred into the working copy. With the bookmark feature, you can set up to nine different bookmarks within documents, spreadsheets, databases, and graphs. You can then jump instantly to any bookmark. The disk utilities module offers a convenient set of file-manipulation tools. Finally, First Choice's built-in macro facility allows you to replace a set of often-used keystrokes with a single key combination.

USING THE BUILT-IN CALCULATOR ━━━

First Choice includes a calculator that performs standard arithmetic calculations, as well as a number of more sophisticated operations. You can use the calculator as a pop-up tool for on-the-spot computations, or you can place the results of a calculation directly into the text at the current cursor position.

The calculator can be called from any of First Choice's modules. However, it can't be called when a menu is displayed on the screen. With one or two exceptions, you can "pop up" the calculator either by pressing the speed key Alt-A, or by selecting *Use calculator* from the Features menu.

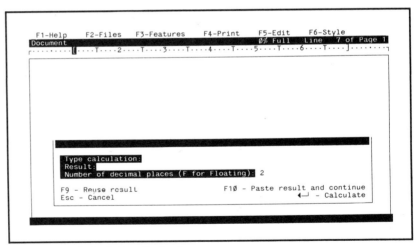

You can exit from the calculator by pressing Esc.

When the calculator is called, the calculation display box shown in Figure 11.1 appears. To use the calculator, enter the calculation on the line after *Type calculation.* For example, to calculate three plus four, type in 3 + 4. To view the result in the calculation display box, press ←. To use the result as the starting point of another calculation, press F9 instead of ←. To place the result into the text at the current cursor location, press F10.

Figure 11.1: Calculation display box

If you've called the calculator from a spreadsheet or a graph, and you press F10 to end a calculation, the result of that calculation will replace whatever is in the current cell. If you've called the calculator from any other module, First Choice moves existing text over to make room for the result (as though the Insert mode were on).

WHAT THE CALCULATOR CAN DO

When using the calculator, you can enter any type of ordinary numeric expression involving the following operators:

+	Addition
-	Subtraction
*	Multiplication
/	Division
^ or **	Exponentiation

For a full discussion of how First Choice does calculations, and its numeric functions, see Chapter 7.

You can use parentheses freely, to make the calculation proceed in a particular order. You can also incorporate into a calculation nearly all of First Choice's built-in numeric and financial functions, except those that refer to ranges of cells or values.

Let's try an example here. Suppose that you are an investment broker, and you want to tell a client what his or her monthly payments will be on a loan of $50,000, payable over 20 years at 10% interest compounded monthly. You could get the result instantly from First Choice by popping up the calculator, then entering the following calculation:

PAYMENT ON 50,000 AT 0.10/12 OVER 20*12

HOW RESULTS ARE FORMATTED

Except for spreadsheets and graphs, when a result is copied to the current cursor position, it always has the following format:

- No currency symbol
- Two decimal places
- No commas
- Variable length, up to 40 characters

For spreadsheets and graphs, the format of a result copied to the cursor position depends on the condition of the cell. If the cell is empty, the format of the copied result conforms to the global format currently in effect. If the cell contains a value, the format of the copied result takes on the format currently being used by that cell. In all cases, results are carried out to a maximum precision of 16 significant digits.

USING BOOKMARKS

Bookmarks can't be used within the report writer or communications modules.

A bookmark is a handy tool that you can use in a variety of ways. You can set up to nine bookmarks within a First Choice document, database, spreadsheet, or graph. Then, no matter what you're doing within First Choice, you can find your way back to that bookmark instantly.

After a bookmark has been set, you can jump to it from within any of the other First Choice modules. If you're working with a long file, such as a document or spreadsheet, using one or more bookmarks is often the quickest way to move from one particular place within that file to another. If you're working with a pair of different files at the same time, setting a bookmark in each allows you to move back and forth between them instantly.

HOW TO SET A BOOKMARK

Setting a bookmark is a simple process, which is the same regardless of which module you're using. Move the cursor to the position where you want to set a bookmark. Select *Set bookmark* from the Features menu. The bookmark display will appear (Figure 11.2). This display indicates which bookmarks are currently in use, and where they are. For instance, in Figure 11.2, bookmark number 2 is set on the second line of the second record in the database CLIENTS.FOL. Select the number of an unused bookmark, either by entering a number or by moving the cursor. Press ◄┘, and the bookmark is set.

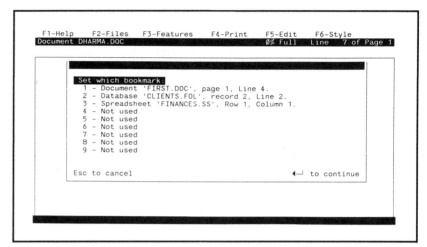

Figure 11.2: Bookmark display

There are several places where you can't set a bookmark. One of these is a document, spreadsheet, etc. that has not yet been stored in a file. Another is a location where a bookmark already exists. Finally, a bookmark can't be set on a blank space in a document or a record.

When a bookmark is set in a document or a record, the character where it's set is highlighted to indicate the bookmark position. However, in spreadsheets and graph data, no bookmark indication is shown on the screen.

If you select a bookmark that's already set someplace else, First Choice moves it from its original position to the location that you've specified.

JUMPING TO A BOOKMARK

When you jump to a bookmark, First Choice automatically performs the following steps. Whatever you're currently working with is saved to its file. If you're building a new application, such as a document or spreadsheet, and you haven't yet saved it to a file, First Choice tells you to assign a file name. First Choice saves your work to that file before retrieving the file containing the bookmark. It then moves the cursor to the bookmark.

The quickest way to jump to a bookmark is to use the speed key Alt-*n*, where *n* is the bookmark number. Alternatively, you can select *Find bookmark* from the Features menu, then specify the bookmark number.

DELETING BOOKMARKS

In general, if a bookmark is set somewhere, and you reset it somewhere else, it's automatically deleted from its original location. There are also other ways to delete a bookmark. If you delete a character on which a bookmark is set, the bookmark is also deleted. If a bookmark is in a block of text that is moved to the clipboard (erasing the text from its original location), the bookmark is deleted.

If a bookmark is set in a spreadsheet or graph cell, it can't be deleted simply by erasing the contents of that cell. This is because the cell itself still exists, and a bookmark is associated with a cell, rather than the contents of the cell. In order to delete the bookmark, you have to delete the actual cell, by deleting either the entire row or column containing that cell. This is less of a problem than it might seem, because leaving a bookmark set has absolutely no effect on anything.

> If you use a DOS command to delete a file in which a bookmark exists, or if you rename that file, the original entry in the Bookmark display isn't modified.

USING THE DISK UTILITIES MODULE

As you work with First Choice, you create and manipulate various types of files: document files, database files, and so on. You treat each type of file according to the type of information it contains.

However, there are certain file operations that apply to any type of file. For example, any file can be copied, renamed, or deleted. Although you can use standard DOS commands for these file operations, you can also perform them within First Choice by using the disk utilities module. Here are the operations that the module provides:

- Display the list of files on a particular disk or directory

- Copy a file to another file, either on the same disk or directory or a different one

- Rename or erase a file
- Create a new directory, or remove an existing one
- Format a new disk
- Copy an entire disk to another one

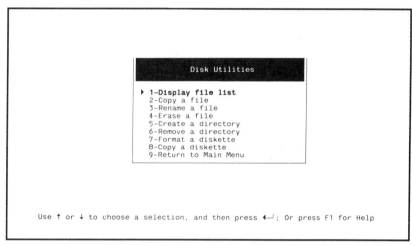

When the module is called from the Files menu, the selections *Format a diskette* and *Copy a diskette* don't appear on the menu.

You can call the disk utilities module either from the Files menu (from within any of First Choice's other modules) or from the Main menu. To select the disk utilities module from the Main menu, choose *Use disk utilities*. The Disk Utilities menu shown in Figure 11.3 appears.

```
                    ┌─────────────────────────────┐
                    │        Disk Utilities       │
                    ├─────────────────────────────┤
                  ▶ │ 1-Display file list         │
                    │ 2-Copy a file               │
                    │ 3-Rename a file             │
                    │ 4-Erase a file              │
                    │ 5-Create a directory        │
                    │ 6-Remove a directory        │
                    │ 7-Format a diskette         │
                    │ 8-Copy a diskette           │
                    │ 9-Return to Main Menu       │
                    └─────────────────────────────┘

   Use ↑ or ↓ to choose a selection, and then press ◀─┘; Or press F1 for Help
```

Figure 11.3: Disk Utilities menu

To exit either to the Main menu or to the module from which the disk utilities module was called, select the *Return to...* option from the Disk Utilities menu.

DISPLAYING LISTS OF FILES

Subdirectories of the current directory are listed in the Other column, followed by <DIR>.

You can display all of the files on the current directory or some other directory, or on a particular floppy-disk drive. You can also display the names of groups of files.

To display the files on the current drive or directory, select *Display file list* from the Disk Utilities menu. The Directory Assistant appears, showing the file list. To display the files on a different disk drive, enter the name of the drive, such as A:, then press ←. To display the files on a different directory, either enter the name of the desired directory or move the cursor to the name of the desired directory, then press ←.

If you want to see if a particular file exists on a disk or in a directory, first enter the name of the disk or directory, then enter the name of the file. If the file is not found, First Choice displays a message near the bottom of the display. If the file is found, no message is displayed.

To list only certain groups of files, you can use the asterisk (*) as a *wildcard*. The asterisk stands for any group of characters. Table 11.1 shows some examples of using wildcards. For example, if you enter the name *.DOC, only files with names ending in .DOC will be listed. Or, if you enter the file name SALES.*, all files with names beginning with SALES. will be printed. When you are done listing files, press the Esc key to return to the Disk Utilities menu.

Table 11.1: Examples of Wildcard Use

FILE NAME SPECIFICATION	FILE NAMES DISPLAYED
WORK.*	WORK WORK.JAN WORK.FEB
*.JAN	WORK.JAN SAMS.JAN ALMS.JAN
W*.*	WORK WORK.JAN WINE.FEB WHISKEY W WS.COM
.	{every file is displayed}

COPYING FILES

You can make a copy of a file to another disk, another directory, or the same disk or directory. If the copy is to another disk or directory, you can use either the same name or a different one for the new file. If the new copy is to be on the same disk or directory as the original, you must use a different name.

To make a copy of a file,

You can also select a directory from the screen with the cursor keys.

- Select *Copy a file* from the Disk Utilities menu. The Directory Assistant appears, displaying a list of the files on the current directory and/or disk.

- To choose a file on a different disk or directory, enter the name of the disk or directory. The list of files on that disk or directory will appear on the screen.

- Enter the name of the file to be copied, or select it by using the cursor keys.

- Enter the name of the new file.

If the new file is to be on a different disk or directory, precede the file name with the name of the disk or directory. You can also enter only the name of the new disk or directory; the corresponding list of files will appear, giving you a chance to see what files are there, before choosing a new file name.

If you select a name for the new file that already exists on the target disk or directory, First Choice issues a warning message. Also, you can back up one step in the copy process at any time by pressing the Esc key.

When the file has been copied, the Disk Utilities menu reappears on the screen.

RENAMING FILES

You can give a new name to a file. Note that this does not change the actual contents of the file. To do this, select *Rename a file* from the Disk Utilities menu. Enter the name of the file to be renamed, or select it with the cursor keys. If the file is on a different disk or directory, precede the file name with the name of the disk or directory. If you're not sure where the file is, you can enter only the name of a disk or directory; the list of files on that disk or directory will appear, and you can scan it to see if your file exists there.

Enter the new name for the file. Note that you don't include a drive or directory name as part of the file name. After First Choice has finished renaming the file, the Disk Utilities menu reappears on the screen.

ERASING FILES

You can permanently delete a file from a disk or directory. This operation should be done with caution, because once a file has been erased, it's gone forever. Because it's not difficult to accidentally erase the wrong file, it's a very good idea to make backup copies of important files. The *Copy a file* option of the disk utilities module is an easy way to make backups.

When the Directory Assistant is displayed on the screen, you can erase a file by first selecting it, then pressing F10. When First Choice asks you to confirm that you want to erase the file, press Y.

To erase a file, select *Erase a file* from the Disk Utilities menu. Enter the name of the file, or select it with the cursor keys. If necessary, select the appropriate disk drive or directory before specifying the file. Before First Choice wipes out the file, it asks you to verify the process. If you press ←⏎, the file is erased; if you press the Esc key, the file is not erased.

Note that erasing a file is not the same as erasing the working copy of a document, spreadsheet, etc. If you obtain a working copy from a disk file, then erase the working copy from the computer's memory, the contents of the original file remain untouched.

CREATING DIRECTORIES

When using a hard disk, you usually divide the files into different directories (sometimes called *subdirectories*) for convenience, placing each group of related files in a separate directory. Directories are arranged in a "tree" structure, in that any directory can itself contain one or more subdirectories as well as a group of files. Directories can also be created on floppy disks. Usually, this isn't done because of the limited storage capacity of a single disk.

When you begin to work with a new group of files, you may want to create a new directory in which to place them. Before creating this new directory, you must first decide where to place it: in the root directory itself (the very top of the tree structure of directories) or in some other directory. This should be given serious thought, because a poorly designed directory structure can be as much of a burden as no structure at all.

A directory name can be up to eight characters long and contain letters, digits, and various special characters.

To create a new directory, select *Create a directory* from the Disk Utilities menu. The Directory Assistant appears, listing the files of the current directory. If you want the new directory to be a subdirectory of the current directory, simply enter the name of the new directory.

If the new directory is to be on a disk other than the current one, enter the name of the disk drive, then press ◄—. The new disk drive name should appear on the line beginning *Directory of.*

If you want the new directory to be a subdirectory of some directory other than the current one, enter the name of that directory, then press ◄—. That directory name should appear on the line beginning *Directory of.* You can then enter the name of the new directory.

If you want the new directory to by directly under the root directory, first press ..◄— as many times as necessary until \ appears on the *Directory of* line. Then enter the name of the new directory.

After you enter the new name, First Choice asks you to verify that it's really all right to create the new directory. You can enter either "Y" or "N," depending on whether or not you've changed your mind. After the directory is created, the Directory Assistant remains on the screen. You can either create additional directories, or exit back to the Disk Utilities menu with the Esc key.

REMOVING DIRECTORIES

You can remove a directory only if it doesn't contain any files. This is a safeguard built into DOS, to prevent disasters. If you want to remove a directory that contains files, you must first erase all of the files.

You can't remove the current directory.

To remove a directory, select *Remove a directory* from the Disk Utilities menu. The Directory Assistant appears on the screen, displaying the files in the current directory. If the current directory is to be removed, you must first exit from it. For example, you can move to its "parent" directory by selecting ..<DIR> with the cursor keys.

Enter the name of the directory to be removed, or select it with the cursor keys (if it's listed on the screen). Subdirectories of the current directory are listed in the Other column. Each subdirectory ends with

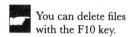
You can delete files
with the F10 key.

<DIR>. Press F10, and First Choice asks you to confirm that you indeed wish to remove the directory.

If the directory that you select contains files, a message to that effect appears on the screen. You can then decide whether or not to delete these files or to copy them to other directories.

After the directory has been deleted, the Directory Assistant display remains on the screen. You can then delete other directories, or you can return to the Disk Utilities menu by pressing the Esc key.

FORMATTING DISKS

Before you can use a new floppy disk (called a *diskette* by First Choice), it must be *formatted*. This is a process during which DOS writes special codes onto the disk. You can think of formatting as creating magnetic "boxes" on the disk, into which data can then be stored and retrieved.

Don't try to reformat a disk that has given you trouble. It's wisest to discard such disks, because there's a good chance that it's sustained permanent physical damage. Any data that you store on it could be lost.

Be sure not to format a disk that contains good data or programs, because the formatting process permanently wipes out everything on the disk.

First Choice allows you to format a disk in either drive A or drive B. You can't format a hard disk from within First Choice.

HARD-DISK COMPUTERS   First Choice must access the DOS program FORMAT.COM (or FORMAT.EXE) to perform disk formatting. To do this, the directory in which FORMAT.COM resides must be included in the currently defined *path*. If no path is defined for your system, or if the path doesn't include this directory, then First Choice won't be able to format disks.

Usually, PATH commands are included in an AUTOEXEC.BAT file that resides in the root directory of the computer. However, if your computer contains the file AUTOEXEC.BAT in the root directory, but it doesn't contain the correct PATH command, you can use the First Choice word processing module to modify the file as follows.

- Select *Get an existing file* from the Main menu.

- Enter the file name \AUTOEXEC.BAT, then press ←.

- Select *ASCII-Preserve carriage returns* for the file type.

- When the file appears, move the cursor to the end, then enter the following on a new line:

  PATH C:*directory*

  where *directory* is the full pathname of the directory containing FORMAT.COM.

- Select *Save as different type of file* from the Files menu.

- Enter AUTOEXEC.BAT for the file name, then press ←. Verify the save by typing "Y."

- Select *ASCII* as the file type.

If your computer has no AUTOEXEC.BAT file, you can create one using the word processing module. Select *Create a document* from the Main menu. Enter the same line described in the preceding paragraph:

PATH C:*directory*

and follow the same steps as above.

FLOPPY-DISK COMPUTERS   To format a disk on a floppy-disk computer, follow these steps:

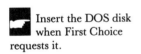
Insert the DOS disk when First Choice requests it.

- Select *Format a diskette* from the Disk Utilities menu.

- Enter either A or B to indicate which disk drive to use.

- Insert the disk to be formatted, then press ←.

When formatting is finished, First Choice asks if you want to format another disk. Enter "Y" or "N." When you've finished formatting disks, press Esc, and the Main menu will appear.

COPYING DISKS

You can make an exact duplicate of a floppy disk, using the procedure outlined below. The disk being copied to must be formatted. Also, make sure that it doesn't contain any valuable files, because they'll be erased during the copy process.

First Choice uses the DOS program DISKCOPY.COM to perform disk formatting. If you're using a hard-disk computer, this program is probably on the disk. If you're using a floppy-disk computer, your DOS disk probably contains the program.

For hard-disk computers, the directory containing the program DISKCOPY.COM must be included in the current path in order for First Choice to be able to find it. See the earlier section "Hard-Disk Computers" for details.

To copy a disk:

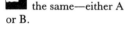
Both drives can be the same—either A or B.

- Select *Copy a diskette* from the Disk Utilities menu.

- Enter the name of the disk drive (A or B) containing the original disk.

- Enter the name of the disk drive (A or B) containing the new disk.

- Follow the instructions on the screen.

After you have finished copying disks, press the Esc key and the Main menu will appear on the screen.

USING MACROS

If you find yourself using the same set of keystrokes over and over, you may be able to use First Choice macros to your benefit. A macro is a single keystroke that "plays back" any set of keystrokes that you wish. For example, suppose that much of your word processing involves typing your name and address at the top of letters. You could create a macro consisting of the keystroke Ctrl-L (L for *letterhead*). Then, at the beginning of each letter, you'd press Ctrl-L, and First Choice would automatically enter your name and address.

You can use macros within any of First Choice's modules. Or, you can set up First Choice so that you can select often-used macros from the Main menu. In addition, you can set up a macro so that it pauses during playback, allowing you to enter text.

CREATING A MACRO

To illustrate how macros work, we'll create one that will help us output a heading each time we want to send a business letter. The heading is shown in Figure 11.4. We'll assign the macro to the keystroke Ctrl-D. Follow these steps:

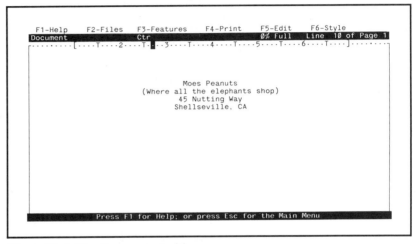

Figure 11.4: Heading created with a macro

1. Exit to the Main menu, then select *Create a document.*

2. Begin creating the macro by pressing Alt-0. The Macro menu shown in Figure 11.5 appears.

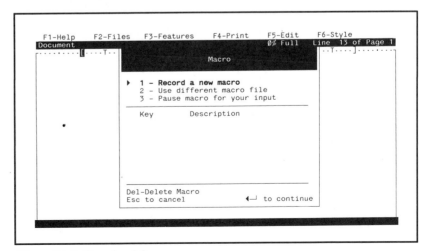

Figure 11.5: Opening Macro menu

3. You want to create a brand-new macro, so select *Record a new macro.*

4. The next display asks you to choose a macro key. Press the key **D**. This means that the final macro will be Ctrl-D. Note the file name, FCMACRO.KEY, at the top of this display. This is the file that will store any macros that you create.

5. Press the Tab key to move to the next line, where you can optionally enter a short description (20 characters maximum) of the macro. Enter the text **Peanut Heading** on this line, then press ⏎.

6. First Choice returns you to the word processor screen. Note that *Recording* appears on the top line. This tells you that each keystroke that you enter is being recorded as part of the macro.

7. Enter the text as shown in Figure 11.4. For simplicity, enter each line starting at the left-hand column. After you've finished, select the entire text, then choose *Center* from the Style menu.

8. To finish the macro recording, press Alt-0. The macro menu shown in Figure 11.6 appears.

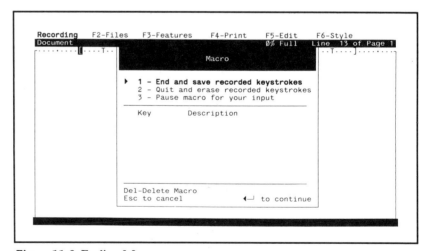

Figure 11.6: Ending Macro menu

9. Choose *End and save recorded keystrokes.*

Your macro has now been saved. Whenever you press Ctrl-D, the heading will "play back" onto the screen. Try it!

RULES FOR MACRO CREATION

You can create a macro from just about anywhere within First Choice: spreadsheet, document, even menus. A macro consists of the Ctrl key used together with any of the function keys or any of the letters A through Z, except H, I, J, or M. In addition, if you want to record a macro while using the communications module, you can use only the macros Ctrl-F1 through Ctrl-F10.

When you begin recording a macro, every keystroke that you enter is recorded as part of the macro. If you make a mistake and then correct it, it's all faithfully recorded.

If you want to make a menu selection during the macro recording, always press the number of the menu item; don't use the cursor keys.

You can stop recording a macro at any time, such as when you've made too many keyboard errors and want to begin again. To terminate recording, press Alt-0, then select *Quit and erase recorded keystrokes.* Verify that you want to quit by pressing ←┘, and you can then start over.

During macro recording, you can have the macro play back itself. For example, if you're recording the macro Ctrl-A, you can type in Ctrl-A. Later, when the macro is played back, it will play itself back endlessly, or until you terminate it with the Esc key. This can be a useful feature. For example, you could write a macro to prompt a user for some input, accept that input (see "Creating a Macro with a Pause"), then output information to the printer. Finally, the macro could call itself, so that the entire process would automatically repeat.

PLAYING BACK A MACRO

You can cause any macro to play back simply by pressing that macro key. Note that you can play any macro from anywhere in First Choice. In other words, if you record a macro in the word processor, you can play it back in the middle of creating a new record or spreadsheet.

Even pressing the Esc key is recorded as part of a macro.

A macro can't play back any macro other than itself.

If you have created a large number of macros, you may forget which one to use for a particular application. If this happens, simply press Alt-0. The Macro menu will display all of the macros that you've recorded. You can select the one that you want with the cursor keys, then press ◄━━┛ to play back the macro.

You can even set up First Choice so that the Main menu displays commonly used macros. To execute the macro, you select that menu item (see ''Running a Macro from the Main Menu''). With this method, you don't even have to remember the name of the macro.

You can also have a macro play back as soon as First Choice runs. To do this, enter the name of the macro along with the call to First Choice. For example, suppose that you want to play back the macro Ctrl-D immediately after First Choice begins running. Instead of calling First Choice with FIRST, type in FIRST -MD (that's a space after the word FIRST, followed by a hyphen). The keys -M stand for *macro,* and the D indicates the macro Ctrl-D.

CHANGING OR DELETING A MACRO

To change an existing macro, you use the macro creation process:

- Begin by pressing Alt-0, then select *Record a new macro.*

- Enter the name of the macro to be changed. First Choice will ask you to verify that you really want to replace the macro. Press ◄━━┛ to indicate *Yes.*

- Record the new keystrokes for the macro.

- Press Alt-0, then select *End and save....*

The new keystrokes will replace the original ones for this macro.

To delete an existing macro, begin by pressing Alt-0 to display the Macro menu. Select the macro with the cursor keys, then press the Del key to delete it. Press Esc to exit from the Macro menu.

CREATING A MACRO WITH A PAUSE

You can have a macro pause while it's playing back, to allow you to enter text. In fact, you can insert as many pauses as you like into a macro. To illustrate this nifty feature, we'll build a macro to help create the screen shown in Figure 11.7. In this figure, the boldfaced text is entered by the macro, and the remaining text by the user. At the end of each boldfaced word, the macro pauses to allow the user to enter information.

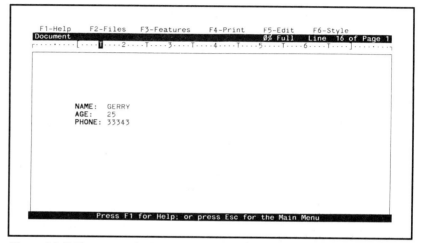

Figure 11.7: Document built with the aid of a macro

Follow these steps to create the macro:

1. Follow steps 1 through 6 in the section "Creating a Macro," creating the macro Ctrl-L.

2. After the word processor screen reappears and macro recording has begun, enter **NAME:** on the first line.

3. Press Alt-0 to bring up the Macro menu.

4. Select *Pause macro for your input.* The word processor screen again appears.

5. Press ⏎ to return to macro recording. The effect of steps 4 and 5 is to insert a pause into the macro after NAME: has been entered.

6. Enter the text **AGE:** and then repeat steps 3 through 5.

7. Enter the text **PHONE:** and then press Alt-0.

8. This time, end the macro recording by selecting *End and save....*

You've now recorded the macro Ctrl-L, containing two pauses for data entry from the keyboard. At each pause, you enter text, then press ⏎ to continue with the macro playback.

Sometimes, you may not want to go to a new line after entering text during a macro pause. You can force the macro to remain on the same line as follows. In steps 5 and 6 above, substitute the keystroke Ctrl ⏎ for ⏎. In this case, when you play back the macro and it pauses for keyboard entry, press Ctrl ⏎ to resume macro playback and also to keep the cursor on the same line. If you press ⏎ instead of Ctrl ⏎, the cursor will move to the next line, but the macro will continue to pause, waiting for the keystroke Ctrl ⏎.

RUNNING A MACRO FROM THE MAIN MENU

You can select frequently used macros from the Main menu. As an example, suppose that you have created the macro Ctrl-P, which selects *Create a document* from the Main menu (by playing back the character "1"), then enters your business heading. Assuming that you've already created the macro Ctrl-P, here's how to make this macro one of the choices on the Main menu.

- Return to the Main menu.

- Select *Set up First Choice*.

- When the Setup menu appears, choose *Set up alternate programs*. A second Setup display will appear (Figure 11.8). This menu is used to add items to the Main menu.

- For *Program name* in item A, enter the following macro description: Create Business letter.

- For *Path* in item A, enter Ctrl-P (that's six characters, starting with the letter C).

- Press ⏎ to exit to the Setup menu, then select *Return to Main Menu*.

You'll now see *Create Business letter* listed as one of the Main menu items. If it's the only addition you've made to the menu, it'll be item A. You can add up to five items to the original Main menu.

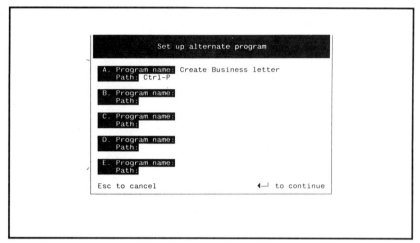

Figure 11.8: Setup display for alternate programs

To run a macro from the Main menu, select that item from the menu. In this example, the word processor would be called, then the business heading entered at the top of the document.

SETTING UP MACRO FILES

Up to now, all of the macros that we've been working with have been stored in the default macro file created by First Choice, namely FCMACRO.KEY. In using only this file for macros, several limitations are imposed on macro use. First, a maximum of 1,024 keystrokes can be recorded for all of your macros. In addition, you're limited to 32 macros. You can remove these restrictions by creating other macro files besides FCMACRO.KEY. Then, each file has the same limitations of 32 macros and 1,024 keystrokes. As an added bonus, you can use the same macro name for different purposes— once within each macro file.

For example, you could set up one macro file, WP.KEY, for word processing, another macro file, DB.KEY, for databases, and so on. Then, you could use the same macro names in each of the files. For instance, in the file WP.KEY the macro Ctrl-D might be used to create a heading on letters; while in the file DB.KEY the macro Ctrl-D could be used to display a particular table view.

To create a new macro file:

- Press Alt-0 to begin macro creation.

- Select *Use different macro file* from the Macro menu.

- When the Directory Assistant appears, enter the name of the new macro file (up to eight characters), then press ←. The extension .KEY is added to the file name by First Choice.

Any new macros that you create will now be added to the new macro file.

To use an existing macro file, follow the first two steps above. Then, when the Directory Assistant appears, select the macro file that you want. You can always tell which macro file is currently in use; when you begin creating a new macro, and First Choice asks you to enter the macro key that you want, the name of the current macro file is displayed at the top of the screen.

SUMMARY

The various tools that we've discussed in this chapter can be used throughout First Choice. They all contribute to the "integrated" feeling that you get as you use the package.

Whenever you need to perform a quick calculation, perhaps for entry into the data that you're working with, the built-in calculator is a handy device. If you need to jump back and forth between different applications, bookmarks can be an invaluable asset. With the disk utilities module, you can perform most of the standard file manipulation features, such as copying, renaming, and deleting. The macro facility offers a useful shortcut if you perform a lot of repetitive operations at the keyboard, and enables you to automate many activities within First Choice.

Appendix
A

...lling

...First

...ice

...chapter describes the preparations for using PFS: First Choice. Installation of ...ackage is straightforward, and only standard off-the-shelf hardware is required. ...chapter also covers various hardware considerations, customizing First Choice ...our computer, and how to get First Choice running.

3599823
14357
3614180

2:00   1:20 ⟩ 1 hr
1:00   12:20 ⟩ 1 hr
12:00   11:20 ⟩ 1 hr
11:00   10:20 ⟩ 1 hr
10:00

ala power
elect cos
elect KWH
FICA SS
HCFA PREM
HOME INS
N GAS COST
N GAS CH FT, 2²
N G COST
PROP TAX
SS PAY
TELEPHON
WATER SEW

APP. A

HARDWARE REQUIREMENTS

When we discuss computers throughout this book, we'll use the following terminology:

Hard-disk computer: Any computer with a hard disk, regardless of the number and type of floppy-disk drives attached to it

Floppy-disk computer: A computer with no hard disk, and at least two floppy-disk drives, regardless of their type

Before installing First Choice, read this section to make sure that you have the appropriate hardware. First Choice is designed to run on a computer that is compatible with the IBM PC, IBM PC/XT, IBM PC/AT, or PS/2. The computer can be either a hard-disk or floppy-disk machine. In addition, the computer must be equipped as follows:

Memory: The computer must have at least 512K of memory, preferably 640K.

If you plan to use First Choice extensively, it's a good idea to use a computer with a hard disk. If your computer does not have one, you might consider purchasing a hard disk for it; the modest investment will be well worth it.

Disks: First Choice will run with a hard disk and one or two floppy-disk drives (5¼-inch, 3½-inch, or one of each); or with two floppy-disk drives of any type.

Monitor: First Choice will work with almost any type of monitor. If your computer has a monochrome monitor, it should also have a Hercules-compatible display adapter (the board that controls the monitor). If you have a color monitor, either a CGA, EGA, or VGA display adapter can be used.

Printer: If you want to get hard copy from First Choice, your computer must be attached to a printer. First Choice directly supports more than 100 printers, but it will work with just about any printer. Even if your printer is old and the manual for it has disappeared, the chances are good that the printer can be used with First Choice.

Plotter: Several different plotters can be driven by First Choice, including those from Hewlett-Packard and Houston Instruments.

Mouse: If you plan to use a mouse with First Choice, either your computer must have a serial port to which the mouse can be connected, or the mouse must come with its own plug-in board. First Choice runs with mice made by Microsoft, PC Mouse Systems, or Logitech.

An *internal modem* is a modem on a board that plugs into the computer's main board. An *external modem* is a small box that plugs into a serial port.

Modem: To use First Choice for communication with remote computers, your computer must have a modem. Many modems are directly supported by First Choice. If you are going to use an external modem, your computer must have a serial port. If your computer has an internal modem, no additional serial port is needed.

If you plan to use both an external modem and a mouse, your computer should have two serial ports. However, if the mouse comes with its own plug-in board, only one serial port is needed (for the modem).

It's possible to share a single serial port between a mouse and an external modem, by plugging in each one as needed. But this quickly gets tiresome, so you might consider purchasing a plug-in board (not very expensive) with a second serial port.

MAKING BACKUPS

Before you install First Choice, you should make backups of the original floppy disks that contain the First Choice programs. A *backup* is a duplicate of an original program. After you've made backups of all the original First Choice disks, you can store the originals in a safe place and use the duplicates for working with the software. Then, if the duplicate disks are damaged in any way, you can make a new set of duplicates from the originals. In this way, you always have a good set of disks stored away safely.

Protect your disks against accidental erasure. If you're using 5¼-inch disks, attach a *write-protect tab* to each of the original First Choice disks. This tab should cover the little rectangular notch along one side of a disk. If you're using 3¼-inch disks, set the write-protect tab to the *protect* position.

Before beginning the backup procedure, obtain as many new disks as you plan to copy.

Making a set of duplicate disks is different on hard-disk and floppy-disk computers. We'll describe each separately.

MAKING BACKUPS ON A HARD-DISK COMPUTER

Before going on, make sure that your computer is running, and that the C prompt (something like C:\>) is showing on the screen. As you follow the steps outlined below, take careful note of the following terminology, which you'll see displayed on your computer's screen:

- SOURCE diskette: The original First Choice disk
- TARGET diskette: The blank disk to become the backup for the original

Here are the steps for copying Program Disk 1 to a blank disk:

The DISKCOPY program can be used to format new disks. For details, see Chapter 11.

1. Type in the following command: **DISKCOPY A: A:** (put a space between the first colon and the second A), then press ←┘. If the screen displays the message *Bad command or file name,* you'll have to get assistance from someone familiar with your computer to find the program DISKCOPY.

2. Insert Program Disk 1 into drive A.

3. Press any key to continue.

4. Continue following the instructions that appear on the screen for inserting and removing disks. You may do a bit of disk switching, so be careful not to get the disks confused.

5. When the copy process is finished, the message *Copy another diskette (Y/N)?* will appear on the screen. Type in **Y**.

6. Remove the backup disk and label it to match the label on the original, adding the word *BACKUP* to the label.

Repeat the above procedure for each original First Choice disk that you have. After you've finished copying the last disk, answer **N** to the question in step 5 above.

After you've finished copying all of the disks, store the originals somewhere safe. You can then start up First Choice, using the backup disks that you've just made.

MAKING BACKUPS ON A FLOPPY-DISK COMPUTER

As you follow the steps outlined below, take careful note of the following terminology, which you'll see displayed on your computer's screen:

- SOURCE diskette: The original First Choice disk
- TARGET diskette: The blank disk to become the backup for the original

The DISKCOPY program formats new disks if necessary.

1. Insert a DOS disk (sometimes called a *system disk*) into drive A, and turn on the machine.

2. After a bit of a wait (possibly as long as one minute for some computers), you'll see the A prompt (something like A:\>) appear on the screen. Enter the time and date as requested, or simply press ←┘ when DOS asks for the time and date.

3. Type in the following command: **DISKCOPY A: B:** (put a space between the first colon and the letter B), then press ←┘. If the screen displays the message *Bad command or file name*, you'll have to get assistance from someone familiar with your computer to find the program DISKCOPY.

4. Remove the DOS disk from drive A, and insert Program Disk 1.

5. Insert a blank disk into drive B.

6. Press any key to continue.

7. When the copy process is finished, the message *Copy another diskette (Y/N)?* will appear on the screen. Type in **Y**.

8. Remove both disks from the computer.

9. Label the backup disk to match the label on the original disk, adding the word *BACKUP* to the label.

10. Repeat steps 3–9 for each original First Choice disk to be copied.

After you've finished copying all of the disks, store the originals somewhere safe. You can then start up First Choice, using the backup disks that you've just made.

INSTALLING PFS: FIRST CHOICE

An advantage of a hard-disk computer is that once First Choice has been installed on the disk, it is there more or less permanently and can be run easily without floppy disks. No special installation is required for floppy-disk computers.

Here are the steps for installation on a hard-disk computer:

1. Turn on the computer (this is also called *booting*). Make sure that you see the DOS prompt, which will look something like C:\>.

Remember: The symbol ◄─┘ means to press the Enter key.

2. Create a new subdirectory. This is where the First Choice programs will be stored. Enter the following commands:

```
MD \PFS ◄─┘
CD \PFS ◄─┘
```

After you've entered the above two DOS commands, you should again see a DOS prompt. You are now "in" the new subdirectory called PFS, and any file manipulations that take place will normally be in and out of this subdirectory.

Now you're ready to copy the First Choice programs into the subdirectory.

3. Insert the backup floppy labeled *Program Disk 1* into drive A. (For 3¹/₂-inch floppies, the label is *Program Disk 1 and Dictionary Disk*).

4. Copy the programs from the floppy onto the hard disk with the following command:

   COPY A:*.*

5. Repeat steps 3 and 4 for each of your backup floppy disks. (You should have a total of either three 5¹/₄-inch or two 3¹/₂-inch disks.)

Your First Choice programs are now "permanently" stored on the hard disk, from which they can be easily started at any time. Store the floppy disks in a safe place. You'll only need them if something accidentally damages the programs on the hard disk.

STARTING PFS: FIRST CHOICE

This section gives detailed instructions on how to get First Choice running. We have provided two sets of instructions, one for each of two possible types of disk-drive configuration:

- A computer with a hard disk and any combination of floppy-disk drives

- A computer with two floppy-disk drives and no hard disk

STARTING FIRST CHOICE ON A HARD-DISK COMPUTER

To get First Choice running, perform the following steps.

1. Turn on your computer. Make sure the DOS prompt (something like C:\ >) appears before you continue.

2. Enter the PFS subdirectory with the following command:

   CD \PFS ↵

3. Start First Choice with the following command:

    FIRST ←┘

You should now see the Main menu of First Choice (Figure A.1).

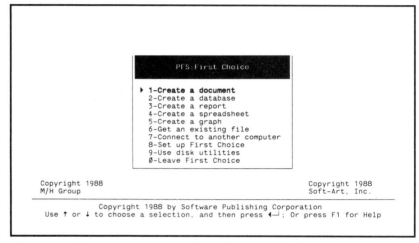

Figure A.1: Main menu display of First Choice

STARTING FIRST CHOICE ON A FLOPPY-DISK COMPUTER

Each time you run First Choice, you'll need to execute the following steps:

1. Insert a DOS disk into drive A and turn the machine on.

2. Enter the time and date as requested. If you prefer, press ←┘ when DOS asks for the date and time. Before going on, make sure that the A> prompt is displayed.

3. Insert the disk labeled *Program Disk 1* into drive A.

4. Start First Choice with the following command:

    FIRST ←┘

You should now see the Main menu of First Choice (Figure A.1). Keep the backup disk labeled *Program Disk 2* handy. From time to time, First Choice may ask you to insert it into drive A.

CUSTOMIZING PFS: FIRST CHOICE FOR YOUR COMPUTER

Depending on the type of equipment being used, you may need to supply First Choice with specific information about the hardware. Once you have done this, First Choice remembers the information so that you don't have to repeat the process unless the hardware changes (with the addition of a new printer or monitor, for example).

The following customization instructions may be skipped *only* if your computer has this equipment configuration:

For the best use of your equipment, we recommend that you glance through the following sections on customization, to see if any apply to you.

- A color or monochrome monitor with a corresponding display adapter (the board that controls the monitors)

- A dot-matrix printer connected to the LPT1 port (if your computer has a single dot-matrix printer, it's probably connected in this way)

- No modem or plotter

MAKING SELECTIONS FROM THE SETUP MENU

In the following sections, you'll learn how to tell First Choice about each type of hardware attached to your computer. If you make a mistake at any point, you can "back out" by pressing the Esc key. Let's begin the customization process.

1. You must have the Main menu display (Figure A.1) on your screen, which you see when you start First Choice. (See "Starting PFS: First Choice" in this appendix.) When this display first appears, the cursor is positioned at the first item, *Create a document.* We'll have a good deal to say about this display later on, but for now we'll choose the menu option that allows you to specify your equipment configuration.

2. Select item 8, *Set up First Choice,* by either pressing the numbered key (8) at the top of the keyboard or by moving the cursor to your selection (item 8 in this case) using the ↑ and ↓ keys.

3. Press ↵ to make the selection. The Setup menu should appear (Figure A.2).

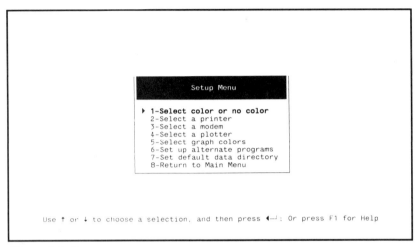

Figure A.2: Setup menu

We'll go through each of the items in this menu in the following sections. You can return to the Setup menu by either pressing the Esc key from any part of the setup process, or by choosing item 8 from the Main menu.

SELECTING COLOR OPTIONS This section applies only to computers with a color monitor.

1. Make sure that the cursor is at item 1, *Select color or no color;* then press ◄┘. A second menu will appear at the bottom of the screen.

2. Select either Color Palette 1 or 2. You can see how one looks on the screen, then view the other to decide which you prefer. As with other hardware options, you can always change your selection later.

SELECTING PRINTER OPTIONS You first need to tell First Choice exactly which type of printer you're using. Also, you must furnish the name of the port to which your printer is attached. If you're not sure which port is being used, find out before doing this part of the equipment setup. Also, try to determine exactly which printer you have.

Finally, if your printer is connected to a serial port (an unlikely situation), try to determine the following details before going on:

Baud rate

Data bits

Stop bits

Parity

Uses XON/XOFF?

To specify the printer options to First Choice, proceed as follows:

1. Choose item 2, *Select a printer,* from the Setup menu. The display shown in Figure A.3 will appear.

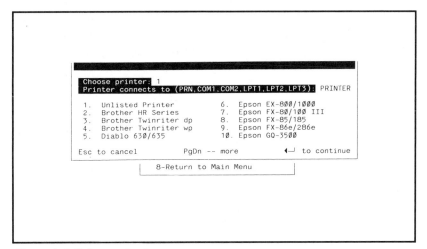

Figure A.3: Printer selection

2. Find your printer on the list by using the PgDn key to scroll through it.

3. When you've found your printer, type in the corresponding number. If you have a dot-matrix printer but can't find it on the list, try one of the following options:

    a. Find a printer close to yours; then type in its number. For example, if you have an Epson printer of unknown vintage, you could try entering **7** for *Epson*

FX-80. If your printer fails to work properly later on, you can return to the Setup menu and select another printer.

b. Select **1**, *Unlisted Printer.* This allows First Choice to use your printer in a minimal fashion that may be adequate for your needs.

If your printer is connected to LPT1, you can skip steps 4–6 and press ⬅ to return to the Setup menu and continue the customization process.

4. Press the Tab key to position the cursor on the line reading *Printer connects to....*

5. Type in the proper port name (LPT2, etc). If you type in either COM1 or COM2 for the port name, you'll be asked to enter still more technical details about your setup. If you have not been able to find out this information, try using the default values supplied on the screen: either they'll be the correct ones and your printer will work all right, or you'll need to find out the correct values from a dealer or the printer manual.

6. When you're done, press ⬅ to return to the Setup menu.

SELECTING MODEM OPTIONS   If you plan to use First Choice for communication with another computer, your computer must have a modem attached to either the COM1 or COM2 port. You must tell First Choice which modem you are using, which port it uses, and the type of telephone line to which it's attached. Proceed as follows:

1. Make sure that the Setup menu is displayed on the screen.

2. Choose item 3, *Select a modem.* The display shown in Figure A.4 should appear on the screen.

3. Locate your modem on the list, using the PgDn and PgUp keys to scroll through it.

4. When you've found your modem, enter its number after the word *Modem* on the screen. If you have an off-brand modem,

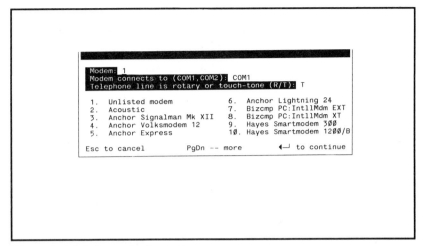

Figure A.4: Modem selection menu

it may not be on the list. In that case, enter the number **1**. This selection works with nearly any modem.

5. Press the Tab key to move the cursor to the next line on the screen.

6. Enter the name of the port to which the modem is attached; this will be either **COM1** or **COM2**. If you plan to use a single port (usually COM1) for both a modem and either a mouse or printer, you must still enter the name of that port here. If you don't know the name of the port, try using COM1. Later, if your modem fails to work properly, return to the Setup menu, select COM2, then try again.

7. Press the Tab key to move the cursor down to the next line.

8. Enter the type of phone line to be used—**T** for touch-tone or **R** for rotary.

9. Press ↵ to return to the Setup menu.

SELECTING PLOTTER OPTIONS   If you're planning to use a plotter, you must tell First Choice its name and also the name of the port to be used. If you can't find some of the information requested in the following steps, leave the standard settings as shown in the Serial

Information menu (from step 7 below). If your plotter fails to work properly, you'll need to locate the appropriate information (perhaps from the dealer or the manufacturer) before you can use the plotter. Proceed as follows:

1. Make sure that the Setup menu is displayed on the screen.

2. Choose item 4, *Select a plotter*. The menu shown in Figure A.5 should appear on the screen.

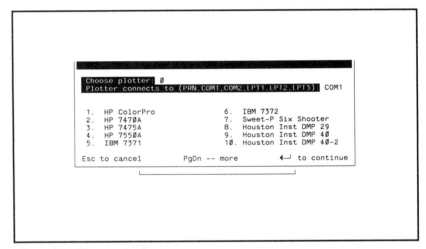

Figure A.5: Plotter selection menu

3. Locate your plotter on the list, using the PgDn key to scroll down if necessary.

4. When you've found your plotter, enter its number after the word *Choose plotter* on the screen.

5. Press the Tab key to move the cursor to the next line on the screen.

6. Enter the name of the port to which the plotter is attached; this will be either **COM1** or **COM2**. Press ↵ to go on.

7. Enter the data requested on the Serial Information menu that appears. This information is usually available in the manual for your plotter.

8. Press ↵ to return to the Setup menu.

SELECTING GRAPH COLORS If you're using a color monitor, First Choice offers you three color combinations that you can use for various displays, such as graphs. You can use item 5 on the Setup menu to select a particular color scheme. Here are the steps:

1. Make sure that the Setup menu is displayed on the screen.

2. Choose item 5, *Select graph colors.*

3. Choose one of the three color schemes. First Choice doesn't give you any clues as to what each color scheme represents; use trial-and-error to see which one suits your needs.

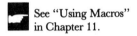 See "Using Macros" in Chapter 11.

SETTING UP ALTERNATE PROGRAMS You can set up First Choice's Main menu to run other programs. To do this, you add a new item to the menu for each program. Then, the program can be run by selecting the corresponding item from the menu. The Main menu can also be used to play back particular macros. Again, you'd do this by adding a menu item for each macro. To play back a macro, you simply select the item from the menu.

If you want to add either programs or macros for selection from the Main menu, choose *Set up alternate programs* from the menu. The display shown in Figure A.6 will appear.

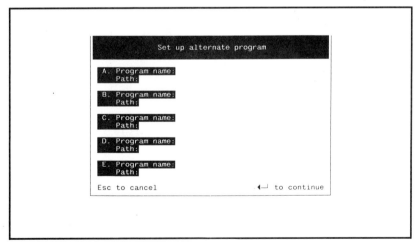

Figure A.6: Alternate Program Setup display

To create a Main menu item for a program:

1. Move the cursor to the first blank entry. If you're entering your first program or macro name, this will be the entry labeled "A."

2. On the line labeled *Program name*, enter a descriptive name for the program. This name will appear on the Main menu. For example, if you were going to run WordPerfect from the menu, you might enter **WordPerfect** here. You can enter up to 27 characters for this name.

3. Press the Tab key to move down to the line labeled *Path* for this entry.

4. Enter the name of the program to be run, including the complete path name. For instance, if the program name is WP.EXE and it is in the directory \WORDPRO, enter the name **\WORDPRO\WP.EXE**.

To create a Main menu item for a macro:

1. Move the cursor to the first blank entry on the Alternate Program Setup menu.

2. On the line labeled *Program name*, enter a descriptive name for the macro. This name will appear on the Main menu. For example, if you are going to run a macro to generate a letter heading, you might enter the phrase *Letter Heading* here.

3. Press the Tab key to move down to the line labeled *Path* for this entry.

4. Enter the name of the macro to be run. For instance, if the macro is Ctrl-D, enter **Ctrl-D** here.

When you're done adding program and macro entries, press ← to return to the Setup menu.

SETTING THE DEFAULT DATA DIRECTORY As you work with First Choice, you'll be creating various data files of different types—spreadsheets, documents, and so on. As a default option, these files are stored the same directory as the First Choice programs. Usually, you'll want to change this so that your data files are stored separately.

If you're using a hard-disk computer, select a separate directory for your data files. If you're using a floppy-disk machine, you'll probably want to select drive B as the repository for your files.

To change the default data directory, begin by selecting *Set default data directory* from the Setup menu. Then follow the appropriate instructions below, depending on which type of computer you have.

For hard-disk computers, the first step is to create a new directory for the data files, and set that directory to be the default. You can do this by using First Choice's disk utilities module:

1. Exit back to the Main menu by pressing Esc until the menu appears.

2. Select *Use disk utilities*.

3. When the Disk Utilities menu appears, select *Create a directory*.

4. When the new screen display appears, enter the name of the new directory. For example, to create the directory \MYDATA under the root directory, enter **MYDATA**, then press ◄──┘. When First Choice asks you to confirm this selection, enter **Y**.

5. Press the Esc key twice to return to the Main menu.

6. Select *Set up First Choice* to reenter the Setup menu.

7. Select *Set default data directory*.

8. Enter the name of the new directory. For example, to select the \MYDATA directory, enter **MYDATA**, then press ◄──┘ to return to the Setup menu.

For floppy-disk computers, first put a floppy disk into the drive to be used for writing data files, then follow these steps:

1. Select *Set default data directory* from the Setup menu.

2. Enter the name of the disk drive on which data will be written. For example, you might enter **B:** (remember to include the colon). Finish by pressing ◄──┘, which returns you to the

Setup menu. If there is no disk in the selected drive, First Choice issues an error message. Put in a disk, close the drive latch, then press ◄◄┘ again.

EXITING THE SETUP MENU

When you have finished specifying your equipment to First Choice, exit by selecting *Return to Main menu* from the Setup menu. The Main menu (Figure A.1) will appear on the screen. If you are somewhere other than the Setup menu, you can find your way back to it by pressing the Esc key until it appears.

If you want to use several devices that require serial ports, or if you'll be using a mouse with First Choice, continue to the next sections. Otherwise, you're ready to use First Choice.

USING MULTIPLE DEVICES WITH COM PORTS

You may want to use as many as four devices (printer, plotter, mouse, and modem), each of which requires a serial port. This is a bit of a problem, because only two serial ports can be installed on a single computer. If you plan to use more than two devices, the two ports will have to be shared by the devices. This can be done as follows:

- Decide which devices will use COM1 and which will use COM2.

- When you use the customization procedures described above for each device, specify either COM1 or COM2—whichever one you've decided to use for that device.

- Whenever you use a device, simply plug it into the correct serial port, and First Choice will know how to communicate with it.

INSTALLING A MOUSE

The First Choice software will run with various types of mice, including those made by Microsoft, Mouse Systems, and Logitech. You may need to consult the manual for your mouse in order to find out how to install it properly.

CHOOSING A PORT FOR THE MOUSE

Some mice run off a serial port (COM1 or COM2); others plug into a special card. A port can be shared by the mouse and another piece of equipment. For example, both a mouse and a serial printer can run off the COM1 port. However, each time you want to use the mouse you'll need to disconnect whatever is attached to the port and then connect the mouse. For this reason, it's a very good idea to have the mouse use its own port exclusively. This may require that you purchase an additional board for your computer.

STARTING THE MOUSE

Before beginning a session with First Choice, you'll need to run a program called a *mouse driver*, which establishes and maintains communication between the mouse and the computer. The manual for your mouse will contain details about this. The mouse driver must be run *before* you run First Choice.

Consult your DOS manual for instructions on setting up a batch file.

If you have a hard-disk computer, you can set up a DOS batch file to run both the mouse driver and First Choice automatically. A *batch file* is a special type of file that contains a set of DOS commands. You can create a batch file with any assortment of commands that you wish. For example, if both the mouse driver and the First Choice programs are in the subdirectory named PFS, you could create the following batch file. (We've assumed that the name of the mouse driver program is MOUSE, and that it's in the directory \MOUSE.)

```
REM  A batch file to run First Choice with a mouse
CD \MOUSE
MOUSE
CD..
FIRST
```

When you run the above batch file, First Choice will run and the mouse will be activated.

USING THE MOUSE WITH FIRST CHOICE

When First Choice begins to run, you'll see the *mouse cursor* in the upper-right corner of the screen. You can drag this cursor around by moving the mouse.

The mouse can be used to make menu selections and perform other operations. To make a menu selection, move the mouse cursor to the appropriate item. As you do, you'll also see the ordinary cursor move. Select the menu item by clicking any button on the mouse.

As we describe the various features of First Choice in this book, we'll mention how to use the mouse whenever appropriate.

Appendix
B

Printers Supported by First Choice

When you install First Choice for your computer system, you need to specify exactly which printer you plan to use. This is so First Choice can send the proper codes to the printer for various functions, such as starting a new line or printing boldface characters. The chart in this appendix lists all of the printers directly supported by First Choice, and the printing features that are supported by each printer.

For example, you can see that First Choice supports the Epson GQ-3500 printer. However, you can't use italics, compressed type, or letter-quality or color printing with this printer.

Note that even if your printer isn't on this list, you may still be able to use it with First Choice with reasonable success. If the manual for your printer indicates that it emulates another printer, you can select that printer during the installation procedure. You also can select a common printer—like the Epson FX-80 or the IBM Graphics—then print a document to see the results. As a last resort, you can choose *Unlisted Printer* from the Printer menu.

First Choice now supports HP LaserJet printers and printers that emulate them. However, note that these printers use default page sizes of 60 lines per inch in Portrait mode, and 45 lines per inch in Landscape mode. If you're using one of these printers, you may want to change the default value for paper length within First Choice's word processor (and perhaps within other modules as well).

		Boldface	Underline	Italics	Super/Sub	Microjust	Compress	Ltr-Qual	Graphics	Color
Brother	Brother HR Series	●	●		●	●	●			
	Brother Twinriter dp	●	●		●	●	●	●	●	
	Brother Twinriter wp	●	●		●	●		●		
Diablo	Diablo 630/635 ECS	●	●		●	●	●			
Epson	Epson EX-800/1000	●	●	●	●	●	●	●	●	●
	Epson FX-80/100 III	●	●	●	●	●	●		●	
	Epson FX-85/185	●	●	●	●	●	●	●	●	
	Epson FX-86e/286e	●	●	●	●	●	●		●	
	Epson GQ-3500	●	●		●	●			●	
	Epson JX-80	●	●	●	●	●	●		●	●
	Epson LQ-800/1000	●	●	●	●	●	●	●	●	
	Epson LQ-850/1050	●	●	●	●	●	●	●	●	
	Epson LQ-1500	●	●	●	●	●	●	●	●	
	Epson LQ-2500	●	●	●	●	●	●	●	●	●
	Epson LX-80	●	●	●	●	●	●		●	
	Epson LX-86/800	●	●	●	●	●	●	●	●	
	Epson MX-80/100 III	●	●	●	●	●	●		●	
	Epson RX-80/100	●	●	●	●	●	●		●	
Fujitsu	Fujitsu DL2400	●	●		●	●	●	●	●	●
	Fujitsu DX2200	●	●	●	●	●	●		●	
HP	HP LaserJet/Plus COUR Landscape	●	●		●	●			●	
	HP LaserJet/Plus COUR Portrait	●	●		●	●			●	
	HP LaserJet/Plus LINE Landscape	●	●		●	●			●	

This table was reprinted by permission from the *PFS: First Choice User Guide* ©1988 by Software Publishing Corporation.

		Boldface	Underline	Italics	Super/Sub	Microjust	Compress	Ltr-Qual	Graphics	Color
	HP LaserJet/Plus LINE Portrait	●	●		●	●			●	
	HP LaserJet/Plus PRES ELITE	●	●		●	●			●	
	HP LaserJet II COUR Landscape	●	●		●	●			●	
	HP LaserJet II COUR Portrait	●	●		●	●			●	
	HP LaserJet II LINE Landscape	●	●			●			●	
	HP LaserJet II LINE Portrait	●	●			●			●	
	HP LaserJet II PRES ELITE	●	●			●			●	
	HP PaintJet	●	●			●	●		●	●
	HP QuietJet	●	●		●	●	●		●	
	HP RuggedWriter (Epson mode)	●	●	●	●	●	●	●	●	
	HP ThinkJet	●	●			●	●		●	
IBM	IBM Color Jetprinter		●			●	●		●	●
	IBM Color Printer	●	●		●	●	●		●	●
	IBM Graphics	●	●		●	●	●		●	
	IBM Proprinter/II/XL	●	●		●	●	●	●	●	
	IBM Proprtr X24/XL24	●	●		●	●	●	●	●	●
	IBM Quickwriter	●	●	●	●	●	●	●	●	
	IBM Quietwriter I, II	●	●		●	●			●	
	IBM Quietwriter III	●	●		●	●	●	●	●	
	IBM Wheelprinter	●	●		●		●			
NEC	NEC 3550	●	●		●	●				
	NEC CP6/CP7	●	●	●	●	●	●	●	●	●
	NEC P2200	●	●	●	●	●	●	●	●	
	NEC P5/P6/P7	●	●		●	●	●	●	●	
	NEC P5XL/P9XL	●	●	●	●	●	●	●	●	●

		Boldface	Underline	Italics	Super/Sub	Microjust	Compress	Ltr-Qual	Graphics	Color
Okidata	Okidata MLine 92/93	●	●		●	●	●	●	●	
	Okidata MLine 182/183	●	●		●	●	●		●	
	Okidata MLine 192/193	●	●	●	●	●	●	●	●	
	Okidata MLine 292/293	●	●	●	●	●	●	●	●	●
	Okidata MLine 294	●	●	●	●	●	●	●	●	●
Panasonic	Pan. KX-P1080i/1091i	●	●	●	●	●	●	●	●	
	Pan. KX-P1524	●	●	●	●	●	●	●	●	
	Pan. KX-P1592/P1595	●	●	●	●	●	●	●	●	
	Pan. KX-3131/3151	●	●		●	●	●			
	Pan. KX-4450	●	●			●			●	
Star	Star NL-10	●	●	●	●	●	●		●	
	Star NX-1000	●	●	●	●	●	●	●	●	
	Star SD/SG/SR Series	●	●	●	●	●	●	●	●	
Tandy	Tandy DMP 106	●	●		●		●		●	
	Tandy DMP 130/430	●	●	●	●			●	●	●
	Tandy DMP 200/400	●	●		●			●	●	●
	Tandy DMP 440/500	●	●		●			●	●	●
	Tandy DMP 2100P/2110	●	●		●	●	●	●	●	
	Tandy DMP 2120	●	●	●	●	●	●	●	●	
	Tandy DWP II/210/410	●	●		●	●				
	Tandy DWP 220/230	●	●		●	●				
	Tandy DWP 520/530	●	●		●	●				
	Tandy LP-1000	●	●		●	●	●	●	●	
Texas Instruments	Texas Instruments 875/877	●	●	●	●	●	●	●	●	●

		Boldface	Underline	Italics	Super/Sub	Microjust	Compress	Ltr-Qual	Graphics	Color
Toshiba	Toshiba P321SL/341SL	●	●	●	●	●	●	●	●	
	Toshiba P341/351	●	●	●	●	●	●	●	●	
	Toshiba P351C	●	●	●	●	●	●	●	●	●
	Toshiba P1350/1351	●	●		●	●	●	●	●	
Xerox	Xerox 4045	●	●		●	●		●	●	

Appendix
C

Using Forms Programs

First Choice allows you to write programs that check data and perform special calculations during data entry. These *forms programs* are powerful tools that can enhance the performance of First Choice. You can write a program to do any or all of the following during entry of a new record:

- Automatic checking of data values. For example, each value entered into an *Age* field can be checked to be sure that it's between 21 and 70. If an incorrect value is found, First Choice will issue an error message.

- Automatic calculation of values for specific fields. For example, the value of a *Bonus* field can be calculated, based on the value input for the *Salary* field of the new record.

- Automatic calculation of unique numbers within records. For example, you can define a field called *Record Number,* and have First Choice insert a unique value into each new record.

You can write several forms programs for a First Choice database, but only one can be current at any time. First Choice automatically runs the current, active forms program each time a new record is added. The program does whatever you have written into it: checks input values for validity and issues appropriate error messages, computes the values of specific fields, and so on. An existing program can be modified or deleted at any time.

If you write a program for a database that already contains records, you can have the program recalculate all of the existing records. You can also use the program to recalculate specific records in the database. For example, suppose that you have a database with many employee records, containing the fields *Name, Salary,* and *Years of Service.* Suppose that you want to increase by 10 percent the salary of those employees who have more than 10 years of service. You could write a forms program to process all of the existing records, updating the *Salary* fields for the appropriate employees.

You should attempt to write forms programs only if you have previous programming experience.

The forms programming language is quite simple (if you've had programming experience), containing only a small number of elements. We'll introduce it with a few program examples, then discuss the general features of the language. Finally, we'll describe how to actually write forms programs.

INTRODUCING THE FORMS PROGRAMMING LANGUAGE

Let's begin by looking at two examples of how the language is used. In our first example, suppose that you have a database with the following fields containing data about your employees:

NAME

AGE

YEARS EMPLOYED

SALARY

BONUS

Suppose that you want to make sure that no record is added with a value of AGE less than 21 (you don't want to hire minors). The following one-line program will do the data checking:

IF AGE < 21 THEN @ERRBOX(AGE, "Value is less than 21")

As each new record is added to the file, the program automatically checks the value input for the AGE field. If the value is less than 21, the program immediately displays an error message on the screen, reading *Value is less than 21.* The user can then reenter a legitimate value for AGE, or perhaps cancel data entry for that record.

This program displays several features of the forms programming language. @ERRBOX(AGE, "Value is less than 21") is an instruction to First Choice to output the string in quotes next to the AGE field. The IF...THEN instruction tests the value of (AGE < 21). If it's TRUE (if AGE is less than 21), whatever follows THEN is executed. In this case, it's the @ERRBOX instruction. If (AGE <21) is FALSE (AGE is equal to or greater than 21), whatever follows THEN is not executed.

Now let's look at another example. Suppose that for the database described above, you would like to include a 10 percent bonus for all employees who have 15 or more years of service. We can enhance the above single-line program to perform this calculation for us:

```
1. IF YEARS_EMPLOYED < 15 THEN GOTO next
2. BONUS = 0.1 * SALARY
3. :next
4. IF AGE < 21 THEN @ERRBOX(AGE, "Value is less than 21")
```

As each new record is added, the above program runs automatically, checking the input values. This program behaves like programs of most other languages: Each statement occupies one line. After a statement has been executed, control moves to the statement on the next line, unless a GOTO statement sends control somewhere else. Let's look at each line.

We've numbered the program lines to facilitate discussion of them; the numbers are not part of the program.

Line 1   Here's another example of an IF..THEN statement. In this case, the value of (YEARS_EMPLOYED < 15) for the current record is tested. If it's TRUE (if YEARS_EMPLOYED is less than 15), then what follows THEN is executed. In this case, it's the GOTO statement, which transfers control to the statement *:next.* If (YEARS_EMPLOYED < 15) is FALSE, what follows THEN is not executed, and the program continues to the second line.

Line 2   The field BONUS is assigned a value equal to 0.1 times the value for the SALARY field. Note that this statement is reached by the program only if the value of YEARS_EMPLOYED is greater than or equal to 15. This is the whole point of the statement in line 1.

Line 3   This statement simply acts as the label *:next.* It functions as a place to which control can be transferred from somewhere else in the program with a GOTO statement.

Line 4   This is the same statement we used in our earlier one-line program. Note that this statement is always reached by the program, regardless of whether or not the statement in line 2 is executed.

After the last line of the program has been executed, the program automatically stops. Any error messages generated as the result of @ERRBOX statements are immediately displayed on the screen.

THE LANGUAGE ELEMENTS

This section describes in detail the parts of the forms programming language. First you'll learn about variables. These are used in program statements, which may also contain field names, arithmetic expressions, constants, logical operators, or functions.

VARIABLES

First Choice provides several types of variables that can be used within a program to help with calculations.

LOCAL VARIABLES   Four local variables can be used for temporary storage of data: @V1, @V2, @V3, and @V4. Each of these can hold either a number or an alphanumeric string. The @ sign in front of each variable name is optional, although it's a good idea to use it to help distinguish these variables from field names.

Local variables are temporary, that is, they exist only during the time a database is open. Each time a database is opened, these variables are set to zero. After that, they retain whatever values are assigned to them by a program. When a database is exited, the current values of the variables are discarded.

FLAG-TYPE VARIABLE   First Choice provides a single flag-type variable, @OLDREC. As you work with a database, you may be adding a new record, or you may be editing an existing one. If you are adding a new one, First Choice sets the value of @OLDREC to FALSE. If you are editing an existing record, the value of @OLDREC is set to TRUE. In this way, a program can determine which type of record it's working with, by inspecting the value of @OLDREC. This is important, because you may want a program to treat existing records differently from new ones.

PERMANENT VARIABLE   First Choice provides one permanent variable, called @DISKVAR, for each database. You can use this variable to hold either a number or a string, and this value is stored permanently along with the database. The most common use of the variable is to keep track of a running counter along with the database. For instance, you could define a special field to contain your own unique record numbers. Each time a new record is added to the database, the program will increase the current value of @DISKVAR by one, then assign that value to the record-number field. Other uses for @DISKVAR might be the automatic assigning of invoice numbers, order numbers and so on.

When a database is first created, the value of @DISKVAR is set to zero by First Choice and stored along with the database. From then on, any changes to @DISKVAR are up to the user.

DECIMALS VARIABLE   The value of this variable determines the number of decimal places displayed on the screen for any values calculated within a program. The value of DECIMALS is assigned with a regular program statement. It can be set either to a simple number, or to the value "FLOAT", as shown in the following examples:

```
DECIMALS = 4
DECIMALS = "FLOAT"
```

In the first example, the variable DECIMALS is set equal to 4, which means that each value calculated by the program will be displayed with four decimal digits. If the value of DECIMALS is set equal to "FLOAT", then any trailing zeros of a calculated number are not displayed.

This variable has no effect on the display of values input by a user, or on the display of preexisting values.

PROGRAM STATEMENTS

Each program consists of one or more statements, and each statement occupies one line. Although the screen can only display 79 characters on a line, a statement can extend to a maximum of 250 characters.

Here are the different types of statements that can be used in a program:

Replacement

Label

GOTO

IF..THEN

@ERRBOX

Comments

REPLACEMENT STATEMENTS This is the most common type of statement. It has the following form:

Var = Expression

where *Var* is the name of a field or variable, and *Expression* is an expression, which can contain the names of constants, fields, functions, or any of the variables discussed above. Here are some examples of replacement statements:

```
AGE = 25
BONUS = 0.1 * SALARY
RECORD_COUNTER = @DISKVAR
```

```
NAME = @V1
FULLNAME = FIRST & LAST
INVOICE_DATE = @NOW
```

Only names of variables or fields are allowed on the left-hand side of an equal sign in a replacement statement. The right-hand side can contain any type of expression that's consistent with the field name on the left-hand side. When field names are used, certain rules apply:

- If a blank is part of a field name, it must be replaced by the underscore (_) character. Note that the original field name remains the same: you only need to modify the name as it appears in an expression.

- If a field containing a string value is used in an expression, that string can't contain more than 240 characters.

- If a field is used for numeric calculations within a program, it must be specified as type N (numeric). If you're using a character type field to hold numeric data, you can redefine the type of the field by selecting *Change form design* from the Features menu, then selecting *Change field types*.

For a more detailed discussion of how First Choice performs its arithmetic operations, see Chapter 7.

If a replacement statement does arithmetic calculations, then the right-hand side will contain an arithmetic expression, consisting of arithmetic operators, what they operate on (for example variables), and parentheses to clarify the meaning of the expression. Here are the arithmetic operators that can be used:

+	Addition
–	Subtraction
*	Multiplication
/	Division
**	Exponentiation

Some examples of arithmetic expressions are

```
AGE * 2
2 * AGE
(SALARY + OVERTIME) * (PAY_RATE + BONUS_RATE)
```

You can perform string manipulations within a program, using any of First Choice's string functions. You can also use the & operator for combining two string values. For example, the following statement could be used for calculating the value of the field NAME:

```
NAME = @TRIM(FIRSTNAME) & ' ' & @TRIM(LASTNAME)
```

In this statement, we've used the @TRIM function to strip off trailing blanks.

If you have fields containing date and time information, you can write replacement statements involving them. For example, suppose that you want the field CURRENT_DATE to contain the date of data entry. You could use the built-in function @NOW to supply the current date as the value of the field:

```
CURRENT_DATE = @NOW
```

A field with Yes/No type data can be assigned values with a replacement statement. For example, the following pair of statements tests the AGE field and, under certain circumstances, assigns the value *Y* to the field ADULT:

```
IF (AGE < 21) THEN GOTO :Next
ADULT = "Y"
    .
    .
```

LABEL STATEMENTS   This type of statement is used for reference by GOTO statements (see below) in the program .A label statement has the following form:

```
:labelname
```

A program can have as many label statements as needed. Each label statement must be on a single line and must begin with a colon.

GOTO STATEMENTS   This type of statement is used to transfer program control to somewhere other than the next line (which would be the normal sequence of program execution). The form of the statement is

```
GOTO label,
```

where *label* is a label statement within the program. A GOTO statement is often used as part of an IF..THEN statement (see below).

IF..THEN STATEMENTS   This type of statement allows control of a program to depend on the outcome of a test. For example, consider the following statement:

IF AGE > 70 THEN @ERRBOX(AGE, "Value of AGE is too large")

An IF..THEN statement always tests a *logical condition*, which comes immediately after the IF part of the statement. If the logical condition is TRUE, the part of the statement following THEN is executed, which in the above example is the generation of an error message (see below for a discussion of @ERRBOX).

An IF..THEN statement can have one of two forms:

IF {*condition*} THEN @ERRBOX(*field*, "*message*")
IF {*condition*} THEN GOTO *label*

Condition can be any logical condition involving variables, field names, constants, and logical operators.

Here are the logical operators that can be used within logical conditions:

=	Equal to
<	Less than
>	Greater than
< =	Less than or equal to
> =	Greater than or equal to
< >	Not equal to

In addition to the above six operators, there are three others that can be used to combine simple logical conditions into more complicated ones. They are AND, OR, and NOT.

The AND operator combines two logical conditions, which we'll call A and B, into one condition. In order for the resulting condition to be TRUE, both A and B must be TRUE. The OR operator is similar, except that if either A or B is TRUE, then the resulting condition is TRUE. The NOT operator negates whatever logical condition immediately follows it. For example, if condition C is FALSE, then NOT(C) is TRUE.

When building a logical condition, it's a good idea to use pairs of parentheses freely in order to improve the clarity of the condition.

Here are some examples of IF..THEN statements:

```
IF AGE < 21 THEN GOTO :youth
IF (AGE < 21) OR (CITY = "Alcatraz") THEN GOTO :illegal
IF NOT (ADULT) THEN @ERRBOX(ADULT, "This person is not
an adult")
```

In the second example, control will transfer to the statement *:illegal* either if the value of the field AGE for the current record is less than 21, or if the value of the field CITY is equal to *Alcatraz*. Notice that two sets of parentheses have been used to improve the clarity of the logical condition.

In the last example, the field ADULT is a Yes/No type. If the value of this field for the current record is *No,* then the error message *This person...* will be displayed.

@ERRBOX STATEMENTS   This type of statement causes an error message to be displayed on the screen next to the specified field. The form of the statement is

@ERRBOX(*field, "message"*)

When this statement is executed, *"message"* will appear on the screen next to the field *field*. Often, this type of statement is used in conjunction with an IF..THEN statement. For each new record added, the value of the specified field is tested; if it is found to be an "illegal" value by the program, the error message is immediately displayed on the screen, giving the person entering the data a chance to correct the input.

COMMENTS   You can enter comments anywhere you like within a program to help document the program for later use. Any line beginning with a semicolon is treated as a comment; that is, it's ignored by First Choice during program execution.

FUNCTIONS

First Choice contains a large number of functions, which are discussed in detail in Chapter 4.

A function (sometimes called a keyword) is a built-in feature of First Choice that can be used to perform a special type of calculation. Any of First Choice's functions can be used in an expression, except for the following ones, each of which deals with ranges of values rather than a single value:

AVERAGE or AVG

COUNT

HLOOKUP

INDEX

MAXIMUM or MAX

MINIMUM or MIN

NPV

STDEV or STD

TOTAL or TOT

VARIANCE or VAR

VLOOKUP

For example, the following program statement would calculate the nearest whole number of the value of the field AGE, and store the result in the variable @V1:

```
@V1 = ROUND(AGE)
```

WRITING AND EDITING A FORMS PROGRAM

To write or edit a forms program, you use First Choice's menus and standard editing commands. The following two sections will explain how.

CREATING A NEW PROGRAM

When you create a new program for a database, it automatically becomes the active program for that database. You can have several programs for a particular database written and stored in files, but only one at a time can be the active program. Here are the steps for creating a new program.

1. Retrieve the database for which a program is to be written.

2. After a blank form appears on the screen, select *Change form design* from the Features menu. First Choice will ask you to confirm your choice, then present you with the Change Form Design menu.

3. Select *Program form* from the menu. If an active program already exists for the database, it will appear on the Edit screen. Otherwise, a blank screen appears. You can save an existing program (see "Storing and Retrieving Existing Programs" below), or erase it by selecting *Erase this record* from the Edit menu. Once you have a blank Edit screen, you can enter the new program. As you proceed, you can use any of First Choice's editing commands.

4. After you've finished, press F10 to store the program.

After you've pressed F10, if you've made any type of error in the program (other than logic errors), First Choice issues an error message and positions the cursor at the line containing the error. Correct the error, then press F10 again. If another error is found, the error message again appears. Continue until all of the errors have been found and corrected.

Make a backup of your database before running a new program.

After First Choice accepts the program as error-free, it asks if you want to recalculate each record in the database with the program. Enter either "Y" or "N." This is a dangerous option, because the default answer is "Y." If you simply press ←⏎, the program will recalculate every record in the database. If your program is not what you really wanted, you could wipe out valuable data!

EDITING AN EXISTING PROGRAM

To edit a program that already exists, follow the steps described for creating a new program. The program will appear on the screen, and you can edit it.

If you want to delete the program, choose *Erase this record* from the Edit menu after the program is displayed on the screen. Press F10 to return to the database.

STORING AND RETRIEVING EXISTING PROGRAMS

You can have more than one program associated with a given database, but only one can be active at any time. Remember that the active program for a database is the one that's automatically attached to the database when it's retrieved. If you want to replace the active program with another one, but you don't want to destroy the active program, you can save it for later retrieval. To save the active program to a disk file:

1. Select *Change form design* from the Features menu and press ←.

2. Select *Program form* from the Change Form Design menu. The active program will appear on the Edit screen.

3. Select *Print this record* from the Print menu.

4. When the Directory Assistant appears, enter the name of the disk file to which the program is to be written. Press ← and the program will be copied to the file.

5. When the Edit screen reappears, select *Erase this record*. You can now enter a new program, or make an existing program the active one.

To retrieve a stored program and make it the active program, begin by following steps 1 and 2 above. Then proceed as follows:

1. If there is already an active program, you can save it as described above in steps 3–4, then erase it by selecting *Erase this record* from the Edit screen.

2. Select *Merge another file* from the Files menu.

3. When the Directory Assistant appears, select the file containing the program you want.

4. Press F10 to return to the database.

USING A PROGRAM TO MAKE GLOBAL CHANGES

Suppose that you want to make a change to a large group of records in a database. The "brute force" method would be to scan through the entire database, changing each desired record. However, you can perform the entire set of changes at once by writing a program to do the modifications, then using the program to recalculate the desired records in the database.

Enter the temporary program (after first saving the active program, as described above). When you've finished, press F10. Use the program to recalculate the database by selecting "Y" when First Choice asks if you wish to recalculate the entire database. After you've finished using the program, you can either erase it or save it on a disk file as described above. Finally, retrieve the program that was originally active.

USING A PROGRAM TO RECALCULATE SELECTED RECORDS

You can also have a program recalculate the current record by pressing the speed key Alt-R.

After a program has been written, it will automatically recalculate each new record that's subsequently entered into the database. You may also use the program to recalculate any existing record or records as follows. Display the desired record on the screen, then select *Run form program* from the Features menu.

Note that when a program recalculates an existing record, the flag variable @OLDREC is assigned a value of TRUE by First Choice. This is how a program can differentiate between an existing record and a new one.

LOOKING AT A SAMPLE PROGRAM

Suppose that you have a database named CLIENTS, which contains several hundred records of client information. After having used the database for some time, you decide that it would be a good idea to write a program to perform data validation on new information as it's input into the database.

Each record consists of the following fields:

NAME

STREET

CITY

STATE

ZIP

PHONE

BALANCE DUE

CREDIT LIMIT

You would like the following restrictions placed on input data for each record:

- The value of STATE must be CA, OR, or WA, because your business is confined to those three states.

- Each value of ZIP must be a valid number, that is, only digits.

- The credit limit must be less than $5,000.

- A value must be entered for the NAME field for each record.

The program is shown in Figure C.1 (Note that the line numbers shown in the figure are not part of the actual program—they are included to simplify our discussion.) Let's look at the program lines.

Lines 1-6   These are comments that describe the purpose of the program.

```
 1.  ; This program validates new data for the CLIENTS database
 2.  ; The following tests are made:
 3.  ; -- Value of STATE must be either "CA", "OR", or "WA"
 4.  ; -- ZIP must be numeric, i.e., only digits are allowed
 5.  ; -- CREDIT LIMIT must be less than $5,000
 6.  ;
 7.  IF (STATE = "CA") OR (STATE = "OR") OR (STATE = "WA") THEN
      GOTO next1
 8.  @ERRBOX(STATE, "Invalid state entered")
 9.  :next1
10.  IF (ZIP>0) AND (ZIP<100000) THEN GOTO next2
11.  @ERRBOX(ZIP, "ZIP must contain only digits")
12.  :next2
13.  IF CREDIT_LIMIT < 5000 THEN GOTO next3
14.  @ERRBOX(CREDIT_LIMIT, "Limit can't exceed $5,000")
15.  :next3
16.  IF TRIM(NAME) <> "" THEN GOTO end
17.  @ERRBOX(NAME, "A name must be entered")
18.  :end
```

Figure C.1: Sample forms program

Line 7   The statement on this line tests the value of the STATE field. If the value is one of the three specified in the statement, then control transfers to the statement *:next1* for the next test. Otherwise, control passes to line 8, which outputs an error message on the screen in the STATE field.

Line 10   This tests the ZIP field to see if a valid number was entered. If so, control passes to line 12 for the next test. Otherwise, an error message is issued.

Line 13   The value of the CREDIT LIMIT field is tested: if it's greater than or equal to 5,000, then an error message is issued. Otherwise, control passes on to the next test.

Line 16   Here, the program tests the NAME field to ensure that a value was entered. The keyword TRIM is used to remove any leading blanks from the value, which is then compared with " ", which means *no value*. If no value was entered, control passes to line 17, which issues an error message. Otherwise, the program ends at line 18.

This program demonstrates several different types of tests, each of which has many different applications. First, the test on the STATE field is a *range test*, which limits the allowable values to a small set (in this case CA, OR, and WA). The test on the ZIP field ensures that each value will contain only digits.

The test on the CREDIT_LIMIT field is another type of range test, which limits the allowable range of values for a numeric field. Finally, the test on NAME is a powerful one; it guarantees that each record is given a value. In other words, you cannot leave the field blank.

USING THE SAMPLE PROGRAM TO CHECK EXISTING RECORDS

The sample program was written to validate new data as it's entered into the CLIENTS database. However, you can also use the same program to check all of the existing records in the database.

To do so, first retrieve the program to the Edit screen by selecting *Change form design* from the Features menu, then choosing *Program form*. When the program appears, press F10. First Choice will ask if you want to recalculate the database; answer "Y." If any record in the database violates any of the tests in the program, the appropriate error message will appear on the screen, and you'll have to correct the data before the program will allow you to proceed.

You can interrupt the data-checking process at any time by pressing the Esc key. You can then choose whether or not to terminate data checking.

USING THE SAMPLE PROGRAM TO CHANGE NEW RECORDS

Now suppose that you decide to add a field called DATE_ADDED to the CLIENTS database. The contents of this field will be the date on which the record was added to the database. You'll have to live with the fact that because you don't know when the existing records were added to the database, this new field must remain empty for those records.

Let's modify the sample program so that for any new records added, the current date will be supplied to the new field. The modified program is shown in Figure C.2. The new statements are shown on lines 19 through 21.

```
1.   ; This program validates new data for the CLIENTS database
2.   ; The following tests are made:
3.   ; -- Value of STATE must be either "CA", "OR", or "WA"
4.   ; -- ZIP must be numeric, i.e., only digits are allowed
5.   ; -- CREDIT LIMIT must be less than $5,000
6.   ;
7.   IF (STATE = "CA") OR (STATE = "OR") OR (STATE = "WA") THEN
     GOTO next1
8.   @ERRBOX(STATE, "Invalid state entered")
9.   :next1
10.  IF (ZIP>0) AND (ZIP<100000) THEN GOTO next2
11.  @ERRBOX(ZIP, "ZIP must contain only digits")
12.  :next2
13.  IF CREDIT_LIMIT < 5000 THEN GOTO next3
14.  @ERRBOX(CREDIT_LIMIT, "Limit can't exceed $5,000")
15.  :next3
16.  IF TRIM(NAME) <> "" THEN GOTO next4
17.  @ERRBOX(NAME, "A name must be entered")
18.  :next4
19.  IF @OLDREC THEN GOTO end
20.  DATE_ADDED = @NOW
21.  :end
```

Figure C.2: Modified forms program

Line 19   The program tests the flag variable @OLDREC, whose value is set by First Choice to TRUE if the program in the record being recalculated is an existing one; when a new record is being recalculated, the value is set to FALSE. This statement ensures that the current date will be entered into the field DATE_ADDED only for new records; for existing records, the statement in line 20 is skipped.

Line 20   Here the program uses the function @NOW to assign the current date to the DATE_ADDED field.

Line 21   The program ends when this statement is reached.

If the DATE_ADDED field is assigned to be a Date type field, the values returned by @NOW are automatically converted to ordinary values (such as 01/02/89).

Appendix
D

Creating
Presentation
Graphics

You can use First Choice's word processor to generate *presentation graphics*. Presentation graphics use a variety of text fonts and sizes, and can incorporate graphs and text. However, the quality of First Choice's presentation graphics is limited, and you'd probably use this feature mainly for "quick-and-dirty" presentations.

To be consistent with First Choice's terminology, we'll use the term *slide* to refer to a single page or screen of presentation graphics output. This output can be directed to either the screen or the printer. From the printed output, you can then produce overhead transparencies. When output is directed to the screen, you can either manually control the movement from slide to slide, or set up timing commands that control how long each page is displayed on the screen.

CREATING THE SLIDE

You'll use First Choice's word processor to create the text and select fonts and sizes. You can then direct the output to either the screen or the printer. You can also save the text as a normal document for later use. To show how easy this process is, we'll create the slide shown in Figure D.1.

```
Joe's Pizza Parlor

        *Pizza
        *Spaghetti
        *All U can eat for $2.95
```

Figure D.1: Sample slide

ENTERING TEXT FOR THE SLIDE

To begin, select *Create a document* from the Main menu, then enter the following lines into the word processor:

Joe's Pizza Parlor

.Pizza
.Spaghetti
.All U can eat for $2.95

Now let's select the font and size for the main heading of the slide:

1. Move the cursor to the beginning of the first line.

2. Select *Change slide font* from the Style menu. The Font menu shown in Figure D.2 appears. You can select the font, character size, and type of spacing from this menu. For this

You'll probably need to experiment to find the right character size. For character spacing, proportional spacing is usually more attractive. However, for tabular output, you'll probably want to choose mono spacing, so that characters line up vertically.

example, select 70 for the character size, Roman font (the default), and proportional spacing.

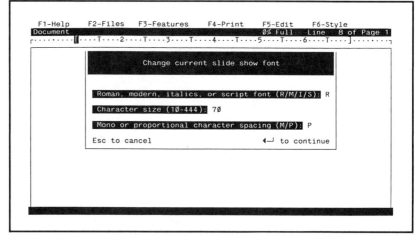

Figure D.2: Font menu

3. When you've finished, press ◄── to return to the word processor display. Notice that the line *font roman 70 Prop* has been inserted. This is a font command, whose contents are determined by your choices above.

4. Move the cursor to the beginning of the line just above *Pizza*.

5. Again select *Change slide font* from the Style menu. This time assign italics font with a character size of 48. Finish up by pressing ◄──.

When you've finished, your screen should look like the one in Figure D.3.

DISPLAYING THE SLIDE

To get an on-screen display of the final slide, select *Display slides from this document* from the Print menu. After a short pause, the final slide will appear. To exit back to the word processor display, press the Esc key.

Generally, the on-screen display of a slide will show the basic features on the slide when printed. If there's too much text on a single

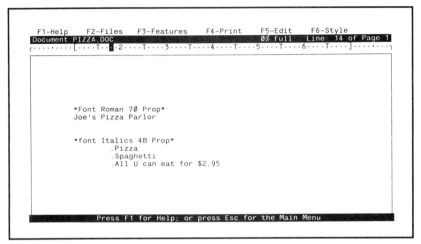

Figure D.3: Final text for slide

line, it'll overflow onto the next line; the amount of text that displays on each line will be the same as that printed out.

If you've got too much text to fit on a single slide, the overflow will automatically go onto the second screen. You can view successive pages on-screen by pressing the PgDn key (or PgUp to view previous slides).

SAVING THE SLIDE TEXT

After you've created the text for a slide, you can save it as a regular document. Later, you can retrieve it for modification and further use. To save the text, select *Save a copy of this document* from the Files menu, then proceed as you would for any other document. If you have several slides in a single document (see below), you would still save the text as a single document.

On the other hand, you can save the text for each slide as a separate document: For each slide, first select its text, then choose *Save selected text only* from the Files menu, and finally assign a file name for the document.

PRINTING AND PLOTTING THE SLIDE

To print your slide, select *Print slides from this document* from the Print menu. The Print Graph Options menu will appear, allowing you to select various printing options. You may find it worthwhile to experiment with these options to determine which combination gives you the best output quality. Note that the selection for orientation and size of the printout (Portrait, etc.) on this menu has no effect on the display of a slide on the screen. Consequently, even though the on-screen display is extremely useful for gauging *relative* sizes and positions, it won't show you exactly how the slide will be printed (see "Controlling Slide Orientation" below).

If you selected *Unlisted printer* when you installed First Choice, then after you select *Print slides from this document* from the Print menu, a screen message will appear that tells you that your printer isn't going to work. Ignore this and go on; your printer should print the slide anyway. If there's too much text on your slide to fit on a single printed page, the overflow prints onto successive pages.

If you have a plotter attached to your computer, and if you've selected it during First Choice installation, you can use it to plot slides. Select *Plot slides from this document* from the Print menu. Follow the screen instructions, and your slides will be plotted.

Some types of printers can't output in the graphics mode; if you have one of these, you're out of luck.

This plotting option only appears if you've selected a plotter during installation.

EDITING SLIDE TEXT

Nearly all of the standard editing features are available for editing the text of slides. However, most of the selections from the Style menu won't work for slides (although they'll still display on the screen as you create the text). For instance, if you boldface a block of text, it'll show on the editing screen, but not when the slide is displayed on-screen or printed. You can, however, use the Center style for centering one or more lines of text; the text will appear centered on-screen, and it'll also be centered properly when displayed or printed.

CREATING FONT COMMANDS

A font command affects the output format of all text following that command, or until another font command is encountered in the document.

Each font command must occupy its own line, as shown in Figure D.3. You can enter your own font commands, rather than letting First Choice do so. Enter each command as shown in this figure. A command contains the word *font,* followed by three options: the font type, character size, and type of spacing. The four legal values for the font type option are *Roman, Modern, Italics,* and *Script* (use any combination of upper- and lowercase). For the font size option, enter a number between 10 and 444. The two values for the spacing option are *Mono* and *Prop.* The entire command must be enclosed in asterisks.

You can include in a font command only those options that you wish to change. If you leave out any of the three options, the current value for that particular option continues. On the other hand, if you enter an illegal value for an option, the entire command is simply treated as ordinary text.

INCLUDING GRAPHS IN A SLIDE

Graphs generated in First Choice's graph module can be included as part of a set of slides. For this to work, the graph must have been saved in First Choice Slide Show format. This type of graph file will have the extension .SLD.

Each graph that's included in a set of slides begins on a new page or screen.

To include a graph in a set of slides, insert the following command:

*SCREEN *filename**

where *filename* is the entire name of the file containing the graph (including the disk drive and extension). As with other commands, each SCREEN command must begin at the far left of a line, and it must be the only text on the line.

PRODUCING A SLIDE SHOW

You can display several slides in succession, by making them part of the same document. To do so, simply insert a page-break between the text for each slide: Select *Start new page* from the Features menu, or type in *new page* on a line by itself, starting at the far left of the line.

VIEWING SLIDES MANUALLY

To start displaying slides, select *Display slides from this document* from the Print menu. You can then use various keystrokes to move from slide to slide:

SLIDE TO BE DISPLAYED	*KEY*
Next slide from the document	PgDn, spacebar, Tab, ⬅, ↓, or F10
Previous slide	PgUp, Shift-Tab, ↑, or F9
First slide	Home
Last slide	End
Slide on which cursor is located in document	C

To interrupt a slide show, press the Esc key.

AUTOMATING A SLIDE SHOW

You can set up a set of slides in a document so that each one is displayed for a preset amount of time, and then the next one is automatically displayed. To control the display time for each slide, insert the following command at the top of the document:

```
*TIMER sec*
```

where *sec* is a number from 1 to 255, representing the display time for each slide.

You can insert several *TIMER sec* commands throughout a document. Each one takes precedence over the previous one. Thus, some slides can be displayed for only a few seconds, while others can be displayed longer.

You also can insert the command *TIMER OFF* wherever you want in the document. You then can control manually the display of slides appearing after that command.

To begin an automated slide show, proceed the same way you would for a manual one: Select *Display slides from this document*. An automated slide show can be interrupted in several ways. If the Esc key is pressed, the show terminates. Or you can immediately display the next slide by pressing almost any other key.

After the last slide in a document has been displayed, the first slide is then displayed again; the cycle continues until interrupted by the Esc key.

CONTROLLING SLIDE ORIENTATION

If you want all of the slides in a document to be printed in the same orientation (portrait, landscape, or small), you can select the *Orientation* option from the Print Graph Options menu. However, you can choose to print some slides in portrait orientation, others in landscape mode. To control this, insert either of the orientation commands, *LANDSCAPE* or *PORTRAIT*, at the beginning of each slide. Each command remains in effect until another orientation command is encountered in the document.

If neither a Landscape or Portrait command appears in the document, the default is Landscape, but this can be overriden by another choice for the *Orientation* option on the Print Graph Options menu. On the other hand, either a Landscape or Portrait command overrides whatever choice was made for the *Orientation* option on the Print Graph Options menu.

If you enter the Portrait command for a slide, it still displays on-screen so that you can easily read it, but it takes up only half the screen width.

Index

– (minus sign)
in arithmetic formulas, 176, 234
in calculator functions, 393
in report field formats, 170
in sorting, 164
% full, as shown in information line, 7
% (percent sign), in cell styles, 216, 219
& (ampersand), as string combination operator, 270
* (asterisk)
in arithmetic formulas, 176, 234
in calculator functions, 393
as error indicator in report calculations, 170
as long length indicator in spreadsheets, 198, 220
as wild card character, 398
+ (plus sign)
in arithmetic formulas, 176, 234
in calculator functions, 393
: (colon), in database form field names, 85, 89
< > (less than/greater than symbols), as relational operators, 118, 280
= (equal sign), as relational operator, 118, 280
? (question mark), as wild card character, 116

. (period), as wild card character, 116
^ (caret)
in arithmetic formulas, 176, 234
in calculator functions, 393
. (decimal point)
in report field formats, 170
in sorting, 164
, (comma)
in calculator functions, 393
in cell styles, 216, 219
in communications module telephone numbers, 343–344
in financial functions, 253
( ) (parentheses)
in calculator functions, 393
in formulas, 176, 234–236
" (quotation marks), as text string separator, 384
/ (slash)
in arithmetic formulas, 176, 234
in calculator functions, 393
in nonmatch search instructions, 119
[] (square brackets), in sort instructions, 135

A

absolute values, calculating, 244–245
addition, 175–177, 234–236, 393
alphanumeric data, 81, 169–170

Alt key, 11
ampersand (&), as string combinatior
    operator, 270
angles, calculating from
    sine/cosine/tangent, 245–246,
    251–252
A prompt, 419
area graphs, 290–291, 313–314. *See
    also* graphs
arguments (in functions), 243
arithmetic
    calculations, 157, 167–171,
        174–177, 241
    within formulas, 234–236
    functions, 234–236, 244–253
Arrow keys. *See* cursor keys
ASCII
    database files in, 141–148
    delimited files, 141–145
    documents in, 65–68
    fixed-length, 141, 146–148
    returning character values in,
        270–271
    spreadsheet importing/exporting,
        228, 383, 386
    telecommunicating files in, 358–360
asterisk (*)
    in arithmetic formulas, 176, 234
    in calculator functions, 393
    as error indicator in report
        calculations, 170
    as long length indicator in
        spreadsheets, 198, 220
    as wild card character, 398
AUTOEXEC.BAT, 402–403
averages, 167, 246
axes (of graphs), 286–287

B

background text, 103
Backspace key, 12, 19

backups
    of database files, 98–100, 130
    of documents, 64–65
    of PFS: First Choice program disks,
        417–420
    of spreadsheets, 227
Bad command or file name message, 418
bar graphs, 286–288, 298–307. *See also*
    graphs
batch files, 433
baud rate, 344, 425
blanks
    in calculations, 176
    in comparisons, 164
    deleting from merged personalized
        form letters, 372
    in formulas, 234
    inserting rows/columns of in
        spreadsheets, 215–216
    preceding stylized text paragraphs,
        42
    in report field formats, 170
    stripping, 275–276
blocks
    copying, 25–26
    defining, 21–23
    deleting, 26
    moving, 23–24
    spell checking of, 59
    of telecommunicated data, 359
boldfacing, 40–42, 224
bookmarks
    in databases, 139–140
    deleting, 396
    in graphs, 334–335
    jumping to, 395–396
    setting, 54–55, 394–395
booting, 420
borders, on graphs, 322
Brother printers, 438
browsing through records, 104–105

built-in functions. *See* functions

bulletin board services, 341–342, 349–350

C

calculations, 157, 167–171, 174–177, 241. *See also* formulas; functions

calculator, 140, 335, 392–394

Caps Lock key, 11

caret (^)
  in arithmetic formulas, 176, 234
  in calculator functions, 393

carriage returns. *See* Enter key

case
  converting, 273–274, 276
  locking in uppercase, 11
  in sorting, 163–164
  in string functions, 270, 272

cell cursor, 193

cells
  constant values in, 238–240
  copying, 214–215
  data entry for, 198–199, 201
  defined, 192
  erasing, 210–211
  formulas in, 201–207
  in graph information forms, 294
  moving, 213–214
  named, 238–240
  naming, 206–207
  selecting ranges of, 209–210
  styles of, 216–222

centering (text), 41, 53

CGA display adapter, 416

character data, 81, 90, 133–134, 278

characters per inch (on printers), 73–74

chat mode for telecommunications, 357

circular graphs, 291–292, 308–313

clipboard, 22–26, 211, 213, 376–377, 379–380

clock, 261. *See also* date functions; time functions

colon (:), in database form field names, 85, 89

color
  printing graphs in, 318–319, 322
  selecting options for, 424

column numbers, as shown in ruler line, 7

columns
  data entry for, 198–199, 201
  deleting, 211–213
  derived, 157, 164, 171, 174–177
  formatting for reports, 162
  headings for, 166–167, 196–201
  inserting, 215–216
  invisible, 168
  totaling by formula, 204–205
  width of, 169, 216–217, 220

COM1/COM2 ports, 340, 426, 432

combining/merging, documents, 67–69

comma-delimited files, 142

comma
  in calculator functions, 393
  in cell styles, 216, 219
  in communications module telephone numbers, 343–344
  in financial functions, 253

comments, in forms programming language, 454

communications module
  accessing information and bulletin board services with, 341–342
  computer settings for, 342–346
  described, 339
  dialing with, 346–349
  file exchange with, 354–356
  interrupts of, 352–353

macro recording in, 407
modem use with, 340–341
monitoring online sessions with,
   352–354
remote computer connections for,
   346–350
Service Information form in,
   343–346
troubleshooting of, 362–363
two-way communications with,
   350–352, 356–362
communication speed, 344–345
comparisons (of strings), 271
compressed type, 71, 161
computations, 157, 167–171,
   174–177, 241
conditional functions, 277–282
constants, in cells, 238–240
context sensitivity, 9
control breaks, 168
Control key (Ctrl), 11, 16
coordinates, of cells, 192
copying
   ASCII files into spreadsheets, 386
   cells, 214–215
   database forms, 128–129
   disks, 403–404
   documents, 64–65
   files, 399
   formulas, 236–240
   records, 129–130, 139
   tables, 111–112
   tables into spreadsheets, 386
   text blocks, 25–26
correcting
   records, 105
   text, 14–19
   typos, 13
correspondence-quality printing, 71,
   73, 161
cosine, 245–246

counts (of items), 167–168, 247
C prompt, 418
Ctrl key, 11, 16
currency symbols, 216, 218–219, 253,
   305, 393
current date and time, 261
current drive, 28
current subdirectory, 28
cursor
   as blinking line, 88. *See also*
      Overwrite mode
   cell, 193
   edit, 194
   mouse, 15, 433–434
   position (as shown in ruler and
      information lines), 7
   text, 6, 15
cursor keys, 5, 14–16, 194–195
cursor movement
   in Graphs Options display, 303
   with mouse, 15
   in spreadsheets, 194–196
   in word processing, 14–16. *See also*
      inside cover

D

data. *See also* forms programs; text
   adding to database records, 93
   automatic checking/calculation with
      forms programs, 445
   conversion between string and
      numeric, 275–276
   entering in graphs, 294–297
   entering in spreadsheets, 198–199
   managing in spreadsheets, 208–216
   types of, 81–82
database files. *See also* database forms;
      forms programs; records; reports
   adding records to, 92–96
   changing design of, 98–103
   creating, 80–83

deleting, 132
described, 77–80
personalizing form letters from, 368–372
printing, 121–123
retrieving, 97–98
retrieving records from, 112–121
size restriction of, 85–86
table generation from, 107–112
target, 128
working with, 103–107
database forms
changing, 98–103, 183
copying, 128–129
creating, 83–89
described, 79
field type selection for, 90–92
saving, 89–90
database key, 82–83
data bits setting for communications, 346, 425
data series (in graphs), 287
date data, 81, 90, 133, 164, 216–217, 219
date functions, 257–262
days of months, 260
dBASE files, importing, 141, 145
DCA files, 65–67
decimal places
in calculator functions, 393
in cell styles, 216–217, 220
setting for reports, 169
decimal point. *See also* period.
in report field formats, 170
in sorting, 164
decimals variable, in forms programming language, 448–450
defaults, for page formatting, 63
deleting
columns, 211–213
database files, 132

directories, 401–402
documents, 65
fields, 100
lines, 21
macros, 408
records, 105–106, 130–132
rows, 211–213
text, 19–21
text blocks, 26
delimited ASCII files, 141–145
Del (Delete) key, 12, 19
depreciation allowance calculations, 253–254, 256–257
derived columns, 157, 164, 171, 174–177. *See also* calculations
Diablo printers, 438
dialing
automatic and manual, 346–348
telephone numbers in a database, 148
troubleshooting of, 348–349
DIR (directory listings), 29
directories
creating/removing, 400–402
default, 430–432
Directory Assistant, 27–29, 97–98
disconnecting a telecommunications session, 355–356
disk
printing documents to, 72
printing graphs to, 333
printing reports to, 160–161, 173
printing spreadsheets to, 224
DISKCOPY.COM, 404, 418
disks
copying, 403–404
formatting, 402–403
PFS: First Choice requirements for, 416
protecting with write-protect tabs, 418

source/target, 419
system, 419
disk utilities module, 396–404
display adapters, 320, 416, 423
ditto feature, 95–96
division, 175–177, 234–236, 393
DOC file extensions, 29
documents. *See also* blocks; files;
    graphs; reports; text
  bookmarks for, 54–55, 139–140,
    334–335, 394–396
  combining with graphs, 382–383
  combining/merging, 67–69,
    377–382
  converting records to, 106–107
  copying, 64–65
  creating, 12–21
  defined, 3
  deleting, 65
  graphs as, 333
  keeping several versions of, 40
  merging, 377–382
  named on information line, 7
  naming, 30
  personalizing form letters, 368–372
  printing, 30–32, 69–70
  replacing, 39–40
  retrieving, 38–39
  saving, 26–30, 40
  size restriction, 69
  spell checking of, 55–59
  thesaurus aid for, 59–60
dot-matrix printers, 73–74, 425. *See*
  also printers
double declining balance method of
  depreciation, 253–254
double spacing, 41, 53, 161
draft-quality printing, 31, 70–71, 161
duplex setting for communications,
  346

E

edit cursor, 194
Edit key (F5), 19–20
editing
  records, 105
  reports, 182
  slides, 469
  text, 13–19
Edit menu, 19–20
EGA display adapter, 416
electronic bulletin boards, 341–342,
  349–350
End key, 16
Enter key (⏎), 4, 13, 194
Epson printers, 438
equal sign (=), as relational operator,
  118, 280
erasing
  cells, 210–211
  files, 65, 400
  ranges (of cells), 210–211
  records, 130–132
  spreadsheets, 213
  and unerasing, 65
  working copy (of documents), 21, 39
ERRBOX statements, in forms
  programming language, 454
ERROR function, 247, 277
ERROR indication in spreadsheet
  cells, 243
errors. *See* corrections; editing
Escape (Esc) key, 5, 10, 21, 39
Escape (printer) codes, 73–74
exact matches (in search instructions),
  115–116
exponentiation, 175–177, 234–236,
  247–248, 393. *See also*
  sub/superscripting
external modems, 417. *See also* modems

F

F1 (Help), 5, 9–10
F2 (Files), 28–30
F3 (Features), 8
F4 (Print), 8–9, 30–32
F5 (Edit), 19–20
F6 (Style), 41–43
FCMACRO.KEY, 411
Features key (F3), 8
fields
  adding/deleting, 100–102
  defined, 79
  invisible, 157
  moving, 100–101
  naming, 88, 102–103
  selecting for reports, 162–165
field types, for database forms, 90–92
file extensions
  described, 29
  .DOC, 29
  .FOL, 99, 129
  .REP, 172, 182
  .SS, 29, 208
  .WKS, 226
files. *See also* ASCII; database files;
  documents
  batch, 433
  combining within PFS: First
    Choice, 375–386
  copying, 399
  described, 29
  displaying lists of, 397–398
  erasing, 65, 400
  importing to PFS: First Choice,
    141, 227–228
  of macros, 411–412
  naming, 30
  printing reports to, 160–161
  renaming, 399–400

  transfering via communications
    module, 354–356, 358–360
Files key (F2), 28–30
financial functions, 253–257
find and replace, 60–62, 141
fixed-length ASCII files, 141,
  146–148
flag-type variables, 449. *See also* forms
  programs
floppy-disk computers, 27, 416,
  419–420, 422
FOL file extensions, 99, 129
fonts, selecting for slides, 466–467,
  469–470
footers and headers, 51–52, 63, 162,
  166–167
FORMAT.COM, 402–403
formatting
  data in database form fields, 91
  dates, 258–259
  disks, 402–403
  lines of text, 12
  reports, 157–159
  spreadsheets, 222–225
  text, 45–54
form for database creation. *See*
  database forms
form letters
  database design considerations for,
    82
  personalizing, 368–372
forms programs
  described, 445–446
  for global changes, 458
  language for, 446–455
  for recalculating selected records,
    458
  retrieving, 457–458
  sample of, 459–462
  saving, 457

using alternate, 429–430
writing and editing, 455–457
formulas. *See also* calculations
arithmetic functions with, 234–236
automatic adjustment of, 241–242
copying, 236–240
in derived columns, 175–177
described, 233
moving, 237–238
PFS: First Choice compatibility with
Lotus 1-2-3, 226
printing, 223
in spreadsheet cells, 201–207
fractions, 248
Fujitsu printers, 438
full duplex setting for
communications, 346
function keys, 5. *See also* F1, F2, etc.
function name, 243
functions. *See also inside cover*
arithmetic, 244–253
date, 257–262
described, 243
financial, 253–257
in forms programming language,
455
logical, 277–282
string, 269–276
table, 265–269
time, 262–265
future value of investment, 254

G

global style, of spreadsheet cells,
216–217
GOTO statements, in forms
programming language, 452–453
*Graph format, 318–320
Graphics menu, 328
graphs. *See also* slides
area, 290–291, 313–314

bar, 286–288
changing types of, 315–316
combining with documents,
382–383
creating, 293–316
data series in, 287
data entry in, 294–297
default settings for, 317–318
described, 285–293
displaying on screen, 319–320
from/to spreadsheet data, 293,
325–334
high/low/close, 292–293, 314–315
legends and labels with, 287,
295–296, 330–331
line, 288–289, 307–308
naming, 329
pie, 291–292, 308–313
point plot, 289
plotting, 323–325
printing, 301, 308, 318–319,
320–322, 332–333
retrieving, 319, 332
saving, 300–301, 308
scatter plots, 289
selecting color options for, 429
slides with, 470
storing, 316–319
trend, 290
less than/greater than symbols ($<>$),
as relational operators, 118, 280
grid lines (of graphs), 287

H

half duplex setting for
communications, 346
hard-disk computers, 416, 418–419,
421–422
hard returns, 17, 142
hardware requirements for PFS: First
Choice, 416–417, 423–434

Harvard Graphics, 317
Hayes Smartmodem, 341
headers and footers, 51–52, 63, 162, 166–167
headings
of spreadsheet columns/rows, 193, 196–201, 226
of spreadsheet pages, 224
Help key (F1), 5, 9–10
Hercules display adapter, 416
Hewlett-Packard LaserJet printers, 437–439
Hewlett-Packard plotters, 417
high/low/close graphs, 292–293, 314–315. *See also* graphs
Home key, 16
host mode for telecommunications, 357, 360
host vs caller, 350
hours, 263. *See also* time functions
Houston Instruments plotters, 417
HP LaserJet printers, 437–439

I

IBM PC/XT/AT computers, 416
IBM PC/XT/AT keyboards, 10–12
IBM printers, 439
if...then (conditional) functions, 279–282
If...then statements, in forms programming language, 453–454
indenting text, 48–49, 63–64, 72
index, for table functions, 269
information line, 7–8, 88, 193–194
inserting
columns, 215–216
rows, 215–216
text, 12
Insert (Ins) mode, 12
Ins key, 12

installing PFS: First Choice
and customizing for your computer, 423–432
hardware requirements for, 416–417, 423–434
importance of backups in, 417–420
with a mouse, 432–434
procedures for, 420–421
startup, 421–422
integers, 248
interest on loans, 254–256
internal modems, 417. *See also* modems
invisible columns, 168
invisible fields, 157
italicizing, 40, 43–44
item counts, 167–168, 247

J

JOIN special command, 69–70
justification (of printed text), 71

K

key, database, 82–83
keyboards, common layouts of, 10–12
keys. *See also inside cover; names of keys;* F1, F2, etc.
for document cursor movement, 5
for graph data editing, 296–297
as macros, 404–412
for remote computer telecommunications, 351–352
for spreadsheet cursor movement, 194–195
key value, 83
keywords, 233, 455

L

labels
in graphs, 295, 330–331

for mailing, 82, 373–375
of spreadsheet cells, 198, 243
label statements, in forms
programming language, 452
landscape style printing, 321
layout. *See* formatting
legends, in graphs, 287, 295–296,
330–331
length, of strings, 272–273
letter-quality printing, 71, 73
line graphs, 288–289, 307–308. *See
also* graphs
line n of Page m message (as shown in
information line), 7
lines
adding blank, 17
deleting, 21
reformatting of, 12
line spacing, 53
lines per inch/page
establishing for reports, 161
establishing for spreadsheets, 224
printer capability for, 49, 54, 73–74,
122–123
local host mode for
telecommunications, 357
local variables, in forms
programming language, 448–449
logarithms, 248–249
logical functions, 277–282
Logitech mouse, 417, 432
lookup functions for tables, 265–269
Lotus 1-2-3, importing/exporting
spreadsheets to/from, 226–228
LPT1/LPT2 ports, 423, 426

M

macro files, 411–412
Macro menu, 408
macros
changing, 408

in communications module, 407
creating, 405–407
deleting, 408
described, 404
displaying in Main menu, 408,
410–411
with a pause, 408–409
playing back, 407–408
mailing labels, 82, 373–375
Main menu, 4, 410–411
margins
default settings for, 63
as shown in ruler line, 7, 45–47
top and bottom, 49–51
matches (in search instructions),
115–121
mathematical calculations, 157,
167–171, 174–177, 241
maximum/minimum values, 247,
305–306
memory
clipboard in, 22
considerations for
telecommunications, 353
document size restriction by, 69
PFS: First Choice requirements for,
416
and spreadsheet size, 193
volatility of, 26–27
memory indicator, 7, 193
menu bar, 8–9, 193
menus, how to use, 4–5
merging
database information into form
letters, 368–372
documents, 67–69, 377–382
Microsoft mouse, 417, 432
Microsoft Word files, 65–67
minimum/maximum values, 247,
305–306
minus sign (−)

in arithmetic formulas, 176, 234
in calculator functions, 393
in report field formats, 170
in sorting, 164
minutes, 264. *See also* time functions
modems
  external, 417
  internal, 417
  PFS: First Choice requirements for,
    340–341, 417
  selecting options for, 426–427
  for telecommunications, 148
modulus, 250
money symbols, 216, 218–219, 253,
  305, 393
monitors
  display adapters for, 416, 423
  display of styles (special print effects)
    on, 41, 43
  PFS: First Choice requirements for,
    416
months, 260. *See also* date functions
mouse. *See also name of mouse*
  block selection with, 23
  cursor movement with, 15
  installing, 432–434
  menu item selection with, 5
  PFS: First Choice requirements for,
    417
mouse cursor, 433–434
mouse driver, 433
Mouse Systems mouse, 417, 432
moving
  cells, 213–214
  fields, 100–101
  formulas, 237–238
  text. *See* blocks
Multimate files, 65–67
multiplication, 175–177, 234–236,
  393

N

named cells, 238–240
naming
  cells, 206–207
  directories, 401–402
  documents/files, 30
  fields in database forms, 84–85
  graphs, 329
NEC printers, 439
net present value of investment, 255
NEW PAGE special command, 54
nonmatches (in search instructions),
  119
numbering pages. *See* page numbers
numeric data, 81, 90, 133, 164,
  169–170, 220–221, 278
numeric keypad, 10
NumLock key, 10–11

O

Okidata printers, 440
1-2-3 (Lotus), importing/exporting
  spreadsheets to/from, 226–228
outputting. *See* printing
Overwrite mode, 12, 17, 88

P

page breaks, 50, 54, 168
page length, 49–51, 63
page numbers, 51–52. *See also* headers
  and footers
Page Size, Headers, and Footers
  Menu, 50
page width, 161, 224
Panasonic printers, 440
paragraph breaks, 17–18
paragraphs creating/deleting, 17–18
parentheses
  in calculator functions, 393

in formulas, 176, 234–236

parity setting for communications, 346, 425

partial matches (in search instructions), 116–118

passwords, 349

pauses
in macro instructions, 408–410
in printing, 223

payment on loans, 255–256

PC Mouse Systems mouse, 417, 432

% full message, as shown in information line, 7

percent sign (%), in cell styles, 216, 219

periodic payment on loans, 255–256

period, as wild card character, 116. *See also* decimal point

permanent variables, in forms programming language, 449

person-to-person mode for telecommunications, 357

PERSONAL.FC dictionary file, 58–59

personalized form letters, 368–372

PFS: First Choice
customizing, 423–432
data transfer between modules of, 367–386
installing, 415–421
starting, 421–422

PgUp/PgDn keys, 5, 9, 15–16

phone numbers, entering for communications module, 343–344

phoning. *See* communications module; dialing

pi, 250

pie graphs, 291–292, 308–313. *See also* graphs

Plot Graph Options menu, 323–324

plotters

PFS: First Choice requirements for, 417

selecting options for, 427–428

troubleshooting use of, 323

plotting
graphs, 323–325
slides, 468–469

plus sign (+)
in arithmetic formulas, 176, 234
in calculator functions, 393

point plots, 289. *See also* graphs

portrait style printing, 321

ports
COM1/COM2, 340, 426, 432
LPT1/LPT2, 423, 426

position indicator, 193

presentation graphics. *See* slides

present value of investment, 256

previewing printouts, 122

Print key (F4), 8–9, 30–32

printers. *See also names of printers*; printing
advanced features of, 73–74
characters per line capabilities of, 47
choosing for reports, 160–161
compressed type on, 71, 161
display of styles (special print effects) on, 43–44
dot-matrix, 73–74, 425
lines per page capabilities of, 49, 54, 73–74, 122–123
list of those supported by PFS: First Choice, 437–441
PFS: First Choice requirements for, 416
and printer codes for, 73–74
selecting options for, 424–426
troubleshooting graph printing on, 322
and Unlisted Printer option, 44

Printer special command, 73–74

Print Graph Options menu, 321
printing. *See also* printers
  advanced features of, 70–74
  correspondence quality, 71, 73, 161
  database records, 121–123
  to disk, 72, 110–111, 160–161, 173,
    224, 333
  documents, 30–32, 69–70
  draft-quality, 31, 70–71, 161
  formulas, 223
  graphs, 301, 308, 318–319,
    320–322, 332–333
  justified text, 71
  in landscape, 321
  letter-quality, 71, 73
  pausing for sheet feeding while, 72
  personalized form letters, 371–372
  in portrait, 321
  records, 106, 121–123, 138
  reports, 173, 183
  to screen, 122, 160–161, 224
  slides, 468–469
  spreadsheets, 222–226
  suppressing repeat printing of
    identical columns/rows, 168
  tables, 110–111
  telecommunicated data, 354
print options, selecting for reports,
  159–162
Print Options menu, 32
Professional Write, working with files
  in, 65–67
programs. *See* forms programs
program statements, in forms
  programming language, 450–454
protocol (for telecommunications),
  354–355
PS/2, 416

Q

question mark, as wild card character,
  116

quick entry feature
  for copying formulas, 240
  for graph data entry, 335
  for spreadsheet data entry, 199–201
quotation marks
  (quote character) in delimited
    ASCII files, 141
  as text string separator, 384

R

random numbers, 250
range matches (in search
  instructions), 120–121
ranges (of cells in spreadsheets),
  209–210, 214–215
records. *See also* database files; forms
  programs; reports
  adding to databases, 92–96
  browsing through, 104–105
  converting documents to, 106–107
  copying, 95–96, 129–130, 139
  defined, 79
  deleting, 105–106, 130–132
  dittoing, 95–96
  editing, 105
  erasing, 130–132
  printing, 106, 121–123, 138
  retrieving, 112–121
  size restriction of, 85–86
  sorting, 82, 133–138
relational operators, 280
relative matches (in search
  instructions), 118–120
reminder line, 194
remote host mode for
  telecommunications, 357
renaming files, 399–400
repeating of string data, 274
.REP file extensions, 172, 182
replacement statements, in forms
  programming language, 450–452
replacing

documents, 39–40
words (search and replace), 60–62
report instructions
  described, 158–159
  for displayed field selection, 162–165
  for headings and calculations,
    166–171
  for print options, 159–162
  repeated use of, 177–180
  saving, 172
reports
  creating, 157–158, 172–174
  described, 154–157
  editing, 182
  improving appearance of, 180,
    182–183
  printing, 183
  sample applications of, 183–186
  saving, 182
  summary, 160, 180–181
retrieving
  database files, 97–98
  documents, 38–39
  files in "foreign" formats, 67
  forms programs, 457–458
  graphs, 319, 332
  records from database files, 112–121
  spreadsheets, 208
  table data, 265–269
Return key. See Enter key
right justification (of printed text), 71
rounding, 250–251
rows
  data entry for, 198–199, 201
  deleting, 211–213
  headings for, 196–201
  inserting, 215–216
ruler line, 7, 45–49, 88

S

Save key (F10), 89

Save record key (F7), 96
saving
  database forms, 89–90
  documents, 26–30, 40
  forms programs, 457
  graphs, 300–301, 308, 316–319
  report instructions, 172
  reports, 182
  slides, 468
  spreadsheets, 207–208
  telecommunicated data, 353
scatter plots, 289. See also graphs
scientific notation, 175–177, 234–236,
  247–248, 393. See also
  sub/superscripting
screen
  displaying graphs on, 319–320
  display of styles (special print effects)
    on, 41, 43
  printing to, 122, 160–161, 224
  scrolling the, 9, 15
scrolling, 9, 15
search and replace, 60–62, 141
search instructions
  for database retrieves, 112–121
  for database sorting, 136–138
  matches in, 118–121
  for report item selection, 157,
    171–172
seconds, 264. See also time functions
series (of data in graphs), 287
Service Information form, 343
Service menu, 342
Setup menu, 423–424, 432
Shift keys, 10
sign-on procedures, 349, 360–362
sine, 245–246, 251
single spacing, 53
slash (/)
  in arithmetic formulas, 176, 234
  in calculator functions, 393

in nonmatch search instructions, 119
slides
  described, 465
  displaying, 467–468
  editing, 469
  entering text for, 466–467
  including graphs in, 470
  orientation of (portrait vs landscape, etc.), 472
  printing and plotting, 468–469
  producing shows of, 470–472
  saving, 468
sorting
  records, 82, 133–138
  report data, 162–164, 166
source diskette, 419
spaces. *See* blanks
spacing, of text lines, 41, 53, 161
special print effects (styles), 40–45, 224–225
speed keys, 20, 25, 215. *See also inside cover*
spell checking
  of database forms, 89
  of database records, 140
  of documents, 55–59
spreadsheets
  converting Lotus 1-2-3 to First Choice, 227–228
  creating, 196–199
  cursor movement in, 194–196
  data entry for, 198–199
  described, 191–194
  erasing, 213
  file input to, 383–386
  formulas in, 201–207
  graphs input to and from, 293, 325–334
  managing data in, 208–216

outputting to disk for document merge, 380–382
printing, 222–226
retrieving, 208
saving, 207–208
square brackets ([]), in sort instructions, 135
square root, 251–252
.SS file extensions, 29, 208
standard deviation, 252
Star printers, 440
startup of PFS: First Choice, 421–422
stop bits setting for communications, 345–346, 425
straight-line method of depreciation, 256–257
string comparisons, 271
string data, 81, 90, 133–134, 278
string functions, 269–276
strings, combining, 270
Style key (F6), 41–43
styles
  adding to form letters, 372
  for special print effects, 40–45, 95
  of spreadsheet cells, 216–222
subaverages, formatting for reports, 168
sub/superscripting, 40–41, 43–44. *See also* exponentiation
subtraction, 175–177, 234–236, 393
sum-of-the-years'-digits method of depreciation, 257
summary reports, 160, 180–181
synonyms, 59–60, 140
system disk, 419

T

Tab key, 16
table functions, 265–269

tables
  copying, 111–112
  copying into spreadsheets, 386
  creating, 107–109
  customizing, 110
  described, 265
  lookup functions for, 265–269
  printing, 110–111
tabs
  default settings for, 63
  as shown in ruler line, 7, 45, 47–48
Tandy printers, 440
tangent, 246, 252
target databases, 128
target diskette, 419
telephone numbers, entering for
    communications module, 343–344
telephoning. *See* communications
    module; dialing
terminal type, 345
terms (number of loan/investment
    payments), 253, 257
Texas Instruments printers, 440
text. *See also* blocks; cursor; data;
    documents
  background, 103
  bookmarks for, 54–55, 139–140,
    334–335, 394–396
  centering, 53
  correcting, 14–19
  deleting, 19–21, 26
  entering, 13–14
  formatting, 45–54
  indenting, 48–49
  inserting, 12
  spell checking of, 55–59
  thesaurus aid for, 59–60
text cursor, 6
thesaurus, 59–60, 140
time data, 81–82, 90, 133, 164,
    216–217, 219

time functions, 262–265
titles
  entering on graphs, 299–300, 331
  for reports, 166
toggle keys, 11
Toshiba printers, 441
totals
  of cell ranges, 252
  formatting for reports, 160, 167–171
  formulas for in spreadsheets,
    204–205
Transmission line, 351
transmission protocol, 354–355
trend graphs, 290. *See also* graphs
true/false data, 82, 90
true/false functions, 277–282
truncation (of data to fit column size),
    169
24-hour clock, 262–263
typestyles, creating commands for
    slides in, 469–470

U

underlining, 40, 43
Unlisted Printer, 44
utilities for disk operations, 396–404

V

values
  automatic checking/calculation with
    forms programs, 445
  in cells, 243
variables, in forms programming
    language, 448–450
variance, 253
Ven-Tel PC Modem, 341
VGA display adapter, 416

W

Wang PC files, 65–67
wild cards, 116–117, 398

.WKS file extensions, 226
WordPerfect files, 65–67
word processing
  described, 3, 10–12
  ending sessions of, 32–33
  as used with spreadsheets, 191
word processing formats and First
  Choice, 65–66
word processing screen, 6–9
words, deleting, 19–20
WordStar files, 65–67
wordwrap, 13
working copy (of documents), 14, 21,
  26–27, 32, 39, 69, 351

write-protect tab, 418

X

Xerox printers, 441
XModem protocol, 355
XON/XOFF setting for
  communications, 346, 425

Y

year, 261–262. *See also* date functions
yes/no data, 82, 90
yes/no functions, 277–282

TO JOIN THE SYBEX MAILING LIST OR ORDER BOOKS
PLEASE COMPLETE THIS FORM

NAME _____ COMPANY _____

STREET _____ STATE _____ ZIP _____

☐ PLEASE MAIL ME MORE INFORMATION ABOUT **SYBEX** TITLES

ORDER FORM (There is no obligation to order)

PLEASE SEND ME THE FOLLOWING:

TITLE	QTY	PRICE
_____	____	____
_____	____	____
_____	____	____
_____	____	____

TOTAL BOOK ORDER   ____ $____

SHIPPING AND HANDLING PLEASE ADD $2.00 PER BOOK VIA UPS   _____

FOR OVERSEAS SURFACE ADD $5.25 PER BOOK PLUS $4.40 REGISTRATION FEE   _____

FOR OVERSEAS AIRMAIL ADD $18.25 PER BOOK PLUS $4.40 REGISTRATION FEE   _____

CALIFORNIA RESIDENTS PLEASE ADD APPLICABLE SALES TAX   _____

TOTAL AMOUNT PAYABLE   _____

☐ CHECK ENCLOSED   ☐ VISA
☐ MASTERCARD   ☐ AMERICAN EXPRESS

ACCOUNT NUMBER _____

EXPIR. DATE _____ DAYTIME PHONE _____

CUSTOMER SIGNATURE _____

CHECK AREA OF COMPUTER INTEREST:

☐ BUSINESS SOFTWARE

☐ TECHNICAL PROGRAMMING

☐ OTHER: _____

THE FACTOR THAT WAS MOST IMPORTANT IN YOUR SELECTION:

☐ THE SYBEX NAME

☐ QUALITY

☐ PRICE

☐ EXTRA FEATURES

☐ COMPREHENSIVENESS

☐ CLEAR WRITING

☐ OTHER _____

OTHER COMPUTER TITLES YOU WOULD LIKE TO SEE IN PRINT:

_____

_____

OCCUPATION

☐ PROGRAMMER	☐ TEACHER
☐ SENIOR EXECUTIVE	☐ HOMEMAKER
☐ COMPUTER CONSULTANT	☐ RETIRED
☐ SUPERVISOR	☐ STUDENT
☐ MIDDLE MANAGEMENT	☐ OTHER:
☐ ENGINEER/TECHNICAL	_____
☐ CLERICAL/SERVICE	
☐ BUSINESS OWNER/SELF EMPLOYED	

CHECK YOUR LEVEL OF COMPUTER USE

☐ NEW TO COMPUTERS

☐ INFREQUENT COMPUTER USER

☐ FREQUENT USER OF ONE SOFTWARE

   PACKAGE:

   NAME _____

☐ FREQUENT USER OF MANY SOFTWARE

   PACKAGES

☐ PROFESSIONAL PROGRAMMER

OTHER COMMENTS:

_____

_____

_____

_____

_____

_____

_____

PLEASE FOLD, SEAL, AND MAIL TO SYBEX

SYBEX, INC.
2021 CHALLENGER DR. #100
ALAMEDA, CALIFORNIA USA
                94501

SEAL

SYBEX Computer Books are different.

Here is why . . .

At SYBEX, each book is designed with you in mind. Every manuscript is carefully selected and supervised by our editors, who are themselves computer experts. We publish the best authors, whose technical expertise is matched by an ability to write clearly and to communicate effectively. Programs are thoroughly tested for accuracy by our technical staff. Our computerized production department goes to great lengths to make sure that each book is well-designed.

In the pursuit of timeliness, SYBEX has achieved many publishing firsts. SYBEX was among the first to integrate personal computers used by authors and staff into the publishing process. SYBEX was the first to publish books on the CP/M operating system, microprocessor interfacing techniques, word processing, and many more topics.

Expertise in computers and dedication to the highest quality product have made SYBEX a world leader in computer book publishing. Translated into fourteen languages, SYBEX books have helped millions of people around the world to get the most from their computers. We hope we have helped you, too.

For a complete catalog of our publications:

SYBEX, Inc. 2021 Challenger Drive, #100, Alameda, CA 94501
Tel: (415) 523-8233/(800) 227-2346   Telex: 336311
Fax: (415) 523-2373

PFS: First Choice
Built-In Functions

Arithmetic

@ABS	Absolute value	@MINIMUM or	
@ACOS	Inverse cosine	@MIN	Minimum value within a range of cell
@ASIN	Inverse sine	@MOD	Remainder after division
@ATAN	Inverse tangent	@PI	The value 3.14159...
@AVERAGE or		@RANDOM or	
@AVG	Average value of a range or cells	@RAND	Random number generator
@COS	Cosine of an angle	@ROUND	Round a number
@COUNT	Number of numeric entries in a range	@SIN	Sine of an angle
@ERROR	Generate the value ERROR	@SQRT	Square root
@EXP	Value of e raised to a power	@STDEV or	
@FRACT	Fractional part of a number	@STD	Standard deviation of values in a rang
@INTEGER	Nearest integer lower than a number	@TAN	Tangent of an angle
@LN	Natural logarithm	@TOTAL or	
@LOG	Common logarithm	@TOT	Sum of cell values in a range
@MAXIMUM or		@VARIANCE or	
@MAX	Maximum value within a range of cells	@VAR	Variance of cell values in a range